ACADIA
NATIONAL PARK

HILARY NANGLE

Contents

Discover Acadia National Park

Mount Desert Island has been luring visitors since French explorers first answered the island's siren song in 1604. Raw, remote, and seductive, it dangles like a pendant into the Atlantic, flashing its voluptuous profile to passing navigators and mainland drivers. Although only 15 miles from north to south and 12 miles from west to east, the island is home to about 30,000 of Acadia National Park's roughly 46,000 acres. It's a miniature masterpiece, a gem of a natural and cultural resource that's laced with hiking trails and carriage roads, etched by a craggy coastline, sprinkled with ponds, and lorded over by bald peaks.

Acadia's appeal is contradictory: It's accessible, and yet it's not. More than two million visitors annually arrive on Mount Desert by car, bus, plane, or cruise ship, all eager to view the park's icons. The park loop road makes that easy. But even on the most crowded days, it's possible to slip away and find solitary peace on a hike or a paddle or a bike ride. Step off the major thoroughfares, and birdsong replaces idle chatter, pine perfumes the air, and signs of civilization disappear from view. Off-the-beaten-path gems might lack the drama of the icons, but they feed the soul, ease the mind, and restore much-needed balance to a hectic life.

Truth is, there is no one Acadia. Beyond Mount Desert Island, more sections of the park beckon. Islesford and Baker Island are connected by passenger ferries and excursion boats, as is the mainland Schoodic section of the park; oh-so-remote Isle au Haut lets the curious view from the safe confines of a boat, while inviting the hardy to hike and camp in near solitude; and Schoodic's pink granite shores receive far fewer visitors than Mount Desert Island.

While the park is the region's flawless gem, it's set amidst other precious ones. If stretched taut, Hancock County – with Acadia as its centerpiece – would have more than 1,000 miles of coastline. No saltwater locale on the entire eastern seaboard can compete with the region's variety of scenery or its natural resources which include the Maine Coastal Islands National Wildlife Refuge, the Donnell Pond Public Reserved Lands, two scenic byways, and countless preserves. It's inspiring scenery that feeds dozens of artists and artisans, whose galleries and studios pepper the region's byways.

A recent quotation put this area in its proper contemporary perspective: "Maine is so lovely," a British visitor to Acadia sighed nostalgically, "I do wish England had fought harder to keep it."

Planning Your Trip

▶ WHERE TO GO

Acadia on Mount Desert Island

Mountains tumbling to the sea, ocean waves crashing upon granite ledges, serene ponds and wildflower-filled meadowlands, the Mount Desert Island section of the park has it all, in spades. Watch the sun rise out of the Atlantic from Cadillac Mountain's summit, drive along the icon-rich Park Loop Road, hike trails through forestlands and up coastal peaks, scale granite cliffs, paddle the coastline's nooks and crannies. Intimate yet expansive, wild yet civilized, Acadia is as accessible or as remote as you desire.

Mount Desert Island Communities

Excursions into the park depart from the surrounding communities, which have attractions of their own: museums, gardens, shops, and theaters. Bar Harbor is the island's hub; tony Northeast Harbor is located at the mouth of Somes Sound, a rare fjord; Southwest Harbor is the heart of the island's quiet side. All edge sections of the park, and, of course, these communities, as well as the smaller fishing villages, are where you'll find a lobster dinner with all the fixings.

Schoodic Peninsula

Everything changes when you continue north on Route 1: the pace slows, fast-food joints and even stoplights disappear, and independence reigns. Schoodic Point's pink granite shores are undoubtedly the highlight of the park's only mainland section, but there are other reasons to mosey off the beaten track. Back roads and scenic byways loop through fishing villages, bisect a mountain-and-lake-speckled wilderness preserve, access a National Wildlife Refuge, and edge those pink shores. It's a bonanza for hikers, bikers, anglers, boaters, and bird-watchers.

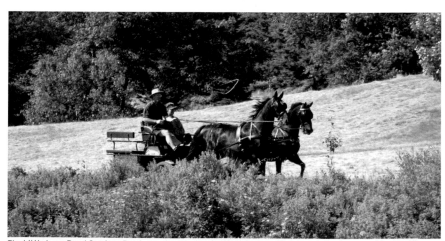

The Little Long Pond Carriage Road, near Seal Harbor, is privately owned but open to hoof, paw, and foot traffic.

Tea and popovers on the lawn at Acadia National Park's Jordan Pond House are a long-standing island tradition.

Blue Hill Peninsula

Water, water everywhere. Around nearly every bend is a river or stream, a cove, a boat-filled harbor, or a serene pond. It's an inspired and inspiring landscape, one dotted with historic homes and forts. Locals, a blend of summer rusticators, genteel retirees, artists, boatbuilders, and back-to-the-landers, have worked diligently to preserve not only the landscape but also the heritage. It's a fine place to kick back, relax, and savor the good life.

Deer Isle and Isle au Haut

If Deer Isle isn't the end of the world, there's a sense that you can see it from here. Tethered to the mainland by a soaring bridge over Eggemoggin Reach, Deer Isle and Little Deer Isle are fishing communities accented by a vibrant arts community. Depart the island's tip by ferry for Isle au Haut, where the most remote and rugged piece of Acadia National Park awaits hikers and those for whom even Deer Isle is a bit too crowded.

Ellsworth and Trenton

To visit Mount Desert Island, you must pass through the madness of Ellsworth and Trenton, a traffic-clogged, curse-inducing strip of mini malls and big-box stores. There are a few gems hidden amidst the sprawl, including historic buildings, trails for hiking, and lakes for boating. Perhaps most delightful is Birdsacre, the former home of ornithologist Cornelia Stanwood, now a preserve, with nature and bird rehab centers. It's a fine place to refuel your soul.

Working piers and wharves edge Corea Harbor.

► WHEN TO GO

Realistically, Acadia National Park is a three-season park (spring, summer, and fall), even though it's open in winter for cross-country skiing, snowshoeing, snowmobiling (with some restrictions), and even camping. Peak travel time for Acadia is the Fourth of July to Labor Day, with the absolute peak around the first week in August.

Spring tends to be something of a blip in Maine; the park starts reawakening only around mid- to late April, when the entire Park Loop Road has reopened (including the Cadillac Mountain road). Even then, some of the carriage roads tend to be fragile and open only for foot traffic, not for bicycles. Trails can be muddy, and ice still coats some of the rocks, but you'll be rewarded by hardy wildflowers poking up here and there. Until about mid-May, you'll also be spared from annoying black flies. In May, the weather can

be unpredictable, and many businesses still haven't opened for the season.

Summer kicks off in late May, but June is relatively quiet until the end of the month. If you yearn to be car-free on Mount Desert, plan to be here in summer, particularly between late June and mid-October, when Acadia's Island Explorer shuttle service operates. Summer means plentiful festivals and fairs, nightlife in Bar Harbor, nature tours, concerts (jazz, classical, and pop), carriage rides, hiking, and whale-watching trips.

Fall is fantastic in the park and on the island—it's my favorite season here. Nights are cool (mid-40s to mid-50s), days are (often) brilliant, and the fall foliage vistas are dramatic (visit www.mainefoliage.com). The grapevine has spread the word, though, so you won't be alone—but the visitor headcount is still far lower than in July and August.

► BEFORE YOU GO

What to Bring

Weather can be unpredictable in the Acadia region, with fog, rain, and temperatures ranging from the low 30s in spring into the 90s during summer. But even summer sees cool, damp days, when a fleece pullover or jacket is quite welcome, and don't forget a lightweight, weatherproof jacket. Other handy items are binoculars for sighting boats, offshore lighthouses, birds, and wildlife; a small backpack for day trips or light hiking; and a small or collapsible cooler for picnics or storing food.

Bicycles are handy when touring offshore islands.

Explore Acadia National Park

▶ THE 3-DAY BEST OF ACADIA NATIONAL PARK

Ready to hit the (Park Loop) Road running? You can pack a lot into three days, taking in the highlights and actually experiencing the park with hikes, bike rides, boat trips, or ranger-led programs. You might even include the Schoodic section of the park. For easiest park access, base yourself in Bar Harbor; even better, stay at one of the park's campgrounds.

Day 1

Pack a picnic, head to the park visitors center, purchase a pass, pick up a Beaver Log, then drive or pedal the Park Loop. Now, you can complete the loop itself in about two hours, but it'll take the better part of the day if you stop at all the sights, including the Nature Center, Wild Gardens of Acadia, and Abbe Museum at Sieur de Monts Springs, as well as Sand Beach, Thunder Hole, Jordan Pond House, and Cadillac Mountain (or save that for sunrise tomorrow). Now make it a whole day by adding a hike. Perhaps stretch your legs with a walk along the Ocean Trail or ascend Great Head or Gorham Mountain. If time permits, visit the Seawall area and Bass Harbor Light. In the evening, if you're not completely exhausted, perhaps attend a ranger-led program at either Blackwoods or Seawall Campgrounds.

Day 2

Rise early and catch sunrise from the summit of Cadillac Mountain. Spend the

Sand Beach

morning exploring one of the park's outly-ing holdings, taking either the ranger-nar-rated cruise to Baker Island or Islesford or catching the ferry to Winter Harbor and exploring the Schoodic section of the park either via bicycle or on the Island Explorer. Upon returning, head to the Jordan Pond House for tea and popovers on the lawn. Work it off with a walk or pedal on the carriage roads. End the day with a sunset horse-drawn carriage ride to the Day Mountain summit.

Day 3

Pursue your interests, mixing and match-ing any of the following: Take a guided sea kayaking tour exploring the western side of the island, departing from Pretty Marsh; take a guided bird-watching tour with Michael Good of Downeast Nature Tours; hike Acadia, St. Saviour, or Flying Mountain, fol-lowed by a refreshing swim in Echo Lake; pedal or walk the Eagle Lake and Witch

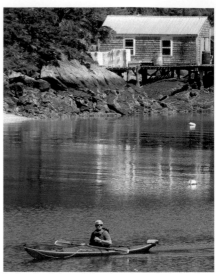

Explore Acadia's coastal nooks and crannies by kayak.

Hole Pond carriage roads; scale Acadia's cliffs on a climbing lesson; or join one or more ranger-led programs.

Acadia's carriage roads are accented with 17 unique stone bridges.

MOUNT DESERT ISLAND WITH KIDS

Acadia National Park is a great place to introduce kids to the great outdoors. Begin at park headquarters, where you can sign them up as **junior rangers.** Then pick and choose from the programs offered, including **ranger-led hikes** that appeal to your family's interests and abilities. Good choices for **easy family hikes** include the Ocean Trail, Jordan Pond Nature Trail, Ship Harbor Nature Trail, and Wonderland. If you're into **geocaching,** ask about the park's EarthCache program. In between park visits, you'll find plenty of other activities with real kid appeal. Here are a few sure bets.

SLIMY SEA CREATURES
You can't beat the wow appeal of **Diver Ed's Dive-In Theater Boat Cruise.** Ed dives to the depths with an underwater camera, while you wait onboard and watch the action. When he resurfaces, he brings along with him a variety of creatures from the depths for passengers to see, feel, and learn about.

OLYMPICS OF THE FOREST
Expert lumberjack Tina Scheer and her crew perform the most amazing skills at **The Great Maine Lumberjack Show.** During the 75-minute performance, two teams compete in 14 events, including ax throwing and log rolling. You can participate in some and even arrange for your youngster to learn how to log roll. Talk about a great story for that "What I did on my summer vacation" assignment.

I SCREAM, YOU SCREAM
The ultimate kid-in-a-candy-store experience, at **Den & Bill's** in Bar Harbor, you can buy not only chocolates made on-site but also to-die-for ice cream in both adult- and kid-pleasing flavors.

CRAFT CRAZY
Need a new teddy bear? Want to make a mug or create a mosaic piece? It's easy for your kids (and you) to express creativity at **All Fired Up!** in Bar Harbor. This rainy day godsend is worth visiting anytime, especially if your kids are craft oriented. There are no specific class times — just walk in and start making your own souvenir.

HANDS-ON NATURE
"Please touch" is the philosophy at the **George B. Dorr Natural History Museum,** a small museum on the College of the Atlantic campus in Bar Harbor. Kids have the opportunity to touch fur, skulls, and even whale baleen.

A WHALE OF A TIME
Skeletons, a model of a prehistoric walking whale, and a video of whales in their natural habitat all enthrall kids at the **Bar Harbor Whale Museum.** If the kids can't get enough (and if they're good on boats and able to handle a three-hour trip), consider pairing the museum visit with a **whale-watching** tour.

FERRY HOPPING
Spend the better part of a day on the **Cranberry Isles,** visiting both Big and Little Cranberry and either walking or biking around, or take the passenger ferry to **Winter Harbor,** and hop on the Island Explorer bus to visit the Schoodic section of Acadia National Park. En route, watch for seals, seabirds, and lobsterboats hauling traps.

NATIVE AMERICAN CULTURE
Check with the **Abbe Museum** in Bar Harbor about special kids' programs scheduled, and time your visit to take advantage of them. There's a resource room for children downstairs and a few other kid friendly exhibits at this Native American history museum, but the events bring it all to life.

LAUGH FEST
Improv Acadia in Bar Harbor stages a family-friendly show every evening.

▶ A 15-DAY ROAD TRIP

Spend 15 days here, and you'll have enough time to visit all sections of Acadia National Park, browse the studios of mega-talented artisans, go whale-watching, hike magnificent trails, kayak along undeveloped coastline, and view working lobstering villages and lighthouses. This driving tour begins in the Schoodic region, then takes in Mount Desert Island before heading to the Blue Hill Peninsula via Ellsworth, with Isle au Haut as the grand finale.

The best air access is via Bangor International Airport. Book your first 2 nights' lodging in the Schoodic region, nights 3 through 10 on Mount Desert Island (perhaps the first four on the east side of the island and the rest on the west side), nights 11 and 12 on the Blue Hill Peninsula, and nights 13 and 14 on Deer Isle.

Day 1

Begin with a drive or bicycle loop around the Schoodic section of Acadia National Park. Depending on your interests, day hike the Schoodic Head Loop or spend the rest of the day sea kayaking.

Day 2

Drive to either Maine Coastal Islands National Wildlife Refuge, on Petit Manan, for bird-watching and easy hiking, or to the

A ranger-led cruise is the best way to visit Baker Island.

ARTISTS AND ARTISANS: A STUDIO TOUR

Given the inspiring scenery, it's no surprise that the Acadia region is home to dozens of immensely talented artists and artisans. Visiting them in their studios allows you to view the region through their eyes. Galleries are abundant on the Blue Hill Peninsula and Deer Isle and in the Schoodic region, and more and more artists and artisans are calling Mount Desert Island home.

MOUNT DESERT ISLAND

- Must-See Contemporary Craft: Island Artisans (page 82) and Shaw Contemporary Jewelry (page 98)
- Must-See Contemporary Art: Redfield Artisans Gallery (page 98)
- Wild About Wildlife: Christopher Smith Galleries (page 98)
- Don't Miss Museum: Wendell Gilley Museum (page 102)

SCHOODIC REGION

- Most Talented Family: Barter Family Gallery (page 148)
- Must-See Contemporary Art: Spring Woods Gallery (page 148)

- Folk Art Favorite: Arthur Smith (page 149)
- Best Sculpture and Sculptor: Ray Carbone (page 149)

BLUE HILL PENINSULA

- Must-See Contemporary Art: Leighton Gallery (page 174)
- Best Sculpture and Sculptor: Jud Hartmann (page 174)
- Smithsonian-Worthy Pottery: Mark Bell Pottery (page 174)
- Dream Weaver: Christine Leith (page 182)

DEER ISLE

- Most Dynamic Duos: Morrow Wilson Studios (page 200) and Greene-Ziner Gallery (page 200)
- Must-See Contemporary Art: The Turtle Gallery (page 201) and Blue Heron Gallery (page 201)
- Just Plain Fun: Nervous Nellie's Jams and Jellies (page 202)
- Furnish Your Future: Geoffrey Warner Studio (page 202)

Peter Beerits's whimsical sculptures accent the tea room at Nervous Nellie's.

The Japanese-influenced Asticou Azalea Garden is a must for garden fans.

Donnell Pond Public Reserved Lands for a day hike followed by a swim. Don't forget a picnic lunch.

Day 3

Browse the numerous artisans' galleries tucked in all corners of the region as you make your way to Mount Desert Island. Begin at Lee Art Glass and move on to Luna Form, Barter Family Gallery, Spring Woods Gallery, and Hog Bay. Stop by the park visitors center when you arrive on Mount Desert Island to purchase a park pass and pick up a *Beaver Log*.

Day 4

Spend the day in Acadia National Park. Begin by driving or bicycling the Park Loop to take in the park's highlights. Stop for a hike along the way—perhaps an easy stroll along the Ocean Trail, a moderate hike up Great Head or Gorham Mountain, a challenging one up one of the trails that leave from Sieur de Monts Spring, or a strenuous climb up a ladder trail. Reward your efforts with tea and popovers at the Jordan Pond House.

Day 5

Another day in the park. Get up early and catch sunrise from atop Cadillac Mountain, then indulge your passions: hiking, sea kayaking, or bicycling. Check the *Beaver Log* to see what naturalist programs are scheduled, and make it a point to take part in one that intrigues you.

Day 6

Spend the day in Bar Harbor. Reserve a spot on a whale-watching trip. Bookend that with visits to the Whale Museum and Abbe Museum, shopping the downtown shops, and strolling the Shore Path. End the day with a sunset carriage tour in the park.

Day 7

Explore Northeast Harbor. Visit the Asticou and Thuya gardens, and perhaps wander out the back gate of Thuya and up Eliot Mountain. Shop downtown and gawk at the yachts in the harbor. Bicycle or drive Sargent Drive along the shores of Somes Sound.

Day 8

Choices, choices: Pack a picnic lunch and either take to the carriage roads on foot or bike or hop aboard a passenger ferry to the Cranberry Isles. If you want to have a sunset dinner on Islesford, make advance reservations and either go on a day when there's a late boat or arrange for a water taxi.

Hop a passenger ferry to the Cranberry Isles.

Day 9

Head for the western side of the island and visit pretty Somesville and Southwest Harbor, allowing time to tour the Wendell Gilley Museum. In the afternoon, hike Acadia, St. Saviour, or Flying Mountain, then refresh

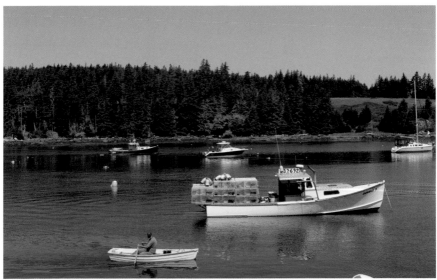
Boats of all types ply the waters of the Isle au Haut Thorofare.

PUFFINS AND EAGLES AND WOODCOCK, OH MY!

If you're looking to add a few species to your life list, the Acadia region is a great place to do so. Throughout the region, the birding is fine. Here is a small selection of some of the best places and activities for bird-watchers. An excellent resource to explore before your trip is www.mainebirding.com; of special interest are the sighting notes.

PETIT MANAN

This section of the **Maine Coastal Islands National Wildlife Reserve** is a must for bird-watchers. The refuge's primary focus is colonial seaboard restoration and management, but its varied habitats – rocky shoreline, fresh- and saltwater marshes, coastal raised peatlands, old hayfields, blueberry barrens, alder thickets, ponds with jack pine stands, and forested lands – provide homes for numerous birds.

Acadia is rich with bird-watching sites.

Neotropical migratory songbirds thrive in the woodlands. Waterfowl, wading birds, and shorebirds hang out in the salt marshes and mudflats. Joining them in the salt marshes are black ducks, great blue herons, and American bitterns, while semipalmated sandpipers, dowitchers, and dunlins prefer the mudflats. Grassland birds, including bobolinks and savannah sparrows, prefer the old hayfields and the blueberry barrens. You also have a good chance of sighting puffins, but for the best opportunities, take one of the commercial excursion boats to **Petit Manan Island** or **Machias Seal Island.**

MOUNT DESERT ISLAND

Various eagles, hawks, and peregrine falcons are among the 338 bird species that have been sighted on Mount Desert Island. This includes more than 20 species of warblers. Each spring, the island hosts a bird-watching weekend filled with events and tours. Mount Desert Island offers so much that perhaps the best solution is to arrange a tour with Michael Good of **Down East Nature Tours.** He knows where to sight native and migrating birds, including bald eagles, osprey, peregrine falcons, shorebirds, and warblers, as well as rare birds, including the Nelson's sharp-tailed sparrow. Especially good spots for birding include the sandbar connecting the Bar Harbor to Bar Island at low tide, **Sieur de Monts Spring,** the **Precipice Trail** for peregrine falcons, and **Cadillac Mountain** for migrating hawks (the park offers programs for the latter two). On the west side, be sure to take Route 102A and visit **Seawall Bog,** a raised coastal peatland; the **Ship Harbor** and **Wonderland** park trails; **Bass Harbor Head Light;** and **Bass Harbor Marsh.** And don't miss the **Wendell Gilley Museum,** in Southwest Harbor.

SCHOODIC POINT AND ISLE AU HAUT

Both of these sections of Acadia National Park are well worth visiting for their birding opportunities. The mix of headlands, rocky coastline, jack pine stands, and spruce forest on Schoodic Point provide for diversity of bird species, including pelagic birds, spruce grouse, and warblers; and outside the park, don't miss **Corea Heath.** Isle au Haut mixes spruce forest with rocky oceanfront, a freshwater pond, marshlands, and headlands. It's renowned for wintering harlequin ducks and, in both locations, you'll see migrating birds and bald eagles. The loop roads circle through varied habitats, so they're good options for multiple sightings – to view specific birds, choose a trail that passes through the appropriate habitat.

yourself with a dip in Echo Lake, followed by dinner at Thurston's Lobster Pound.

Day 10

Drive out to Bass Harbor Lighthouse, then continue to the village and take the luncheon nature cruise to Frenchboro with Island Cruises (be sure to make advance reservations). Or if you're an experienced cyclist, take a bike aboard the state ferry to Swans Island for the day.

Day 11

Depart Mount Desert for the Blue Hill Peninsula. En route, visit Birdsacre, a peaceful preserve and bird refuge. You could also put the region in perspective with a plane or glider flight. Spend the afternoon in Blue Hill, beginning with a tour of the Parson Fisher House. Afterward, if time permits, visit some of the many galleries in town. Do ask locally to see if the Flash in the Pans are performing during your days on the peninsula, and make it a point to hear them.

Day 12

Your choice: Hike Blue Hill Mountain, followed by more time for visiting galleries; hike Great Pond Mountain, followed by a visit to the Craig Brook National Fish Hatchery; or mosey over to Castine and pick up a brochure for a self-guided walking or bicycling tour followed by a guided sea kayaking tour.

Day 13

Explore Deer Isle and Stonington, allowing plenty of time to browse the galleries along the way. Hike the Edgar Tennis or Barred Island preserves, and, if your timing's right, visit the Haystack Mountain School of Crafts.

Day 14

Another day in the park, this time the Isle au Haut section. Plan in advance and book a seat on the early boat, then spend the day hiking. Don't forget a picnic lunch or water; supplies are limited on the island.

Day 15

Visit Fort Knox and the Penobscot Narrows Bridge and Observatory in the morning, before heading home. If you're flying out of Bangor, you can either mosey up Route 15 or connect via Route 174 to Route 1A north.

Penobscot Narrows Bridge and Observatory

▶ LOBSTER, LIGHTHOUSES, AND L.L.BEAN

Yes, you can hit the three Ls in the Acadia region. Book your first three nights on Mount Desert, nights four and five in the Blue Hill region, and nights six and seven on Deer Isle.

Day 1

Make your first stop on Mount Desert Island the Acadia National Park visitors center to purchase your park pass, pick up a copy of the *Beaver Log,* and chat with a ranger. Tonight, head to Thurston's Lobster Pound for the Real Thing, a lobster dinner with all the fixings.

Day 2

Rise early and beat the crowds on the Park Loop Road. In the afternoon, take a trip on *LuLu,* and learn everything there is to know about lobsters. Afterwards, stroll up Main Street to Ben & Bill's for a lobster ice cream

Long Pond, on the western side of Mount Desert Island, is a quiet spot for a hike or paddle.

Explore the islands around Deer Isle and Isle au Haut by sea kayak.

cone (it's a good idea to ask for a taste first). Still want more? Head to Maggie's for lobster crepes.

Day 3

Take a spin out to Bass Harbor to see the lighthouse, then board Island Cruises' *R.L. Gott* for the luncheon tour to Frenchboro. There's no finer place for a lobster or lobster roll than Lunt's.

Day 4

Book a morning whale- and puffin-watching cruise that includes Petit Manan Light on its itinerary. Afterwards, leave Mount Desert Island for the Blue Hill Peninsula, stopping at L.L.Bean's factory store in Ellsworth. It's nowhere near as big or complete as the mother ship in Freeport, but it will provide a taste of what the gigunda outdoor-oriented retailer offers. After your shopping spree, it's on to the Blue Hill region.

Day 5

Head to Castine, pick up a walking tour brochure at a local business, and take a leisurely stroll around town, making sure to see Dyce's Head Lighthouse. For lunch, order a lobster roll at The Breeze, a waterfront takeout stand. Spend the afternoon pursuing your interests: perhaps a hike up Blue Hill Mountain, a sea kayaking tour, gallery browsing throughout the peninsula, or visiting the WoodenBoat School in Brooklin.

Day 6

On to Deer Isle. When you cross the bridge onto Little Deer Isle, bear right at the info booth and head to the end of the road for views of Pumpkin Island Light. Then mosey on down the peninsula to Stonington, a bona fide lobstering community. Spend the afternoon with Captain Walter Reed's Guided Island Tours (be

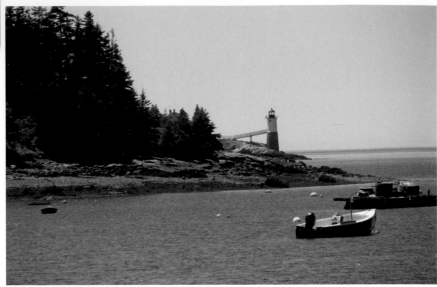

Isle au Haut Light, built in 1907, is now listed on the National Historic Register.

sure to book in advance and tell him what you want to see—lighthouses and lobster fishing). Finding a lobster dinner in these parts is easy.

Day 7

Pack a picnic lunch and take the ferry to Isle au Haut, and spend the day hiking in Acadia National Park. Go for one last lobster dinner in Stonington or Deer Isle before heading home tomorrow.

ACADIA ON MOUNT DESERT ISLAND

Rather like an octopus, or perhaps an amoeba, Acadia National Park extends its reach here and there and everywhere on Mount Desert Island. The park was created from donated parcels—a big chunk here, a tiny chunk there—and slowly but surely fused into its present-day size of more than 47,000 acres (nearly 36,000 are owned by the National Park Service; the balance are privately owned lands under conservations easements managed by the park). Permanent boundaries do exist (Congress certified them in 1986), but they can be confusing to visitors. One minute you're in the park, the next you've stepped into one of the island's towns. This symbiotic relationship is a reminder that Acadia National Park, covering a third of the island, is the major presence here on Mount Desert. It affects traffic, indoor and outdoor pursuits, and, in a way, even the climate.

Acadia's history is unique among national parks and indeed fascinating. Several books have been written about the high-minded (in the positive sense) and high-profile personalities who provided the impetus and wherewithal for the park's inception and never flagged in their interest and support. Just to spotlight a few, we can thank George B. Dorr, Charles W. Eliot, and John D. Rockefeller Jr. for what we have today.

© HILARY NANGLE

HIGHLIGHTS

Park Ranger Programs: Make it a point to join one of the numerous programs, from hikes and photography tours to natural history programs and children's activities, offered daily by park rangers (page 31).

Park Loop Road: If you do nothing else on Mount Desert, drive this magnificent road that takes in many of Acadia National Park's highlights (page 33).

Sieur de Monts Spring: This lovely oasis is home to the Wild Gardens of Acadia, the Nature Center, the Sweet Waters of Acadia spring, and the original Abbe Museum, as well as the base for hiking Dorr Mountain (page 37).

Sand Beach: Spread a blanket on one of the few beaches in this region of Maine (page 38).

Thunder Hole: Time your visit right to see the tide surge and explode through this geological formation (page 38).

Jordan Pond House: Come for tea and popovers and ice cream on the lawn, but allow time to walk or ride the carriage roads or explore the nature trail (page 39).

Cadillac Mountain: Acadia's prime feature is the highest point on the eastern seaboard, allegedly where the sun's first rays land. You can drive, bike, or hike to the 1,530-foot summit for stunning views (page 39).

Carriage Roads: On the eastern side of Mount Desert Island, 57 miles of meandering, crushed-stone paths, crossing 17 handsome stone bridges, welcome walkers, bikers, horseback riders, snowshoers, and cross-country skiers (page 39).

Eagle Lake: A mountain backdrop and undeveloped shores contribute to Eagle's popularity. A small-boat launch and a carriage road make it easy to explore (page 41).

Gorham Mountain Trail: This trail requires a minimum amount of effort to produce maximum rewards, and it's an excellent family hike – kids love the Cadillac Cliffs (page 49).

LOOK FOR (TO FIND RECOMMENDED SIGHTS, ACTIVITIES, DINING, AND LODGING.

Exploring the Park

INFORMATION CENTERS

There are two major centers on Mount Desert Island for Acadia National Park information. Some Acadia information is also available from the Bar Harbor Chamber of Commerce's two offices (one on Route 3 in Trenton, as you approach the island; the other on the Town Pier in Bar Harbor), the Southwest Harbor Chamber of Commerce, and the Mount Desert Chamber in Northeast Harbor.

Thompson Island Information Center

As you cross the bridge from Trenton toward Mount Desert Island, you might not even notice that you arrive first on tiny Thompson Island, site of a visitors center established jointly by the chambers of commerce of Mount Desert Island's towns and Acadia National Park.

The rustic building (on your right as you head south on Route 3) has walls lined with brochures for accommodations, restaurants,

PARK RULES

All parks have rules, and Acadia is no exception. Most are just common sense; some are specific to Acadia's situation and needs.

- It's forbidden to disturb or remove any public property – plants, minerals, artifacts, animals, etc. This extends to the rocks on the beaches, and you'll see signs here and there reminding you of that.

- Pets are allowed in Acadia, with some exceptions, but they must be on a leash (6 feet or shorter) or physically restrained. Voice control is not acceptable. They must not be left unattended. Pets are not allowed on Sand Beach, on the beach at Echo Lake, or in the Duck Harbor campground on Isle au Haut. They are also banned from the park's ladder trails and from the visitor centers and other public buildings. Pets should not be taken on Park Ranger tours. (Service dogs, of course, are always exempted from the rules.)

- In-line skating, rollerskiing, and skateboarding are allowed only on roads closed to automobiles.

- Bicycles are not allowed on any hiking trails. They're allowed on 45 miles of park carriage trails, but *not* on 12 miles of sign-posted (Green Rock Company) private carriage roads.

- Motorized vehicles are not allowed on park trails and carriage roads; ATVs are not allowed anywhere in the park. Electric wheelchairs *are* allowed on the carriage roads.

- Camping within park boundaries is allowed only at the park's two campgrounds on Mount Desert Island and one on Isle au Haut. There is no backcountry camping in the park or anywhere else on Mount Desert Island, but outside the park, the island has a dozen commercial campgrounds.

- Camp stoves and grills are allowed only in designated campgrounds and picnic areas; fires are allowed only in fire rings and fireplaces at these sites.

- Alcohol use is not allowed at Sand Beach, at Echo Lake beach, along the Lake Wood shoreline, or within a quarter-mile of the swimming areas at the southeastern end of Long Pond.

- Hunting is not allowed in the park.

- Federal law requires the use of seatbelts by drivers and passengers in national parks.

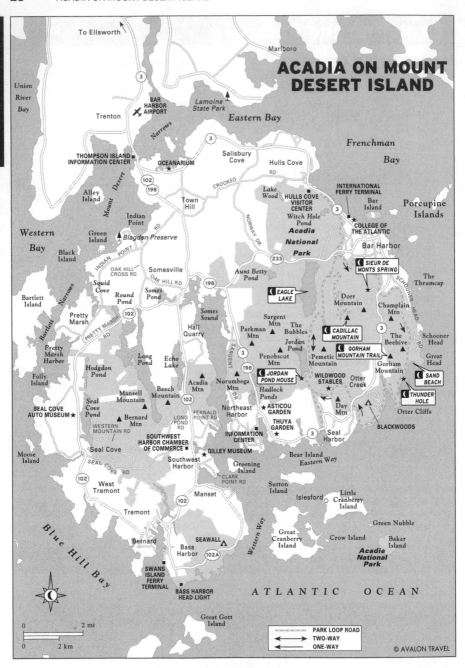

and activities. There are also restrooms. Across Route 3 is a picnic area overlooking Mount Desert Narrows.

If you've arrived without a place to stay (particularly in July and August), the welcoming staffers here are incredibly helpful. They keep track of lodging vacancies throughout Mount Desert Island and will go to great lengths to funnel you somewhere. In high season, don't expect to be overly choosy, though—room rates are high, vacancies are few, and you take your chances.

The center opens for the season in mid-May and is open 8 A.M.–6 P.M. daily. Everything wraps up soon after Columbus Day, when the center closes for the season.

In season, a park ranger is usually posted on Thompson Island to answer questions and provide basic advice on hiking trails and other park activities, but consider this a stopgap—be sure also to continue on to the park's main visitor center. You can purchase your Acadia pass here, too ($20 for all passengers in one vehicle late June–mid-Oct., when the Island Explorer bus is running; $10 mid- to late Oct. and May 1–late June; valid for seven days; an individual one-week pass is $5, a better value at $10 total for couples).

Hulls Cove Visitor Center

The modern Hulls Cove Visitor Center (Rte. 3, Hulls Cove, 207/288-3338) is eight miles southeast of the head of Mount Desert Island and well signposted. Here you can buy your park pass; rendezvous with pals; make reservations for ranger-guided natural and cultural history programs; watch a 15-minute film about Acadia; study a relief map of the park; buy books, park souvenirs, and cassette guides; and use the restrooms. Pick up a copy of the **Beaver Log,** the tabloid-format park newspaper that lists park activities, plus tide calendars and the entire schedule for the excellent **Island Explorer** shuttle bus system, which operates from late June to Columbus Day. The Island Explorer is supported by park entrance fees, as well as by Friends of Acadia and L.L.Bean. If you have children, enroll them in the park's

© HILARY NANGLE

Most of the programs led by park rangers are free.

Junior Ranger Program (a nominal fee may be charged). They'll receive a booklet, either one for ages eight and older or one for ages seven and younger. To earn a Junior Ranger Patch, they must complete the activities in the booklet and join one or two Ranger-led programs or walks.

Parking is usually ample at the visitor center, although the lot gets mighty full in midsummer, when as many as 9,000 people a day visit. Day-trippers also leave their cars in the lot and hop on the Island Explorer bus. The bus stops at the base of the winding stairway from the parking lot to the center, which is open daily, 8 A.M.–4:30 P.M. mid-April through late June and October, until 6 P.M. in July and August, and until 5 P.M. in September.

Acadia Park Headquarters

From November to mid-April, information is available at Acadia National Park Headquarters on Eagle Lake Road (Route 233), about 3.5 miles west of downtown Bar Harbor. These months, the headquarters office is open 8 A.M.–4:30 P.M. daily except Thanksgiving, December 24 and 25, and New Year's Day. During the summer, park publications are also available here, but the office is open only weekdays.

Park headquarters is also the meeting point for the three-times-weekly volunteer work projects organized by the park and Friends of Acadia.

PARK ENTRANCE FEES

A single glance at the map of Acadia National Park immediately raises the question: How do you sell passes and count heads in a park that has patches of land here and there and everywhere—even on a section of the mainland and on offshore islands? The answer: Not easily.

So…let's look at the picture another way. Thanks to action by Congress, about 80 percent of the fees Acadia collects are now returned to the park for much-needed maintenance and educational projects. The private Friends of Acadia organization and other donors often match these funds to make the money even more effective. Consider just a few of the projects your pass helps fund:

- Trail and carriage road reconstruction and rehabilitation

- The Island Explorer bus system

- New and improved restroom facilities

- Repairs to historic stone bridges

- New and improved informational exhibits

- Rock wall reconstruction

- Campground rehabilitation

At many of the project sites, you'll see brown Park Service signs: This Project Funded by Your Park User Fee. Think of them as Acadia's thank-you note for your support.

Where to Buy Your Park Pass

- The **Hulls Cove Visitor Center,** the park's visitor information center from May through October. (No entrance fees are collected from November through mid-April.)

- The Acadia National Park information office opposite the **Village Green** in downtown Bar Harbor. It also faces the hub for the propane-powered Island Explorer bus system.

- The **Sand Beach Park Entrance Station,** on the Park Loop Road, between the Schooner Head Overlook and Sand Beach.

- The **Blackwoods and Seawall Campgrounds,** the park's only camping areas.

- **Thompson Island Information Center** (Rte. 3, Trenton).

- **Acadia National Park Headquarters** (Eagle Lake Rd., Rte. 233, Bar Harbor), open weekdays in summer.

- Within the park, you can purchase your pass at the **Jordan Pond House** and at the summit of **Cadillac Mountain.**

Park Fees and Passes

- **Entrance fee:** $20 per vehicle (car or RV), late June through mid-October (when the Island Explorer is running). It covers everyone in the vehicle and is valid for seven days. From May 1 to late June and for all of October, the fee is $10. If you're traveling solo or want to buy an individual pass, the fee is $5 for seven days.

- **Acadia Annual Pass:** $40, valid for one year from the day you buy it. If you're in Acadia more than one week in any given year, you'll easily amortize this fee.

- **America the Beautiful Annual Pass:** $80, allowing unlimited entrance for one year to all national parks and other federal recreation sites with entrance or vehicle fees.

- **Senior Pass:** $10, for U.S. citizens and permanent residents who are 62 or older, allowing lifetime entrance to the more than 300 national parks, historic sites, and monuments. It also entitles you to half-price camping. This is an incredible bargain. Purchase has to be made in person, with proof of age (driver's license, passport, etc.). The pass covers everyone in the passholder's vehicle.

- **Access Pass:** free for any U.S. citizen or permanent resident who is blind or permanently disabled (a temporary disability, such as a broken arm or leg, does not qualify). It allows lifetime entrance to all national parks, as well as Fish and Wildlife, Forest Service, and Bureau of Land Management sites. It also allows half-price camping. The pass covers everyone in the passholder's vehicle.

GUIDED TOURS

The variety of guided activities in the park and nearby is astonishing—park ranger walks and talks and cruises, bus tours, bicycling tours, sea kayaking tours, birding expeditions, guided hikes, horse-drawn carriage rides, and even deluxe camping outfitters.

◖ Park Ranger Programs

When you stop at the Hulls Cove Visitor Center and pick up the current issue of the park's *Beaver Log* newspaper (or download it ahead of time at www.nps.gov/acad/), you'll find a whole raft of possibilities for learning more about the park's natural and cultural history.

The best way to see Baker Island Light is on the ranger-narrated Acadia National Park Baker Island Tour.

The Park Ranger programs, lasting one to three hours, are great—and most are free. During July and August, there are dozens of programs each week, all listed in the *Log*. Included are early-morning (7 A.M.) birding walks; mountain hikes (moderate level); tours of the historic Carroll Homestead, a 19th-century farm; Cadillac Mountain summit natural-history tours; children's expeditions to learn about tide pools and geology (an adult must accompany kids); trips for the wheelchair-borne; and even a couple of tours a week in French. Some tours require reservations, while others do not. (Reservations can be made up to three days in advance.)

Reservations and fees are required for several different boat cruises with park rangers who provide natural-history narration. The specific cruises can vary from year to year, but they usually include **Baker Island, Dive-In Theater, Frenchman Bay,** and **Islesford.**

Park rangers also give evening lectures during the summer in the amphitheaters at Blackwoods and Seawall Campgrounds. And the good news is that between late June and mid-October, you can join almost every ranger program via an Island Explorer bus.

Bus and Trolley Tours

The veteran of the Bar Harbor–based bus tours is **Acadia National Park Tours** (tickets at Testa's Restaurant, Bayside Landing, 53 Main St., Bar Harbor, 207/288-3327, www.acadiatours.com), operating May–October. A 2.5-hour, naturalist-led tour of Bar Harbor and Acadia departs at 10 A.M. and 2 P.M. daily from downtown Bar Harbor (look for the green-and-white bus across from Testa's). The bus makes three 15-minute stops in the park. Reservations are wise in midsummer and during fall foliage season (late Sept.–early Oct.); pick up reserved tickets 30 minutes before departure. The cost is $25 for adults, $15 for children under 12.

If you have a time crunch, **Oli's Trolley** (1 West St., Bar Harbor, 208/288-9899 or

PEREGRINE FALCONS

One of Acadia's great success stories is that of a seasonal mountain dweller, the peregrine falcon. DDT and other pollutants caused a decline in the falcons until the last breeding pair in Acadia was observed in 1956. (Before DDT, peregrines were depleted by trappers, hunters, and nest robbers.) The peregrine was listed as a federal endangered species in the early 1970s and removed from that list in 1999; it remains an endangered species in Maine. In the 1980s, biologists worked to reintroduce the falcons to Acadia. Their efforts proved successful when, in 1991, a breeding pair of falcons settled on the east-facing cliffs of Champlain Mountain and produced young. Since then, there have been up to three breeding pairs of falcons nesting in Acadia (at Champlain, Jordan Cliff, and Beech Cliff).

Their nests, or scrapes, are shallow ledges on cliffsides, which provide them with an unimpeded view of potential prey (other birds) below. Their high-speed pursuits of prey thrill those who are lucky enough to witness them.

During the spring and summer, park staff are stationed at the Precipice Trail Parking Area each morning (weather permitting), 9 A.M.-2 P.M., with spotting scopes to help anyone who stops by view the peregrines and their scrapes and to provide information about their habits. Check the park newspaper, the *Beaver Log,* for the latest information.

During breeding and fledging season (Apr.-mid-Aug.), the trailhead for the **Precipice Trail** is gated, with an informational sign explaining the history and status of peregrines in the park. (When you arrive, other trails may be closed for the same reason; check at the Hulls Cove Visitor Center.)

Contributed by Kristen Britain.

866/987-6553, www.acadiaislandtours.com) operates a one-hour trolley-bus tour four times daily (between 10 A.M. and 3:30 P.M.) in July and August, including Bar Harbor mansion drive-bys and the Cadillac summit. The cost is $15 for adults, $10 for children under 12. Oli's also offers 2.5-hour tours daily at 10 A.M. and 2 P.M. ($29 adults, $15 children under 12). Purchase tickets at One Harbor Place, next to the Town Pier on the waterfront; aboard the trolley; or at Oli's Trolley Ice Cream on Cottage Street. Dress warmly; it's an open-air trolley.

Note that while the Island Explorer buses do reach a number of key park sights, they are not tour buses. There is no narration, the bus cuts off the Park Loop at Otter Cliffs, and the routes exclude the summit of Cadillac Mountain.

Birding and Nature Tours

For private tours of the park and other parts of the island, contact Michael Good at **Down East Nature Tours** (207/288-8128, www.downeastnaturetours.com). A biologist and Registered Maine Guide, Good is simply batty about birds. He's spent more than 25 years studying the birds of North America, and he's even turned his home property on Mount Desert Island into a bird sanctuary. Good specializes in avian ecology in the Gulf of Maine, paying special attention to native and migrating birds. Whether you're a first-timer wanting to spot eagles, peregrine falcons, shorebirds, and warblers or a serious birder seeking to add to your life list, perhaps with a Nelson's sharp-tailed sparrow, Good's your man. Prices begin at $40 per adult, $20 per child for a two-hour wetland ecology tour; they increase to $75 per person for a four-hour "Discover the Native Birds of Mount Desert Island and Down East Maine" tour. Other options are available. Rates include transportation from your lodging. Family rates are available. Bring your own binoculars, but Michael supplies a spotting scope.

Carriage Tours

A fabulous way to recapture Acadia's early carriage-roads era is to take one of the horse-drawn open-carriage tours run by Ed Winterberg's **Carriages in the Park,** departing from Wildwood Stables, 0.5 mile south of the Jordan Pond House, on the Park Loop Road (207/276-3622, www.acadia.net/wildwood). Don't pooh-pooh this as too touristy—on a gorgeous day, the vistas are everything, and you won't be disappointed. Half a dozen one- and two-hour trips start daily at 9:30 A.M., mid-June through Columbus Day. Reservations are encouraged, especially at the height of summer. The best outing is the two-hour **Sunset at the Summit** trip to the top of Day Mountain; call for departure times. Trip prices are $18–22 per adult, $9–10 ages 6–12, and $5–7 ages 2–5. If you take the two-hour carriage ride to Jordan Pond House, departing daily at 1:15 P.M., you're guaranteed a reserved lawn chair for tea and popovers (not included in rate).

You also can arrange for a private carriage road tour of 1–4 hours. A one-hour trip is $180 for up to four passengers, plus $35 for each additional passenger; two hours is $240 plus $50; three hours is $360 plus $50; and four hours is $480 plus $50. Wildwood has no trail rides, but you can bring your own horse and stable it here at $25 a night for a box stall. (A basic campground has sites for stall renters for $15 a night.)

DRIVING TOUR

The ideal way to fully appreciate Acadia is to hike the miles of trails, bike the carriage roads, canoe the ponds, swim in Echo Lake, and camp overnight. It seems rather a shame to treat Acadia as a drive-through park, but circumstances—time, health, and other factors—sometimes dictate that.

◖ Park Loop Road

Logically, then, a driving tour of Acadia would follow the 20-mile Park Loop Road (open Apr. 15–Nov. 30, weather permitting).

It begins at the Hulls Cove Visitor Center, winds past several of the park's scenic highlights (with parking areas), ascends via a 3.5-mile spur to the summit of Cadillac Mountain, and provides overlooks of magnificent vistas. Allow a couple of hours so you can stop along the way. You can rent an audio tour on cassette or CD for $12.95 (including directions, an instruction sheet, and a map) at the Hulls Cove Visitor Center. Another option is to pick up the drive-it-yourself tour booklet, **Motorist Guide: Park Loop Road** ($1.50), available at the Thompson Island and Hulls Cove Visitor Centers.

Start at the parking lot below the Hulls Cove Visitor Center and follow the signs; part of the loop is one-way, so you'll be doing the loop clockwise. Traffic gets heavy at midday in the height of summer, so aim for an early morning start if you can. The maximum speed is 35 mph, but be alert for gawkers and photographers stopping without warning and pedestrians dashing across the road from stopped cars or tour buses. If you're out at midday in summer, don't be surprised to see cars and RVs parked in the right lane in the one-way sections; it's allowed when the designated parking lots are filled (and even when they aren't).

Along the route are trailheads and overlooks, as well as **Sieur de Monts Spring** (Acadia Nature Center, Wild Gardens of Acadia, Abbe Museum summer site, and the convergence of several spectacular trails), **Sand Beach, Thunder Hole, Otter Cliffs, Fabbri picnic area** (there's one wheelchair-accessible picnic table), **Jordan Pond House, Bubble Pond, Eagle Lake,** and the summit of **Cadillac Mountain.** Just before you get to Sand Beach, you'll see the Park Entrance Station, where you'll need to purchase a pass if you haven't already done so. (If you're here during nesting/fledging season—April to mid-August—be sure to stop in the Precipice Trail Parking Area; see the *Peregrine Falcons* sidebar.)

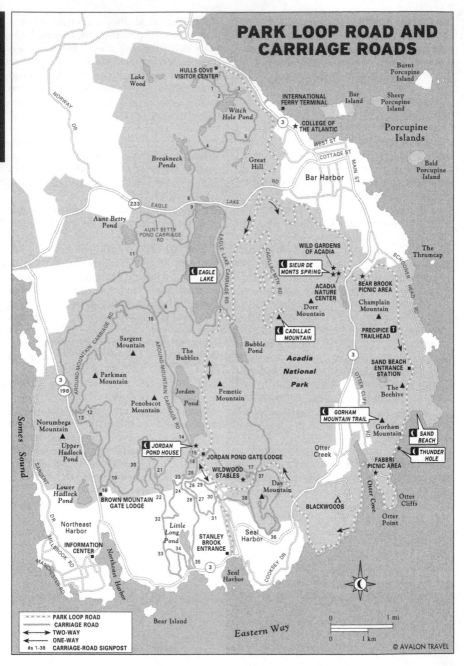

PARK LOOP ROAD AND CARRIAGE ROADS

Lake Wood

HULLS COVE VISITOR CENTER

Witch Hole Pond

Breakneck Ponds

Great Hill

Burnt Porcupine Island

INTERNATIONAL FERRY TERMINAL

Bar Island

Sheep Porcupine Island

COLLEGE OF THE ATLANTIC

WEST ST

COTTAGE ST

Porcupine Islands

Bald Porcupine Island

Bar Harbor

NORWAY DR

233 EAGLE

Aunt Betty Pond

AUNT BETTY POND CARRIAGE RD

EAGLE LAKE

LAKE

The Thrumcap

WILD GARDENS OF ACADIA

SIEUR DE MONTS SPRING

ACADIA NATURE CENTER

Dorr Mountain

BEAR BROOK PICNIC AREA

Champlain Mountain

PRECIPICE TRAILHEAD

SCHOONER HEAD RD

CADILLAC MTN RD

CADILLAC MOUNTAIN

Acadia National Park

SAND BEACH ENTRANCE STATION

The Beehive

Sargent Mountain

The Bubbles

Bubble Pond

Parkman Mountain

AROUND-MOUNTAIN CARRIAGE RD

AROUND MOUNTAIN CARRIAGE RD

EAGLE LAKE CARRIAGE RD

Jordan Pond

Pemetic Mountain

GORHAM MOUNTAIN TRAIL

Gorham Mountain

SAND BEACH

Penobscot Mountain

3 198

Norumbega Mountain

Upper Hadlock Pond

SARGENT DR

Somes Sound

Lower Hadlock Pond

JORDAN POND HOUSE

JORDAN POND GATE LODGE

WILDWOOD STABLES

Day Mountain

THUNDER HOLE

Otter Creek

FABBRI PICNIC AREA

OTTER CLIFF RD

BROWN MOUNTAIN GATE LODGE

Northeast Harbor

MILLBROOK RD

MANCHESTER RD

INFORMATION CENTER

Northeast Harbor

Little Long Pond

STANLEY BROOK ENTRANCE

Seal Harbor

BLACKWOODS

Otter Cove

Otter Cliffs

Otter Point

Seal Harbor

3

COOKSEY DR

Bear Island

Eastern Way

Legend:
- ======= PARK LOOP ROAD
- ——— CARRIAGE ROAD
- ←→ TWO-WAY
- ← ONE-WAY
- #s 1-38 CARRIAGE-ROAD SIGNPOST

0   1 mi
0   1 km

© AVALON TRAVEL

Island Tour

If you still have time for and interest in more driving after you've done the loop, take a spin around the rest of the island. Exit the Park Loop Road (near Bar Harbor) onto Route 233, heading west. Continue to Route 198 and go left (south). After just over a mile, watch for a smallish sign for **Sargent Drive**. (Only cars are allowed on this road—no RVs.) Take Sargent Drive, skirting gorgeous **Somes Sound,** into Northeast Harbor.

Leave Northeast Harbor via Route 198, northward, until you reach the head of Somes Sound. Go left around the head of the sound, to **Somesville,** a gem of a historic hamlet, then continue southward on Route 102 to Southwest Harbor. If you have time, take the Route 102A loop, which offers a chance to see **Bass Harbor Head Light.** You'll want to walk from the parking lot to get the best view; one trail has you scampering down steps to the ledges and rocks below it, while the other is a paved drive to near the light's base. Otherwise,

---

THE CAR-FREE PARK

Every way you look at it, the **Island Explorer** bus system is a success. Since 1999, when the fare-free propane-fueled buses began running throughout Mount Desert Island, more than 2.5 million riders have used the system, reducing car and RV usage and their resultant pollutants.

Since the service began on an experimental basis, it's been dramatically expanded, in great part thanks to the backing of L.L.Bean, which has pledged $2 million since 2002. Service now begins in late June and lasts until Columbus Day (the Schoodic Peninsula route, established on a trial basis in 2003, continues through September).

"The little bus system that could," as Friends of Acadia president Ken Olson called it, transports passengers to ferry landings, saves hikers and bikers from backtracking, gets commuters to work, and generally has revolutionized the summertime traffic patterns on Mount Desert Island.

Why spend valuable vacation time looking for a place to park your car? Why be disappointed when you reach a hiking trailhead and find the parking lot full? Take the bus. Feeling unsteady and unable to hike or bike? Tour the park and the island on the bus. Each bus can handle two bikes and a wheelchair, and there's even a dedicated bike shuttle operating between the Bar Harbor downtown hub and Eagle Lake.

The fleet is operated by the nonprofit Downeast Transportation (www.exploreacadia.com), with support from your park entrance fees, Friends of Acadia, and area towns and businesses.

Two caveats: First, these aren't tour buses, and there is no narration, nor do they climb Cadillac Mountain, so don't use them as a substitute for a guided tour or as a way to see all park highlights. Second, although the buses are free, riders traveling into the park must have a park pass.

The Island Explorer hub is the Bar Harbor Village Green, where all of the routes (except Schoodic) begin or end. Between late June and Labor Day, service begins at 6:45 A.M., although not every route starts that early. But, like the Energizer bunny, the buses keep going and going and going...until late into the summer evening (last bus leaves downtown Bar Harbor about 11 P.M. for the campgrounds at the northern end of the island). A geolocator system provides tracking information at the Village Green, at the Hulls Cove Visitor Center, and online.

Specific stops are listed on the schedule, but drivers will pull over and pick you up or drop you off anywhere they feel it's safe. Don't hesitate to request a stop or flag down a bus.

So pick up a schedule – copies are everywhere on Mount Desert – and use the Island Explorer to explore the island!

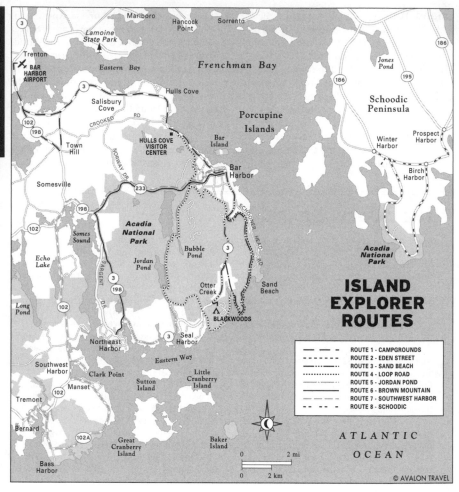

continue on Route 102 to Tremont (with a possible detour into Bernard for great lobster on the wharf), then go clockwise around to West Tremont, Seal Cove, Pretty Marsh, and back to Somesville. From there, you can go directly north to leave the island via Route 102/198, or go to Bar Harbor by heading eastward (follow signs).

Sights

The **Park Loop Road** will lead you to the major sights on the east side of the park—Sieur de Monts Spring, Sand Beach, Thunder Hole, Otter Cliffs, and the summit of Cadillac Mountain—but then there's also the fantastic carriage road system. As you explore the rest of the park acreage on Mount Desert, particularly its west side, you'll come upon still more surprising spots.

◖ SIEUR DE MONTS SPRING

About two miles from Bar Harbor and close to the often-busy Park Loop Road, Sieur de Monts Spring is an oasis in a tranquil woodland setting. Named after 17th-century French explorer Pierre du Gua, Sieur de Monts, the spring is the centerpiece of a 10-acre parcel donated in 1916 for a future national park by George Bucknam Dorr, the Father of Acadia.

The original Abbe Museum at Sieur de Monts Spring is filled with Native American artifacts.

It was Dorr who erected the pretty Italianate Spring House and dubbed this "The Sweet Waters of Acadia"—after the Sweet Waters of Europe and the Sweet Waters of Asia, two springs that had deeply impressed him on a visit to Constantinople. (The water here, incidentally, is not safe to drink—nor, for that matter, is the water in those Istanbul springs.)

Also here is the Acadia **Nature Center,** containing exhibits on flora and fauna and explanations of the ongoing efforts to preserve the park's natural resources. The center is open mid-May through mid-October (9 A.M.–5 P.M. daily in July and Aug.). Admission is free.

While at the Nature Center, take time to walk through the adjacent **Wild Gardens of Acadia,** touted as "an outdoor field guide" to the island's plant life. George B. Dorr acquired and named the land in 1909, and in 1961 then–park superintendent Harold Hubler proposed the wildflower garden. It was initially sponsored by the Bar Harbor Garden Club, and the book *Wild Flowers of Mt. Desert Island,* published in 1918, was used to determine the plantings. Walking paths lace the gardens, which are divided into a dozen different habitats containing more than 400 indigenous wildflower species. It's now supported by the park and the Friends of Acadia and maintained by volunteers as well as a park-sponsored college student during the summer months. The gardens are open mid-May through mid-October (9 A.M.–5 P.M. in July and Aug., shorter hours early and late in the season).

An important feature of this lovely area is the privately run **Abbe Museum** (207/288-3519, www.abbemuseum.org, 9 A.M.–4 P.M. daily, late May–mid-Oct., $2 adults, $1 ages 6–15), the original home of Dr. Robert Abbe's extensive personal collection of prehistoric and historic archaeological artifacts, some dating back 11,000 years. Opened in 1928, the museum outgrew this building (which is on the National Register of Historic Places) and now has a handsome year-round structure in downtown Bar Harbor. Inside are exhibits on Maine archaeology and the history of the museum. Tickets purchased here can be applied toward admission to the main campus of the museum in Bar Harbor.

The Sieur de Monts Spring area provides access to several Acadia trails. To the west of the Spring House are strenuous trails leading up **Dorr Mountain** (originally Dry Mountain, then Flying Squadron Mountain). To the north is the easy **Jesup Path**—two to three miles in the valley between Dorr Mountain and Huguenot Head. The Jesup Path (also called the Jesup Trail) is particularly spectacular during the fall foliage season. You can also access the Tarn and Hemlock Trails at Sieur de Monts.

Sieur de Monts Spring is accessible on the Island Explorer via either Route 3/Sand Beach or Route 4/Blackwoods.

◖ SAND BEACH

Below the Park Loop Road and the newly spiffed-up Park Entrance Station, Sand Beach is the park's only large sandy beach on saltwater—*cold* saltwater. Well, it's not really sand, as a sign posted here will tell you—it's composed of zillions of crushed shells, pulverized so they look like sand. If you haven't purchased your park entrance pass by this point, you'll need to do it here. Via the Island Explorer bus (Route 3/Sand Beach), Sand Beach is about 25 minutes from Bar Harbor. It's a bit quicker than that by car before and after the bus season. You can access the **Great Head** and **Ocean** trails from here.

◖ THUNDER HOLE

Thunder Hole gets pumped up as a spectacular attraction, and it is—but only if your timing is right. If not, it's more of, as one ranger snickered, a gurgling gulch. When the wind is coming from the south or southeast, when a storm has churned up the sea, or when the tide is rushing inward—then you'll hear (and feel) how Thunder Hole got its name. As the water rushes into a narrow slot in the rocks, it creates a powerful roar,

On a hot summer day, some folks actually brave the cold waters of Sand Beach.

© HILARY NANGLE

shoots into the air, and often showers the closest bystanders.

If your schedule is flexible, check the tide tables in the local paper (or in the park's *Beaver Log* newspaper) and try to be here for the incoming tide, preferably about midtide.

Because of the sea spray, the steps leading down toward Thunder Hole are often very slippery. Take particular care with small children and anyone who tends to be unsteady.

From May through late October, the park operates an information station here, open daily 9 A.M.–5 P.M.

JORDAN POND HOUSE

Afternoon tea on the lawn at the rustic Jordan Pond House (207/276-3316, www.jordanpond .com, 11:30 A.M.–9 P.M.) was a summer tradition in the late 19th century, and it's still on everyone's list of Acadia highlights. You can even arrive by carriage and re-create the car-free era. While tea (with hot-from-the-oven popovers and strawberry jam and homemade ice cream) is the most popular choice here, the restaurant—now in a modern building—also serves lunch and dinner between mid-May and mid-October. From late June to Columbus Day, the Island Explorer bus (Route 5/Jordan Pond) will get you here from Bar Harbor in 20 minutes. (In summer, the last bus for Bar Harbor leaves the restaurant at 8:50 P.M.)

The Jordan Pond House is a great base for using the area's carriage roads. Also here is a short nature path.

CADILLAC MOUNTAIN

As the highest point (1,530 ft.) in Acadia, the Cadillac summit receives the day's first ray of sunlight between early October and early March. A couple of trails will get you to the Cadillac summit (including one from Blackwoods Campground), and you can get a good mountain-bike workout on the road (bikes aren't allowed on trails), but in the end, most summiteers tend to get there by car—a seven-mile round-trip via paved road. (The Island Explorer bus does not go to the Cadillac summit.)

Formerly named Green Mountain, Cadillac was topped by the wooden Summit Hotel, built by an ambitious developer who eventually fell on hard times and went into bankruptcy. Some might say he deserved it for blighting the landscape. Before his decline in the late 19th century, however, his 6,000-foot Green Mountain Cog Railway transported guests to the summit, where the view was just as spectacular as it is today. (Photos of the Cog Railway era are part of the collection at the Bar Harbor Historical Society, on Ledgelawn Street.) The summit road was built in 1931.

At the height of summer, sunrise, midday, and sunset are the busiest times on the summit; if you're not looking for bragging rights about sunrise or sunset, try to be here an hour or two after sunrise or an hour or two before sunset.

At the top are head-swiveling vistas and a gift shop and restrooms. Be sure to walk the paved 0.3-mile Summit Trail loop for the full effect, but *please stay on the trail* to preserve the summit's fragile plants and soil.

From late August to mid-October, the park runs the **Hawkwatch** program near the Cadillac summit. (The observation site is on the Cadillac North Ridge Trail, about 600 feet from the summit parking lot.) Each day during the Hawkwatch, 9 A.M.–2 P.M., weather permitting, park interpreters are on hand to help you identify the various species of hawks, falcons, eagles, and ospreys that migrate through Acadia each fall. Since the Hawkwatch project began in 1995, the annual raptor count here during the migration season has averaged about 2,500, but 2007 witnessed a record-breaking 3,697.

CARRIAGE ROADS

Bare summits, woodlands, gemlike ponds, 17 handsome stone bridges, and dazzling vistas—you'll see them all as you walk or bike the fantastic 57-mile carriage road network that makes Acadia unique among America's national parks.

Forty-five miles of the broken-stone roads—all on the east side of the island, between the Hulls Cove Visitor Center in the north and

JORDAN POND HOUSE

In the late 19th century, when Bar Harbor was in the throes of becoming "the great new place" to escape the heat of Washington, New York, Philadelphia, and the Midwest, gentle ladies and men patronized an unassuming farmhouse/teahouse on the shores of Jordan Pond. By 1895 or 1896, under the stewardship of Thomas McIntire, it became Jordan Pond House – a determinedly rustic establishment, with massive fieldstone fireplaces, serving afternoon tea and leisurely luncheons during the summer and fall.

And rustic it remained, well into the late 20th century – until leveled by a disastrous fire in the summer of 1979. At that point, it was owned by Acadia. John D. Rockefeller Jr. had bought it in the 1930s and donated it to the park in the early 1940s. Since then, it's been managed on behalf of the park by concessionaires – currently the Acadia Corporation (which also operates gift shops in several locations).

Today, Jordan Pond House, the only restaurant within Acadia National Park, must rely on its framed antique photos to conjure up a bit of nostalgia for the bygone era. The building is modern and open, the pace in summer is frenetic, and the food is average. But the view from the lawn over Jordan Pond and the astounding Bubbles is incredible. Surely *it* hasn't changed.

So, at least once, brave the crowds and have afternoon tea on the lawn at Jordan Pond House. Order tea or Oregon Chai or even cappuccino and fresh popovers (two) with extraordinary strawberry jam. You might even splurge and add a scoop of Jordan Pond Ice Cream. Expect to pay $11 or more, but how much would you pay for the view?

Lunch (salads, sandwiches, and entrées include a popover) and afternoon tea are served 11:30 A.M.-5:30 P.M. daily, inside or on the lawn. Dinner (entrées $17-25) begins at 5:30 P.M. – inside or on the porch. The reservation system is as follows: call 207/276-3316, any time from 9:15 A.M., which puts you "on the list." You'll probably still have to wait when you arrive, so stop in the gift shop for a jar of jam to take home.

Perhaps because of all the sweet drinks and jam served outdoors, patrons at the lawn tables sometimes find themselves pestered by bees. They don't usually sting unless you pester them back, but if you're allergic to bee stings, or are with anyone who is, be alert.

You can buy a package of popover mix along with the jam in the gift shop, but if you don't and you need a popover fix when you return home, here's the Jordan Pond House recipe:

JORDAN POND HOUSE POPOVERS

2 large eggs

1 cup whole milk

1 cup all-purpose flour (pre-sifted)

½ teaspoon salt

⅛ teaspoon baking soda

Preheat oven to 425°F. Beat eggs with electric mixer at high speed for three minutes. Reduce mixer speed to lowest setting and very gradually pour in half the milk. In separate bowl, combine sifted flour, salt, and baking soda and sift again.

With mixer still running at slowest speed, add dry ingredients to egg-and-milk mixture. Turn off mixer and use rubber spatula to blend mixture thoroughly.

Set mixer to medium speed and very gradually pour in remaining milk, blending for one minute. Raise mixer speed to highest setting and beat 10 minutes.

Strain batter through fine-mesh strainer to remove lumps, then pour into well-buttered popover or custard cups. Bake 15 minutes. Without opening oven, reduce heat to 350°F and bake 15 more minutes (20 minutes if oven door has a window).

Serve immediately, with fresh jam and room-temperature butter. Recipe makes two popovers. Increase as desired, but be sure to measure carefully. Popovers turn out significantly better if baked in ovenproof cups rather than in metal or glass.

a picturesque stone bridge in Acadia

BASS HARBOR HEAD LIGHT

At the southern end of Mount Desert's western "claw," follow Route 102A to the turnoff toward Bass Harbor Head. Drive or bike to the end of Lighthouse Road, walk down a steep wooden stairway, and look up and to the right. Voilà! Bass Harbor Head Light—its red glow automated since 1974—stands sentinel at the eastern entrance to Blue Hill Bay. A paved path with interpretational signage departs from the other end of the parking lot and leads to near the tower's base. Built in 1858, the 26-foot tower and lightkeeper's house are privately owned, but the dramatic setting is a photographer's dream. Winter access to the parking lot may be limited, but otherwise the area is open all year. Not far from the light (east along Route 102A) are the trailheads for the easy Ship Harbor and Wonderland nature trails, part of Acadia National Park (see *Hiking*).

Seal Harbor in the south—are open for walking, bicycling, and horseback riding (and in winter for cross-country skiing and snowshoeing). Twelve additional miles, on private land owned by the Green Rock Company, are open for walking and horseback riding but not biking (be alert for the No Bikes signs when you're cycling; all of the private roads are south of the Jordan Pond House).

◖ EAGLE LAKE

The largest lake on the eastern half of the island, Eagle Lake is entirely within the park, so its shoreline is undeveloped. Cadillac, Pemetic, and Sargent Mountains and the Bubbles surround it. You can pedal or walk around Eagle on a carriage road or launch a canoe or kayak and paddle its waters. Or just find a rock to sit on and enjoy the scenery. You might spot osprey, eagles, great blue heron, loons, and other wildlife here. Two parking lots off Route 233 make access easy (one by the boat launch and a larger one on the other side of the road).

Bass Harbor Head Light is off the beaten path, but worth a visit.

MOUNT DESERT ISLAND

MR. ROCKEFELLER'S ROADS

Imagine being able to build your own network of pathways where you could step into a horse-drawn carriage and meander through matchless terrain. Petroleum heir John D. Rockefeller Jr. did just that on Mount Desert Island – and, thanks to him, we can all walk and bike these roadways, and even go for our own horse-drawn carriage rides.

The story of Acadia's car-free carriage roads has been told and retold, but Rockefeller's granddaughter, Ann R. Roberts, had the inside track when she wrote *Mr. Rockefeller's Roads: The Untold Story of Acadia's Carriage Roads & Their Creator* (see *Suggested Reading*). Her book relates a fascinating saga of benevolence and sensitivity and talent and organization. The carriage road system is one of Acadia's most valued cultural resources – listed since 1979 on the National Register of Historic Places.

Between 1913 and 1940, Rockefeller was involved in the purchase of acreage and the design and construction of more than 57 miles of carriage roads on Mount Desert Island. (Forty-five miles of these roads are now within Acadia National Park boundaries and 12 are on private land but open to the public.)

And "involved" is the operative word here. Not only did he conceptualize the project, finance it, and consult on every aspect of the road and bridge designs, he was on hand during the construction and landscaping phases. No detail escaped his scrutiny.

Rockefeller's passion for road engineering and landscaping came from watching and working with his father, John D. Rockefeller Sr., who planned carriage roads and rustic stone bridges for the family's estate near Cleveland. Later, father and son created carriage roads through Pocantico Hills, their vast Hudson River estate. Lessons learned from those undertakings laid the groundwork (literally and figuratively) for the even more ambitious project on Mount Desert.

Rockefeller Jr. first visited Mount Desert as a Brown University student in 1893, but it was his 1908 trip to Seal Harbor – with his wife Abby – that shaped his lifelong love for the island. In 1910, they bought The Eyrie, a Seal Harbor estate that still remains in the family, and he soon began other land acquisitions that continued until 1940. Around 1913, he began laying out his astonishing network of carriage roads, stepping up the pace in 1916 when he

PRETTY MARSH PICNIC AREA

Picnic spots are everywhere on Mount Desert, but an Acadia National Park site that many people miss is the Pretty Marsh Picnic Area, overlooking Pretty Marsh Harbor, on the opposite side of the island from Bar Harbor. Dense woods shelter grills and tables, and you can walk down to the shoreline and even launch a sea kayak. Kids love this place, but be prepared with insect repellent. The picnic area is just west of Route 102 (Pretty Marsh Rd.), on the westernmost shore. Pretty Marsh is not on an Island Explorer bus route; you'll need a car or bike to get here.

BAKER ISLAND

The best way to get to—and to appreciate—history-rich Baker Island is on the ranger-narrated Acadia National Park Baker Island Tour aboard the *Miss Samantha,* booked through **Bar Harbor Whale Watch Co.** (1 West St., Bar Harbor, 207/288-2386 or 888/942-5374, www.barharborwhales.com, $36 adult, $18 ages 6–14, $5 age 5 and younger). The half-day tours depart Monday–Saturday late June through mid-September and include access via skiff to the 130-acre island with farmstead, lighthouse, and intriguing rock formations. The return trip provides a view of Otter Cliffs (bring binoculars and look for climbers), hired Charles P. Simpson as his chief engineer. In 1922, Simpson turned over the task to his son Paul ("Chip"), who remained chief engineer until 1940. Renowned landscape architect Beatrix Farrand worked with Rockefeller on roadside plantings, and dozens of other people – noted and not-so-noted – became part of the team at some point during the nearly three-decade-long project.

Distinctive features of the roads are 17 handsome rough-stone bridges (with single, double, and triple arches; no two alike), 16-foot-wide broken-stone roadbeds that required more man-hours than anyone could count, and tasteful carved trail markers. A holdover from Rockefeller's previous carriage road experience was the use of roadside borders of squared-off granite coping stones – known at Acadia as "Mr. Rockefeller's teeth."

And then there are the two stone gate lodges (or gate houses) – Brown Mountain Gate Lodge and Jordan Pond Gate Lodge – heralding entrances to the original carriage road system. (Many more access points exist today.) Designed by Grosvenor Atterbury in a whimsical French Romanesque style, the handsome structures are startling, to say the least.

It's hard not to smile when you come upon them (near Northeast Harbor and near Jordan Pond, respectively). During the carriage road building, engineer Paul Simpson and his family occupied the Jordan Pond Gate Lodge.

Until his death in 1960 (when Acadia assumed responsibility for 45 miles of the carriage road system), John D. Rockefeller Jr. continued his magnanimity by financing the maintenance of the carriage road network. By the early 1990s, however, the roads, bridges, and drainage systems had seriously deteriorated, and the fabulous vistas had become overgrown. Enter Friends of Acadia, an amazing nonprofit organization that helped the park obtain federal funding and then maximized the grant with matching private funds – generating enough to cover the $6 million face-lift and begin a carriage road endowment. Funding maintenance are annual contributions from FOA of more than $200,000 from the endowment and a portion of park user fees. In addition, volunteers log countless hours.

As one carriage road admirer put it: "The roads are just the way God would have made them if he only had the money."

Thunder Hole, Sand Beach, and Great Head from the water.

History buffs, lighthouse lovers, and naturalists will love this trip. Baker was settled in the early 1800s by Hannah and William Gilley, who rowed here from Mount Desert Island, accompanied by their three young children, goats, and household goods. They built a home and farm and reared 12 children here, with Hannah schooling them in the three Rs and rowing them to church in Southwest Harbor every Sunday. When the lighthouse was built on the island in 1828, William became its first keeper, at an annual salary of $350. He was removed from that post in 1848 for political reasons, and that's where the story gets really interesting.

Note that because the Park Service contracts with an independent boat company, there have been years when this trip hasn't been available. In that case, the only way to Baker Island is via charter or your own boat. In any case, pack a lunch. Check the *Beaver Log* or a visitors center for tour status. Or visit virtually: Go to www.nps.gov/acad and click on "Photos and Multimedia," then "Virtual Tour."

Hiking

It would take weeks of nonstop all-day hiking to cover every trail in the Mount Desert Island acreage of Acadia National Park. And it would consume most of this book to write about them. Not a bad idea—but few of us have enough free time to manage such a feat. (Island resident Tom St. Germain, author of *A Walk in the Park,* somehow finds time to hike each of the trails at least once a year. More power to him!) Best to do as much as you can when you're here—and return as often as possible to do more.

What follows, therefore, is a selection of choice hikes, ranging from very easy to strenuous. Evaluate your schedule, your skills and limitations (especially the capabilities of your least-sturdy hiking partners), gather your gear, pack a picnic and plenty of water, and head out.

As you take your first step on your first park trail, however, keep in mind the Leave No Trace philosophy that governs all recreation in the park—but especially hiking. Stick to it for yourself, your family, and the generations to come.

Until the establishment of the **Island Explorer** bus system, hikers had to do loop trails in order to return to their cars or bikes, or they had to make elaborate arrangements for pickup or shuttling. The bus schedule now has created all kinds of other options. It allows you to skip the backtracking—and in some cases lets you pick up transport along the way if you (or the kids) wear out earlier than expected. (Of course, this holds true only during the bus season, late June through early October, and the schedule is reduced after early September.) Even if your destination or locale isn't on the bus schedule, you can request a stop or flag down a bus anywhere that's safe for the driver to pull over. The bus schedules vary slightly

A trail edges the water in the western section of the park.

© HILARY NANGLE

each year. Pick up the latest schedule at the Hulls Cove Visitor Center or download it before you leave home (www.exploreacadia.com). Then take advantage of the system while you're on Mount Desert Island.

All of the hikes described here follow Acadia National Park hiking trails. (See the *Mount Desert Island Communities* chapter for info on the in-town Shore Path, which is not part of the park.) The separate but sometimes interconnected carriage roads, which also are open for hiking (more like strolling, in many cases)—as well as horseback riding and bicycling—are described later, under *Biking*.

The hikes that follow are divided into two sections—the east side of Mount Desert Island and the west side. Because Somes Sound nearly bisects the island, none of the trails cross from one side of the island to the other, and almost every one of the peaks' ridgelines runs in a north-south (or south-north) direction. The hikes are described below in the order of difficulty, from very easy to strenuous; lengths of hikes vary within each category (length, of course, doesn't always determine the difficulty). Ratings are based on park advisories and personal experience.

While you plan, bear in mind that most visitors tend to spend more time on the east side of the island, for a variety of reasons—more trails, a range of easy-to-moderate trails, the carriage road network, the auto road to the Cadillac summit, the Park Loop Road, the park's only restaurant (Jordan Pond House), and so on. So heading for the west-side trails, even at the height of summer, can provide you with quieter spaces and some truly great hikes.

You'll find a number of commercial maps available. I like the *Acadia National Park Trails, Carriage Roads, Hiking, Biking* map ($4.95), published by Map Adventures L.L.C. (www.mapadventures.com), because it's easy to read. The only drawback is it doesn't include the entire island, making it a bit difficult to easily figure out locations if you're not familiar with the area. There's also a waterproof version available for $9.95.

EAST-SIDE TRAILS
Jordan Pond Nature Trail

- Distance: 1 mile round-trip
- Duration: 30–45 minutes
- Elevation gain: Minimal
- Effort: Very easy
- Trailhead: Jordan Pond Parking Area (Island Explorer Route 5/Jordan Pond)

This oh-so-easy trail is perfect for little ones. You can pick up a brochure detailing 10 numbered sites at the trailhead ($0.50 donation), so you can pepper the walk with fun info and quiz the kids along the way. Reward them afterward with ice cream at the Jordan Pond House.

The trail loops from the Jordan Pond overflow/hikers' parking lot through the woods and down to the pond, following its shore for a bit before looping back to the starting point.

Ocean Trail

- Distance: 4 miles round-trip
- Duration: 1–1.5 hours
- Elevation gain: Level
- Effort: Very easy
- Trailhead: Take the Park Loop Road to either the Sand Beach or the Otter Point parking lot. The Island Explorer bus (Route 3/Sand Beach) stops at Sand Beach and Otter Cliffs Parking Areas, so you can begin the walk at either end. If you want to do the trail once, rather than backtracking, get off the bus at one end or the other, then pick up another bus when you're ready to continue onward—mix and match, if you will.

Because this trail is so easy, and easy to reach, it's extremely popular. In fact, lovely as it is, you'd have to be crazy to be on it between 10 A.M. and 3 P.M. at the height of summer. At the risk of divulging the solution, the last time I walked it, at 7 A.M. on a bright June day, I had the path all to myself—a minor miracle, actually—and

TIPS FOR DAY HIKING

Since Acadia has no backcountry camping, all the hikes in the park are day hikes – guaranteeing, at least, a load off your back! You need little gear for a half-day or daylong hike, but don't be complacent or stupid – use common sense and be prepared for emergencies. That way, they probably won't happen.

Experienced hikers and backcountry campers won't need my advice here, but a few reminders never hurt, and it's worth noting the "maps and guides" information specific to Acadia.

In general, the gear you carry (and the size of your day pack) depends on your plans for the day – following a short nature trail then calling it quits; hiking for a few hours then stopping for a swim; hiking all day with a noontime picnic. Here's a checklist that should help you get organized (divvy up the items if you're hiking with friends or family):

- **Identification,** such as a driver's license. Even if you don't carry your regular wallet, be sure you have your health insurance card.

- **Maps and guides.** Purchase a trail map at the park's visitor center. The National Park Service map of Acadia that's available free at the visitor center will give you the lay of the land and useful general info, and it's serviceable if you're planning only to drive or bike the Park Loop Road, but *do not* rely on it for hiking. The map published by Jim Witherell is particularly good (contour interval 20 feet), as is the Parkman Publications map, published in conjunction with Friends of Acadia (contour interval 50 feet). On the east side of the island, even if you are planning to stick to the hiking trails, *be sure* also to carry a map of the park's carriage roads to avoid confusion where carriage and hiking trails meet and cross.

- Purchase and use a trail guide as well. I recommend *A Walk in the Park* by Tom St. Germain ($11.95) and *Hiking Acadia National Park* by Dolores Kong and Dan Ring ($16.95). Both provide useful detailed maps and elevations for each hike. Also valuable is the Appalachian Mountain Club's *Discover Acadia National Park,* by Jerry and Marcy Monkman ($16.95), which comes with a foldout map (contour interval 100 feet). Besides hikes, the Appalachian Mountain Club guide includes information on bike and paddling routes as well as other recreational activities in the park.

- Between late June and Columbus Day, carry a copy of the **Island Explorer bus schedule,** which you can find almost anywhere on the island (or download it before you leave home: www.exploreacadia.com). Stuff it in your day pack, even if you're getting to your trailhead by car. If someone in your hiking party wants to quit early, you'll want to know the nearest spot (and time) to catch a bus.

- **Water and food.** Even though some ponds in the park are used as drinking-water sources for surrounding towns, it's treated before they get it. Don't risk intestinal problems; carry your own water. If you're worried about carrying weight, and can stand the taste, include iodine tablets. To avoid excessive thirst, don't bring salty snacks – carry gorp or energy bars (without chocolate, so you don't have to deal with a melting mush). If you're carrying picnic fare, don't be overambitious (or greedy) if you're planning a strenuous hike. Be sure to pack any mayo-based food in a flexible insulated bag; peanut-butter-and-jam (jelly for the kids) sandwiches are a safer bet.

- A couple of wastebasket-size **trash bags** – carry in, carry out. A spare bag can also come in handy for protecting maps, a camera, binoculars, etc., in the event of a sudden squall (not unheard of during a Maine summer).

- A **compass or GPS,** particularly if you're directionally challenged or are planning a lengthy hike. If you own a cell phone, carry it, but *turn it off* and use it *only* in an emergency. Wireless service can be iffy in some parts of Acadia; check when you arrive.

- A small **first-aid kit** (in a waterproof or zip-top bag) containing a few basic items: adhesive bandages, aspirin or acetaminophen, ibuprofen, perhaps an elastic bandage. Even though bees don't tend to be a problem in Acadia (except perhaps on the lawn at Jordan Pond House), be sure you're carrying a prefilled epinephrine syringe to prevent anaphylaxis if you're allergic to bee stings (or, for that matter, shellfish). Include a few wooden matches and a whistle in case of emergency.

- **Moist towelettes** for various cleanup tasks, or for cleansing minor scrapes.

- A **Swiss Army knife.** Carry the kind with a corkscrew if you're planning on having wine with a picnic. Or you could decant white wine into a plastic water bottle to save weight – but go easy on the alcohol. Not only will it dehydrate you, but you're more prone to tripping and falling.

- A full-brimmed **hat** and decent **hiking shoes** (not sandals, which provide no ankle support).

- **Sunblock, lip balm** (the kind with UV protection), and **insect repellent.** Lewey's, a natural repellent, is a good choice, especially for children. Ben's and Cutter's tend to be widely available.

- A **camera** (and a spare battery) and **binoculars.** Take plenty of film or memory cards if you're planning to be out all day. Most of the island's summits are bare, allowing fabulous views – photo ops are everywhere in Acadia.

- A **mini-flashlight** and spare batteries (just in case).

- Depending on your plans for the day, carry a change of socks, a rain jacket or windbreaker, maybe a fleece vest, and perhaps a swimsuit for a hike such as Penobscot and Sargent Mountains, where you can pause for a swim in Sargent Pond.

- Most importantly, don't hike alone, or if you do, tell someone – a friend, a relative, your lodging manager, a campground ranger, your shrink, anyone – or leave a note to say where you are headed. If for any reason you don't return, the park rangers at least will know where to start looking.

- Remember, bikes are banned from *all* hiking trails. Dogs must be leashed (not always convenient on strenuous scrambles), and they are banned from Sand Beach and hiking trails with ladders ("ladder trails"). Best advice: Don't bring a dog. If you do, hike only the shorter, easier trails – and *do* come equipped to clean up after your pet.

- And a health note: Lyme disease has been reported here, so when you return from hiking, check for ticks.

the tide was at just the right height for Thunder Hole to live up to its name.

The first bus doesn't arrive at Sand Beach until 9:25 A.M., so if that's your mode of transport, consider doing this trail later in the day at the height of summer.

The trail runs close to the shore for about half of its length and takes in several of the Park Loop Road's highlights—Sand Beach, Thunder Hole, Otter Cliffs, and the giant sea stack in Monument Cove—not to mention gorgeous sea-level views of Frenchman Bay.

Along here, it's especially tempting to "liberate" rocks from the shore—resist the urge. Remember the slogan, "Leave the rocks for the next glacier." If you forget, a few judiciously placed national park signs will remind you.

Compass Harbor

- Distance: 1 mile round-trip

- Duration: 30 minutes

- Elevation gain: Level

- Effort: Very easy

- Trailhead: Compass Harbor section of the park, off Main Street, approximately one mile south of the intersection with Mount Desert Street.

This is an easy stroll through an oft-ignored section of the park. You can easily walk from downtown, if you want to lengthen the hike without adding any difficulty. The path loops through old-growth forest to a point on Compass Harbor and by the ruins of George B. Dorr's summer cottage. There are plenty of nice spots for a picnic here.

Great Head Trail

- Distance: 1.4 miles round-trip

- Duration: 1 hour

- Elevation gain: 145 feet

- Effort: Moderate

- Trailhead: Take the Park Loop Road to the

Sand Beach Parking Area (Island Explorer Route 3/Sand Beach)—the lower parking area is closer to the beach, but it fills up first. Walk down the steps to the beach and across it to the far (eastern) side, where you'll see the trailhead marker. You'll need to cross a rivulet here to reach the trailhead. If you're not here at low tide, and you don't have waterproof shoes, remove your shoes so you won't be hiking with wet feet.

First take the trail to the right, which climbs a few dozen steps (the "moderate" part), then continue right toward the headland ("head"), from which you can see the beach and the prominent mound of the Beehive. Out in Frenchman Bay is Egg Rock Light and beyond it is Schoodic Point. Continue on the trail counterclockwise, following the perimeter of the head, perhaps pausing for a picnic near the ruins of the mid-19th-century stone teahouse. Continue the loop around the head, then return back to Sand Beach.

You can reach Sand Beach (and therefore the Great Head Trail) via the Island Explorer bus, but since the Park Loop Road is one-way at this point, you won't be able to return to Bar Harbor the way you came. You'll need to grab a bus and continue the loop back to Bar Harbor, but the time is the same: 25 minutes from Bar Harbor to Sand Beach, 25 minutes back to the Village Green from Sand Beach. If you're staying in Bar Harbor, consider bicycling to the trail via the relatively quiet Schooner Head Road, off Route 3, just south of town.

Option: Another (easier) way to hike Great Head is to begin on the north side of the head and go in a clockwise direction. Take Main Street (Route 3) southward out of Bar Harbor, and about 0.8 mile after the athletic field, bear left onto Schooner Head Road, which roughly parallels the Park Loop Road. Continue just beyond the turn for the Schooner Head Overlook, park at the dead end, and begin your hike from this end of Great Head. There are actually two loops, which could end up taking you 1.8–2 miles. Keep bearing left (clockwise) to skirt the perimeter of Great Head.

Jordan Pond Shore Path

• Distance: 3.3 miles round-trip

• Duration: 1 hour minimum

• Elevation gain: Level

• Effort: Easy to moderate

• Trailhead: Jordan Pond

This mostly level counterclockwise circuit of Jordan Pond is a great way to walk off a Jordan Pond House lunch (including those popovers). Or do the hike first and reward yourself with afternoon tea. Start on the east side, the easiest; the west side has the only moderate section—rocky and rooty and, depending on recent weather, possibly a bit squishy. Log bridges have been installed in a number of spots.

Jordan Pond is part of the island's drinking-water supply, so no swimming (or even wading) is permitted here.

As if the summer setting here weren't enough, this trail is even more beautiful in the fall, when stands of birches add gold to the palette. Plus, the trail is far less crowded in late September and early October (except perhaps for Columbus Day weekend).

Option: The giant glacial erratic known as **Bubble Rock** is enough of a phenomenon that you may want to detour from the shore trail to see it, via the Bubble Rock Trail (at the northeast corner of the pond). It's a slightly steep 0.8-mile round-trip, up and back on the trail. At the risk of perpetuating a cliché, I'll add that the classic photo here is a Sisyphus imitation—the mythological fellow relentlessly pushing the boulder up a mountain, only to have it roll back. Fortunately, this one doesn't move, since it's the size of an SUV. There must be thousands of photo albums (and probably CDs) all over the world containing this image. Needless to say, kids love it.

In the summer of 2003, trail areas around Jordan Pond House and Jordan Pond were upgraded for wheelchair access, part of a major public-private collaborative effort to increase accessibility in the park. The improved access is on the east side of Jordan Pond.

By car from Bar Harbor, take the Park Loop Road (the two-way west side of the loop) to the Jordan Pond parking lot. An Island Explorer bus follows the same route. (In midsummer, another auto option is to take Route 3 south from Bar Harbor to Seal Harbor, then take the Stanley Brook entrance to the park, going north toward Jordan Pond.) Park and head toward the boat-launching ramp; you'll see the trailhead to the right.

◖ Gorham Mountain Trail

• Distance: 1.8 miles round-trip

• Duration: 1.5–2 hours

• Elevation gain: 525 feet

• Effort: Moderate

• Trailhead: On the one-way section of the Park Loop Road, continue past Sand Beach and Thunder Hole to the Gorham Mountain Parking Area. The Island Explorer bus (Route 3/Sand Beach) can drop you off here, or walk a short distance along the Ocean Trail after getting off the bus at the Thunder Hole stop. The trailhead is at the back of the parking lot.

The round-trip distance specified here covers the trail directly to the summit, then a return the same way with a short detour via Cadillac Cliffs. (You can also continue onward from the Gorham summit, following part of the Bowl Trail down to the Park Loop Road, then walk along the Ocean Trail back to your car, if you've left it in the Gorham lot.)

Follow cairns across ledges up from the trailhead to a fork, where you'll see a plaque commemorating Waldron Bates, the ingenious pathmaker who instigated the strategic use of granite staircases and iron ladders for Acadia's trails.

Bates was a lawyer for his day job, but his summer avocation as head of the Roads and Paths Committee for the Bar Harbor Improvement Association (1900–1909) gave him the greatest pleasure. Think of him as you navigate the Cadillac Cliffs Trail, one of his projects.

WITH A LITTLE HELP FROM OUR FRIENDS . . .

As we watch federal funding for national parks lose headway year after year, every park in America needs a safety net like **Friends of Acadia (FOA),** a dynamic organization headquartered in Bar Harbor. Propane-powered shuttle-bus service needs expanding? FOA finds a million-dollar donor. Well-used trails need maintenance? FOA organizes volunteer work parties. New connector trails needed? FOA gets them done. No need seems to go unfilled.

FOA – one of Acadia National Park's greatest assets – is both reactive and proactive. It's an amazingly symbiotic relationship. When informed of a need, the Friends stand ready to help; when they themselves perceive a need, they propose solutions to park management and jointly figure out ways to make them happen. It's hard to avoid sounding like a media flack when describing this organization.

Friends of Acadia was founded in 1986 to preserve and protect the park for resource-sensitive tourism and myriad recreational uses. Since 1995, FOA has contributed more than $10.5 million to the park and surrounding communities for trail upkeep, carriage road maintenance, seasonal park staff funding, and conservation projects. Plus FOA cofounded the Island Explorer bus system and instigated the Acadia Trails Forever program, a joint park-FOA partnership for trail rehabilitation. In 2003, for instance, FOA and the park announced the reopening (after considerable planning and rebuilding) of the Homans Path, on the east side of Dorr Mountain. The trail, built around 1916 and named after Eliza Homans, a generous benefactor, fell into disuse in the 1940s. It ascends via a granite stairway to a ledge with a commanding view of the Great Meadow and Frenchman Bay. More recently, FOA reconstructed the East Cliffs Trail on Sargent Mountain and reopened the abandoned Penobscot Mountain Trail. As part of its Tranquility Project to reduce traffic congestion on the island, FOA purchased land in Trenton for an off-island transit and welcome center and has sold approximately 150 acres

to the Maine Department of Transportation for the facility.

The Schoodic Committee of Friends of Acadia (www.friendsofschoodic.org) does much of the same type of work to preserve and protect the Schoodic section of the park. It also assists in maintaining the Schoodic Education and Research Center buildings, inventorying natural resources, and counting visitors.

You can join FOA and its 3,000 members and support this worthy cause for $35 a year, or $100 for a family (43 Cottage St., P.O. Box 45, Bar Harbor 04609, 207/288-3340 or 800/625-0321, www.friendsofacadia.org). You can also lend a hand (or two) while you're here. FOA and the park organize volunteer work parties for Acadia trail, carriage road, and other outdoor maintenance three times weekly between June and Columbus Day: 8:20 A.M.-12:30 P.M. Tuesday, Thursday, and Saturday. Call the recorded information line (207/288-3934) for the work locations, or 207/288-3340 or 800/625-0321 for answers to questions. The meeting point is Park Headquarters (Eagle Lake Rd., Rte. 233, Bar Harbor), about three miles west of town. This is a terrific way to give something back to the park, and the camaraderie is contagious. Be sure to take your own water, lunch, and bug repellent. Dress in layers and wear closed-toe shoes. More than 8,000 volunteer hours a year go toward this effort.

Each summer, Friends of Acadia also sponsors a handful of **Ridge Runners,** who work under park supervision and spend their days out and about on the trails repairing cairns, watching for lost hikers, and handing out Leave No Trace information.

If you happen to be in the region on the first Saturday in November, call the FOA office to register for the annual carriage road cleanup, which usually draws 250 or so volunteers. Bring water and gloves; there's a free hot lunch at midday for everyone who participates. It's dubbed Take Pride in Acadia Day – indeed an apt label.

For now, though, bear left (saving the Cadillac Cliffs route for the return) and head for the open-ledge summit (525 ft.; the third-lowest of Acadia's peaks). A signposted cairn marks the spot. From here, you'll see Sand Beach, Egg Rock Light in Frenchman Bay, the Beehive, Champlain Mountain, and lots more—a fabulous view.

Return via the same route, but make the short detour left onto the U-shaped Cadillac Cliffs Trail, featuring stairs, rocky footing, granite "tunnels," and even an ancient sea cave, now high and dry. (This sea cave once was filled with beach cobbles, but slowly, slowly it's been cleaned out by hikers—a prime example of the damage done by removing "just one.")

Beachcroft Trail

- Distance: 1.6 miles round-trip
- Duration: 1.5–2 hours
- Elevation gain: 1,100 feet
- Effort: Moderate to difficult
- Trailhead: The Tarn parking area, just north of Route 3, near Sieur de Monts Spring, and just west of the Park Loop Road, near the Jackson Laboratory (or take the Island Explorer bus, Route 4/Blackwoods).

The Beachcroft Trail on Huguenot Head leads up the west side of Champlain. Also called the Beachcroft Path, the trail is best known for its nearly 1,500 beautifully engineered granite steps, built by the Civilian Conservation Corps (CCC). It's a moderate climb via switchbacks to the granite ledges of Huguenot Head and its views to the Atlantic. Take in the views and replenish yourself with a snack to prepare for the next section. The trail descends briefly before climbing steeply over rocks to the Champlain's summit. The views are stupendous. From there, you can connect with the Bear Brook or Precipice Trails.

Penobscot and Sargent Mountains

- Distance: 6 miles round-trip
- Duration: 4 hours
- Elevation gain: 1,200 feet
- Effort: Difficult to strenuous
- Trailhead: Park your car in the overflow lot at Jordan Pond House, go left of the restaurant, and look for the carved trail signpost.

You'll cross Jordan Stream and a carriage road before starting on the rough part—heading upward rather steeply with rocky, ledgy footing. Handholds have been installed in strategic spots. (This part is even less fun on the return route.) But the rewards are worth the effort. Continue on to the Penobscot summit (1,194 ft.; the fifth-highest in the park), with wide-open views. In August, you'll have wild blueberries (but leave some for others) en route to the top.

The best feature of this hike is that you get to reach one summit then go for a swim in gorgeous little Sargent Pond before tackling the next one. From Penobscot's summit, it's only 10 minutes downhill to the pond. (If you're retracing your route, you can even have a second swim on the way back.) This is a long hike, however; if you're hiking with kids, be sure they're up to the challenge. For that matter, be sure *you* are.

From Sargent Pond, head upward on the South Ridge Trail to the summit of Sargent Mountain (1,373 ft.; the second-highest in the park).

Don't rush the return—the vistas are superb up here—but when you're ready, go back the same way.

Dorr Mountain via Homans Path and Dorr Mountain East Face

- Distance: 2.8 miles round-trip
- Duration: 1.5–2 hours
- Elevation gain: 1,200 feet
- Effort: Difficult to strenuous

- Trailhead: Take Hemlock Trail from the beginning of the Sieur de Monts parking lot (look for the split rail fence) and follow it to the intersection with the Jesup Path. Continue on the Hemlock Trail another few yards to the trailhead on your left. You can also take the Hemlock Trail from Bar Harbor to the trailhead.

Avid hiker Tom St. Germain, author of *A Walk in the Park,* rediscovered the Homans Path, originally built in 1915, while searching for abandoned trails in the early 1990s and wrote about it in another book, *Trails of History.* He deserves a big thanks, and Friends of Acadia and the Park Service also deserve accolades for restoring the trail, which reopened in 2004.

The Homans Path ascends rapidly via steps and switchbacks 0.3 mile to the intersection with the Dorr Mountain East Trail. It's a beautiful trail that weaves through narrow passages in the granite ledges and even under slabs of granite. From the intersection with the East Trail, the Homans Path continues its climb over rocky terrain. Along the way, expect nice views over Frenchman Bay.

Option: On the return, follow the East Face Trail all the way down to the Sieur de Monts Spring parking lot or veer off on Kurt Diederich's Climb, which also returns to the lot.

Other Recommended East-Side Trails

For an easy hike, consider **Jesup Path,** a 2–3-mile hike through the lovely area around Sieur de Monts Spring. Also, the **Seaside Path** (or Seaside Trail) runs about two miles through the woods (use insect repellent) between Seal Harbor and the Jordan Pond House. Use the Island Explorer bus to make this a one-way hike, or retrace your route for a longer hike.

A choice moderate hike is **Conner's Nubble,** with super views down to Eagle Lake and the mountains off to the east. For a moderate-to-strenuous hike, try **Parkman Mountain**—not too difficult but difficult enough to make it worthwhile, especially with the views from the

bald summit. It's what you might call an "all-purpose hike."

You can access the **Cadillac South Ridge Trail** from Blackwoods Campground. Start the trail at the entrance to the campground and do a 7.4-mile round-trip. The hike is moderate to strenuous (1,530-ft. elevation gain), with a couple of quite easy stretches (the last part is the steepest).

Experienced, serious hikers seeking real challenges in the *strenuous* category should consider the **Beehive** and **Precipice** trails. These two "ladder trails" (no pets allowed) are the park's toughest routes, with sheer faces, iron ladders, and strenuous ratings. As already mentioned, Champlain Mountain's 1.6-mile round-trip Precipice Trail is often closed (usually from mid-April into August) to protect nesting peregrine falcons. Avid hikers consider the 0.8-mile round-trip Beehive a "must-do." If challenges are your thing, you're not acrophobic, and these trails are open (check beforehand at the Hulls Cove Visitor Center), go ahead. Both trailheads are on the Park Loop Road (Island Explorer Route 3/Sand Beach).

WEST-SIDE TRAILS
Wonderland

- Distance: 1.4 miles round-trip

- Duration: 45 minutes

- Elevation gain: Minimal

- Effort: Easy

- Trailhead: The Wonderland trail begins on the south side of Route 102A, a mile west of the Seawall Campground. Walk from Seawall; if you're staying elsewhere, ask the Island Explorer bus driver (Route 7/Southwest Harbor) to drop you off (it's not a regular stop).

The shortest and easiest of the park's trails, Wonderland follows an old fire road and is more a walk than a hike—a great starter-upper for a family ensconced at Seawall Campground. Most of the route is wooded—trees gnarled from the wind, branches laden with moss—with the rugged shoreline and a small cobble beach as your reward at the end.

Across Route 102A from the Wonderland trailhead is the 420-acre Big Heath, considered one of Maine's "critical areas." Because of its sensitive peatland—wet and squishy and fragile underfoot (not to mention its battalions of mosquitoes)—avoid it. (You'll be skirting its edges, though, if you walk the Hio Trail from the back of Seawall Campground.)

Ship Harbor Nature Trail

• Distance: 1.3 miles round-trip

• Duration: 45–60 minutes

• Elevation gain: Level

• Effort: Easy, some uneven ground

• Trailhead: The parking area (with restrooms) for Ship Harbor is less than half a mile west of the Wonderland Parking Area. The trail is on the south side of Route 102A. As with Wonderland, you can be dropped off by an Island Explorer bus (Route 7/Southwest Harbor) or flag one down after your hike.

The Ship Harbor Nature Trail isn't quite as easy as Wonderland—roots can snag you along the way, and rocks can be slippery if it has rained or the tide has receded—but it's even more educational as a family hike. At the Thompson Island Information Center, the Hulls Cove Visitor Center, or at Seawall Campground, pick up a copy of the park's 12-page *Ship Harbor Nature Trail* booklet and use it along the way.

Legend has it that the harbor earned its name during the Revolutionary War, when an American privateer, seeking refuge, became stranded here.

If the tide has gone out, follow the trail along the shore first (counterclockwise) so the kids can check out what's been left in the tide pools. If the tide is high, perhaps you'll want to follow the booklet's suggested clockwise route. Or you can do a figure-eight route. In any case, you won't get lost.

Option: Since Wonderland and Ship Harbor are so close together, consider doing both trails in a morning or afternoon. Carry a picnic and enjoy it on the shore.

The higher you hike, the better the vistas, as this view over Somes Sound from Flying Mountain shows.

© TOM NANGLE

Flying Mountain Trail

- Distance: 1.5 miles round-trip
- Duration: 1 hour
- Elevation gain: 200 feet
- Effort: Moderate, some steep sections
- Trailhead: The trail begins at the end of Fernald Point Road, 0.8 mile east of Route 102 (at the northern edge of Southwest Harbor). If you're driving from the Bar Harbor area, slow down after passing Echo Lake and take the next left. Drive to the end of the road, park in the Valley Cove lot, and begin at the carved signpost. Fernald Point was the site of the early 17th-century St. Sauveur mission settlement established by French Jesuits. The Island Explorer bus headed to or from Southwest Harbor can drop you off or pick you up at the corner of Route 102 and Fernald Point Road; from there, walk down the road to the trailhead.

At 284 feet, Flying Mountain is the lowest of Acadia's 26 summits, so it shouldn't have one of the best views—but it does. With minimum effort (some minor scrambling up and over, but the trail is level at the end), you're surveying the mouth of Somes Sound, including Northeast and Southwest Harbors and Greening Island between them. It hardly gets better than this (well, it does, but this is pretty spectacular).

From the trailhead, the rise through the trees is a bit steep, with some stepped ledges, but it's quick (why rush, though?). At the summit, relax and take photos, then descend toward Valley Cove. You'll encounter roots and rocks, and your knees may complain a bit, but again, it's really not strenuous and it doesn't last long. At the bottom, bear left onto the woods road and return to the parking area.

You can hike the Valley Cove Trail as an extension of the Flying Mountain Trail, but it may be closed April–mid-August, as peregrine falcons have been nesting there in recent years.

Beech Mountain Trail

- Distance: 1.2 miles round-trip
- Duration: 1–1.5 hours
- Elevation gain: 700 feet
- Effort: Moderate
- Trailhead: From Route 102 in Somesville, take the Pretty Marsh Road westward to Beech Hill Road. Turn left and continue to the end, climbing gradually to the parking area for Beech Cliff and Beech Mountain. (This trail is not accessible via the Island Explorer.)

Several hiking routes merge and converge in the Beech Mountain area. Some begin from a trailhead on the southern side of Beech and can be more strenuous than this one. This hike starts from the northern side. None of the Beech Mountain hikes are particularly convenient to the Island Explorer bus system.

A short distance from the beginning of the Beech Mountain Trail, you'll reach a fork—the Beech Mountain loop. Bear right to do the loop counterclockwise—the rewarding vistas over Long Pond come sooner, and it's less steep this way.

At the summit (839 ft.) stands the park's only fire tower, now disused. During unseasonably hot summers, when the ranger-posted fire-danger level is high, volunteers come up to keep an eye on things, but small charter planes do most of the fire patrols these days. Besides the great views of Long Pond, from here you can see as far as Blue Hill to the northwest and the Cranberry Isles to the south. A knob near the summit is a prime viewing spot for the migration of hawks (and other raptors) in September.

From the summit, continue your counterclockwise route or backtrack the way you came, heading down to the trail junction and back to the parking area.

Option: If you're particularly fascinated by mosses and lichens (and have brought insect repellent), consider a three-mile round-trip to Beech Mountain that begins with a lovely walk-in-the-woods starting at the same trailhead. Instead of taking the Beech Mountain Trail, follow the Valley Trail on fairly level ground for just under a mile. Then bear right onto the Beech Mountain South Ridge Trail and start climbing stone steps (lots of them) toward the summit. Descend from the summit via the Beech Mountain loop route, going clockwise (left) to take advantage of the Long Pond vistas.

Acadia Mountain Trail

• Distance: 2.5 miles round-trip

• Duration: 1.5–2 hours

• Elevation gain: 1,050 feet

• Effort: Difficult

• Trailhead: From Somesville (west of Bar Harbor), take Route 102 southward for just over three miles, alongside Echo Lake, until you see the signposted Acadia Mountain parking lot. Cross the road to the trailhead. (The Island Explorer's Route 7/Southwest Harbor goes right along Route 102; request

a stop to start your hike and flag down the bus when you've finished the hike.)

Climb the steps and continue to the junction with the St. Sauveur Mountain Trail. (If you're up for a much longer hike, do an Acadia and St. Sauveur loop, for a four-mile round-trip.) Continue left on the Acadia Mountain Trail, where it's briefly deceptively flat and lovely. After you cross a fire road (your eventual return route), begin the rocky, ledgy ascent, following cairns.

It's less than a mile to the open summit—with fantastic views up and down Somes Sound. (Actually, there's a sort of double summit, with the second one only slightly lower than the 641-foot maximum height.) In summer, you'll find wild blueberries. The descent toward the Sound is longer and quite steep—take it slowly. At the bottom, when you reach the spur to Man o' War Brook, detour briefly to follow the brook to Somes Sound. Allegedly, Revolutionary War vessels stocked up on water here during their exploits along the Maine coast. Return to the trailhead via an easy walk on the mile-long fire road.

Biking

Bicycling on Mount Desert Island is a joy, but you have to pedal in the right locations. The island is mountainous, and that includes the roads; many have serious ups and downs. Serious, experienced road cyclists will have a blast. Mountain bikers, casual bikers, families, and everyone else will be more than pleased with the carriage roads. These gravel roads lace through the heart of the park and are punctuated with beautiful stone bridges. They provide a variety of challenges, and you can create a ride of practically any length by linking them together.

Information about rental bikes, organized rides, and tours appears in the Bar Harbor, Northeast Harbor, and Southwest Harbor sections of the *Mount Desert Island Communities* chapter.

You'll find a number of commercial maps available. I prefer the *Acadia National Park Trails, Carriage Roads, Hiking, Biking* map ($4.95 paper, $9.95 waterproofed) published by Map Adventures L.L.C. (www.mapadventures .com), because I find it easiest to read, it details in-town roads, and it shows some of the dirt roads described below. One big drawback for cyclists is that this map doesn't include the entire island; the northern third is simply lopped off, so if you're cycling that section, you'll need another map as well.

ROAD BIKING

Road biking on Mount Desert Island is best left to the experienced. Roads are often narrow, shoulders frequently nonexistent or soft, and gawking visitors often aren't paying attention to the road while driving. Families, once-a-year pedalers, and casual bicyclists will do best on the carriage roads. That said, serious road bikers do have a few choices. Stop in at one of Bar Harbor's bike shops for recommendations or to find out about group rides. If you go by yourself, timing is critical. For the best ride with the least traffic, get up at the crack of dawn and start pedaling once it's truly light outside. It's very important to wear reflective clothing on these roads. It's also wise to drive the roads before cycling them to check conditions. If it's been a while since they've been resurfaced, you might be in for a very rough ride.

Park Loop Road

Since bikes are not allowed on hiking trails in Acadia, the **Park Loop Road** provides a good workout for mountain or road bikers. Its prime drawback is the volume of car and RV exhaust fumes you'll be inhaling if you take this route in the middle of the day at the height of summer. So don't. (Park-wide ozone alerts are not common, but they do occur in Acadia.) Nor are the Park Loop's shoulders as wide as they might be to comfortably accommodate a great many bikes. Besides, on most of the one-way sections of the Park Loop, overflow auto parking is allowed in the right lane. Dodging cars ain't fun. The 27-mile route is indeed spectacular, so if you want to bike it, plan your pedaling for early in the day (around 7 A.M. in summer), late in the day (around "happy hour," when everyone else has packed it in and headed for bars or restaurants), or during "shoulder" months (June, September, or even October).

Southeast Quarter of the Island

This route dips you in and out of the park. Begin in Bar Harbor and follow Route 3 to Schooner Head Road, then follow signs to Park Loop Road. Ride the Park Loop to the end of the one-way section in Seal Harbor, go right on Jordan Pond Road heading to Seal Harbor, then pick up Route 3 to the intersection with Route 198 in Northeast Harbor. Go left on Route 198 into Northeast Harbor, taking Harborside Road to Joy Road to Manchester Road. Go right. Manchester Road merges into Sargent Drive. Follow it until it meets Route 198, go left, and continue to the intersection with Route 233. Go right, and follow Route 233 back to Bar Harbor.

You can increase the mileage by exploring some of the back roads of Seal Harbor (watch out for Martha Stewart) or Northeast Harbor. Another option is to take the Duck Brook Road off Route 233, just after the Eagle Lake parking lots. The road meanders into Bar Harbor, merging onto West Street; careful though, it's a popular local bypass road.

Routes 102/102A

Experienced riders who are accustomed to traffic might consider this loop around the western half of Mount Desert Island. It passes through Somesville, Southwest Harbor, Bass Harbor, Tremont, and Pretty Marsh. While little mileage on this route is actually in the park, quite a few offshoots do venture into it (in most cases on dirt roads). If you do the full loop, it's about 26 miles. Unless you're intent on getting in mileage, plan time to stop and explore along the way. Expect nonexistent or soft shoulders on much of the route and moderate to heavy traffic.

To add to the distance, venture down some of the side roads along the way, such as Ripples Road to Beech Hill Road (dead ends) or Hall Quarry Road (loop), or detour north in Pretty Marsh on the Indian Point Road, which ends at Routes 198/102.

CARRIAGE ROADS

The better alternative for most aspiring bicyclists is to bring, borrow, or rent a bike and take advantage of the spectacular carriage road system—57 miles of crushed-rock roadways with nary a car in sight. (Bikes are allowed on only 45 of the 57 miles; 12 miles are on private land, so be alert for signs.)

At every junction in the carriage road system stands a tall wooden post with a number and directional signs. Use these numbers, together with the park's free carriage road map, to navigate the network. Also very helpful are a couple of portable books—*A Pocket Guide to the Carriage Roads of Acadia National Park,* by Diana Abrell, and *A Pocket Guide to Biking on Mount Desert Island,* by Audrey Minutolo.

Periodically, carriage roads and their bridges undergo necessary repair, and since such work is possible only in decent weather, you may encounter closures. When you obtain the carriage road map at the Hulls Cove Visitor Center, ask a ranger to indicate any sections that are under repair or closed.

Some sections of the carriage roads are fine for wheelchairs, particularly near Eagle Lake and Bubble Pond. Since these are multiuse roadways, bicyclists in particular should remember and adhere to the rules:

- Bikes yield to everyone (pedestrians, horses, wheelchairs, strollers); pedestrians yield to horses. Horses tend to become skittish around bikes, so be particularly cautious when you're pedaling near them. Better still, pull off to the right, stop, and let them pass.

- Wear a helmet.

- Keep to the right and signal clearly when passing on the left.

- Do *not* speed; speeders are a danger to walkers, horses, children, the disabled, and sometimes themselves.

- Pets must be leashed.

As with the park's hiking trails, it would take a whole book just to focus on all the options on the carriage roads. While the carriage roads make wonderful walking paths, they are the best places in the park for bikes. So most of the route suggestions that follow are geared to cyclists.

It cannot be said often enough: *There is no off-road biking in Acadia, and bikes are not allowed on the hiking trails.*

At the end of the *Jordan Pond and Bubble Pond* section, there is one recommended carriage road loop for walking—on private land where bikes are not allowed.

Eagle Lake and Witch Hole Pond

These two loops are probably the most popular in the park—because they're not difficult (good for families) and they're close to Bar Harbor, where so many visitors stay. Thus, if you decide to do either of these in the middle of summer, *get an early start.* If you're planning to rent bikes, rent them the night before, so you can be on your way right after breakfast.

If you're doing this anytime between late June and Columbus Day, check the schedule for the Island Explorer bus and use it to get to and from your starting points.

For the Eagle Lake loop, the Route 6/ Northeast Harbor bus makes a stop at the head of Eagle Lake on Route 233, or you can pedal or drive from downtown Bar Harbor via Mount Desert Street. At the end of the street, cross over to Route 233 (Eagle Lake Road) and follow it to the beginning of this route. (Park in the Eagle Lake Parking Area, across Route 233 from the beginning of the carriage road.)

To reach the Witch Hole Pond loop from downtown Bar Harbor, take West Street to its end, cross Route 3, then continue on West Street Extension. Take a right on Duck Brook Road and continue from there to the carriage road (starting at numbered signpost 5).

Option: Drive to the Hulls Cove Visitor Center, park there, and bike (or walk your bike) up the steep trail to the first carriage road intersection, number 1. From there, continue to 2 and then veer right to make the circuit via signposts (junctions) 4 and 5 and then to 3, making a loop back to 1. From there, it's pretty much downhill to your car.

Each of those rides is about six miles. If you'd prefer to double your hiking mileage, park at the Eagle Lake Parking Area and do both loops from there.

Jordan Pond and Bubble Pond

To ride this loop, take the Island Explorer bus to the Jordan Pond Parking Area or drive there via the Park Loop Road (use the Jordan Pond lot, not the Jordan Pond House Parking Area). Pedal back along the Park Loop Road (follow bike rules and stay with the traffic; it's two-way here) to the handsome stone Jordan Pond Gate Lodge. Now you have two choices—a clockwise route or a counterclockwise one.

The counterclockwise route allows you a downhill coast along Jordan Pond near the end of your 8.5-mile circuit. Enter the carriage road next to the gatehouse and continue to signpost (junction) 17. Head north, passing Bubble Pond along its west shore—practically in the water—to signpost 7. Bear left around the bottom of Eagle Lake, to signpost 8, continue to 10, then turn south, skirting Jordan Pond, to signpost 14. Continue south to 15 and 16, exiting onto the Park Loop Road across from where you entered.

After these warm-up rides, you'll have a good sense of this amazing network. And now how about a walk on private carriage roads, where you won't be dodging bikes? (Bikes are banned from the 12 miles of private Green Rock Company carriage roads; you're free to walk there, however.)

Amphitheatre Loop

This is a fabulous 5.5-mile loop that takes you into the heart of the park, far from the noises of traffic and civilization. You'll pass over two bridges—the gently curving Amphitheatre Bridge, which, at 236 feet, is one of the longest in the system, and Little Harbor Brook Bridge, which must be one of the smallest. The route has some steady climbs, but the rewards are panoramic views to the Cranberry Islands. Follow a clockwise route beginning at the Brown Mountain Gatehouse parking lot on Route 198 (one mile north of Northeast Harbor). Enter the carriage road system and bear right at signposts 18 and 19 and keep straight or left at signpost 20. Keep right again at signposts 21 and 22. When you return to signpost 20, go left and keep left until you're back at the parking area.

Option: Hikers can enjoy the 0.8-mile Amphitheatre Trail connecting the two bridges. It's a lovely walk in the woods paralleling and often crossing Harbor Brook as it babbles and descends over waterfalls into small pools—perfect for cooling hot, tired feet. Don't take this trail during spring run-off periods or after heavy rains, when that sweet brook might be a raging torrent.

Around the Mountain

This 11-mile loop is an outstanding ride for experienced mountain bikers. It circumnavigates several of the park's major peaks, including Sargent, Penobscot, Cedar Swamp, Parkman, and Gilmore, and it passes numerous bridges and waterfalls. The views are glorious. It's not an easy ride, however, as it climbs many hills. Begin at the Parkman Mountain parking lot on Route 198 by heading right. At signpost 13, go left, and then go left at signpost 12. You're now on the Around the Mountain road. At signpost 10, turn right and then keep right, staying on the Around the Mountain road, at signposts 14, 21, 20, and 19. At signpost 12, turn left, then turn right at signpost 13 to return to the parking lot. You can also access this route from the Jordan Pond area.

FIRE ROADS
Hio Trail

This old Acadia fire road begins at the back of the Seawall Campground (behind Loop C) and goes over to Route 102. It's an easy four-mile round-trip. The path is mostly wooded, passing near the Big Heath, so if you take the trail late in the day, be sure to use insect repellent. It's a great family ride, with plenty of bird- and wildlife-watching opportunities.

Long Pond Fire Road

This five-mile loop off Route 102 just south of Pretty Marsh Picnic Area (park there) follows a dirt road to Long Pond and back, with a short section on Route 102 to close the loop. The terrain is moderate, with many long hills. Spruce and fir trees line most of the route, and you'll pass boggy areas as well as a few ponds. This is prime moose territory in the park, so be on the lookout for the gangly beasts. If you see one, observe from a distance; if it starts coming toward you, move away quietly.

Other Recreation

CALM-WATER PADDLING

Both **Eagle Lake** and **Jordan Pond** have boat ramps. The Eagle Lake put-in is off Route 233; the Jordan Pond put-in is adjacent to the hiker parking lot near the Jordan Pond House, on the Park Loop Road. No swimming is allowed in either lake.

Another fine pond for paddling is **Seal Cove Pond,** in Tremont. Route 102 skirts the western edge of the 1.5-mile-long pond, and the shoreline has plenty of houses, but most of the forested eastern shore is in the park. The primary access point is off the Western Mountain Road. To find it, take the Seal Cove Road from Seal Cove, go left on the first park road, and follow it to its intersection with the Western Mountain Road. Go right; the road ends at the put-in. You might also be able to find a parking spot or two with easy access on Route 102.

SWIMMING

Acadia has a limited number of swimming areas; they and their parking lots are mighty crowded on hot days. Go early in the day or take your chances.

Don't assume you can swim in any freshwater pond or lake you encounter in the park or even elsewhere on the island. Six island locations—Upper and Lower Hadlock Ponds, Bubble and Jordan Ponds, Eagle Lake, and the southern half of Long Pond—are drinking-water reservoirs where swimming and windsurfing are banned (but boating is allowed). Don't let your dog swim in these ponds, either. Five of the six are within the park; Long Pond borders the park.

Also see *Penobscot and Sargent Mountains* under *Hiking;* Sargent Pond is a lovely spot to cool off mid-hike.

Sand Beach

Located slightly below the Park Loop Road (take Island Explorer Route 3/Sand Beach), Sand Beach is the park's (and the island's) biggest sandy beach. Lifeguards are on duty during the summer, and even then the

© TOM NANGLE

Lake Wood's grassy beach is a favorite among locals.

biggest threat can be hypothermia. The saltwater is terminally glacial—in mid-July, it still might not reach 60°F. By September, it's usually warmer, though the air will be cooler. Even though kids seem not to notice, they can become chilled quickly; keep an eye on their condition. The best solution is to walk to the far end of the beach, where a warmer, shallow stream meets the ocean. Also, if you arrive here on the incoming tide, after the sun has warmed up the cove's bottom, the water temperature is marginally higher. On a hot August day, arrive early; the parking lot fills up. Bring a picnic. There are changing rooms and restrooms. Dogs are *not* allowed on Sand Beach.

After hiking nearby Great Head on a hot day, go for a swim at Sand Beach—you'll be surprisingly grateful for the chilly water.

Echo Lake

The park's most popular freshwater swimming site, staffed with a lifeguard and inevitably crowded on hot days, is Echo Lake, south of Somesville on Route 102 and well signposted (take Island Explorer Route 7/Southwest Harbor). Pets are not allowed on the beach.

Swimming Holes

If you have a canoe, kayak, or rowboat, you can reach swimming holes in **Seal Cove Pond** and **Round Pond,** both on the western side of Mount Desert. Both have shorelines bordering the park. The eastern shore of **Hodgdon Pond** (also on the western side of the island) is accessible by car (via Hodgdon Road and Long Pond Fire Road).

Another popular swimming hole is **Lake Wood,** at the northern end of Mount Desert. It has a small sand beach and a grassy area, a toilet by the parking area, and auto access. To get to Lake Wood from Route 3, head west on Crooked Road for just over half a mile to Lake Wood Pond Road. Turn left and continue to the parking area, which will be crowded on a hot day, so arrive early.

ROCK CLIMBING

Acadia has a number of splendid sites prized by climbers: the sea cliffs at Otter Cliffs and Great Head, South Bubble Mountain, Canada Cliff (on the island's western side), and the South Wall and the Central Slabs on Champlain Mountain. The climbing season usually runs May–October. Occasionally, it can be extended at either end, but you'd have to be on or near the island to be able to catch the decent weather before it deteriorated. (Heck, that can happen even in summer.)

Some park regulations you need to know for Acadia climbing:

- Don't leave your dog tied up or on the loose while you're climbing.

- The park's bridges are off-limits for climbing or bouldering.

- From April to mid-August, while peregrine falcons are nesting, the Central Slabs area on the Precipice is almost always closed.

- Sign in at the registration box at climbing sites—registration is required at Otter Cliffs, the South Wall, and Canada Cliff.

If you've forgotten any climbing gear or need replacements, the best source is **Cadillac Mountain Sports** (26 Cottage St., Bar Harbor, 207/288-4532, www.cadillacsports.com), on the ground floor next to Atlantic Climbing School (ACS).

Climbing Schools and Guides

If you haven't tried climbing, *never* do it yourself without instruction. The best advice is to contact one of Bar Harbor's two climbing operations. **Acadia Mountain Guides Climbing School** (198 Main St., Bar Harbor, 207/288-8186 or 888/232-9559, www.acadiamountainguides.com) offers all levels of instruction and guided climbs for individuals and families from mid-May to October. The American Mountain Guides Association–accredited school is directed by AMGA-certified rock and alpine guide Jon Tierney. A private full-day guided climb is $225; a half day is $125.

© HILARY NANGLE

Otter Cliffs is accessible from the Park Road or the Ocean Trail.

Family rates ($190 half day; $290 full day for up to four people) are available for families with kids younger than 10.

Atlantic Climbing School (ACS) (24 Cottage St., 2nd Fl., Bar Harbor, 207/288-2521, www.climbacadia.com) provides basic half-day courses (3.5 and 4.5 hours), including a "family climbing experience," all by reservation (minimum age is eight). You'll learn just enough to introduce you to the sport and do an initial basic climb—with guides and in line with park rules. ACS also offers a series of courses for intermediate climbers and a half- or full-day guided course for experienced climbers. Half-day courses are $70 each for three people, $80 each for two people, and $125 for a private course. The family course is $250 for up to four related students. Full-day guided courses are $110 per person for three, $130 per person for two, or $225 for a private outing. All gear is provided by both firms.

Jeff Butterfield, the owner of ACS, wrote the must-have book for experienced climbers: *Acadia: A Climber's Guide,* which covers all the best-known routes as well as some lesser-known crags. Routes are described and rated (with maps and symbols), and there's all kinds of other essential information. For instance, the book recommends that South Bubble climbers wear helmets for protection from rocks dropped ("by yahoos," as he puts it) from hiking trails overhead. At $25 for a 160-page book, it's expensive—but it may save your life. How valuable is that? (It's even entertaining just reading the route names: Selfless Bastard, Homosexual Armadillo, Fear of Flying, Arms Race, Pickled Amnesiac, and dozens more.)

GEOCACHE

Although traditional geocaching, with hidden prizes, is forbidden in the park, if you have your own GPS unit, you can participate in Acadia's **EarthCache Program** (www.nps.gov/acad/earthcache.htm). Instead of directing you to stashes of trinkets, it leads to some of the park's significant geological sites. Full details, including coordinates for the first stop, are available on the park's website.

WINTER SPORTS

As mentioned earlier, these miles of car-free carriage roads are fantastic for cross-country skiing and snowshoeing. The only problem is that even though Acadia gets about five feet of snow during an average winter, it's not like a ski resort, where there's a base and more snow keeps piling on top of it. Here, it might snow one day and rain or thaw the next. But now and then, a bumper crop of snow creates a winter wonderland for days or even weeks. Acadia's proximity to the ocean and its Gulf Stream current means that you take your chances with snow. January and February can be good bets…but then again, you never know. The park publishes a very handy *Winter Activities Guide,* a foldout map/brochure that explains what you can and cannot do and where you can and cannot go.

Cross-country skis and snowshoes are available for rent from **Cadillac Mountain Sports** (26 Cottage St., Bar Harbor, 207/288-4532, www .cadillacsports.com), which is open all year.

For carriage road information and other visitor information about Acadia during the winter, when the Hulls Cove Visitor Center is closed, contact **Park Headquarters** (Eagle Lake Rd., Rte. 233, Bar Harbor, 207/288-3338, www.nps.gov/acad/), which is open all year. In winter, it's open 8 A.M.–4:30 P.M. daily except Thanksgiving, December 24 and 25, and January 1; in summer, it's closed on weekends.

Forty-five miles of carriage trails are open to Nordic skiing and snowshoeing, and volunteers sometimes groom trails; check with the park or online for grooming reports. Dog sledding and skijoring are permitted, but there are restrictions. Check with park officials or online for current info. Unplowed park roads also are open, but many of these are shared with snowmobilers, so use caution. Snowmobilers can ride the 27-mile Park Loop Road, two miles of the carriage roads, and the road to Cadillac's summit.

Any hardy souls up for experiencing Acadia in winter can stay at the **Blackwoods Campground** (Rte. 3, Otter Creek, five miles south of Bar Harbor), the park's only year-round campground.

Practicalities

CAMPING

Mount Desert Island has at least a dozen private (commercial) campgrounds, but there are only two—**Blackwoods** and **Seawall**—within park boundaries on the island. (A third park campground is on Isle au Haut.)

Blackwoods and Seawall have *no* hookups. Most sites at both are for tents, but some do accommodate pop-ups, vehicle campers, and RVs up to 35 feet in length. Both campgrounds have seasonal restrooms (no showers) and dumping stations. Less than half a mile from Blackwoods, and even closer to Seawall, are coin-operated hot showers and small markets for buying incidental supplies.

Both campgrounds are wooded, with no sea views but not far from the water. In June, be prepared for black flies; in July and August, bring insect repellent for mosquitoes. Maximum capacity at each site is six persons, one vehicle, and one large tent (or two small ones). Quiet time in both campgrounds is 10 P.M.–6 A.M.

Both campgrounds also have **amphitheaters,** where park rangers present free, hour-long evening programs (various starting times) during the summer on a variety of natural- and cultural-history topics. Noncampers are also welcome at these events, and there's wheelchair access. Some of the programs have included "Forces of Nature," "Avian Mysteries,"

"Acadia's Treasures," "The French in Acadia," and "All Things Furry." Even sing-alongs are sometimes on the schedule. Blackwoods has programs several nights a week; Seawall programs tend to be on weekend evenings.

Firewood collection is no longer allowed within Seawall's grounds. Rather than scrounge for what little duff remains around the campgrounds in order to build a campfire, stop on your way to Acadia and pick up a stash of firewood. All along Route 3 in Trenton and along Route 3 on Mount Desert (near the clusters of commercial campgrounds), you'll see signs for firewood for sale (usually around $3). Do *not* bring firewood from home, as it may contain bugs that threaten park resources.

The propane-powered Island Explorer buses serve both Blackwoods (Route 4/Blackwoods) and Seawall (Route 7/Southwest Harbor) between late June and early October. Leave your vehicle at your campsite and do your park and island exploring by bus.

Blackwoods Campground

With more than 300 campsites, Blackwoods Campground, just off Route 3, five miles south of Bar Harbor, is open all year. Because of its location on the east side of the island, it's also the more popular of the two campgrounds. Reservations, handled by the National Recreation Reservation Service (877/444-6777, www.recreation.gov, credit card required), can be made up to six months in advance and are suggested from May 1 through October 31. The fee is $20 per site per night; you cannot reserve specific sites or adjoining sites. Campsites cost $10 in April and November, open weather permitting; from December through March it's free, but only few primitive sites are available (portable toilet, hand pump for water, access only by hiking in from Route 3). No reservations are taken for the shoulder or off seasons. (These dates and regulations are subject to change, so call to check to not be disappointed.)

If you're staying at Blackwoods, consider adding the **Cadillac South Ridge Trail** to your hiking list. Of course, you can drive to the Cadillac summit and get the same fabulous 360-degree views, but this hike makes you feel you earned them.

Seawall Campground

Reservations are not accepted at Seawall Campground, on Route 102A in the Seawall district, four miles south of Southwest Harbor—it's first-come, first-served. But in midsummer, you'll need to arrive as early as 8:30 A.M. (when the ranger station opens) to secure one of the 200 or so sites. Seawall is open from late May through September. The cost is $20 per night for drive-up sites and $14 per night for walk-in sites.

FOOD

The only restaurant within the park is the **Jordan Pond House** (Park Loop Rd., 207/276-3316, 11:30 A.M.–8 P.M. daily mid-May–late Oct., to 9 P.M. late June–early Sept.), a modern facility in a spectacular waterside setting (see *Jordan Pond House* sidebar). Jordan Pond House is on the Island Explorer's Route 5/Jordan Pond. It's also a hub for the carriage roads and accessible via hiking trails. Parking is limited. If you must arrive by car, there is an overflow lot just north of the main site, with a connecting trail through the woods.

EMERGENCIES

If you have an emergency while in the park, call **911.** The park's general information number is 207/288-3338. If you're in a remote location, it helps if you're carrying a cell phone, but *please* keep it turned off while hiking or biking; save it for an emergency. The nearest hospital, in downtown Bar Harbor, is Mount Desert Island Hospital, with a 24-hour emergency room. The nearest major medical center is in Bangor (Eastern Maine Medical Center), via a congested route that can take an hour or longer at the height of summer. (Bangor, however, is one of the state's bases for a LifeFlight medevac helicopter.)

The best advice for averting emergencies is to be cautious and sensible in everything you undertake in the park. Wear a helmet while biking. Don't hike alone or go off the trails—nearly every year, some-one is seriously injured or killed falling from the cliffs. Keep a sharp eye on children.

ACCESSIBILITY

The park publishes an *Access Guide* that provides accessibility information about general facilities, programs, and services. If you have other questions, call 207/288-3338, 8 A.M.– 4:30 P.M. Monday–Friday. Information also is available on the park's website.

GETTING AROUND

The free **Island Explorer** (207/667-5796, www.islandexplorer.com) operates seven routes on Mount Desert Island that connect villages and campgrounds and access most areas of the park. It operates from late June through early October.

MOUNT DESERT ISLAND COMMUNITIES

Perhaps no national park has as symbiotic a relationship with its feeder towns as Acadia National Park. Is it a chicken-and-egg situation? Not really. Whereas other national parks have served as magnets for the creation of clusters of new towns, the towns that surround Acadia are long-termers. These island communities made do and eked out a living from fishing and boat-building long before the first 19th-century "rusticators" unloaded their families and steamer trunks—and long before the first chunk of pristine island real estate was donated to the nation.

Mount Desert Island's official towns (tax-collecting entities with all the bureaucracy that ensues) are **Bar Harbor, Mount Desert, Southwest Harbor,** and **Tremont.** Within each of these towns are villages—some with post offices and zip codes, some without. Bar Harbor, for instance, includes the villages of Hulls Cove, Salisbury Cove, Town Hill, and Eden (all in the northern sector of the island), and part of the village of Otter Creek.

The town of Mount Desert can be the most confusing, since it includes the villages of Seal Harbor, Hall Quarry, Pretty Marsh, Beech Hill, Somesville, Northeast Harbor, and part of Otter Creek.

Be sure to drive or bike (or take the Island Explorer bus between late June and Columbus Day) around the smaller villages, especially Somesville, Bass Harbor, and Bernard. Views are fabulous, the pace is slow, and you'll feel you've stumbled upon "the real Maine."

© TOM NANGLE

HIGHLIGHTS

◖ **Abbe Museum:** In downtown Bar Harbor, the Abbe Museum and its seasonal museum at Sieur de Monts Spring are fascinating places to while away a few hours and learn about Maine's Native American heritage (page 69).

◖ **Oceanarium:** Visit a lobster hatchery and learn about ocean ecology on this fascinating tour (page 69).

◖ **Dive-In Theater Boat Cruise:** Got kids? Don't miss this tour, where Diver Ed brings the undersea world aboard (page 78).

◖ **Whale-Watching Excursions:** Board a high-speed catamaran and cruise well offshore to view whales and the puffin colony at Petit Manan Light (page 79).

◖ **Somes Sound:** It's worth the journey to the quiet side of the island to see this spectacular inlet (page 94).

◖ **Asticou and Thuya Gardens:** Magical and enchanting best describe these two peaceful gardens. While Zen-like Asticou is best seen in spring, Thuya delivers color through summer and also has hiking paths (page 94).

◖ **Wendell Gilley Museum:** Gilley's intricately carved birds, from miniature shorebirds to life-size birds of prey, are a marvel to behold (page 102).

◖ **The Seal Cove Auto Museum:** A must for fans of antique automobiles, the museum hosts one of the largest collections of Brass Era vehicles in the country, including a few extremely rare models (page 113).

◖ **Island Cruises:** Adults and kids alike enjoy Captain Kim Strauss's extremely informative and fun nature cruises (page 114).

◖ **Cranberry Isles:** Do make it a point to cruise to at least Islesford for a taste of island life (page 120).

LOOK FOR ◖ TO FIND RECOMMENDED SIGHTS, ACTIVITIES, DINING, AND LODGING.

PLANNING YOUR TIME

Arrive in **Bar Harbor** in mid-July these days, and you'll find it tough to believe that the year-round population is just shy of 5,000. Bar Harbor is liveliest (in both positive and negative senses) in July and August, but the season keeps stretching. Many clued-in travelers try to take advantage of September's prime weather, relative quiet, and spectacular foliage, although even September and October activity has stepped up. Cruise ships have "discovered" Bar Harbor in recent years, many opting for September and October visits. You won't be competing with the passengers for beds, but about 80 percent of them make a perfunctory visit to Acadia, usually by chartered bus. (The cruise visits add about $10 million annually to the island's coffers.) In the dead of winter, the town is close to moribund, kept alive by devoted year-rounders, including students and faculty at the College of the Atlantic (a unique four-year liberal-arts college geared to environmental studies) and the 1,200 or so staff members at the internationally recognized Jackson Laboratory for Mammalian Research.

If you're traveling with children, Bar Harbor can be a very convenient base of operations for exploring Acadia National Park and the rest of the island. In the smallish downtown area, kids can walk around, play in the parks, hang out at the waterfront, buy ice cream, and hit the movies. It's also a source for sporting-gear rentals and the starting point for boat, bus, kayaking, and walking tours. Staying downtown can be a real plus, but the high cost of even ordinary lodging can be a minus—especially for families. Bar Harbor Chamber of Commerce staffers are particularly adept at rounding up rooms, but don't abuse their helpfulness; contact them well ahead if you're planning a peak-season holiday.

The **Southwest Harbor** area also serves as a very convenient base for exploring Acadia National Park, as well as the island's less-crowded villages and offshore Swans Island, Frenchboro, and the **Cranberry Isles.**

Bar Harbor and Vicinity

In 1996, Bar Harbor celebrated the bicentennial of its founding (as the town of Eden). In the late 19th century and well into the 20th, the town grew to become one of the East Coast's fanciest summer watering holes.

In those days, ferries and steam yachts arrived from points south, large and small resort hotels sprang up, and exclusive mansions (quaintly dubbed "cottages") were the venues for parties thrown by summer-resident Drexels, Du Ponts, and Vanderbilts and prominent academics, journalists, and lawyers. The "rusticators" came for the season, with huge entourages of servants, children, pets, and horses. The area's renown was such that by the 1890s, even the staffs of the British, Austrian, and Ottoman embassies retreated here from summers in Washington DC.

The establishment of the national park in 1919 and the arrival of the automobile changed the character of Bar Harbor and Mount Desert Island; two world wars and the Great Depression took an additional toll in myriad ways; but the coup de grâce for Bar Harbor's era of elegance came with the Great Fire of 1947.

Nothing in the history of Bar Harbor and Mount Desert Island stands out like the Great Fire of 1947, a wind-whipped conflagration that devastated more than 17,000 acres on the eastern half of the island and leveled gorgeous mansions, humble homes, and more trees than anyone could count. Only three people died, but property damage was estimated at $2 million. Whole books have been written about the October inferno; fascinating scrapbooks

COMMUNITIES

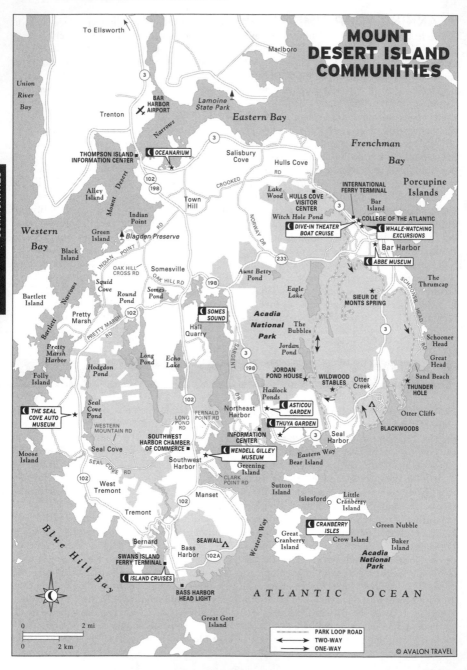

MOUNT DESERT ISLAND COMMUNITIES

To Ellsworth

Marlboro

Union River Bay

3

BAR HARBOR AIRPORT

Lamoine State Park

Trenton

Narrows

Eastern Bay

THOMPSON ISLAND INFORMATION CENTER

OCEANARIUM

3

Salisbury Cove

Hulls Cove RD

Frenchman Bay

Porcupine Islands

102 198

Alley Island

Mount Desert

Town Hill

CROOKED

Lake Wood

HULLS COVE VISITOR CENTER

Witch Hole Pond

INTERNATIONAL FERRY TERMINAL

3

Bar Island

COLLEGE OF THE ATLANTIC

Indian Point

NORWAY DR

DIVE-IN THEATER BOAT CRUISE

WHALE-WATCHING EXCURSIONS

Western Bay

Green Island

Blagden Preserve

INDIAN POINT RD

Bar Harbor

Black Island

OAK HILL CROSS RD

Somesville

233

SCHOONER HEAD RD

ABBE MUSEUM

The Thrumcap

Squid Cove

OAK HILL RD

198

Aunt Betty Pond

Eagle Lake

SIEUR DE MONTS SPRING

Round Pond

Somes Pond

Bartlett Island

102

Narrows

PRETTY MARSH RD

Hall Quarry

SOMES SOUND

Acadia National Park

The Bubbles

Schooner Head

Pretty Marsh

Long Pond

Echo Lake

Jordan Pond

Great Head

Pretty Marsh Harbor

Hodgdon Pond

SARGENT DR

3

198

JORDAN POND HOUSE

WILDWOOD STABLES

Otter Creek

Sand Beach

THUNDER HOLE

Folly Island

Seal Cove Pond

Hadlock Ponds

ASTICOU GARDEN

Otter Cliffs

THE SEAL COVE AUTO MUSEUM

WESTERN MOUNTAIN RD

LONG POND RD

FERNALD POINT RD

Northeast Harbor

THUYA GARDEN

BLACKWOODS

Moose Island

SOUTHWEST HARBOR CHAMBER OF COMMERCE

INFORMATION CENTER

3

Seal Harbor

102

Seal Cove

SEAL COVE RD

WENDELL GILLEY MUSEUM

Eastern Way

Eastern Bear Island

West Tremont

Southwest Harbor

Greening Island

CLARK POINT RD

Sutton Island

Little Cranberry Island

102

Manset

Islesford

Green Nubble

Tremont

Bernard

SEAWALL

Western Way

CRANBERRY ISLES

Blue Hill Bay

SWANS ISLAND FERRY TERMINAL

Bass Harbor

102A

Great Cranberry Island

Crow Island

Baker Island

Acadia National Park

ISLAND CRUISES

BASS HARBOR HEAD LIGHT

ATLANTIC OCEAN

Great Gott Island

0   2 mi

0   2 km

PARK LOOP ROAD

TWO-WAY

ONE-WAY

© AVALON TRAVEL

in the Bar Harbor Historical Society dramatically relate the gripping details of the story. Even though some of the elegant cottages have survived, the fire altered life here forever.

SIGHTS

Acadia National Park comes right up to the edge of town, but the Bar Harbor area has plenty of attractions of its own.

◖ Abbe Museum

The fabulous Abbe Museum is a superb place to introduce children (and adults) to prehistoric, historic, and contemporary Native American tools, crafts, and other cultural artifacts, with an emphasis on Maine's Micmac, Maliseet, Passamaquoddy, and Penobscot tribes. Everything about this privately funded museum, established in 1927, is tasteful. It has two campuses. The main campus (26 Mount Desert St., Bar Harbor, 207/288-3519, www .abbemuseum.org, 9 A.M.–5 P.M. Apr.–Dec., call ahead off-season as hours may change, $6 adults, $2 ages 6–15), built in 2001 and incorporating the former YMCA, is home to a collection spanning nearly 12,000 years. Museum-sponsored events include craft workshops, hands-on children's programs, archaeological field schools, and the **Native American Festival** (held at the College of the Atlantic; usually the first Saturday after July 4). The museum's gift shop has an especially nice selection of Native American–made baskets.

Admission to the in-town Abbe also includes admission to the museum's original site in the park, about 2.5 miles south of Bar Harbor, at Sieur de Monts Spring, where Route 3 meets the Park Loop Road (9 A.M.–4 P.M. mid May–mid-Oct.). Inside a small but handsome National Historic Register building are displays from a 50,000-item collection. Admission to only the Sieur de Monts Spring Abbe is $2 adults, $1 ages 6–15.

While you're at the original Abbe Museum site, take the time to wander the paths in the adjacent **Wild Gardens of Acadia,** a 0.75-acre microcosm of more than 400 plant species native to Mount Desert Island. Twelve separate display areas, carefully maintained and labeled by the Bar Harbor Garden Club, represent native plant habitats; pick up the map/brochure that explains each.

St. Saviour's Episcopal Church

St. Saviour's (41 Mount Desert St., Bar Harbor, 207/288-4215, http://ellsworthme.org/ssaviour, 7 A.M.–dusk), close to downtown Bar Harbor, boasts Maine's largest collection of Tiffany stained-glass windows. Ten originals are here; an 11th was stolen in 1988 and replaced by a locally made window. Of the 32 non-Tiffany windows, the most intriguing is a memorial to Clarence Little, founder of the Jackson Laboratory and a descendant of Paul Revere. Images in the window include the laboratory, DNA, and mice. In July and August, volunteers regularly conduct free tours of the Victorian-era church (completed in 1878); call for the schedule or make an appointment for an off-season tour. The church is open for self-guided tours—pick up a brochure in the back. If old cemeteries intrigue you, spend time wandering the 18th-century town graveyard next to the church.

◖ Oceanarium

At the northern edge of Mount Desert Island, 8.5 miles northwest of downtown Bar Harbor, is this understated but fascinating spot, also called the **Maine Lobster Museum and Hatchery** (1351 Rte. 3, Bar Harbor, 207/288-5005, www.theoceanarium.com, 9 A.M.–5 P.M. Mon.–Sat. mid-May–mid-Oct.), one of the island's two related oceanariums. This low-tech, high-interest operation awes the kids, and it's pretty darn interesting for adults, too. David and Audrey Mills have been at it since 1972 and are determined to educate visitors while showing them a good time. At this facility (there's also a sister site in Southwest Harbor that may or may not be open; it varies year to year), visitors on tour view thousands of tiny lobster hatchlings, enjoy a museum, and meander along a salt marsh walk, where you can check out tidal creatures and vegetation. All tours begin on the hour and half hour. Allow

CHANGING THE WORLD, ONE MIND AT A TIME

Wherever you turn on Mount Desert Island, you'll find evidence of **College of the Atlantic.** The students are highly visible; graduates have established numerous island businesses; and the college itself is an integral part of the year-round island community. In addition to its Bar Harbor campus, COA owns marine research facilities on two offshore islands with lighthouses, Mount Desert Rock and Great Duck Island. And it has an 85-acre Maine Organic Farmers and Gardeners Association-certified organic farm in Mount Desert, dedicated to sustainable agriculture, that provides produce for the school's kitchen as well as for local businesses and its own farmstand.

Founded in 1969, COA is an accredited, four-year independent college with a graduate program. Despite being a small school – it has fewer than 300 students – it has a far-reaching reputation. The 2007-2008 student body hailed from 49 states and 38 foreign countries. The school and the curriculum are built around the concept of sustainability. COA awards two degrees, the bachelor of arts and the master of philosophy. Both are in human ecology, which the college defines as "the study of the interconnected relationships between people and our natural, social, and constructed environments." That translates to programs designed for long-term results that help people and nature flourish.

Many of the innovative school's alumni remain on the island to start new businesses or take over existing ones. COA alumni are behind the Dive-In Theater Boat Cruise, Gulf of Maine Expedition Institute, Reel Pizza Cinerama, Wildwood Stables, Criterion Theatre, and several restaurants, including Burning Tree, Café This Way, Havana, Morning Glory Bakery, and Rupununi. That's just skimming the top. Town Hill Market, Sunflower Gardens & Greenhouses, Sweet Pea's Farm Store, and more than a dozen services are COA-graduate initiatives. And that's just on the island.

The college's admission policy, like its curriculum, is geared to the individual student, and interested students are encouraged to visit the campus, take a tour, and talk with faculty and staff. Even if you're not interested in pursuing the COA's educational opportunities, the gorgeous 35-acre oceanfront campus is well worth a visit. It houses a museum, a gallery, gardens, and a shorefront path.

© HILARY NANGLE

The seaside garden at The Turrets, on the College of the Atlantic campus, is a quiet spot.

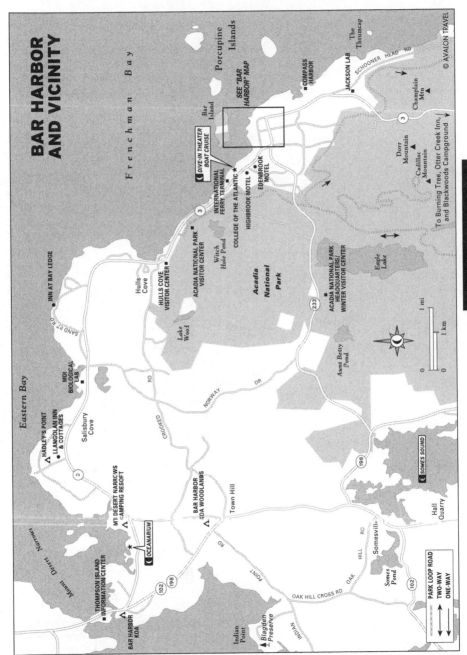

BAR HARBOR AND VICINITY

Frenchman Bay

Porcupine Islands

Bar Island

SEE "BAR HARBOR" MAP

The Thrumcap

COMPASS HARBOR

JACKSON LAB

SCHOONER HEAD RD

Champlain Mtn

3

© AVALON TRAVEL

DIVE-IN THEATER BOAT CRUISE

INTERNATIONAL FERRY TERMINAL

COLLEGE OF THE ATLANTIC

HIGHBROOK MOTEL

EDENBROOK MOTEL

Dorr Mountain

Cadillac Mountain

To Burning Tree, Otter Creek Inn, and Blackwoods Campground

3

ACADIA NATIONAL PARK VISITOR CENTER

Witch Hole Pond

Hulls Cove

HULLS COVE VISITOR CENTER

INN AT BAY LEDGE

SAND PT RD

Acadia National Park

Lake Wood

233

ACADIA NATIONAL PARK HEADQUARTERS/ WINTER VISITOR CENTER

Eagle Lake

MDI BIOLOGICAL LAB

HADLEY'S POINT

LLANGOLLAN INN & COTTAGES

Salisbury Cove

Eastern Bay

3

NORWAY DR

CROOKED RD

Aunt Betty Pond

1 mi

1 km

0

0

MT DESERT NARRCWS CAMPING RESOFT

OCEANARIUM

BAR HARBOR KOA WOODLANDS

Town Hill

198

SOMES SOUND

Hall Quarry

Mount Desert Narrows

THOMPSON ISLAND INFORMATION CENTER

BAR HARBOR KOA

102

198

POINT RD

OAK HILL CROSS RD

OAK HILL RD

Somesville

Somes Pond

102

Indian Point

Blagden Preserve

INDIAN POINT RD

PARK LOOP ROAD

TWO-WAY

ONE-WAY

COMMUNITIES

COMMUNITIES

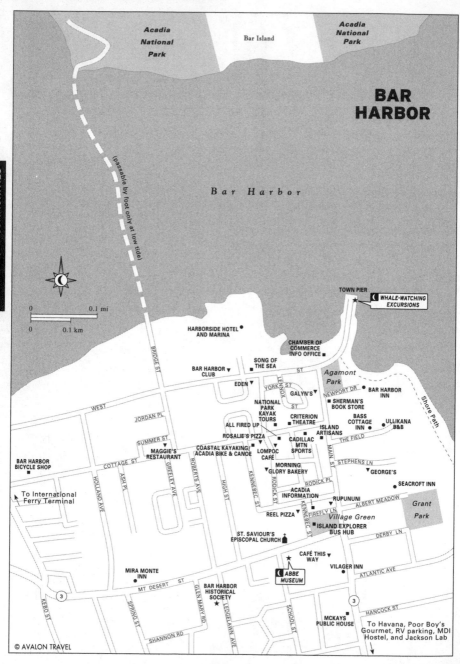

Acadia National Park

Bar Island

Acadia National Park

BAR HARBOR

Bar Harbor

(passable by foot only at low tide)

0   0.1 mi
0   0.1 km

TOWN PIER ★ ➤ WHALE-WATCHING EXCURSIONS

HARBORSIDE HOTEL AND MARINA ●

CHAMBER OF COMMERCE INFO OFFICE ■

BAR HARBOR CLUB ▼

SONG OF THE SEA

EDEN ▼

Agamont Park

NEWPORT DR. ● BAR HARBOR INN

YORK ST.
LENOX ST.

GALYN'S ▼

■ SHERMAN'S BOOK STORE

NATIONAL PARK KAYAK TOURS

CRITERION THEATRE ■

BASS COTTAGE INN ●

ULLIKANA B&B ●

ALL FIRED UP ■

ROSALIE'S PIZZA ▼

CADILLAC MTN SPORTS

ISLAND ARTISANS ■

THE FIELD

COASTAL KAYAKING/ ACADIA BIKE & CANOE

LOMPOC CAFÉ ▼

MAGGIE'S RESTAURANT

STEPHENS LN.

MORNING GLORY BAKERY ▼

GEORGE'S ▼

BAR HARBOR BICYCLE SHOP ■

ACADIA INFORMATION ■

RUPUNUNI ■

SEACROFT INN ●

To International Ferry Terminal

REEL PIZZA ■

ALBERT MEADOW

Village Green

Grant Park

ISLAND EXPLORER BUS HUB ■

DERBY LN.

ST. SAVIOUR'S EPISCOPAL CHURCH ⌂

CAFÉ THIS WAY ★

VILAGER INN ●

ATLANTIC AVE.

MIRA MONTE INN ●

ABBE MUSEUM

BAR HARBOR HISTORICAL SOCIETY ★

3

HANCOCK ST.

3

MCKAYS PUBLIC HOUSE ■

To Havana, Poor Boy's Gourmet, RV parking, MDI Hostel, and Jackson Lab

BRIDGE ST.
WEST
JORDAN PL.
SUMMER ST.
COTTAGE ST.
HOLLAND AVE.
ASH PL.
GREELEY AVE.
ROBERTS AVE.
HIGH ST.
KENNEBEC ST.
RODICK ST.
FIREFLY LN.
RODICK PL.
MAIN ST.
SHORE PATH
KEBO ST.
SPRING ST.
MT. DESERT ST.
GLEN MARY RD.
LEDGELAWN AVE.
SCHOOL ST.
SHANNON RD.

© AVALON TRAVEL

1–2 hours to see everything. Tickets are $12 adults, $7 children 4–12 for a program with two talks; an expanded program includes a 45-minute Marsh Walk for $14 adults, $8 children. If the Southwest Harbor site also is open, a discount pass to both may be available.

College of the Atlantic

A museum, a gallery, and a pleasant campus for walking are reasons to visit the college (105 Eden St., Rte. 3, Bar Harbor, 207/288-5015, www.coa.edu), which specializes in human ecology, or humans' interrelationship with the environment. In a handsome renovated building, the **George B. Dorr Natural History Museum** showcases regional birds and mammals in realistic dioramas made by COA students. The biggest attraction for children is the please-touch philosophy, allowing kids to reach into a touch tank and to feel fur, skulls, and even whale baleen. Tickets are $3.50 adults, $2.50 seniors, $1.50 teenagers, and $1 ages 3–12. The museum is open 10 A.M.–5 P.M. Monday–Saturday mid-June to Labor Day; off-season by appointment. The museum also sponsors an excellent and very popular **Family Nature Camp**—six one-week programs—between late June and mid-August; well-in-advance registration is essential (800/597-9500 or www.coa.edu/summer). Families are housed and fed on the campus ($900 per adult, $450 ages 5–15; covers almost everything). The museum gift shop has a particularly good collection of books and gifts for budding naturalists.

Across the way is the **Ethel H. Blum Gallery** (207/288-5015 ext. 254, 10 A.M.–4 P.M. Tues.–Sat. in summer, 9 A.M.–4 P.M. Mon.–Fri. during the academic year), a small space that hosts some intriguing exhibits.

Also on campus is a **Beatrix Farrand Garden,** which is undergoing restoration. The garden, designed in 1928, contained more than 50 varieties of roses and was the prototype for the rose garden at Dumbarton Oaks in Washington DC. Both are known for Farrand's use of garden rooms, such as the terraces in this garden.

Also open is the first floor of **The Turrets,** a magnificent 1895 seaside cottage that's now an administration building. Don't miss the gardens in front, either.

The college and its museum are a half mile northwest of downtown Bar Harbor. They're on Route 2/Eden St. of the Island Explorer.

Bar Harbor Whale Museum

For a whale of a good time, don't miss the small, but jam-packed Bar Harbor Whale Museum (52 West St., Bar Harbor, 207/288-0288, 9 A.M.–9 P.M., hours may vary off-season), operated by research associates affiliated with College of the Atlantic's Allied Whale program. Features include a life-sized model of a prehistoric walking whale, a 29.5-foot humpback whale skeleton, seals, marine birds, a 22-foot-long minke porpoise, and interactive

Bar Harbor Whale Museum is filled with exhibits pertaining to whales and sea life, and the staff are all affiliated with Allied Whale.

exhibits on whales and climate change. There's also a mesmerizing video of whales in their habitat. Admission is free, but donations support marine mammal research and conservation. While here, ask about COA's **Adopt A Finback or Humpback Whale** program. Biologists from Allied Whale have identified more than 1,000 finbacks and more than 6,000 humpbacks. Your $40–50 contribution

---

ADOPT A WHALE

Here's a trump card: When everyone else is flashing photos of kids or grandkids, you can whip out images of your very own adopted whale. And for that you can thank the **Adopt-a-Whale** program at College of the Atlantic (COA) in Bar Harbor.

In 1972, COA established Allied Whale, a marine-mammal laboratory designed to collect, interpret, and apply research on the world's largest mammal. Although Allied Whale's primary focus is the Gulf of Maine, its projects span the globe, involving international scientific collaboration. Since 1981, part of the research has involved assembling an enormous photo collection (more than 25,000 images) for identification of specific humpback and finback whales (with names such as Quartz and Elvis) and tracking of their migration routes. The photo catalog of finbacks already numbers more than 1,000.

And here's where the adoption program comes in – a way to support the important research being done by Allied Whale and its colleagues. If you sign up as an adoptive "parent" for a year, you'll receive a Certificate of Adoption, a large color photo and a biography of your whale, its sighting history, an informational booklet, and a subscription to Allied Whale's newsletter. It's a superb gift for budding scientists. The adoption fee is $40 for a single whale or $50 for a mother and calf.

For further information, contact **Allied Whale** (College of the Atlantic, 105 Eden St., Bar Harbor 04609, 207/288-5644, www.coa.edu/html/adoptawhale.htm).

---

supports research and nets you a color photo of your whale, a brief history of it, and a book, as well as an adoption certificate and newsletter subscription. The museum's gift shop is green—lots of good choices here for budding naturalists—and the museum uses no plastic.

The Bar Harbor Historical Society

The Bar Harbor Historical Society (33 Ledgelawn Ave., Bar Harbor, 207/288-0000, http://barharborwhalemuseum.org, 1–4 P.M. Mon.–Sat. mid-June–mid-Oct., free), in its own National Historic Register building, has fascinating displays, stereopticon images, and a scrapbook about the 1947 fire that devastated the island. The photographs alone are worth the visit. Also here are antique maps, Victorian-era hotel registers, and other local memorabilia. In winter, it's open by appointment.

For a sample of Bar Harbor before the great fire, wander over to upper West Street, which is on the National Historic Register thanks to the remaining grand cottages that line it.

Hulls Cove Tool Barn and Sculpture Garden

Part shop, part nature center, part art gallery, the Hulls Cove Tool Barn and Sculpture Garden (17 Breakneck Rd., behind Hulls Cove General Store, Hulls Cove, 207/288-5126, www.jonesport-wood.com, 9 A.M.–5 P.M. daily June–Labor Day, Thurs.–Sun. Labor Day–Columbus Day, Sat. and Sun. in winter) is just one of creative Skip Brack's enterprises. Inside the barn is an extensive selection of old tools, with an emphasis on woodworking hand tools. Paths lace through perennial gardens, woods, and fields at the Davistown Museum Sculpture Garden, which surrounds the barn and continues across the street. Throughout the garden are sculptures by noted Maine artists and found-object creations by Brack. Take the Island Explorer Route 1/Campgrounds and request a stop at the Hulls Cove General Store, then walk up the road.

Research Laboratories

Some of the world's top scientists live here year-round or come to Bar Harbor in summer to work at two prominent scientific laboratories.

World renowned in genetic research, scientists at **The Jackson Laboratory for Mammalian Research** (600 Main St., Rte. 3, Bar Harbor, 207/288-6000, www.jax.org) study cancer, diabetes, muscular dystrophy, heart disease, Alzheimer's disease, and other diseases—with considerable success. The nonprofit research institution, locally called "JAX" or just "the lab," is also renowned for its genetics databases and for producing genetically defined laboratory mice, which are shipped to research labs worldwide. Free scheduled public tours (limited to 15; call for details and reservations) begin in the lab's visitor lobby and visit the lab's three main research wings. These show the evolution of facilities over the decades, beginning with the 1980s, and the guide discusses the genetic research occurring in each. The lab is 1.5 miles south of downtown Bar Harbor.

No less impressive is the **Mount Desert Island Biological Laboratory** (159 Old Bar Harbor Rd., Salisbury Cove, 207/288-3605, www.mdibl.org), one of the few scientific research institutions in the world dedicated to studying marine animals to learn more about human health and environmental health. It is the only comprehensive effort in the country to sequence genomes. Public tours are offered twice weekly, from late June through late August; call for schedule. The program begins at Maren Auditorium with a presentation by a laboratory scientist about the lab's history and research and a short video. Then a naturalist talks about animal life in Frenchman Bay and how it pertains to the lab's research. It includes a hands-on presentation at the touch tank, filled with marine animals from Frenchman Bay, a visit to a 15-foot glass tank of other marine creatures, and a stroll through the visitor center, where there are smaller tanks. The tour takes about 1.5 hours. To avoid crowds, go on a nice day. The lab also presents a summer evening lecture series. Most are serious scientific talks, but there's also usually a family program or two. The lab is six miles north of Bar Harbor off Route 3.

PARKS AND PRESERVES

Shore Path

A real treat is a stroll along downtown Bar Harbor's Shore Path, a well-trodden, granite-edged byway built around 1880. Along the craggy shoreline are inviting granite-and-wood benches, town-owned **Grant Park** (great for picnics), birch trees, and several handsome mansions that escaped the 1947 fire. Offshore are the four Porcupine Islands. The path is open 6:30 A.M.–dusk, and leashed pets are okay. Allow about 30 minutes for the one-mile loop, beginning next to the town pier and the Bar Harbor Inn and returning via Wayman Lane, near the Bar Harbor Hospital. There's also access to the path adjacent to the Balance Rock Inn.

Bar Island

Check local newspapers or the Bar Harbor Chamber of Commerce visitor booklet for the times of low tide, then walk across the gravel bar (wear hiking boots or rubberized shoes) to wooded **Bar Island** (formerly Rodick's Island) from the foot of Bridge Street in downtown Bar Harbor. Archaeologists have confirmed that Native Americans enjoyed this turf in the distant past. (Part of the island now belongs to Acadia National Park.) You'll have the most time to explore the island during new-moon or full-moon low tides, but plan on no more than three hours—about 90 minutes before and 90 minutes after low tide. *Be sure* to wear a watch so you don't get trapped by the tide (for up to 10 hours). The foot of Bridge Street is also an excellent kayak-launching site.

Compass Harbor

About a mile southeast of downtown, along Main Street (Route 3), is Compass Harbor, a section of the park where you can stroll through woods to the water's edge and explore the overgrown ruins of park co-founder George Dorr's home.

© HILARY NANGLE

Bar Harbor's famed Shore Path edges the waterfront.

Indian Point Blagden Preserve

In the far northern corner of the island (still within the Bar Harbor town limits) is a lovely preserve owned by The Nature Conservancy. From the junction of Routes 3 and 102/198, continue 1.8 miles to Indian Point Road and turn right. Go 1.7 miles to a fork and turn right. Watch for the preserve entrance on the right, marked by a Nature Conservancy oak leaf.

Four trails wind through forested, 110-acre Indian Point Blagden Preserve, a rectangular parcel with island, hill, and bay vistas and more than 1,000 feet of frontage on Western Bay. Seal-watching and birding are popular—harbor seals on offshore rocks and six species of woodpeckers and 12 species of warblers (plus more than 100 other species) in blowdown areas. To spot the seals, plan your hike around the time of low tide, when they'll be sprawled on the rocks close to shore. Wear rubberized shoes or boots. Bring binoculars or use the telescope installed here for that purpose. To keep from disturbing the seals, watch quietly and avoid jerky movements. Park near the preserve entrance and follow the Big Woods Trail, running the length of the preserve. A second parking area is farther in, but then you'll miss walking through much of the preserve. When you reach the second parking area, just past an old field, bear left along the Shore Trail to see the seals. Register at the caretakers' house (just beyond the first parking lot, where you can pick up bird and flora checklists), and respect private property on either side of the preserve. Open dawn–6 P.M. daily, year-round.

RECREATION

Acadia National Park of course steals the limelight for most of Mount Desert Island's recreation, but Bar Harbor has its own pursuits—plus several outfitters for anyone headed to Acadia. (See the *Acadia on Mount Desert Island* chapter for information on rock-climbing guides in Bar Harbor.)

Great Meadow Loop

This easy walk connects downtown Bar Harbor with the park's Jesup Path, which leads to Sieur de Monts Spring. From there, you have access to the Dorr Mountain trails. It's a fine pre- or post-breakfast walk and a gentle introduction to hiking for those nervous about straying too far from civilization. To find the Great Meadow Loop trailhead, walk up Mount Desert Street from the Village Green to Spring Street. Follow Spring Street to the Cromwell Harbor Road and turn left. At the edge of Ledgelawn Cemetery, you'll see the signed trail. It meanders through the woods for a bit, before emerging on Ledgelawn Avenue. Turn right and walk along the road until the trail re-enters the woods across the road. The trail never strays too far from pavement. It parallels the road for a bit before re-crossing it and shadowing the Park Loop Road; the Kebo Valley Golf Club will be on your right. Just before the trail crosses Harden Farm Road, you'll see the Jesup Path trailhead on your left, across the Park Loop Road. Take that if you want to head to Sieur de Monts Spring (0.6 mile). Otherwise, continue along the trail as it follows and crosses Harden Farm Road and wraps around the golf course. (There's a portable toilet near one green). At the intersection with Cromwell Harbor Road, turn right, and return to Spring Street and follow it back to Mount Desert Street and the Village Green. It's just shy of two miles round-trip.

Biking

With all the great biking options, including 45 miles of carriage roads (12 of the total 57 miles are off-limits to bicycles) and some of the best roadside bike routes in Maine, you'll want to bring a bike or rent one here. Two rental firms based in downtown Bar Harbor also handle repairs. Expect to pay around $22 per day for a rental bike, including helmet, lock, and map; more for a performance model. It's wise to make advance reservations.

The Minutolo family's **Bar Harbor Bicycle Shop** (141 Cottage St., Bar Harbor, 207/288-3886, www.barharborbike.com), on the corner with Route 3, has been in business since 1977 and has earned an excellent reputation. If you have your own bike, stop here for advice on routes—the Minutolos have cycled everywhere on the island and can suggest the perfect mountain-bike or road-bike loop based on your

ability and schedule. The shop also sponsors the **Downeast Bicycle Club** (www.downeastbicycleclub.org), which organizes weekly group rides, including a free Sunday morning one, with moderate and fast options, usually 9 A.M.–noon, and a Friday late-afternoon carriage road ride, usually at 4:30 P.M. from the Eagle Lake parking lot. For details, call the shop or check the calendar section of the club's website. The shop has rentals ranging from standard mountain bikes to full-suspension models and even tandems ($44) as well as all the accessories and gear you might need. Hours in summer are 8 A.M.–8 P.M. daily, other months 9 A.M.–5:30 P.M. Tuesday–Saturday. The shop stays open March through Christmas.

Acadia Bike & Canoe (48 Cottage St., Bar Harbor, 207/288-9605 or 800/526-8615, www.acadiabike.com) also rents bikes. Reserve ahead with a credit card for a better rate. The shop opens daily at 8 A.M. in spring, summer, and fall.

For a low-key, insider bicycle tour of the region, you can't do better than **Maine Coast Bicycle Tours** (48 Cottage St., Bar Harbor, 207/288-0050 or 888/412-2453, www.mainecoastbicycletours.com), a division of Acadia Bike & Canoe. Locally owned and operated, Maine Coast specializes in all-inclusive bicycle tours of Mount Desert Island, with forays to Schoodic Point and Swans Island. These folks know the island and are willing to share their insider info. The six-day tour costs about $1,700. That fee covers most meals (usually in top-rated restaurants), a 24-speed rental bicycle and related gear, a guide and a support vehicle, an afternoon guided sea kayak or hiking tour, a guided walking tour of downtown Bar Harbor, a welcome reception at an oceanfront private home, a sunset tour of Cadillac, round-trip ferry to Swans Island, and five nights of upscale hotel lodging. This is not for super-serious cyclists; trips cover a mere 15 to 25 miles each day, allowing plenty of time to enjoy the scenery and relax.

If you're headed to Southwest Harbor, perhaps for a day trip to Swans Island, see the information on Southwest Cycle in the

Southwest Harbor and Vicinity section farther on in this chapter.

Sea Kayaking

Sea kayaking is wildly popular along the Maine coast, and Bar Harbor has become a major kayaking destination. No experience is necessary to join tours operated by any of the firms in Bar Harbor.

Bob Mensink and Robert Shaw established **National Park Kayak Tours** (39 Cottage St., Bar Harbor, 207/288-0342 or 800/347-0940, www.acadiakayak.com) in 1993, and they limit their Registered Maine Guide–led tours to a maximum of six tandem kayaks per trip. Four-hour morning, mid-day, afternoon, or sunset paddles are offered, including shuttle service, a paddle/safety lesson, and a brief stop. Paddlers are shuttled to the quiet, west side of the island (usually Western or Blue Hill Bay, occasionally Somes Sound), with location determined by wind and weather. Rates are $48 per person in July and August, $44 off-season. Most trips cover about six miles. Multi-day camping trips also are offered. It's best if you make reservations at least one day in advance. Trips are offered from Memorial Day weekend through early October.

Half-day ($48), full-day ($72; bring your own lunch), and multi-day sea-kayak tours are on the schedule organized by **Coastal Kayaking Tours** (48 Cottage St., Bar Harbor, 207/288-9605 or 800/526-8615, www.acadiafun.com). The best option for beginners is the 2.5-hour harbor tour, beginning at 9 A.M. ($38). By prearrangement, special half-day family tours, departing at 1:30 P.M., can handle kids eight and over ($48). A 2.5-hour sunset cruise begins around 5 P.M. (depending on season), at $38; a three-day island-camping adventure is $399, including equipment and meals; and a three-day inn-to-inn tour is $649, including all meals. Other kayak trips are offered mid-May through September. All trips are weather-dependent, and reservations are essential. Rental canoes ($30), ruddered kayaks ($45 solo, $55 tandem), and open cockpits ($25 single, $35 double) are available.

Three other firms in Bar Harbor do sea kayak tours and rentals. New tour operators spring up often; opt for experience. Other companies operate elsewhere on the island; see the *Southwest Harbor and Vicinity* and *Tremont* sections.

If you've brought your own kayak, one place to launch it is **Hadley Point Beach** (Hadley Point Rd., Bar Harbor). This pebbly beach on Mount Desert Narrows has a couple of picnic tables, a portable toilet, and parking. Careful, though—the currents are very strong. To find the put-in, continue south from the Thompson Island Visitor Center on Route 3 for about four miles. The Hadley Point Road will be on your left. Follow it to the end.

Golf

Duffers first teed off in 1888 at **Kebo Valley Golf Club** (100 Eagle Lake Rd., Rte. 233, Bar Harbor, 207/288-5000, www.kebovalleyclub.com, May–Oct.), Maine's oldest club and the eighth-oldest in the nation. The 17th hole became legendary when it took President William Howard Taft 27 tries to sink the ball in 1911. Kebo is very popular, with a gorgeous setting, an attractive clubhouse, and decent food service, so tee times are essential; you can reserve up to six days in advance. Greens fees ($85 peak season) are the highest on the island, but afternoon and twilight rates are available.

Mount Desert Island YMCA

Here's a lifesaver on a stormy day. The MDI YMCA (21 Park St., Bar Harbor, 207/288-3511, www.mdiymca.org) has an indoor pool, gym, track, fitness room, and recreation room. Rates are $9 adult (19–59); $6 full-time student and senior; or $16 per family, covering two adults and up to three kids. Summer hours are 5:30 A.M.–9 P.M. Monday–Friday, 8 A.M.–4 P.M. Saturday, and 8 A.M.–2 P.M. Sunday.

EXCURSION BOATS

Please note: Prices are given as a guide and will fluctuate with the cost of fuel.

◖ Dive-In Theater Boat Cruise

You don't have to go diving in these frigid

waters; others will do it for you. When the kids are clamoring to touch slimy sea cucumbers and starfish at various touch tanks in the area, they're likely to be primed for Diver Ed's Dive-In Theater Boat Cruise (P.O. Box 870, Bar Harbor, 207/288-3483, www .divered.com), departing from the College of the Atlantic pier (105 Eden St., Bar Harbor). Former Bar Harbor harbormaster and College of the Atlantic grad Ed Monat heads the crew aboard the 46-passenger *Seal,* which goes a mile or two offshore and sends down two professional divers (including Ed) with video cameras. You and the kids stay on deck, all warm and dry, and watch the action on a TV screen. There's communication back and forth, so the kids can ask questions as the divers pick up urchins, starfish, crabs, lobsters, and other sea life. When the diver surfaces, he or she brings a bag of touchable specimens—another chance to pet some slimy creatures (which go back into the water after show-and-tell). Great concept. Watch the kids' expressions—this is a big hit. The two-hour trips depart three times daily

Monday–Friday, twice daily Saturday, and once on Sunday, from early July through early September; fewer trips are made in spring and fall. Cost is $35 adults, $30 seniors, $25 children ages 5–12, $10 younger than 5. Usually twice weekly there's a park ranger or naturalist on board and the tour lasts for three hours—check the park's *Beaver Log* newspaper or Diver Ed's website for the schedule and reservation information—these trips cost an additional $5. Advance reservations are strongly encouraged.

◖ Whale-Watching Excursions

Whale-watching boats go as far as 20 miles offshore, so no matter what the weather in Bar Harbor, dress warmly and bring more clothing than you think you'll need—even gloves, if you're especially sensitive to cold. I've been out on days when it's close to 90°F on island, but feels more like 30°F in a moving boat on open ocean. Motion-sensitive children and adults should plan in advance for appropriate medication, such as seasickness pills or patches.

© TOM NANGLE

Whale-watching and nature cruises depart from Bar Harbor's waterfront.

COMMUNITIES

Adults are required to show a photo ID when boarding the boat.

Whale-watching, puffin-watching, and combo excursions are offered by **Bar Harbor Whale Watch Company** (1 West St., Bar Harbor, 207/288-2386 or 800/942-5374, www .barharborwhales.com), sailing from the town pier (1 West St.) in downtown Bar Harbor. The company operates under various names, including Acadian Whale Watcher, and has a number of boats. Most trips are accompanied by a naturalist (often from Allied Whale at the College of the Atlantic), who regales passengers with all sorts of interesting trivia about the whales, porpoises, seabirds, and other marine life spotted along the way. In season, some trips go out as far as the puffin colony on Petit Manan Light. Trips depart daily from late May through late October, but with so many options, it's impossible to list the schedule, so call. Tickets are $49–53 adults, $26 children 6–14, $8 children under six. A portion of the ticket price benefits Allied Whale, which researches and protects marine animals in the Gulf of Maine.

Trips may extend longer than the time advertised. Don't plan anything else too tightly around the trip. However, try to visit the Whale Museum, either before or afterward.

Scenic Nature Cruises (1.5–2 hours) and kid-friendly Lobster and Seal Watch Cruises (1.5 hours) also are offered. Rates for these are $23–26 for adults, $16 children, $5 kiddies.

Sailing

Captain Steve Pagels, under the umbrella of **Downeast Windjammer Cruises** (207/288-4585 or 207/288-2373, www.downeastwindjammer.com), offers 1.5- to 2-hour day sails on the 151-foot steel-hulled *Margaret Todd,* a gorgeous four-masted schooner with tanbark sails that he designed and launched in 1998. Trips depart daily at 10 A.M. and 2 P.M. and around sunset mid-May to mid-October (weather permitting), from the Bar Harbor Inn pier, just east of the town pier in downtown Bar Harbor. You'll get the best wildlife

sightings on the morning trip; better sailing on the afternoon trip; and live music on the sunset one. Some morning sails are narrated by a park ranger. Buy tickets either at the pier or at 27 Main Street or online with a credit card; plan to arrive at least half an hour early. Cost is $32 adults, $22 ages 11 and younger. Dogs are welcome on all sails.

Sea Venture Cruise

Captain Winston Shaw's custom boat tour by Sea Venture (207/288-3355, www.svboattours .com) lets you design the perfect trip aboard *Reflection,* a 20-foot motor launch. Captain Shaw, a Registered Maine Guide and committed environmentalist, specializes in nature-oriented tours. He's the founder and director of the Coastal Maine Bald Eagle Project, and he was involved in the inaugural Earth Day celebration in 1970. He's been studying coastal birds for more than 25 years. You can pick from 10 recommended cruises lasting from one to eight hours or design your own. In any case, the boat is yours. Boat charter rate is $95 per hour for one or two people, $110 for three or four, and $150 for five or six. Captain Shaw can also arrange for picnic lunches. On longer trips, restroom stops are available. The boat departs from the Atlantic Oakes Motel pier, off Route 3.

Lobster Cruise

When you're ready to learn The Truth about lobsters, sign up for a cruise aboard Captain John Nicolai's *Lulu,* a traditional Maine lobster boat. Operating daily from May to September, *Lulu* departs from the Harborside Hotel and Marina in Bar Harbor (55 West St., 207/963-2341 or 866/235-2341, www.lululobsterboat .com), and makes two to five two-hour trips daily. Captain Nicolai provides an entertaining commentary on anything and everything, but especially about lobsters and lobstering. He hauls a lobster trap and explains intimate details of the hapless critters. (Lobstering is banned on Sundays June–August; the cruises operate, but there's no hauling that day.)

Reservations are required. Cost is $27 adults, $24 seniors and military, $15 children 2–12. No credit cards. Free parking is available in the hotel's lot.

ENTERTAINMENT AND EVENTS

At the height of the summer season, plenty of live entertainment varies from pub music to films to classical concerts.

The **Bar Harbor Town Band** performs free Monday and Thursday evenings (8 P.M.) July to mid-August on the Village Green (Main St. and Mount Desert St., Bar Harbor).

Above Rupununi restaurant, **Carmen Verandah** (119 Main St., Bar Harbor, 207/288-2766) is the weekend place to be and be seen. Everything gets rolling about 9:30 P.M.—blues, rock, salsa, funk, zydeco, ska, reggae, you-name-it—and there's lots of space for dancing. Other nights, there's a DJ. Darts and billiards round out the picture. It's open all year.

You never know quite what's going to happen at **Improv Acadia** (15 Cottage St., Bar Harbor, 207/288-2503, www.improvacadia .com, $15 adults, $10 kids age 12 and younger). Every show is different, as actors use audience suggestions to create comedy sketches. Shows are staged once or twice a night, mid-June to mid-October. Dessert, snacks, and drinks are available.

The **Bar Harbor Music Festival** (207/288-5744 in July and August, 212/222-1026 off-season, www.barharbormusicfestival.org), a summer tradition since 1967, emphasizes up-and-coming musical talent in a series of classical, jazz, and pop concerts, usually Fridays and Sundays early July to early August, at various island locations, including local inns and an annual outdoor concert in Acadia National Park. A relatively new addition to the schedule is an opera, which received rave reviews in its debut season. Tickets are $25–35 adult, $15 student, and can be purchased at the festival office building (59 Cottage St., Bar Harbor). Pre-concert dinners are also sometimes available at $35. Reservations are wise.

Theaters

Built in 1932 and listed on the National Register of Historic Places, the beautifully refurbished **Criterion Theatre and Arts Center** (35 Cottage St., Bar Harbor, 207/288-3441 for films or 207/288-5829 for concerts, www .criteriontheatre.com) is a gem. In 2007, it gained nonprofit status with a mission to make arts and theater more accessible through diverse programs. Now, in addition to screening films, the Criterion puts on concerts, plays, and other special events. You'll soak up the nostalgia in this art deco classic with nearly 900 seats (including an elegant floating balcony).

Combine pizza with your picture show at **Reel Pizza Cinerama** (33 Kennebec Pl., Bar Harbor, 207/288-3811 for films, 207/288-3828 for food). Two films are screened nightly on each of two screens. All tickets are $6; pizzas are $13–20. Doors open at 4:30 P.M.; get there early for the best seats.

Create Your Own Art

Definitely worthy of the *Entertainment* category is **All Fired Up!** (44 Cottage St., Bar Harbor, 207/288-3130, www.acadiaallfiredup .com), the perfect answer to "What do we do in the rain?" Solution: Paint your own pottery, make mosaics, or create a critter (stuffed animal). You'll often see three generations sharing a booth as they work away at their projects in this bright, airy space. Here's the drill for pottery: Select a mug or bowl or whatever from one of the 500 or so white-bisque pottery pieces ($2 and up). Figure out a design (check out "the inspiration center"), choose your colors, and work away. If you opt for a glaze instead of paint, so you can dine off your masterpiece, you'll need to leave it for a few days so it can be kiln-fired (and shipped to your home if you prefer). Studio time (including all the supplies) is $10 per adult, $7 per child. Owner Nina Zeldin inspires even the artistically challenged, and it's all great fun. Open all year. Summer hours (late June to Labor Day) are 9 A.M.–8 P.M. daily, to 10 P.M. in July and August.

COMMUNITIES

Events

Bar Harbor is home to numerous special events. Here's just a sampling. For more, call 207/288-5103 or visit www.barharbormaine.com.

In mid-June, the annual **Acadia Birding Festival** attracts birders with guided walks, boating excursions, tours, talks, and meals.

In late June, **Legacy of the Arts** is a week-long celebration of music, art, theater, dance, and history, with tours, exhibits, workshops, concerts, lectures, demonstrations, and more.

The **Fourth of July** is always a big deal in Bar Harbor, celebrated with a blueberry-pancake breakfast (6 A.M.), a parade (10 A.M.), a seafood festival (11 A.M. on), a band concert, and fireworks. A highlight is the Lobster Race, a crustacean competition drawing contestants such as Lobzilla and Larry the Lobster in a four-lane saltwater tank on the Village Green. Independence Day celebrations in the island's smaller villages always evoke a bygone era.

The Abbe Museum, the College of the Atlantic, and the Maine Indian Basketmakers Alliance sponsor the annual **Native American Festival,** 10 A.M.–4 P.M. the first Saturday after July 4, featuring baskets, beadwork, and other handicrafts for sale, and Indian drumming and dancing (free admission; held at College of the Atlantic, Bar Harbor).

In even-numbered years, the **Mount Desert**

Garden Club Tour presents a rare chance to visit some of Maine's most spectacular private gardens on the second or third Saturday in July (confirm the date with the Bar Harbor Chamber of Commerce).

The **Directions Craft Show** fills a weekend in late July or early August with extraordinary displays and sales of crafts by members of Directions. You'll find it at Mount Desert Island High School (Rte. 233, Eagle Lake Rd., Bar Harbor). Hours are Friday 5–9 P.M., Saturday and Sunday 10 A.M.–5 P.M.

SHOPPING

Bar Harbor's boutiques—running the gamut from attractive to kitschy—are indisputably visitor-oriented; many shut down for the winter, even removing or covering their signs and blanketing the windows. Fortunately, the island has enough of a year-round community to support the cluster of loyal shopkeepers determined to stay open all year, but shop-till-you-droppers will be happiest here between Memorial Day weekend and Columbus Day, and particularly in July and August. (Remember, too, that Bar Harbor isn't Mount Desert's only shopping area.)

Galleries

Downtown Bar Harbor's best craft gallery is **Island Artisans** (99 Main St., Bar Harbor,

© HILARY NANGLE

Find the perfect basket at the annual Native American Festival in early July.

207/288-4214, www.islandartisans.com). More than 100 Maine artists are represented here, and the quality is outstanding. Don't miss it. You'll find basketwork, handmade paper, wood carvings, blown glass, jewelry, weaving, metalwork, ceramics, and more. (Island Artisans also has a summertime branch at 119 Main St. in Northeast Harbor.)

For more than three decades, **Alone Moose Fine Crafts** (78 West St., Bar Harbor, 207/288-4229, www.finemainecrafts.com) has lured collectors and browsers with its selection of sculpture, pottery, jewelry, and other works.

Newer on the scene is **Aragona Designs** (150 Main St., Bar Harbor, 207/288-2120, www.aragonadesigns.com), where Jodie Aragona shows and sells her jewelry as well as a carefully chosen selection of glasswork, pottery, fiber arts, and other contemporary craft.

It's worth the brief detour off the beaten path to find **Rocky Mann Studio & Gallery** (38 Breakneck Rd., Bar Harbor, 207/288-5478, www.rockymann.com) to see Mann's porcelain and raku pottery along with paintings by Carol Shutt.

Books

Toys, cards, and newspapers blend in with the new-book inventory at **Sherman's Book Store** (56 Main St., Bar Harbor, 207/288-3161). Even some fusty clutter is here, but it's all user-friendly. Sherman's is just the place to pick up maps and trail guides for fine days and puzzles for foggy days.

Find a whodunit at **Mystery Cove Book Shop** (1 Dewey St., Hulls Cove, 207/288-4665), the overflow of an Internet business specializing in mysteries, from rare books to popular titles.

Souvenir Gifts

Souvenir shops are *everywhere* on Mount Desert Island, so why single out the Acadia Shops? If you need Maine-made mementos for Uncle Harry and Aunt Mary, or if the kids need trinkets for friends back home, the Acadia Corporation has several shops in downtown

Bar Harbor that can cover it all. Price range is broad, quality is fairly high, and clerks are especially friendly at **The Acadia Shop** (85 Main St., Bar Harbor, 207/288-5600, www.acadiashops.com). Another branch, **Acadia Outdoors** (45 Main St., Bar Harbor, 207/288-2422), features sportswear and outdoor accessories.

Musical Instruments

Most vacationers don't expect to shop for musical instruments, but everyone with an affinity for folk music gravitates toward **Song of the Sea** (47 West St., Bar Harbor, 207/288-5653, www.songsea.com), a unique, jam-packed harborfront shop where you can find guitars, banjos, harmonicas, and tin whistles—but also such esoterica as hammered dulcimers, doumbeks, didgeridoos, psalteries, and Chilean rainsticks. Ed and Anne Damm are extremely knowledgeable and helpful, even to the point of playing instruments over the phone for call-in orders.

ACCOMMODATIONS

If you're not planning to camp in one of Acadia National Park's two campgrounds (there are no other lodgings, and there's no backcountry camping), you'll need to search elsewhere on the island for a place to sleep. Bar Harbor alone has thousands of beds in hotels, motels, inns, B&Bs, cottages, and two hostels—and the rest of the island adds to that total, with a dozen private campgrounds thrown into the mix. Nonetheless, lodgings can be scarce at the height of summer (particularly the first two weeks in August), a stretch that just happens to coincide with an outrageously high spike in room rates (sorta like gasoline hikes that "just happen" to occur just before long holiday weekends). Off-season, there's plenty of choice, even after the seasonal places shut down, and rates are always lower—often dramatically so. (The Bar Harbor Chamber of Commerce and the Thompson Island Visitor Center will give you a list of lodgings open year-round, and both offices are helpful for finding beds even at peak times.) Rates noted reflect peak season, usually

MDI ON A BUDGET

At first glance, Mount Desert Island might seem an expensive place to visit, especially if you're not a fan of camping. Truth is, you can afford to visit the island, even if your budget is tight.

Consider this: Once you've paid for your park pass, your recreation is free. There are no further fees to hike, canoe, bicycle, or swim, unless you need to rent equipment. If so, plan ahead and ask about any deals. Some sports outfitters offer a discount for advance reservations or multi-day rentals. Some will allow you to rent a bike after a certain time and keep it for the next day, charging you for only one day. That allows you to get in an extra evening ride – ideal at the peak of summer when daylight lasts well into the evening.

Outside of the park, many of the recommended sights detailed here are free. Perhaps you can't afford to take the family to the Oceanarium, but you certainly can visit the MDI Biological Laboratory. Most of the Park Ranger programs are free (check the *Beaver Log*), including evening ones presented in the park's campgrounds. Free concerts and lectures are regularly presented at many locations around the island; check local newspapers or ask at information centers.

You must eat, but you can keep prices down, even when dining out. For starters, opt for lodging with an in-room refrigerator if possible. Then, stock up on breakfast and sandwich and salad staples (milk, cereal, bread, luncheon meats and cheeses, vegetables, fresh fruit, etc.) at the supermarket. If you don't have a refrigerator, a cooler will do, but remember to keep it stocked with ice. (Collapsible coolers are available and easy to pack or carry on an airplane, or purchase an inexpensive Styrofoam one.) You can survive on this; I've done so. Even better is to have access to boiling water to make instant soups or ramen noodles, to which you can add all kinds of vegetables for a healthful meal.

If you want to dine out, lunch is almost always less expensive than dinner. For dinner, look for restaurants with early-bird specials; many places have very reasonable meals available before 6 or 6:30 P.M. Or consider combining your meal with evening entertainment at Reel Pizza. When you do dine out, take home any leftovers (assuming you have a refrigerator or cooler). Other inexpensive options are public suppers; look for notices on bulletin boards and in local newspapers.

As for lodging, in general the farther you get from the key sights or downtowns, the less it will cost. If you're staying for a week or longer, your best move is to find a cottage rental. (Hint: Prices for many rentals drop the week before Labor Day.) Another option is to consider a camping cabin. These rustic shelters generally do not have any plumbing – you'll have to walk to a shared bathhouse – but they are clean and dry and have real beds; some even provide linens or minimal cooking facilities. What you sacrifice in privacy is more than offset by the folks from around the world you'll meet.

Wherever you go, whatever you do, always ask about any applicable discounts: automobile clubs, seniors, military, family rates, etc. And finally, ditch the car and use the free Island Explorer bus to get around. Not only does doing so save you money on gasoline and avoid parking hassles, but – big bonus points – it benefits the environment.

July and August. Unless noted otherwise, properties are seasonal.

Hostels

The **Bar Harbor/Mount Desert Island Hostel** (321 Main St., Bar Harbor, 207/288-5587, www.barharborhostel.com, $25 dorm, $80 private room, $10 per person for a tent platform) is listed for sale, and given its prime location, it's unlikely to remain a hostel, but check online to be sure. It is the island's only hostel.

Not officially a hostel, but with a hostel-style atmosphere, and only for women, the **MDI YWCA** (36 Mount Desert St., Bar Harbor, 207/288-5008, $30–40) has second- and third-floor single and double rooms, as well as a seven-bed solarium (dorm). Located in a historic downtown building next to the library and across from the Island Explorer bus hub, "the Y" has bathrooms on each floor, as well as a laundry room (coin-operated machines), a TV room, and shared kitchen facilities. Free parking; no pets. There's zero tolerance for smoking, alcohol, and drugs (you'll need to sign an agreement). For July and early August reservations, call way ahead, as the Y is popular with the island's young summer workers.

Inns and Bed-and-Breakfasts

Few innkeepers have mastered the art of hospitality as well as Roy Kasindorf and Hélène Harton, owners of the **(Ullikana Bed & Breakfast** (16 The Field, Bar Harbor, 207/288-9552, www.ullikana.com, $165–335), a 10-room, Victorian Tudor inn, built by Alpheus Hardy, Bar Harbor's first "cottager," in 1885. They genuinely enjoy their guests. Hélène's a whiz in the kitchen; after one of her multicourse breakfasts, usually served on the water-view patio, you won't need lunch. She's also a decorating genius, blending antiques and modern art, vibrant color with soothing hues, folk art and fine art, with a result like a finely tuned orchestra. Roy excels at helping guests select just the right hike, bike route, or other activity. Afternoon refreshments provide a time for guests to gather and share experiences. Ten comfortable rooms all have private baths; many have working fireplaces, and some have private terraces with water views. Hélène and Roy also own The Yellow House, next door, with six lovely rooms decorated in old Bar Harbor style and a huge living room filled with antique wicker. They're at a quiet downtown location close to Bar Harbor's Shore Path. Both are open from late May to late October.

Right next door is the fabulously renovated and rejuvenated **(Bass Cottage** (14 The Field, Bar Harbor, 207/288-1234 or 866/782-9224, www.basscottage.com, $210–360). Corporate refugees Teri and Jeff Anderholm

The Ullikana Bed & Breakfast is tucked in a quiet downtown location, just steps from Main Street and the waterfront.

purchased the 26-room 1885 cottage in 2003 and spent a year gutting it, salvaging the best of the old and blending in new to turn it into a luxurious and stylish 10-room inn. It retains its Victorian bones, yet it is most un-Victorian in style. Guest rooms are soothingly decorated with cream and pastel-colored walls and have phones, Wi-Fi, and TV with DVD (a DVD library is available—a godsend on a stormy day); many rooms have fireplaces and whirlpool tubs. The spacious and elegant public rooms—expansive living rooms, cozy library, porches—flow from one to another. Teri puts her culinary degree to use preparing baked goods, fruits, and savory and sweet entrées for breakfast and evening refreshments. A guest pantry is stocked with tea, coffee, and snacks. Open mid-May to late October.

Situated on one oceanfront acre in the West Street Historical District, **The Saltair Inn** (121 West St., Bar Harbor, 207/288-2882, www.saltairinn.com, $155–360) was originally built in 1887 as a guesthouse. Innkeepers Kristi and Matt Losquadro and their young family now welcome guests in four spacious rooms, three of which face Frenchman Bay. It's elegant, yet informal. Rooms have flat-screen TVs and Wi-Fi, but truthfully, it will be hard to tear yourself away from the Adirondack chairs perched at the water's edge on the long expanse of lawn.

Energetic Marian Burns, a former math and science teacher, is the reason everything runs smoothly at **Mira Monte Inn** (69 Mount Desert St., Bar Harbor, 207/288-4263 or 800/553-5109, www.miramonte.com, $170–290), close (but not too close) to downtown. Born and raised here, and an avid gardener, Marian's a terrific resource for island exploring. Try to capture her during wine and cheese (5–7 P.M.), and ask about her experience during the 1947 Bar Harbor fire. And don't miss her collection of antique Bar Harbor hotel photos. The 13 Victorian-style rooms have air-conditioning, cable TV, and either a balcony or a fireplace, and some have whirlpool tubs. Two efficiency suites and one fully equipped apartment-style unit in a separate building are ideal for families. Rates include an extensive hot-and-cold breakfast buffet. Open early May to early November (the two suites are available all year).

Much less pricey and a find for families is the **Seacroft Inn** (18 Albert Meadow, Bar Harbor, 207/288-4669 or 800/824-9694, www.seacroftinn.com, $99–139), well situated between Main Street and the Shore Path. All rooms in Bunny and Dave Brown's white, multi-gabled cottage have a phone, TV, refrigerator, and microwave, and a breakfast basket is delivered to your room each morning (subtract $5 from the rate if you don't want breakfast). Some rooms can be joined as family suites. Closed from mid-November until April 1; no breakfast or housekeeping April 1 until mid-May.

Outside of town, in a serene location with fabulous views of Frenchman Bay, is Jack and Jeani Ochtera's ☾ **Inn at Bay Ledge** (150 Sand Point Rd., Bar Harbor, 207/288-4204 in summer and 207/875-3262 in winter, www.innatbayledge.com, $150–475), an oasis of calm tucked under towering pines and atop an 80-foot cliff. Terraced decks descend to a pool and hot tub and onto the lawn, which stretches to the cliff's edge. Stairs descend to a private stone beach below. It's an elegant, casual retreat. Almost all guest rooms have water views. Beds are topped with down comforters and feather beds; some rooms have whirlpool tubs, and second-floor rooms have private decks. A sauna and steam shower are available. Also available are cottages, which lack the view but have use of the inn's facilities. The newest addition is the adjacent Summer House at Bay Ledge, a shingled cottage with a deck 25 feet from the edge of Frenchman Bay. It's available from late May to October ($375–475).

On a budget? Consider the pleasant but few frills **Llangolan Inn & Cottages** (865 Rte. 3, Bar Harbor, 207/288-3016, www.llangolan.com), seven miles from downtown. The well-cared-for property includes a B&B and cottages. Five rooms, one with private bath and four sharing two baths, are comfortable and welcoming and go for a bargain $75–85, including a continental breakfast. Also available are basic housekeeping cottages sleeping two to five, each with kitchenette, TV, and heat ($85–130). Pets are permitted ($10 per night). This property is right on Route 3, so expect traffic noise. Ask for rooms facing the back or for a cottage well away from the road. Even then, you'll probably hear the passing *vroom*.

Another budget choice is the **Otter Creek Inn** (Rte. 3, Otter Creek, 207/288-5151 or 800/845-5852, www.ottercreekme.com), a well-maintained complex with a small motel-like inn, an apartment, and cottages. The inn's six guest rooms ($105) each have a mini-fridge and TV and include continental breakfast. A two-bedroom apartment rents for $175; two housekeeping cabins are $125. There are laundry facilities, and all accommodations are adjacent to the Otter Creek Market, which has everything from camping supplies to lobster and wine.

Hotels and Motels

One of the town's best-known, most visible, and best-situated hotels is the **Bar Harbor Inn** (Newport Dr., Bar Harbor, 207/288-3351 or 800/248-3351, www.barharborinn.com, $199–379), a sprawling complex on eight acres overlooking the harbor and Bar Island. The 153 rooms and suites vary considerably in style, from traditional inn to motel, and are in three different buildings. Continental breakfast is included, and special packages, with meals and activities, are available—an advantage if you have children. The kids also will appreciate the heated outdoor pool; adults might enjoy the full-service spa. Service is attentive. Open from April to November. Other Bar Harbor lodgings under the same management and ownership (www.bar-harbor-hotels.com) are the fancypants **Bluenose Inn** (90 Eden St., Bar Harbor, 207/288-3348, www.barharborhotel.com); the less expensive, family-oriented **Acadia Inn** (98 Eden St., Bar Harbor, 207/288-3500, www.acadiainn.com); and **Bar Harbor Grand Hotel** (269 Main St., Bar Harbor, 207/288-5226, www.barharborgrand.com), a four-story neo-Victorian, opened in 2003 and modeled on Bar Harbor's 19th-century Rodick House, looming over Lower Main Street.

The newest and fanciest hotel in town is **Harborside Hotel & Marina** (55 West St., Bar Harbor, 207/288-5033 or 800/238-5033, www.theharborsidehotel.com, $199–329), fronting the water in downtown Bar Harbor. Almost all of the 185 rooms and suites have a water view and semi-private balconies. Some have whirlpool tubs; deluxe rooms have marble baths, and some have large outdoor hot tubs. Deluxe studios have one to three bedrooms, and penthouse suites have full kitchens. Rates include a continental breakfast buffet. A fine-dining restaurant and full-service spa are located in the beautifully restored Bar Harbor Club. An Italian restaurant is in the hotel. Facilities also include an outdoor heated pool and Jacuzzi and a pier.

At the opposite end of the budgetary scale is the **Edenbrook Motel** (96 Eden St., Rte. 3, Bar Harbor, 207/288-4975, www.edenbrookmotelbh.com, $70–100, two-bedroom suite $120), with an excellent location 1.5 miles from Acadia's main entrance, one mile from downtown, and 500 yards from the ferry servicing Canada. Four tiers of buildings are built on a hillside; rooms on the second floor in the highest building have balconies with panoramic views over Frenchman Bay. The 47 rooms are basic motel style but spacious, and all have phones, TV, air-conditioning, and in-room coffee.

A little fancier and right next door is the **Highbrook Motel** (94 Eden St., Rte. 3, Bar Harbor, 207/288-3591 or 800/338-9688, www.highbrookmotel.com, $89–132), with 26 rooms in two hillside buildings. Each room has air-conditioning, TV, telephone, Wi-Fi, and a coffeemaker, and most have refrigerators. The nicest rooms are in the quiet back building. Coffee, tea, juice, and breakfast pastries are available in the morning.

Seasonal Rentals

Contact **L. S. Robinson Co.** (337 Main St., Southwest Harbor, 207/244-5563, www.lsrobinson.com) or **Maine Island Properties** (Mount Desert, 207/244-4308, fax 207/244-0588, www.maineislandproperties.com) for

COMMUNITIES

listings of houses and cottages available by the week or month. In July and August, rates run from $700–6,000 a week or more, plus tax and deposit. Both agencies handle rentals in all parts of Mount Desert. (If you decide to stay, they also have residential listings.) The Bar Harbor Chamber of Commerce's annual guide also has listings of cottages—some private, others that are part of cottage colonies.

Camping

Mount Desert Island's private campgrounds are located at the northern end of the island, down the center, and in the southwest corner. Most are also on the routes of the free Island Explorer bus service, making it easy and economical—and preferable—to leave your car (or RV) at your campsite and avoid parking panic (between late June and Columbus Day). The Thompson Island and Hulls Cove Visitor Centers have a listing of private campgrounds.

Near the Thompson Island Visitor Center are two well-sited campgrounds, both large, well maintained, and on an Island Explorer bus route. Next to the causeway, and 10 miles northwest of Bar Harbor, **Bar Harbor KOA** (136 County Rd., Bar Harbor, 207/288-3520 or 888/562-5605, www.barharborkoa.net, mid-May to mid-Oct.) occupies 32 acres with 2,500 feet of shorefront. Many of the 200 open, grassy, and wooded tent and RV sites have terrific views. Facilities include coin-operated showers and laundry, a playground, a beach, game areas, an on-site sea kayak and canoe rental and tour outfitter, and a small shop. Pets are allowed. Also under this campground's umbrella is a second camping area, one mile up the road, and not on the ocean. It's geared more to smaller RVs and tents, but campers have full use of the other campground's facilities. Rates begin around $42 for a tent site.

Mount Desert Narrows Camping Resort (1219 Rte. 3, Bar Harbor, 207/288-4782, www.narrowscamping.com, $30–80 per site varying with location and hookups, May–late Oct.), 1.5 miles east of the causeway, has a fantastic view over Thomas Bay and the Narrows.

The 40-acre campground has 239 wooded and open tent and RV sites (many oceanfront), a heated pool, a convenience store, canoe and kayak rentals, volleyball and basketball courts, a playground, coin laundry, free movie nights and hay rides, and live entertainment from mid-June to Labor Day. Pets are allowed.

The Baker family has operated **Hadley's Point Campground** (33 Hadley Point Rd., Bar Harbor, 207/288-4808, www.hadleyspoint .com, May 15–mid-Oct.) since 1969. Tent sites are $27, sites with water and electric are $35, and full hookups are $40 (seventh night free on a week-long stay). Tent sites are nicely spaced in the woods and have a sense of privacy; big-rig sites, located in fields, are tight. Facilities include a laundry, a heated pool, shuffleboard courts, horseshoes, and a playground. A public saltwater beach with a boat launch is within walking distance. The campground is eight miles from Bar Harbor.

FOOD

You won't go hungry in Bar Harbor, and you won't find chain fast-food places. The summer tourism trade and the College of the Atlantic students have created a demand for pizzerias, vegetarian bistros, brewpubs, and a handful of creative restaurants. But of course almost every restaurant has some variant of lobster. And even if you're using Bar Harbor as a base of operations, don't miss opportunities to explore restaurants elsewhere on the island.

The island's best collection of good, inexpensive restaurants, most open year-round, are along Rodick Street, from Reel Pizza down to Rosalie's, which actually fronts Cottage Street. You'll find a good ethnic mix here, from Mexican to Thai to Italian—not a lobster in sight.

Local Flavors

Only a masochist could bypass **Ben & Bill's Chocolate Emporium** (66 Main St., Bar Harbor, 207/288-3281 or 800/806-3281, 9 A.M.–10 P.M. daily), a long-running taste-treat-cum-experience in downtown Bar Harbor. The homemade candies and more than 50 ice cream flavors (including a dubious lobster flavor) are nothing short of outrageous; the whole place smells like the inside of a chocolate truffle. Some of the chocolate candies find their way into the ice cream; for example, the butter crunch ice cream contains butter crunch chocolate made in the shop.

That said, the most creative flavors come from **MDI Ice Cream** (7 Firefly La., Bar Harbor, 207/288-0999, and 325 Main St., Bar Harbor, 207/288-5664, www.mdiic.com). It's made in small batches, just five gallons at a time, using the finest ingredients. We're talking ultra creamy, ultra rich, ultra delicious.

Probably the least-expensive lunch or ice cream option in town is the **West End Drug Co.** (105 Main St., Bar Harbor, 207/288-3318), where you can get grilled cheese sandwiches and other old-fashioned white bread basics as well as frappes (a Maineism—frappes are made with ice cream, milk shakes aren't) and sundaes at the fountain.

Equally inexpensive, but with a healthful menu, is the **Blair Dining Hall** at College of the Atlantic (105 Eden St., Bar Harbor, 207/288-5015, www.coa.edu). Known as Take-A-Break, the hall serves breakfast, lunch, and dinner weekdays, and while there are individual choices, the best deal is the all-you-can eat breakfast, lunch, or dinner ($5–10). There are always vegetarian, vegan, and meat choices, and the selection includes organic and local foods whenever possible.

Bar Harbor has a super natural foods store, the **Alternative Community Market** (16 Mount Desert St., Bar Harbor, 207/288-8225, 7 A.M.–10:30 P.M. daily), with a deli, where you can purchase breakfast bagels and wraps, sandwiches and paninis, espresso, or even fruit smoothies. There's limited seating indoors and on the deck.

J. H. Butterfield Co. (152 Main St., Bar Harbor, 207/288-3386) is a fine place to pick up fixings for a fancy picnic.

Between Mother's Day and late October, the **Eden Farmers Market** operates out of the YMCA parking lot off Lower Main Street in Bar Harbor each Sunday, 9 A.M.–noon. You'll find fresh meats and produce, local cheeses and maple syrup, yogurt and ice cream, bread, honey, preserves, and even prepared Asian foods.

Brewpubs and Microbreweries

Bar Harbor's longest-lived brewpub is the **Lompoc Café** (36 Rodick St., Bar Harbor, 207/288-9392, www.lompoccafe.com, 11:30 A.M.–9 P.M. late Apr.–mid-Dec.), serving creative lunches and dinners daily ($8–24). How about a lobster and avocado quesadilla? After 9 P.M., there's just beer and thin-crust pizza until about 1 A.M. The congenial cafe has a beer garden, a bocce court, open mic night Thursdays, and live entertainment (blues, bluegrass, and jazz) Fridays and Saturdays May through October.

Lompoc's signature Bar Harbor Real Ale and five or six others are brewed by the **Atlantic Brewing Company** (15 Knox Rd., Town Hill, in the upper section of the island, 207/288-2337 or 800/475-5417, www.atlanticbrewing.com). Free brewery tours, including tastings, are given daily at 2, 3, and 4 P.M. Memorial Day to Columbus Day. Also based here in summer is **Mainely Meat Bar-B-Q** (207/288-9200, 11:30 A.M.–8 P.M., $8–16), offering pulled pork, chicken, ribs, and similar fare daily for lunch and dinner and an extremely popular all-you-can-eat barbecue on Saturdays for $15.

Bar Harbor Brewing Company & Soda Works (8 Mt. Desert St., Bar Harbor, 207/288-4592, www.barharborbrewing.com), begun in 1990 by Tod and Suzi Foster as a mom-and-pop operation, remains a small, friendly, hands-on enterprise producing five kinds of beer and ale. It began in their basement, but in 2008 the microbrewery moved downtown into a spacious shop, where tours and tastings are held most afternoons; stop by or call for the schedule. Kids can sample Bar Harbor Blueberry Soda or Root Beer.

Tom St. Germain founded **Maine Coast Brewing Company** (102 Eden St., Rte. 3, Bar Harbor, 207/288-5214, www.bhmaine.com) in 1994 and opened Jack Russell's Brewpub, at the same location, in 1995. Burgers are the specialty, and there's a beer garden. Lunch is served noon–4 P.M.; dinner starts at 5 P.M. Free tours and tastings are offered. Tom's the guy who wrote *A Walk in the Park,* an excellent hiking guide to Mount Desert Island.

Casual Dining

An unscientific but reliable local survey gives the best-pizza ribbon to **Rosalie's Pizza & Italian Restaurant** (46 Cottage St., Bar Harbor, 207/288-5666, 11:30 A.M.–11 P.M., closed Sun., hours vary with season), where the Wurlitzer jukebox churns out tunes from the 1950s. Rosalie's earns high marks for consistency with its homemade pizza (in four sizes or by the slice), calzones, and subs—lots of vegetarian options. If you need something a bit heartier, try the Italian dinners—spaghetti, eggplant parmigiana, and others—all less than $10, including a garlic roll. Beer and wine are available. Here's a hint: Avoid the downstairs lines by heading upstairs and ordering at that counter or call in your order.

Combine a pizza with a first-run or an art flick at **Reel Pizza Cinerama** (33 Kennebec Pl., Bar Harbor, 207/288-3811 for films, 207/288-3828 for food, www.reelpizza.net), where you order your pizza, grab an easy chair, and watch for your number to come up on the bingo board. Most films are screened twice nightly. Pizzas ($12–20 or by the slice) have cinematic names—Zorba the Greek, The Godfather, Manchurian Candidate. Then there's Mussel Beach Party—broccoli, tomatoes, goat cheese, and smoked mussels. You get the idea. Reel Pizza opens daily at 4:30 P.M. and has occasional Saturday matinees; closed Monday in winter. Be sure to arrive early; the best chairs go quickly.

Efficient, friendly, cafeteria-style service makes **EPI Sub and Pizza Shop** (8 Cottage St., Bar Harbor, 207/801-2516, 11 A.M.–9 P.M., to 8:30 P.M. July and Aug.) an excellent choice for picnics or a quick break from sightseeing. The dozen-plus sub-sandwich choices at EPI's (short for "epicurean") are bargains (try the Cadillac); also available are salads, pizza, and Italian dinners. If the weather closes in, there

are always the pinball machines in the back room. Credit cards are not accepted.

For a light meal, you can't go wrong at **Morning Glory Bakery** (39 Rodick St., Bar Harbor, 207/288-3041, 7 A.M.–7 P.M. daily). Espresso and other fancy coffees, fresh-squeezed juices, smoothies, fresh-baked goodies ($1–2), soups, quiches, and sandwiches (most are about $8) are all made from scratch. There's some seating inside, but why not take it to go and head for the park?

Far less fancy is **Adelmann's Deli** (224 Main St., Bar Harbor, 207/288-0455, 6 A.M.–3 P.M.). Build-your-own egg sandwiches are $3.99; build-your-own lunch sandwiches are $7.45. Choose from a variety of breads, Boar's Head-brand meats and cheeses, veggies, condiments, and more.

The (Spot) Grill (33 Cottage St., Bar Harbor, 207/288-1233, 7 A.M.–9 P.M. daily, to 2 A.M. Fri. and Sat.) is just the spot to pick up breakfast, lunch, dinner, or late-night nibbles. The order-at-the-counter menu leans toward the Mediterranean, but the options are many. Take it to go or eat here. Box lunches also are available.

Just a few doors down is **Café Milagro** (37 Cottage St., Bar Harbor, 207/288-9552, www.milagrocoffee.com, 6:30 A.M.–10 P.M.), a two-fer, with one side serving crepes and gelato and the other serving organic, shade-grown, fair trade coffees as well as smoothies and accompaniments.

If you happen to be on Route 102 in the Town Hill area around lunchtime, plan to pick up picnic fare at **Mother's Kitchen** (Rte. 102, Town Hill, Bar Harbor, 207/288-4403, www.motherskitchenfoods.com). The plain, minuscule building next to Salsbury's Organic Garden Center (look for the Real Good Food sign) is deceiving—it's been operating since 1995 and turns out 20 different sandwiches, as well as deli salads, scones, breakfast sandwiches, great cookies, and pies. They'll even pack up box lunches. Calling ahead would save time, but the whimsically named sandwich combos are tough to describe over the phone. (How about Charlie Noble—homemade chicken salad with walnuts and tarragon, cranberry sauce, and lettuce on onion-walnut-dill bread.) If you're desperately hungry, there are a few picnic tables outside, but you can find better picnic settings elsewhere. Mother's Kitchen is open 8 A.M.–2 P.M. Monday–Friday, mid-April through October.

Family Friendly

Once a Victorian boarding house and later a 1920s speakeasy, **Galyn's Galley** (17 Main St., Bar Harbor, 207/288-9706, www.galynsbarharbor.com, 11:30 A.M.–10 P.M., Mar.–Nov.) has been a popular eatery since 1986. Lots of plants, modern decor, reliable service, a great downtown location, and several indoor and outdoor dining areas contribute to the loyal clientele. The cuisine is consistently good if not outstandingly creative (dinner entrées $14–31). Reservations are advisable in midsummer.

Just up the street from Galyn's, **Rupununi** (119 Main St., Bar Harbor, 207/288-2886, www.rupununi.com, 11 A.M.–1 A.M. daily) gets its name from a river in Guyana—the inspiration of owner Mike Boland, a College of the Atlantic grad. Billed as "an American bar and grill," Rupununi draws a lively, fun crowd for great burgers (even ostrich burgers), veggie and meat dinner entrees ($18–29), some Caribbean and Mediterranean touches, and about two dozen beers on tap. The daily poacher's special usually means buffalo or venison. On Sunday, jazz is part of the mix; on Friday nights, acoustic guitar.

Set back from the road behind a garden is the very popular **McKays Public House** (231 Main St., Bar Harbor, 207/288-2002, www.mckayspublichouse.com, 11:30 A.M.–3 P.M. and 5–10 P.M.), a comfortable pub with seating indoors, in small dining rooms or at the bar, or outdoors, in the garden. Classic pub fare includes Reuben sandwiches, shepherd's pie with lamb, burgers, and fish and chips ($8–10). At dinner, fancier entrées, such as coq au vin and seafood risotto, are also available, most in the $17–30 range.

Fifties memorabilia and old toys fill **Route 66 Restaurant** (21 Cottage St., Bar Harbor, 207/288-3708, www.bhroute66.com, 11 A.M.–9 P.M., $8–20), a fun restaurant that's a real hit with kids (check out the train running around just below the ceiling). Pardon the pun, but it's decent road food, with a wide-ranging menu that includes sandwiches, burgers, pizza, steak, chicken, seafood, and kids' options.

Good food at a fair price reels them into **Poor Boy's Gourmet** (300 Main St., Bar Harbor, 207/288-4148, www.poorboysgourmet.com, opens daily at 4:30 P.M.). Until 6 P.M. it serves an Early Bird menu with a half dozen entrées as well as another 10 all-you-can-eat pasta choices for $8.95. The price jumps just a bit after that, with most entrees running $11–15. There's even a lobster feast for $18.95.

Eclectic Fare

In 2005, **Café This Way** (14 Mount Desert St., Bar Harbor, 207/288-4483, www.cafethisway.com) received a welcome makeover. The college-funk decor has been updated with a more sophisticated look and a wall of doors now opens to the porch, providing much-needed ventilation, but the casual friendly service and fabulous food remain the same. The breakfast menu is a genuine wake-up call ($5–9). Dinner entrées are in the $14–23 range, but you can just as easily create a mix-and-match meal out of the enticing appetizers. The wine list is very selective and the desserts are outstanding. In summer and fall, Café This Way serves breakfast (7–11 A.M. Mon.–Sat. and 8 A.M.–1 P.M. Sun.) and dinner (5:30–9:30-ish P.M. daily).

For breakfast or lunch, you can't beat **2 Cats** (130 Cottage St., Bar Harbor, 207/288-2808 or 800/355-2828, www.2catsbarharbor.com, 7 A.M.–1 P.M.). "Fun," "funky," and "fresh" best describe both the restaurant and the food. Dine inside or on the patio. Dinner is also served at 2 Cats—call for nights and hours. Three upstairs guestrooms are available for $125–195, with breakfast, of course.

Although off the beaten tourist path, you'll need reservations at **Town Hill Bistro** (Rte. 102 and Crooked Rd., Bar Harbor, 207/288-1011, 5:30–9:30 P.M. Tues.–Sat.). It promises interesting, creative cuisine served with a sense of humor, and it delivers. Possibilities include small and large plates, making it easy to please mixed appetites, and menu items fluctuate with what's fresh and available. The intimate, cabin-like dining area is simply adorned, anchored by a fireplace at one end and a bar at the other.

Ethnic and Vegetarian Fare

For Thai food, **Siam Orchard** (30 Rodick St., Bar Harbor, 207/288-9669, 11 A.M.–11 P.M. daily) gets the locals' nod. House specials run $14–18; curries and noodle dishes, such as pad Thai, run $11–15. Lunch specials are around $8 and a sushi two-for-one happy hour runs 3–5 P.M. There are plenty of choices for vegetarians. Siam Orchard serves beer and wine only and is open all year.

Sharing the same building is **Gringo's** (30 Rodick St., Bar Harbor, 207/288-2326, 11 A.M.–9 P.M. Mon.–Sat.), a Mexican hole-in-the-wall specializing in takeout burritos, wraps, homemade salsas, and smoothies, with almost everything—margaritas and beer, too—less than $7. For a real kick, don't miss the jalapeño brownies.

There's a good chance that (**Eden** (28 West St., Bar Harbor, 207/288-4422, www .barharborvegetarian.com, 5–9:30ish P.M.) could make a vegetarian out of even the most die-hard meat lover. This small restaurant (reservations highly recommended) is dedicated to using organic ingredients from area farms and preparing vegan entrées such as pistachio-crusted soy seitan cutlets, Korean hot pot, firecracker BBQ tempeh, and a bento box with grilled tofu, seasoned edamame, baby bok choy, sesame seaweed salad, umeboshi nori roll, and citrus ponzu. Too green? Try spaghetti alla carbonara, with sunchoke and smoked dulse cream, fresh peas, and sun-dried tomatoes. Entrées run $14–19.

"American fine dining with Latin flair" is the slogan at (**Havana** (318 Main St., Bar Harbor, 207/288-2822, www.havanamaine .com, 5–10 P.M. daily May–late Oct., Wed.–Sat. the rest of the year), where the innovative, Cubanesque menu (entrées $16–35) changes

almost daily to take advantage of what's locally available. Inside, bright orange walls and white tablecloths set a tone that's equally festive and accomplished. It's easy to make a meal of appetizers here. More substantial choices might include black bean and Dijon–crusted rack of lamb, lobster paella with chicken and chorizo, or flash-seared tuna. Save room for the chocolate torte or the mojito cheesecake. Reservations are essential on weekends.

For a taste of Italy, segue into **Guinness & Porcelli's** (191 Main St., 207/288-0030, www .guinnessporcellis.com, 4:30–9 P.M.). Pastas and a few other dishes are available in two serving sizes, a real plus.

Fancy to Fine Dining

Fresh, fresh, fresh seafood—that's what you'll find at **Maggie's Restaurant** (6 Summer St., Bar Harbor, 207/288-9007, www.maggiesbarharbor.com, 5–9:30 P.M. Mon.–Sat. June–Oct.). The restaurant grew out of owner Maggie O'Neil's experiences as a fishmonger, and much of the equally fresh produce comes from Maggie's own farm. Most entrées, such as halibut with orange chive beurre blanc or bronzed salmon with ginger lime butter, run around $20; a notable exception are the lobster crepes, which reflect market rates and may be around $30, but oh, my, are they worth it! Soft music and good service complement the dining experience.

Five miles south of Bar Harbor, in the village of Otter Creek (which itself is in the town of Mount Desert), is the inauspicious-looking (**Burning Tree** (Rte. 3, Otter Creek, 207/288-9331, 5–10 P.M. Wed.–Mon. late June–early Oct., also closed Mon. after Labor Day), which is anything but nondescript inside. Chef-owners Allison Martin and Elmer Beal Jr. have created one of Mount Desert Island's best restaurants. Bright and airy, with about 16 tables crowded in three areas, it serves a casually chic crowd. Reservations are essential in summer. Specialties are imaginative seafood entrées—such as curry pecan flounder and cioppino—and vegetarian dishes made from organic produce. Scallop kebabs have *lots* of scallops, the specialty crab cakes are 90 percent crabmeat, and edible flowers garnish the entrées ($18–25). The homemade breads and desserts are delicious. At the height of summer, service can be a bit rushed and the kitchen runs out of popular entrées. Solution: Plan to eat early; it's worth it.

INFORMATION AND SERVICES

The **Bar Harbor Chamber of Commerce** (1201 Bar Harbor Rd./Rte. 3, Trenton, 207/288-5103 or 888/540-9990, www .barharbormaine.com) is open daily in summer, weekdays off-season. From late May to mid-October, you'll find a branch chamber office at Harbor Place, 1 West Street, next to the town pier. (Some Bar Harbor information is also available at the Thompson Island Information Center, just after you cross the bridge from Trenton toward Mount Desert Island.) Bar Harbor's annual visitor information booklet is usually off the presses in January—a big help in making early plans for a summer vacation.

Once you're on Mount Desert, if you manage to bestir yourself early enough to catch sunrise on the Cadillac summit (you won't be alone—it's a popular activity), stop in at the Chamber of Commerce office and request an official membership card for the **Cadillac Mountain Sunrise Club** (they'll take your word for it).

Libraries

Jesup Memorial Library (34 Mount Desert St., Bar Harbor, 207/288-4245, www.jesup.lib .me.us) is open all year. The library holds its annual book sale on the third Saturday in August.

Public Restrooms

Downtown Bar Harbor has public restrooms in the Harbor Place complex at the Town Pier, in the municipal building (fire/police station) across from the Village Green, and on the School Street side of the athletic field, where there is RV parking. Restrooms are also at the Mount Desert Island Hospital and the International Ferry Terminal.

Parking

Make it easy on yourself, help improve the air quality, and reduce stress levels by leaving your car at your lodging (or if day-tripping, at the Bar Harbor Chamber of Commerce on Rte. 3 in Trenton) and taking the Island Explorer.

RVs are not allowed to park near the town pier; designated RV parking is alongside the athletic field, on Lower Main and Park Streets, about eight blocks from the center of town.

Northeast and Seal Harbors

Ever since the late 19th century, the upper crust from the City of Brotherly Love has been summering in and around Northeast Harbor. Sure, they also show up in other parts of Maine, but it's hard not to notice the preponderance of Pennsylvania license plates surrounding Northeast Harbor's elegant "cottages" from mid-July to mid-August. (In the last decade or so, the Pennsylvania plates have been joined by growing numbers from Washington DC, New York, and Texas.)

Actually, even though Northeast Harbor is a well-known name with special cachet, it isn't even an official township; it's a zip-coded village within the town of Mount Desert, which collects the breathtaking property taxes and doles out the municipal services.

The attractive boutiques and eateries in Northeast Harbor's small downtown area cater to a casually posh clientele, while the well-protected harbor attracts a tony crowd of yachties. For their convenience, a palm-sized annual directory, *The Redbook,* discreetly lists owners' summer residences and winter addresses—but no phone numbers. The directory also includes listings for the village of

COMMUNITIES

Seal Harbor—an even more exclusive village a few miles east of Northeast Harbor, where Princess of Perfection Martha Stewart bought Edsel Ford's palatial estate in 1997, much to the chagrin of long-timers.

Except for two spectacular public gardens and two specialized museums, not much here is geared to budget-sensitive visitors—but there's no charge for admiring the spectacular scenery.

Note that a devastating fire destroyed three Main Street buildings in midsummer 2008 and rebuilding efforts are ongoing.

SIGHTS
❰ Somes Sound

As you head toward Northeast Harbor on Route 198 from the northern end of Mount Desert Island, you'll begin seeing cliff-lined Somes Sound on your right. Experts disagree as to whether Somes is a true fjord, but in any case, it's a lovely chunk of real estate. The glacier-sculpted sound juts five miles into the interior of Mount Desert Island from its mouth, between Northeast and Southwest Harbors. Watch for the right-hand turn for Sargent Drive (no RVs allowed), and follow the lovely, granite-lined route along the east side of the sound.

Halfway along, a marker explains the geology of this spectacular natural inlet, which may be the only fjord on the eastern seaboard. There aren't many pullouts en route, and traffic can be fairly thick in midsummer, but don't miss it. An ideal way to appreciate Somes Sound is from the water—sign up for an excursion out of Northeast or Southwest Harbor.

❰ Asticou and Thuya Gardens

If you have the slightest interest in gardens (even if you don't, for that matter), allow time for Northeast Harbor's two marvelous public gardens. Information about both is available from the local chamber of commerce (18 Harbor Rd., Northeast Harbor, 207/276-5040, 8 A.M.–5 P.M. mid-June–mid-Oct.). If gardens are extra-high on your priority list, inquire locally about visiting the private Rockefeller garden, accessible on a very limited basis.

One of Maine's best spring showcases is the **Asticou Azalea Garden,** a 2.3-acre pocket where about 70 varieties of azaleas, rhododendrons, and laurels—many from the classic Reef Point garden of famed landscape designer Beatrix Farrand—burst into bloom. When Charles K. Savage, beloved former innkeeper of the Asticou Inn, learned the Reef

For the best views of Somes Sound, drive or pedal Sargent Drive.

© HILARY NANGLE

Point garden was being undone in 1956, he went into high gear to find funding and managed to rescue the azaleas and provide them with the gorgeous setting they have today, across the road and around the corner from the inn. Serenity is the key—with a Japanese sand garden, stone lanterns, granite outcrops, pink gravel paths, and a tranquil pond. Try to visit early in the season and early in the morning, to savor the effect. The garden is on Route 198, at the northern edge of Northeast Harbor, immediately north of the junction with Peabody Drive (Rte. 3). Watch for a tiny sign on the left (if you're coming from the north), marking access to the parking area. Asticou is open daily, from sunrise to sunset, between May and November. Blossoming occurs here from May through August, but the prime time for azaleas is roughly mid-May to mid-June. A small box suggests a $1 donation, and another box contains an attractively designed garden guide ($2). Pets are not allowed in the garden. Take Island Explorer Route 5/Jordan Pond or Route 6/Brown Mountain and request a stop.

Behind a carved wooden gate on a forested hillside not far from Asticou lies an enchanted garden also designed by Charles K. Savage, and inspired by Beatrix Farrand. Special features of **Thuya Garden** are perennial borders and sculpted shrubbery. On a misty summer day, when few visitors appear, the colors are brilliant. Adjacent to the garden is **Thuya Lodge** (207/276-5130), former summer cottage of Joseph Curtis, donor of this awesome municipal park. The lodge, with an extensive botanical library and quiet rooms for reading, is open 10 A.M.–4:30 P.M. Monday–Saturday and noon–4:30 P.M. Sunday from late June to Labor Day. The garden is open 7 A.M.–7 P.M. daily. A collection box next to the front gate requests a $5 per adult donation. To reach Thuya, continue on Route 3 beyond Asticou Azalea Garden and watch for the Asticou Terraces parking area (no RVs; two-hour limit) on the right. Cross the road and climb the Asticou Terraces Trail (0.4 mile) to the garden. Or drive 0.2 mile beyond the Route 3 parking area, watching for a minuscule Thuya Garden

© HILARY NANGLE

COMMUNITIES

The Japanese-influenced Asticou Azalea Garden is a must for garden fans.

sign on the left. Go half a mile up the steep, narrow, and curving driveway to the parking area. Take Island Explorer Route 5/Jordan Pond and request a stop.

After you've visited Thuya Garden, open the back gate, where you'll see a sign for the **Eliot Mountain Trail,** a moderately difficult (lots of exposed roots) 1.4-mile round-trip trail. Near the summit, Northeast Harbor spreads out before you. If you're here in August, sample the wild blueberries. Much of the Eliot Mountain Trail is on private land, so stay on the path and be respectful of private property.

Petite Plaisance

On Northeast Harbor's quiet South Shore Road, Petite Plaisance is a special-interest museum commemorating noted Belgian-born author and college professor Marguerite Yourcenar (pen name of Marguerite de Crayencour), the first woman elected to the prestigious Académie Française. From the early 1950s to 1987, Petite Plaisance was her home, and it's hard to believe she's no longer here; her intriguing possessions and presence fill the two-story house—of particular interest to Yourcenar devotees. Free, hour-long tours of the first floor are given in French or English, depending on visitors' preferences. (French-speaking visitors often make pilgrimages here.) The house is open for tours daily June 15–August 31. No children under 12 are allowed. Call 207/276-3940 at least a day ahead, between 9 A.M.–4 P.M., for an appointment and directions, or write: Petite Plaisance Trust, P.O. Box 403, Northeast Harbor 04662. Yourcenar admirers should request directions to Brookside Cemetery in Somesville, seven miles away, where she is buried.

Great Harbor Maritime Museum

Annual exhibits focusing on the maritime heritage of the Mount Desert Island area are held in the small, eclectic Great Harbor Maritime Museum (125 Main St., Northeast Harbor, 207/276-5262, 10 A.M.–5 P.M. Tues.–Sat. late June to Labor Day, plus weekends Sept.–Oct., $3), housed in the old village fire station and municipal building. ("Great Harbor" refers to the Somes Sound area—Northeast, Southwest, and Seal Harbors, as well as the

Cranberry Isles.) Yachting, coastal trade, and fishing receive special emphasis. Look for the canvas rowing canoe, built in Veazie, Maine, between 1917 and 1920; it's the only one of its kind known to exist today. Special programs and exhibitions are held during the summer.

RECREATION

Hardy folks can test the cold Atlantic waters at the small saltwater beach at the head of the harbor in **Seal Harbor** (Island Explorer Route 5/Jordan Pond). Bicycle rentals are available at **Island Bike Rental** (1 Main St., Northeast Harbor, 207/276-5611), sharing space with Shirt Off Your Back, a laundry service tucked down a stairway in an alley at the head of Main Street. Bikes are $15 for a half day or $20 for a full day. Shirt Off Your Back is located next door to the National Bank of Bar Harbor.

Hiking

LONG POND CARRIAGE ROAD TRAIL

- Distance: 3.4 miles round-trip

- Duration: 1.5–2 hours

- Elevation gain: Minimal

- Effort: Easy

Pond's End, at the northern end of Long Pond, is a fine spot to launch a canoe or kayak.

© TOM NANGLE

• Trailhead: South end of Long Pond, west of Seal Harbor. From Bar Harbor, take the Island Explorer Route 5/Jordan Pond bus and get off at Seal Harbor Beach. Then walk west a very short distance to Little Long Pond and enter the carriage roads there. Or drive from Bar Harbor either on the Park Loop Road (the two-way section) or on Route 3, via Otter Creek, and park in a small lot on the north side of Route 3 at the bottom of Little Long Pond.

This loop—part of the 12 miles of carriage roads on private land (but open to the public)—is easy, a "walk-in-the-woods" kind of experience. (If you do this late in the day, use insect repellent.) The pond is officially named Long Pond, but it's known as **Little Long Pond** to distinguish it from the far larger Long Pond on the west side of the island. Head north, on the east shore of the pond, passing signpost 35 and continuing to signpost 28. Bear left toward signpost 24 (and the lovely Cobblestone Bridge), then start heading west and south, meandering to signpost 32. Turn south (left) to signpost 33, where you'll bear left toward 34 and back to Route 3. (You can also do the loop in a clockwise direction, but counterclockwise gets you near the pond right at the start.) If you're using the bus, flag it down or walk back to the Seal Harbor Beach stop.

This section of the carriage roads is not open to bicyclists.

Golf
The 18-hole **Northeast Harbor Golf Club** (15 Golf Club Rd., 207/276-5335, http://nehgc .com) is open to visitors. The first nine, designed by Donald Ross, opened in 1916; the second nine, designed by Herbert Strong, opened in 1925.

EXCURSION BOATS
Northeast Harbor is the starting point for a couple of boat services headed for the **Cranberry Isles.** (Other boats depart from Southwest Harbor; see below.) The vessels leave from the commercial floats at the end of the concrete Municipal Pier on Sea Street. See the *Cranberry*

Isles section for information on the regular ferry/mailboat service between Northeast Harbor and the Cranberries. (The ferries are slightly less expensive, but there's no narration.)

Sea Princess
The 75-foot *Sea Princess* (207/276-5352, www .barharborcruises.com) carries visitors as well as an Acadia National Park naturalist on a 2.5-hour morning trip around the mouth of Somes Sound and out to Little Cranberry Island (Islesford) for a 50-minute stopover. The boat leaves Northeast Harbor at 10 A.M. daily mid-May to mid-October ($25). A narrated afternoon trip departs at 1 P.M. on the same route. A scenic 1.5-hour Somes Sound cruise departs at 3:45 P.M. daily from late June to early September. The same months, two sunset cruises are offered. The three-hour sunset/dinner cruise departs for the Islesford Dock Restaurant on Little Cranberry (Islesford) at 5:15 P.M. Dinner is on your own at the restaurant. A 1.5-hour sunset cruise of Somes Sound departs at 7 P.M. Cost for all tours is $20–25 adult, $15 children 5–12, $5 for children under 5. Reservations are advisable for all trips, although even that provides no guarantee, since the cruises require a rather hefty 15-passenger minimum. Arrive at least half an hour before departure to buy tickets at the booth next to the harbormaster's office, at the head of the municipal pier.

Sailing
Sail aboard an original Friendship sloop. Captain Wilson Fletcher's *Blackjack* (207/288-3056, www.downeasthost.com/blackjack) has been sailing since 1900. Four 90-minute cruises are offered daily, Monday through Saturday, sailing from the Town Dock in Northeast Harbor. Cost is $35 per person, and the 33-foot sloop takes a maximum of six passengers; reservations are required.

ENTERTAINMENT
Since 1964, the **Mount Desert Festival of Chamber Music** (207/276-3988, www .mtdesertfestival.org) has presented concerts.

COMMUNITIES

They are staged in the century-old Neighborhood House on Main Street in Northeast Harbor at 8:15 P.M. on Tuesdays from mid-July to mid-August. Past musicians have included the Borromeo String Quartet and the Miami String Quartet. Tickets ($25 general admission, $10 student section) are available at the Neighborhood House box office on Mondays and Tuesdays during the concert season or by phone reservation.

SHOPPING

Upscale shops, galleries, and boutiques, with clothing, artworks, housewares, antiques, and antiquarian books, line both sides of Main Street in Northeast Harbor, making for intriguing browsing and expensive buying (but be sure to check the sale rooms of the clothing shops for bona fide bargains). The season is short, though, with some shops open only in July and August.

Galleries

You'll enter another world at **Shaw Contemporary Jewelry** (100 Main St., Northeast Harbor, 207/276-5000 or 877/276-5001, www.shawjewelry.com). Besides the spectacular silver and gold beachstone jewelry created by Rhode Island School of Design alumnus Sam Shaw, the work of more than 100 other jewelers is displayed exquisitely. Plus there are sculptures, Asian art, and rotating art exhibits. It all leads back toward a lovely, light-filled garden. Prices are in the stratosphere, but appropriately so. As one well-dressed customer was overhead saying to her companion: "If I had only one jewelry store to go to in my entire life, this would be it." The gallery is open all year, with a varying schedule depending on the season.

A seasonal branch of Bar Harbor's **Island Artisans** (119 Main St., Northeast Harbor, 207/276-4045, www.islandartisans.com) carries an exceptional selection of locally made fine crafts.

For more than a quarter century, **Redfield Artisans Gallery** (125 Main St., Northeast Harbor, 207/276-3609) has been selling high-

end art and crafts to the area's discriminating buyers.

Next door, at **Christopher Smith Galleries** (125B Main St., Northeast Harbor, 207/276-3343, www.smithbronze.com), browse through an array of bronze wildlife sculptures and fountains. Smith was featured in 2005 on the cover of *Wildlife Art Magazine.*

Gifts and Clothing

The tony shops here are worth a visit and maybe even a major splurge. You'll find plenty of pink and lime green; Lilly Pulitzer is big here.

Early and late in the season, the summer crowd shops at **The Kimball Shop & Boutique** (135 Main St., Northeast Harbor, 207/276-3300, www.kimballshop.com) to stock up on wedding and Christmas gifts. It's all very tasteful.

At **Local Color** (147 Main St., Northeast Harbor, 207/276-5544 or 888/582-2250), you'll find—just for a start—stunning silk and chenille sweaters and jackets and exquisite jewelry. Owner Jayn Thomas has impeccable taste. Quality is high, and so are prices.

Antiques and Antiquarian Books

A small but select inventory of pre-owned hardcover books lines the walls at **Wikhegan Old Books** (117 Main St., Northeast Harbor, 207/276-5079 or 244-7060). Specialties include nautical books, Native American lore, women's studies, poetry, and antiques. The shop doubles as **Pine Bough,** offering a small but well-chosen selection of antiques and decorative arts.

ACCOMMODATIONS
Inns

If money's no object and a haute ambience appeals, spring for the **Asticou Inn** (Rte. 3, Northeast Harbor, 207/276-3344 or 800/258-3373, www.asticou.com, $140–340). Built in 1883 and refurbished periodically, the classic harbor-view inn has 31 second-, third-, and fourth-floor rooms and suites in the main building, plus 16 rooms and suites in several

COMMUNITIES

The classic Asticou Inn overlooks yacht-filled Northeast Harbor.

more modern cottages. Rooms vary widely, from tiny to luxe, but all retain old-fashioned charm, if you love it (outdated decor, if you don't). Facilities include clay tennis courts, an outdoor pool, and access to the Northeast Harbor Golf Club. The elegant, mural-lined dining room, open to the public for Sunday brunch (11:30 A.M.–2:30 P.M.) and dinner (6–10 P.M.) by reservation, has fabulous views of the harbor. Jackets and ties are advised for dinner. Lunch is also open to the public, served 11:30 A.M.–5 P.M.; reservations aren't needed, but you may have to wait on a gorgeous July or August day. Try to plan a late May or early June visit; you're practically on top of the Asticou Azalea Garden, and Thuya Garden is a short walk away, and the rates are lowest. The Asticou is a popular wedding venue, so if you're looking for a quiet weekend, check the inn's wedding schedule before you book a room.

Bed-and-Breakfasts

Less pricey and far less formal, **The Maison Suisse Inn** (144 Main St., Northeast Harbor, 207/276-5223 or 800/624-7668, www.maison-suisse.com, $145–395) is a lovely shingle-style inn set off the street behind a rustic garden. Ten rooms and suites are in the main inn, another five in the guest cottage behind it. All have private baths, TV, and phone; some have a fireplace or porch. Breakfast is provided at a restaurant across the street.

The casual elegance of a bygone era still exists at **Grey Rock Inn** (Rte. 3/198, Northeast Harbor, 207/276-9360 in summer, 207/244-4437 in winter, www.greyrockinn.com, $110–375, mid-May–late Oct.), an antiques-filled mansion with to-die-for views over Northeast Harbor to the outer islands. Guest rooms are comfortable and large; many have fireplaces. Common rooms, most with fireplaces, flow from one to another. Trails lace the property's seven acres, which are bordered by Acadia

National Park on two sides. Head out for a hike, perhaps to the summit of Norumbega Mountain, or stroll down the street to downtown Northeast Harbor. Rates include a full breakfast.

In 1888, architect Fred Savage designed the two shingle-style buildings that make up the three-story **Harbourside Inn** (Main St., Northeast Harbor, 207/276-3272, www.harboursideinn.com, $125–295, mid-June–mid-Sept.). The Sweet family has preserved the old-fashioned feel by decorating the 11 spacious rooms and three suites with antiques, yet modern amenities include some kitchenettes and phones. Most rooms have working fireplaces. A continental breakfast is served. Trails to Norumbega Mountain and Upper Hadlock Pond leave from the back of the property. Do note that over the years the waterfront property has been sold, so despite the inn's name, only glimpses of the harbor can be seen.

Three miles from Northeast Harbor, in equally tony Seal Harbor, is a true bargain, the **Lighthouse Inn and Restaurant** (12 Main St./Rte. 3, Seal Harbor, 207/276-3958, www.lighthouseinnandrestaurant.com, $50–75). Sure, the three rooms are a bit dated, but at these prices, who cares! All have private baths, and downstairs is a restaurant (8 A.M.–9 P.M. Mon.–Sat., to 4 P.M. Sun.), where breakfast, lunch, and dinner are available at equally reasonable prices. It's a short walk to Seal Harbor Beach and the Seal Harbor entrance to the Park Loop Road.

Motels
Although it's a bit dated—every room has two double beds—and the decor is uninspired, you can't beat the location of the **Kimball Terrace Inn** (10 Huntington Rd., Northeast Harbor, 207/276-3383 or 800/454-6225, www.kimballterraceinn.com, $67–190, May–late Oct.). The three-story motel faces the harbor, and every room has a patio or private balcony (ask for a harbor-facing room). Do bring binoculars for yacht-spotting. The motel has a pool,

a restaurant serving three meals daily, and a lounge, and it is a short walk to Northeast Harbor's downtown. It is a popular wedding venue, so ask if there are any groups in-house before you book, if that's a concern. The best deals are early and late season, when rates plummet, and there are some wallet-friendly packages.

FOOD
Hours listed below are for peak season, early July through early September. If you're visiting at other times, call, as most restaurants are open fewer days and hours during slower periods.

Local Flavors
In the **Pine Tree Market** (121 Main St., Northeast Harbor, 207/276-3335, 7 A.M.–7 P.M. Mon.–Sat., 8 A.M.–6 P.M. Sun.), you'll find gourmet goodies, a huge wine selection, a resident butcher, fresh fish, a deli, homemade breads, pastries, sandwiches, and salads. The market offers free delivery to homes and boats.

A seasonal branch of **Little Notch Bakery** (Main St., Northeast Harbor) sells their famous breads.

Pop into **Full Belli Deli** (5 Sea St., Northeast Harbor, 207/276-4299, 8 A.M.–4 P.M. Mon.–Sat., to 2 P.M. Sun.) for soups, fat sandwiches, and breakfast fare.

From June well into October, the **Northeast Harbor Farmers Market** is set up each Thursday, 9 A.M.–noon, across from the Kimball Terrace Inn on Huntington Road. Look for the usuals, as well as cheeses, cider, maple syrup, breads, cookies, yarns and related fiber products, and prepared Asian foods.

Casual Dining
Real local color and crab cakes and crab sandwiches are *the best* at the **Docksider** (14 Sea St., Northeast Harbor, 207/276-3965, 11 A.M.–9 P.M., summer only), a low-key, family-friendly, unassuming, hole-in-the-wall inevitably jammed with devoted locals and summer

folk. Just up the hill from the chamber office, the Docksider has an outside deck, plus a couple of veteran (since forever) waitresses, no view, and a reputation far and wide. Prices reflect market rates, with burgers and sandwiches beginning around $7, and more popular options in the $15–28 range. (Early-bird specials and a 10 percent discount are offered 4:30–6 P.M.) If you're smitten, buy one of the T-shirts, featuring an upright lobster announcing, "Frankly, I don't give a clam."

Tucked in a shady corner of a parking lot behind Shaw's Jewelry is a taste of the Mediterranean. **Bassa Cocina de Tapeo** (3 Old Firehouse La., Northeast Harbor, 207/276-0555, www.bassacocina.com), a perfect choice for a hot, sultry night, lets you pick and choose from a tapas menu ($6–12) or splurge on entrées ($15–35), all representing the flavors of the Mediterranean: Spain, France, Italy, and Morocco. A wine bar serves grappas, sherries, and Mediterranean wines. Dine inside or on the patio. It opens for dinner at 5 P.M. daily in season.

Casual, yet sophisticated, **C Redbird Provisions** (11 Sea St., Northeast Harbor, 207/276-3006, 11:30 A.M.–2:30 P.M. and 6–9 P.M., www.redbirdprovisions.com) is the perfect neighborhood restaurant—if your neighbors are the yachting type. Inspired lunches and dinners ($14–26) reflecting seasonally available ingredients are served in a renovated house and on the weatherized patio. At lunch, the flatbread pizza topped with taleggio cheese, black trumpet mushrooms, and parsley and drizzled with truffle oil ($15) is fabulous; split it paired with soup or salad.

An overwhelming menu and big portions at fair prices are the draw at **Tan Turtle Tavern** (151 Main St., Northeast Harbor, 207/276-9898, 11 A.M.–10 P.M. daily). The menu lists more than 200 choices, with the bulk in the $8–15 range. All-you-can-eat specials include barbecue on Monday nights for $12 and Tex-Mex on Thursday nights for $10.

Fine Dining

The elegant, mural-lined dining room at the **Asticou Inn** (Rte. 3, 207/276-3344 or 800/258-3373, 7–9 A.M., 11:30 A.M.–2 P.M., and 6–9 P.M. daily) is open to the public for breakfast, lunch, Sunday brunch, and dinner ($27–35). Lunch is served on the harborside deck, with serene views over Northeast Harbor. Jackets and ties are advised for dinner.

INFORMATION AND SERVICES

The harborfront Chamber Information Bureau (also called the Yachtsmen's Building) of the **Mount Desert Chamber of Commerce** (18 Harbor Rd., Northeast Harbor, 207/276-5040, 8 A.M.–5 P.M. mid-June–mid-Oct.) covers the villages of Somesville, Northeast Harbor, Seal Harbor, Otter Creek, Pretty Marsh, Hall Quarry, and Beech Hill. The staff can provide information on Northeast Harbor's gardens, museums, and trails, in addition to food and lodging. They even rent tennis rackets (reserve court time here, too). Coin-operated hot showers ($1.50, quarters only), designed primarily but not exclusively for the boating crowd, are available here around the clock. You can even rent a hair dryer. The coffee and tea are free. Request a free copy of the annual *Mount Desert Chamber of Commerce Village/Island Guide & Northeast Harbor Port Directory.*

Public Restrooms

Restrooms are at the end of the building housing the Great Harbor Maritime Museum, in the town office on Sea Street, and at the harbor.

GETTING AROUND

Northeast Harbor is serviced by Route 5/Jordan Pond and Route 6/Brown Mountain of the Island Explorer bus system.

Southwest Harbor and Vicinity

Southwest Harbor considers itself the hub of Mount Desert Island's "quiet side." In summer, its tiny downtown district is probably the busiest spot on the whole western side of the island (west of Somes Sound), but that's not saying a great deal. "Southwest" has the feel of a settled community, a year-round flavor that Bar Harbor sometimes lacks. And it competes with the best in the scenery department.

The quirky nature of the island's four town boundaries creates complications in trying to categorize various island segments. Officially, the town of Southwest Harbor includes only the villages of Manset and Seawall, but nearby is the precious (really!) hamlet of Somesville. The Somesville National Historic District, with its distinctive arched white footbridge, is especially appealing, but Route 102 traffic gets congested here, so rather than just rubbernecking, plan to stop and walk around.

Be sure to drive or bike around the smaller

villages, especially Somesville, Bass Harbor, and Bernard, to take advantage of the gorgeous views and slower pace of life.

SIGHTS
◖ Wendell Gilley Museum

In the center of Southwest Harbor, the Gilley Museum (Herrick Rd., corner of Rte. 102, Southwest Harbor, 207/244-7555, www.wendellgilleymuseum.org, 10 A.M.–4 P.M. Tues.–Sun. June–Oct., to 5 P.M. in July and Aug., Fri.–Sun. in May, Nov., and Dec., $5 adults, $2 kids 5–12) was established in 1981 to display the life work of local woodcarver Wendell Gilley (1904–1983), a one-time plumber who had gained a national reputation for his carvings by the time of his death. The modern, energy-efficient museum houses more than 200 of his astonishingly realistic bird specimens carved over more than 50 years. He was pretty much self-taught, but he benefited from tips

The gently curving footbridge is a Somesville icon.

© HILARY NANGLE

COMMUNITIES

SOUTHWEST HARBOR AND TREMONT

© AVALON TRAVEL

0.5 mi
0.5 km

*Main map labels:*

Greening Island

Western Way

Ferry to CRANBERRY ISLES

THE MOORINGS
SHORE DR
Western Way

SEE DETAIL

Southwest Harbor

Norwood Cove
HERRICK RD
MAIN ST
102

Southwest Harbor

XYZ RESTAURANT

Manset
SEAWALL RD
102A

Seawall Point

SEAWALL MOTEL

SEAWALL

Ho Trail

Wonderland Trail

Ship Harbor Nature Trail

Ship Harbor

Big Heath

QUIET SIDE

BASS HARBOR HEAD LIGHT

To Somesville and Hall Quarry

FREEMAN RIDGE RD

WHITE BIRCHES
ISLAND HOUSE

2

Acadia National Park

SEAL COVE RD

WESTERN MTN RD

102

BASS HARBOR COTTAGES

Bass Harbor

ANN'S POINT INN & SPA

ISLAND CRUISES

Tramont

BERNARD RD

THURSTON'S

ISLAND ASTRONOMIC INSTITUTE

Bernard

Bass Harbor

Ferries to Swan's Island and Frenchboro

Mitchell Cove

Lopaus Point

Duck Cove

West Tremont

KELLEYTOWN RD

102

Seal Cove

Goose Cove

To THE SEAL COVE AUTO MUSEUM and Pretty Marsh

CAVE RD

Seal Cove

Dodge Point

Southwest Harbor

Norwood Cove

HIGH RD

(8)GO RD

CLARK POINT RD

HARBOUR COTTAGE INN

CLAREMONT HOTEL

Clark Point

SOUTHWEST HARBOR OCEANARIUM

Southwest Harbor

CAUSEWAY LN

HERRICK RD

LINDENWOOD INN

RED SKY

HARBOR VIEW MOTEL & COTTAGES

SOUTHWEST HARBOR/TREMONT CHAMBER OF COMMERCE

MAIN ST

WENDELL GILLEY MUSEUM

EAT-A-PITA/CHEF MARC

LITTLE NOTCH CAFE

FOREST

WESLEY AVE

OCEAN WAY

INN AT SOUTHWEST

FIDDLER'S GREEN

102

DECK HOUSE CABARET

SEAL COVE RD

and instruction provided by local artists. Before he began carving, he practiced taxidermy, so he had a special understanding of birds' structure and musculature. Summer exhibits also feature other wildlife artists. Many days, a local artist gives woodcarving demonstrations, and members of the local carving club often can be seen whittling away. The gift shop carries an ornithological potpourri—from books to binoculars to carving tools. Kids over eight appreciate this more than younger ones. If you're bit by the carving bug, workshops are available, ranging from 90-minute introductory lessons for adults and children ($25), offered most weekdays during the summer, to multi-day classes on specific birds ($70).

Southwest Harbor Oceanarium

Touching a sea cucumber or a starfish may not be every adult's idea of fun, but kids sure enjoy the hands-on experience at the Oceanarium (Clark Point Rd., Southwest Harbor, 207/244-7330, http://theoceanarium.com), sister site to the Bar Harbor Oceanarium. A knowledgeable naturalist introduces creatures from a watery touch tank during a tour of the oceanarium. Twenty tanks hold a range of sea creatures. In addition, exhibits line the walls of the intriguing, low-tech museum. It's located next to the Coast Guard station. Note: This site did not open in 2008, and exhibits were moved to the Bar Harbor location. That was planned to be temporary, but call before venturing over to find out about the current situation.

Mount Desert Island Historical Society Museum

This tiny museum (Rte. 102, Somesville, 207/276-9323, 1–4 p.m. Tues.–Sat., seasonal) is adjacent to the gently curving white bridge in Somesville, so there's a good chance you're going to stop, if just for a photo. In season, the heirloom garden, filled with flowering plants and herbs of the 19th and early 20th centuries, is worth a photo or two in and of itself. The tiny one-room museum has local artifacts and memorabilia displayed in a themed exhibit that changes annually. You can purchase a walking tour guide to Somesville in the museum. If you're especially interested in history, ask about the museum's programs, which include speakers, demonstrations, and workshops. No admission fee, but donations are welcomed.

Charlotte Rhoades Park and Butterfly Garden

It's easy to miss the Charlotte Rhoades Park and Butterfly Garden (Rte. 102, Southwest Harbor, 207/244-5405), but that would be a mistake. This tiny seaside park was donated to the town in 1973, and the butterfly garden was established in 1998. It's maintained entirely by volunteers. The park is seldom busy, and it's a delightful place for a picnic. A kiosk is stocked with butterfly observation sheets. The park is located on the water side of Route 102 between the Causeway Golf Club and the Seal Cove Road.

RECREATION

Acadia National Park, of course, is the recreational focus throughout Mount Desert Island; on the island's western side, the main nonpark recreational activities are bike-, boat-, and picnic-related.

A broad swath of Acadia National Park cuts right through the center of this side of the island, and many of its hiking trails are far less congested than those elsewhere in the park. A connector trail from Southwest Harbor makes access to park trails easy. Seawall Campground, as well as the Wonderland and Ship Harbor Trails, lie within the town limits of Southwest Harbor.

At the Southwest Harbor/Tremont Chamber of Commerce office, or at any of the area's stores, lodgings, and restaurants, pick up a free copy of the *Trail Map/Hiking Guide,* a very handy foldout map showing more than 20 hikes on the west side of Mount Desert Island. Trail descriptions include length, time required, and skill level (easy to strenuous). In 2001, thanks to a group effort spearheaded by Friends of Acadia, the half-mile-long Western Mountain Connector was opened a few miles north of downtown Southwest Harbor to provide easier access to several Acadia trails on this side of the island.

Biking

A veteran business with a first-rate reputation, **Southwest Cycle** (370 Main St., Southwest Harbor, 207/244-5856 or 800/649-5856, www.southwestcycle.com) rents bikes by the day and week and is open all year (June–Sept. hours are 8:30 A.M.–5:30 P.M. Mon.–Sat. and 9:30 A.M.–4 P.M. Sun.). The staff will fix you up with maps and lots of good advice for three loops (10–30 miles) on the western side of Mount Desert. (See *Islands near Mount Desert* to plan biking day trips to Swans Island or the Cranberry Isles.) Rentals begin around $16 for a half day and $22 for a full day, with multi-day discounts available. The shop also rents every imaginable accessory, from baby seats to jogging strollers.

Sea Kayaking

On the outskirts of Southwest Harbor's downtown is **Maine State Kayak** (254 Maine St., Southwest Harbor, 207/244-9500 or 877/481-9500, www.mainestatekayak.com). Staffed with experienced, environmentally sensitive kayakers (several are Registered Maine Guides), the company offers four-hour trips (8:30 A.M.–12:30 P.M., 10 A.M.–2 P.M., 2 P.M.–6 P.M., and a sunset tour) with a choice of half a dozen routes (depending on tides, visibility, and wind conditions). The trip is $48 per person ($44 in June and September) and it includes shuttle transportation, paddling equipment, and a guide. Most trips also include island or beach breaks. Maximum group size is six tandems; minimum age is 12. Neophytes are welcome.

Calm-Water Paddling

Just west of Somesville (take the Pretty Marsh Rd.), and across the road from Long Pond, the largest lake on Mount Desert Island, **National Park Canoe & Kayak Rental** (145 Pretty Marsh Rd., Rte. 102, Mount Desert, 207/244-5854 or 877/378-6907, www.nationalparkcanoerental.com, mid-May–mid-Oct.) makes canoeing and kayaking a snap. Just rent the boat, carry it across the road to Pond's End, and launch it. Be sure to pack a picnic. Half-day rate (8:30 A.M.–12:30 P.M. or 1–5 P.M.) for a canoe is $25, full-day rate is $40, and weekly rate is $135. A solo kayak is $25 for a half day, $38 for a full day, and $135 per week. A tandem kayak is $27 for a half day, $50 for a full day, and $180 per week. A do-it-yourself sunset canoe or kayak tour (from 5 P.M. to sunset) is $16 per person. Late fee is $10 per half hour. Reservations are advisable, and essential in July and August.

If you've brought your own canoe (or kayak), launch it here at Pond's End and head off. It's four miles to the southern end of the lake. If the wind kicks up, skirt the shore; if it *really* kicks up from the north, don't paddle too far down the lake, as you'll have a devil of a time getting back.

Another option is to launch your canoe on the quieter, cliff-lined southern end of the lake, much of which is in the park. To find the put-in, take the Seal Cove Road (on the east end of downtown Southwest Harbor). Go right on Long Cove Road to the small parking area at the end near the pumping station. You can also put in from the Long Pond Fire Road, off Route 102, in Pretty Marsh.

Almost the entire west side of Long Pond is Acadia National Park property, so plan to picnic and swim along there; tuck into the sheltered area west of Southern Neck, a crooked finger of land that points northward from the western shore. Stay clear of private property on the east side of the lake.

Friendship Sloop Charters

Charter a traditional Friendship sloop with **Downeast Friendship Sloop Charters** (Dysert's Great Harbor Marina, Apple Lane, Southwest Harbor, 207/266-5210, www.downeastfriendshipsloop.com). Private charters start at $125 per hour, including an appetizer; shared trips are $50 per person for two hours, $75 per person for three hours. A sunset sail is a lovely way to end a day. One of the boats used is the oldest known Friendship sloop still sailing.

COMMUNITIES

Deep Sea Fishing

Go fishing with the **Masako Queen Fishing Company** (Beal's Wharf, Clark Point Road, Southwest Harbor, 207/244-5385, www .masakoqueen.com) aboard the 43-foot *Vagabond,* and you might return with a lobster. The boat goes 8–20 miles offshore for mackerel, bluefish, codfish, and more, but on each trip every passenger is assigned a lobster trap. When that trap is hauled, any legal-sized lobster in your trap is yours (an arrangement for cooking is possible). Half day or full day, the cost is the same: $59 adult, $39 ages 5–12. All equipment is included. Dress warmly.

Sailing

Mansell Boat Rental Co. (135 Shore Rd., Manset, next to Hinckley, 207/244-5625, www.mansellboatrentals.com) rents sailboats and power boats by the day or week. A keel day sailor is $195 per day. A 13.6 Boston Whaler is $175 per day. Plenty of other choices are available. Also available are sailing lessons: $195 for a two-plus-hour sail lesson cruise for two, which includes rigging and unrigging the boat; $100 per hour for private lessons, minimum two hours.

Half-day, full-day, and longer power boat rentals are also available from **Manset Yacht Service** (113 Shore Rd., Manset, 207/244-4040, www.mansetyachtservice.com). Rates begin at $185 for a half-day rental of a standard 18-foot Horizon; $265 for a 22-foot T-top Angler.

Golf

Play a quick nine at the **Causeway Club** (Fernald Point Rd., 207/244-3780), which edges the ocean. Be forewarned: It's more challenging than it looks.

EXCURSION BOATS

Southwest Harbor is the starting point for a couple of boat services headed for the Cranberry Isles. See the *Cranberry Isles* section for information on these.

Play a quick nine at the waterfront Causeway Club.

© HILARY NANGLE

ENTERTAINMENT AND EVENTS
Life Is a Cabaret

It's not too far to drive from Southwest Harbor to Bar Harbor for dinner and evening entertainment, but Southwest has a cabaret theater that draws customers in the reverse direction for great entertainment and so-so food: **The Deck House Restaurant and Cabaret Theater** (Great Harbor Marina, 11 Apple La., off Rte. 102, Southwest Harbor, 207/244-5044, www.thedeckhouse.com). Try to arrive for dinner by 6:30 P.M. to enjoy the spectacular harbor view and order your meal (entrées are $17–27). The cathedral-ceilinged dining room holds 140, and the table is yours for the evening for an additional $10 per person cover charge (reservations are essential in midsummer). At about 8:15 P.M., the young waitstaff, chameleonlike, unveil their other talents— singing, dancing, even storytelling and puppetry. After hearing the dozen or so numbers, you won't be surprised to learn that many Deck House staff have moved on to Broadway and beyond. The performers aren't compensated, so be prepared to leave a tip. The Deck House is open mid-June to mid-September.

Repertory Theater

Somesville is home to the **Acadia Repertory Theatre** (Rte. 102, Somesville, 207/244-7260 or 888/362-7480, www.acadiarep.com, $22 adults, $16 seniors, students, and military, $10 kids under 16), which has been providing first-rate professional summer stock on the stage of Somesville's antique Masonic Hall since the 1970s. Classic plays by Wilde, Neil Simon, and even Molière, have been staples, as has the annual Agatha Christie mystery. Performances in the 144-seat hall run from late June to late August, Tuesday–Sunday at 8:15 P.M., with 2 P.M. matinees on the last Sunday of each play. Special children's plays occur Wednesday and Saturday at 10:30 A.M. in July and August. Tickets for children's theater programs are $8 adults, $5 kids. (No credit cards are accepted; pay at the box office before the performance.)

Lecture Series

During July and August, the Claremont Hotel (22 Claremont Rd., Southwest Harbor, 207/244-5036 or 800/244-5036, www.theclaremonthotel.com) sponsors a free weekly lecture series on Thursday evenings at 8 P.M. Past topics have ranged from Arab-Israeli peace possibilities to wildlife on Mount Desert Island.

Events

During July and August, the Wednesday **Pie Sale** at the Somesville Union Meeting House is always a sellout. Go early; the doors open at 10 A.M.

In early August, the annual Claremont Croquet Classic, held on the grounds of the classic hotel, is open to all ages.

In September, Smuggler's Den Campground, on Route 102 in Southwest Harbor, is home to the annual **MDI Garlic Festival,** with entertainment and opportunities to savor the stinking rose, and in October, the campground hosts the annual **Oktoberfest and Food Festival** (207/244-9264 or 800/423-9264, www.acadiachamber.com), a one-day celebration with crafts, food, games, music, and about two dozen Maine microbrewers presenting about 80 different brews.

SHOPPING

The best shopping locale on this side of the island is Southwest Harbor. Mind you, there aren't *lots* of shops, but the small selection is interesting. You'll also find a few (okay, very few) shops in Somesville.

Crafts and Gifts

In the middle of Southwest Harbor's small shopping area is **Sand Castle Ocean and Nature Store** (360 Main St., Southwest Harbor, 207/244-4118), a delightful shop with a huge range of handcrafted items, most with a marine theme. Representing the work of several dozen artisans, the shop has wind chimes, jewelry, ceramics, ship models, and lots of other surprises.

More than 50 coastal Maine artisans sell their crafts at **Flying Mountain Artisans** (28 Main St., Rte. 102, Southwest Harbor, 207/244-0404), a cooperatively owned shop with a good range of creative goods from quilts to blown glass. Also here is a gallery showing the works of more than 20 artists. Consider stopping in after a hike on Flying Mountain.

Art and Jewelry

Fine art of the 19th and early 20th century is the specialty at **Clark Point Gallery** (46 Clark Point Rd., Southwest Harbor, 207/244-0920, www.clarkpointgallery.com). Most works depict Maine and Mount Desert Island.

Jewelry approaches fine art at **Aylen & Son Jewelers** (332 Main St., Rte. 102, Southwest Harbor, 207/244-7369, www.peteraylen.com). For more than 25 years, Peter and Judy Aylen have been crafting and selling jewelry in 18-karat gold and sterling silver and augmenting it with fine gemstones or intriguing beads.

COMMUNITIES

Books, Charts, and Music

You can stop in at the **Hinckley Ship' Store** (130 Shore Rd., Southwest Harbor, 207/244-7100 or 800/446-2553, www .hinckleyshipstore.com) and pick up books, charts, and all sorts of Hinckley-logo gear. The Hinckley Company, a name of stellar repute since the 1930s, is one of the nation's premier boatbuilders. There are no tours of the Hinckley complex, but most yachters can't resist the urge to look in at the yard.

Don Gooding's **Mainely A Cappella** (11 Seal Cove Rd., Southwest Harbor, 800/827-2936, www.a-cappella.com) is the largest source of *a cappella* music in the world, with more than 3,000 *a capella*–related items. Available are CDs, sheet music, videos, songbooks, instructional materials, and more from all over the globe.

ACCOMMODATIONS

As the Asticou Inn is to Northeast Harbor, the Claremont is to Southwest Harbor. On the other end of the lodging scale, there are several commercial campgrounds in this part of the island, plus an Acadia National Park campground.

Inns

When you're ready to splurge, **The Claremont** (22 Claremont Rd., Southwest Harbor, 207/244-5036 or 800/244-5036, www.theclaremonthotel.com) may well be your choice. The most popular time is the first week in August, during the annual Claremont Croquet Classic. An elegant grande dame, dressed in yellow clapboard, the Claremont dominates a six-acre hilltop overlooking Somes Sound and caters to honeymooners, yuppies, and gentrified folk. The views are stupendous. Guests have access to croquet courts, a clay tennis court, bikes, rowboats, and a library. Dating from 1884, the main building has 24 rooms, most of them recently refurbished, yet pleasantly old-fashioned and not fancy. Additional rooms are in the Phillips House and Cole Cottage. Rooms in these buildings are $120–255 including buffet breakfast. Also on the premises are 14 cottages ($155–310); they can go for as high as $3,675 a week in midsummer. A hefty 15 percent service charge is added to all rates. Children are welcome. The hotel and dining room are open early June to mid-October; cottages are open late May to mid-October.

Bed-and-Breakfasts

Many of Southwest Harbor's B&Bs are clustered downtown, along Main Street and the Clark Point Road.

Set on a corner, well back from the Clark Point Road, is **⟨ Harbour Cottage Inn** (9 Dirigo Rd., Southwest Harbor, 207/244-5738 or 888/843-3022, www.harbourcottageinn .com), appealingly revamped in 2002, when Javier Montesinos and Don Jalbert took over the reins. Built in 1870, it was the annex for one of the island's original hotels and housed the increasing numbers of rusticators who patronized this part of the island. It has evolved into a lovely B&B with eight rooms ($187–197) and three suites ($248–294), decorated in a colorful and fun cottage style. Most rooms have whirlpool baths or steam-sauna showers, some have fireplaces, and all have telephones, TV, and Wi-Fi. Rates include a multicourse breakfast and the use of beach bicycles. The inn stocks a nice selection of wine and beer. Also part of Harbour Cottage is **Pier One,** which offers five weekly waterfront suites ($1,414–1,624), including a studio cottage, all with kitchens, TV, and phone. Guests have private use of a 150-foot pier, and they can dock or launch canoes or kayaks or other small boats from right outside their doors; dockage is available for larger boats. It's all within walking distance of downtown.

The linden-blossom fragrance can be intoxicating in summer at the **Lindenwood Inn** (118 Clark Point Rd., Southwest Harbor, 207/244-5335 or 800/307-5335, www .lindenwoodinn.com, $155–325). Jim King, the Australian owner, has imaginatively decorated the inn's nine rooms and poolside bungalow with artifacts from everywhere in a style that's sophisticated, yet comfortable. After you hike Acadia's trails, the heated pool and hot tub are especially welcome, and after that, perhaps the inn's full bar. Some rooms have harbor views. It's open all year.

At the Victorian **Inn at Southwest** (371 Main St., Rte. 102, Southwest Harbor, 207/244-3835, www.innatsouthwest.com, $135–185) guests gather for games, reading, conversation, and afternoon tea in a huge living room with a fireplace and comfortable couches. Built in 1884 as the Freeman Cottage, the elegant building has 13 dormers and a wraparound veranda furnished with wicker. Seven second- and third-floor guest rooms—named for Maine lighthouses and full of character—are fitted out with wicker furniture, ceiling fans, down comforters, and lots more. Some have gas stoves or limited water views. The inn is wired for Wi-Fi and open from May through October. Breakfast is a feast, with such treats as cheesecake crepes and eggs Florentine.

Across the lane, **The Kingsleigh Inn 1904** (373 Main St., Southwest Harbor, 207/244-5302, www.kingsleighinn.com, $150–195) is a very attractive and artsy Queen Anne manse with eight well-thought-out rooms on three floors. If you're sensitive to street noise, request a back-facing (harbor-view) room, although air-conditioners and in-room sound machines muffle the sound in summer. The huge turret suite, with a fireplace, a TV, a telescope, a large bathroom, and lots of comfortable wicker furniture, is $245–305, depending on the season. Breakfast is an elegant, three-course affair, served on the water-view porch, weather permitting. Afternoon refreshments are served, and chocolate truffles or chocolate raspberry rum balls and port wine are replenished daily in guest rooms. Guests have access to a telephone and Wi-Fi throughout the inn.

In 2004, Ann and Charlie Bradford sold the family home that had housed their longtime B&B and reopened a petite version of the **Island House** (36 Freeman Ridge, Southwest Harbor, 207/244-5180, www.islandhousebb.com) in their new custom home, built atop a ridge in a quiet neighborhood about a mile from downtown. They've downsized the guest space to just two comfy rooms available for $115, plus a guest living/dining room all on one level (a great place for anyone with mobility problems, although it's not wheelchair accessible). Anne's warm hospitality and delicious full breakfasts remain the same. Also available is a separate two-bedroom apartment above the garage ($150), with a tiny deck offering glimpses of distant islands. The Island House is open all year.

Even glimpsed through the trees from the road, **The Birches** (46 Fernald Point Rd., Southwest Harbor, 207/244-5182, www.thebirchesbnb.com, $105–150) is appealing. A wooded drive winds down to the large home fronting the ocean, near the mouth of Somes Sound. It's just 350 yards to the Causeway Golf Club and a short walk to the Flying Mountain trailhead. Built as a summer cottage in 1916, The Birches retains that casual summer ease, right down to the stone fireplace in the living room and the croquet court on the lawn. Guest rooms are large and minimally decorated. Hosts Dick and Rocky Homer serve a full breakfast.

In Manset, adjacent to the Hinckley Yacht complex and with jaw-dropping views down Somes Sound, is **The Moorings** (133 Shore Rd., Manset, 207/244-5523 or 800/596-5523, www.mooringsinn.com), owned and operated by the King family since 1960. The oceanfront complex is part motel, part cottage rental, and part old-fashioned B&B, and the rates are terrific. Nine rooms, including two singles, in the Main House are named after locally built sailing vessels. Rates ($90–150) include juice, coffee, and doughnuts. The Lighthouse View Wing ($125) has motel-style rooms with refrigerators, microwaves, waterfront decks, and incredible views (spend the afternoon counting the Hinckley yachts). Also on the property are cottage units, a combination of rooms and efficiencies ($115–175). Bikes, canoes, and kayaks are available for guests, so you can paddle around the harbor; Mansell Boat Rental Co.

COMMUNITIES

(see *Recreation*) is also on the premises. One mile distant is Eagle Watch Cottage ($200), with two bedrooms and harbor views, and King's Mark, with two apartments ($150). Dogs are permitted with permission.

Motels and Cottages

Right smack on the harbor and just a two-minute walk from downtown is the appropriately named **Harbor View Motel & Cottages** (11 Ocean Way, Southwest Harbor, 207/244-5031 or 800/538-6463, www.mainesunshine .com/harbview). The family-owned complex comprises motel rooms ($75–123 per day, $335–785 per week) spread out in a two older one-story buildings and a newish three-story structure that fronts the harbor. A continental breakfast is served to motel guests from July 1 through Labor Day. Also on the premises are seven housekeeping cottages with kitchenettes (weekly rentals only; $485–1,195), ranging from studios to two-bedrooms. The property is open mid-May through mid-October. Pets are welcome in some units for $10 per day or $60 per week.

Right across from the famed seawall and adjacent to the park is the **Seawall Motel** (566 Seawall Rd./Rte. 102A, Southwest Harbor, 207/244-9250 or 800/248-9250, www .seawallmotel.com, $75–110). The no-surprises, two-story motel (upstairs rooms have the best views) has free Wi-Fi, in-room phones, and cable TV. A continental breakfast is included mid-May through October. Kids 12 and younger stay free. The location is excellent for birdwatchers—there's a freshwater pond, a heath bog, a pine forest, and the ocean. The motel is also home to the Acadia Workshop Center (207/244-3020 or 800/248-9250, www.acadia-workshopcenter.com), which offers five-day art classes from May into October. Packages are available that include lodging, meals, airport transportation, the workshop, and a park tour.

L. S. Robinson Co. (337 Main St., Southwest Harbor, 207/244-5563, www.lsrobinson .com) has an extensive list of cottage rentals in the area. The Southwest Harbor/Tremont Chamber of Commerce also keeps a helpful listing of privately owned homes and cottages

available for rent. The chamber's annual summer guide usually contains a couple of pages of ads with photos.

Camping

On the eastern edge of Somesville, just off Route 198, at the head of Somes Sound, the **Mount Desert Campground** (516 Somes Sound Dr., Rte. 198, Somesville, 207/244-3710, www.mountdesertcampground.com) is especially centrally located for visiting Bar Harbor, Acadia, and the whole western side of Mount Desert Island. The campground has 152 wooded tent sites, about 45 on the water, spread out on 58 acres. Reservations are essential in midsummer—one-week minimum for waterfront sites, three days for off-water sites in July and August. (Campers book a year ahead for waterfront sites here.) This deservedly popular and low-key campground gets high marks for maintenance, noise control, and convenient tent platforms. Another plus is The Gathering Place, where campers can relax, play games, and purchase coffee and fresh-baked treats or ice cream. Summer rates are $36–49 a night ($49 for the waterfront sites) for two adults and two children younger than 18. Electrical hookups are available for $2 per night. (No pets July–early Sept. No trailers over 20 feet. Kayak and canoe rentals available. The campground is open mid-June to mid-Sept.)

Just outside of town, on a quiet road cutting through the woods and adjacent to the park is **White Birches Campground** (195 Seal Cove Rd., Southwest Harbor, 207/244-3797 or 888/716-0727, www.mainecamper.com), with sites in a field and in the woods. This is a great location if you're going to concentrate your hiking efforts on the western side of the park. Rates for two adults and two children younger than 16 are $29 for a tent, $35 with water and electric, $60 for a camping cabin, $75 for an RV rental. With the exception of camping cabins and RV rentals, the seventh night is free. Facilities include a heated outdoor pool, a playground, and free hot showers.

Built on the site of an old quarry, on a hillside descending to rocky frontage on Somes

Sound, **Somes Sound View Campground** (86 Hall Quarry Rd., Mount Desert, 207/244-3890 or off-season 207/244-7452, www.ssvc .info, $29–55) is among the smallest campgrounds on the island, with 60 tent and RV (maximum 28 feet) sites. Facilities include hot showers (if you're camping on the lowest levels, it's a good hike up to the bathhouse), a heated pool, a boat launch, kayak and paddleboat rentals, and a fishing dock. You can swim in the sound (from a rocky beach). Leashed pets are allowed (vaccinations must be up to date). No credit cards are accepted. The campground is open from late May to mid-October. It's two miles south and east of Somesville and a mile east of Route 102.

Smuggler's Den Campground (Rte. 102, Southwest Harbor, 207/244-3944, www .smugglersdencampground.com) is a mid-sized campground between Echo Lake and downtown Southwest Harbor. It's also the site of the annual Oktoberfest. Trails access back roads to both Echo Lake (1.25 miles) and Long Pond (1 mile). Big rig sites are grouped in the top third; pop-ups and small campers are in the middle third; tenting sites are in the lower third and in the woods rimming the large recreation field. Summer rates covering four adults vary from $30 (tent) to $49 (full hookups and concrete pad) for the 96 sites, 54 of which are designated for tents. Also available are four camping cabins that rent for $500 per week. Facilities include a heated pool and a kiddie pool, laundry, free hot showers, lobster and ice cream sales, and entertainment. Well-behaved pets are a possibility.

FOOD
Local Flavors
Lots of goodies for picnics can be found at **Sawyer's Market** (344 Main St., Southwest Harbor, 207/244-7061, 5:30 A.M.–7:30 P.M. Mon.–Sat.) or across the street at **Sawyer's Specialties** (353 Main St., Southwest Harbor, 207/244-3317), which specializes in wine and cheese.

The students at College of the Atlantic run **Beech Hill Farm** (Beech Hill Rd., Mount Desert, 207/244-5204, 8 A.M.–5 P.M. Tues.–Sat.), a five-acre, MOFGA-certified organic farm that also has acres of heirloom apple trees and 65 acres of forestland. (MOFGA stands for Maine Organic Farmers and Gardeners Association.) Visit the farmstand for fresh produce as well as other organic or natural foods, such as cheeses and baked goods.

When you don't want to cook, **Pectic Seafood** (153 Hall Quarry Rd., Southwest Harbor, 207/244-7544, 8 A.M.–6 P.M. daily in summer, closed Sun. spring and fall) has you covered. This family operation makes dinner easy, with just-heat foods ranging from crab cakes and smoked salmon to soups and chowders to casseroles (including vegetable lasagna, lobster Newberg, and baked stuffed haddock). Prices are reasonable and quality is high.

Casual Dining
Some of the island's most creative sandwiches and pizza toppings emerge from Arthur and Kate Jacobs's **Little Notch Cafe** (340 Main St., Southwest Harbor, 207/244-3357, 11 A.M.–8 P.M. Mon.–Sat. May–Oct., 11 A.M.–7 P.M. weekdays Nov.–Apr.), next to the library in Southwest Harbor's downtown. How about a broccoli, sausage, and black olive pizza? Or a prosciutto sandwich with asiago cheese and roasted peppers? All this plus Little Notch Bakery's famed breads, a couple of pasta choices, and homemade soups, stews, and chowders make the cafe a winner (but skip the overpriced and flavorless cookies).

By day, **Eat-a-Pita** (326 Main St., Southwest Harbor, 207/244-4344, 8 A.M.–9 P.M.) is a casual, order-at-the-counter restaurant, serving breakfast and lunch. At night, it morphs into **Café 2,** a full-service restaurant. The pleasant dining room is furnished with old oak tables and chairs; there's also patio seating outside and an outdoor bar. Start the day with a Greek or Acapulco omelet. Lunch emphasizes pita sandwiches and salads (delicious—call in advance for take-out); dinner choices ($9–26) include salads, light meals, a half dozen pastas, and entrées such as poached Atlantic salmon and boneless lamb loin. Desserts are homemade.

Good food, good coffee, and good wine mix with a Mediterranean-influenced menu at **Sips** (4 Clark Point Rd., Southwest Harbor, 207/244-4550, 6:30 A.M.–9:30 P.M.). Small- and large-plate and tapas-style choices range $8–25; the risottos are especially good.

Earning high praise for its internationally accented fare, good service, fabulous views over the harbor, and incredible martinis is **Fiddlers' Green** (411 Main St., Southwest Harbor, 207/244-9416, www.fiddlersgreenrestaurant .com, 11 A.M.–2 P.M. and 5:30 P.M.–close daily). House specialties, such as Asian vegetarian hot pot, Creole-spiced chicken, and lobster pot pie, range $16–27, but you can also make a meal of small plates, soups, and salads.

Check your email, sip espresso, or order ice cream, pizzas, or paninis at **Harbor Treats** (19 Clark Point Rd., Southwest Harbor, 207/244- 0313, 8 A.M.–9 P.M.), a casual Internet cafe and coffeehouse. In addition, you can pick up pre- pared Asian foods made by Chiaolin and Ken Korona: sushi, sesame noodles, pad Thai, and other specialties.

Ethnic Fare

Craving a taste of Mexico? **XYZ Restaurant** (80 Seawall Rd., Rte. 102A, Manset, 207/244- 5221, 5:30–9 P.M.) delivers the real thing. No gloppy Mexican fare here; rather, this popu- lar spot (do make reservations) delivers the flavors of interior Mexico: Xalapa, Yucatán, and Zacatecas (hence "XYZ"). Most popu- lar dish? *Cochinitas*—citrus-marinated pork rubbed with achiote paste (it's worthy of its reputation). Entrées are $24; all come with a green salad and tortillas. The margaritas are classic—requiring, allegedly, 1,100 pounds of fresh limes each year. For dessert, try the exqui- site XYZ pie. Dine inside or on the porch.

From the outside, it doesn't look like much, but locals know you can count on **DeMuro's Top of the Hill** (Rte. 102, Southwest Harbor, 207/244-0033, 4:30 P.M.–close) for a really good meal at a very fair price. Dine in the coun- try-style pine dining room or on the weather- ized patio. The Italian-influenced menu (try the excellent veal Italiano) has something in all price ranges ($10–25), but twilight specials, served until 6 P.M. are the best deal; most are $9–11. Ask about the Lobster Paloozah spe- cial, a multicourse chowder-to-blueberry-cake bonanza built around a lobster.

Ultra family-friendly **Presto's Italian Family Restaurant** (386 Main St., Southwest Harbor, 207/244-0555, 4–9 P.M. daily, $8–18) serves red-sauce Italian favorites such as lasa- gna and chicken parmigiana along with other classics, including shrimp scampi and chicken marsala. Light meals, vegetarian fare, and even gluten-free pasta are available. All en- trées include salad and bread. Kids have their own menu as well as toys, books, and games to keep them busy while the food cooks and adults chat.

Fine Dining

Red sky at night, diners delight. Gold walls, artwork, wood floors, and a giant hearth set a chic tone for splurge-worthy **Red Sky** (14 Clark Point Rd., Southwest Harbor, 207/244-0476, www.redskyrestaurant.com, 5:30–9:30 P.M. daily), one of the island's premier restaurants. The creative fare (entrées $19–30) emphasizes fresh seafood, hand-cut meats, and local or- ganic produce, and there's always a vegetarian choice. Bread is baked daily and the desserts are homemade. The restaurant is open from Valentine's Day to New Year's Eve.

The dreamy views from **Claremont Dining Room** (22 Claremont Rd., Southwest Harbor, 207/244-5036 or 800/244-5036, 5:30–9 P.M. daily) descend over the lawns and croquet courts to the boathouse and dock, and beyond, to the water backed by mountains. It's truly a special place for an elegant meal complemented by an old-fashioned grace. Unfortunately chefs seem to change annually, so it's hard to pre- dict the quality; it's best to ask locally (jackets and ties requested for dinner, entrées $19–29). Dining room reservations are wise in midsum- mer. In July and August, informal lunches and cocktails are served in the shorefront Boat House, also open to the public.

Lobster-in-the-Rough

In 2008, the appropriately named **Head of the Harbor** (433 Main St., Southwest Harbor, 207/244-5222, 11 A.M.–9 P.M. daily) became a sibling of renowned Thurston's, in Bernard. Unlike Thurston's, it's full service and the menu includes steak, pastas, and fried foods in addition to the usual seafood—and lobster—fare. The pleasant indoor dining room has big windows to soak in those harbor views.

Putting the "rough" in lobster-in-the-rough is **The Captain's Galley at Beal's Lobster Pier** (182 Clark Point Rd., Southwest Harbor, 207/244-7178 or 207/244-3202, 9 A.M.–8 P.M., closes at 5 P.M. after Labor Day), where you eat on covered picnic tables on the working dock. In addition to lobster, steamers, and fresh fish, you'll find chowders, sandwiches, ice cream, and baked desserts. It's at the end of the road, adjacent to the Coast Guard base. (Early morning hours are not for breakfast—they allow customers to order lobster shipped nationwide.)

INFORMATION AND SERVICES

Information

Near the public parking lots and fire station (behind Sawyer's Market) is the **Southwest Harbor/Tremont Chamber of Commerce** (Village Green Way, Southwest Harbor, 207/244-9264 or 800/423-9264, www.acadiachamber.com).

Check out **Southwest Harbor Public Library** (338 Main St., Southwest Harbor, 207/244-7065, www.swhplibrary.org).

Public Restrooms

In downtown Southwest Harbor, public restrooms are at the southern end of the parking lot behind the Main Street park and near the fire station. Across Main Street, Harbor House also has a restroom, and there are portable toilets at the town docks.

GETTING AROUND

Southwest Harbor, Tremont, and Bass Harbor are serviced by Route 7/Southwest Harbor of the Island Explorer bus system.

COMMUNITIES

Tremont: Bass Harbor, Bernard, and Seal Cove

The "quiet side" of the island becomes even more quiet as you round the southwestern edge into Tremont, which includes the villages of Bernard; Bass Harbor, home of **Bass Harbor Head Light** and ferry services to offshore islands; and Seal Cove. Tremont occupies the southwesternmost corner of Mount Desert Island. It's about as far as you can get from Bar Harbor, but the free Island Explorer bus service, Route 7/Southwest Harbor, comes through here on a regular basis.

SIGHTS
Country Store Museum

Stepping inside the former general store that's now headquarters for the Tremont Historical Society (Shore Rd., Bass Harbor, 207/244-

9753, www.tremontmainehistory.us) is like stepping into the 1800s. Displays highlight the local heritage. If you're lucky, the society's president, seventh-generation islander Muriel Davidson, might be on duty and regale you with stories about her aunt, author Ruth Moore. You can buy copies of Moore's books here—good reads all. The museum, across from the Seafood Ketch, is open July to mid-October, but hours vary by season, so call; donations appreciated.

◖ The Seal Cove Auto Museum

On the westernmost side of the island, but easily accessible from Southwest Harbor, a nondescript blue building camouflages the Seal Cove Auto Museum (Pretty Marsh Rd.,

© TOM NANGLE

Lobster traps crowd Bass Harbor's wharves.

Rte. 102, Seal Cove, 207/244-9242, www
.sealcoveautomuseum.org, 10 A.M.–5 P.M.
daily June 1–early Sept., $5 adults, $2 kids
under 12). It houses the late Richard C.
Paine Jr.'s Brass Era (1905–1917) collection,
one of the largest in the country. All are in
as-found condition; this ranges from fresh-
from-the-barn to meticulously restored. It's
easy for kids of any age to spend an hour here,
reminiscing or fantasizing. Among the highlights are a 1907 Chadwick Touring Car and
a 1910 Chadwick Racer, two of only three
Chadwicks still in existence; a 1915 F.R.P.,
the fifth of only nine built and the only one
still in existence; an original 1903 Ford Model
A, the first car commercially produced by the
Ford Motor Co., and a 1909 Ford Model T
"Tin Lizzie," from the first year of production. The oldest car in the collection is an
1899 DeDion-Bouton, one of the earliest cars
produced in the world. The museum is about
six miles southwest of Somesville. Or, if you're
coming from Southwest Harbor, take Route

102 north to Seal Cove Road (partly unpaved)
west to the other side of Route 102 (it makes a
giant loop) and go north about 1.5 miles. This
is not on the Island Explorer route.

RECREATION
Sea Kayaking
If you have your own boat, consider putting
in at either the park's Pretty Marsh Picnic
Area, off Route 102, in Pretty Marsh, or at
the public boat launch at the end of Bartlett's
Landing Road, off the Indian Point Road near
the Route 102 end. From either put-in, you can
paddle around privately owned Bartlett Island.
For a longer trip, head north along the shoreline past Black and Green Islands, both privately owned, to Alley Island, which is open
for day access.

◖ Island Cruises
High praise goes to Captain Kim Strauss's
Island Cruises (Little Island Marine,
Shore Rd., Bass Harbor, 207/244-5785,

FRENCHBORO, LONG ISLAND

Since Maine has more Long Islands than anyone cares to count, most of them have other labels for easy distinction. Here's a case in point – a Long Island known universally as Frenchboro, the name of the village that wraps around Lunts Harbor. With a year-round population hovering at 50, Frenchboro has had ferry service only since 1960. Since then, the island has acquired phone service, electricity, and satellite TV, but don't expect to notice much of that when you get here. It's a very quiet place where islanders live as islanders always have – making a living from the sea and proud of it. In 1999, when more than half the island (914 acres, including 5.5 miles of shorefront) went up for sale by a private owner, an incredible fund-raising effort collected nearly $3 million, allowing purchase of the land in January 2000 by the Maine Coast Heritage Trust. Some of the funding has been put toward restoration of the village's church and one-room schoolhouse; islanders and visitors will still have full access to all the acreage, and interested developers will have to look elsewhere.

Frenchboro is a delightful day trip. A good way to get a sense of the place is to take the 3.5-hour lunch cruise run by Captain Kim Strauss of **Island Cruises** (Little Island Marine, Shore Rd., Bass Harbor, 207/244-5785, www .bassharborcruises.com), see *Island Cruises* under *Tremont*. For an even longer day trip to Frenchboro, plan to take the passenger ferry *R. L. Gott* during her weekly run for the Maine State Ferry Service. Each Friday from early April to late October, the *Gott* departs Bass Harbor at 8 A.M., arriving in Frenchboro at 9 A.M. The return trip to Bass Harbor is at 6 P.M., allowing nine hours on the island. The Maine State Ferry Service uses the ferry *Captain Henry Lee* (same one used on the Swans Island route) for service to Frenchboro on Wednesday, Thursday, and Sunday, but the service is only over-and-back (50 minutes each way) – no chance to explore the island.

When you go, take a picnic with you, or stop at **Lunt's Dockside Deli** (207/334-2922), open in July and August only. It's a very casual establishment – order at the window, grab a picnic table, and wait for your name to be called. Lobster rolls and fish chowder are the specialties, but there are plenty of other choices, including sandwiches, hot dogs, and even vegetable wraps. Of course, you can get lobster, too. Prices are low, the view is wonderful, and you might even get to watch lobsters being unloaded from a boat.

The **Frenchboro Historical Society Museum,** just up from the dock, has interesting old tools, other local artifacts, and a small gift shop. It's usually open afternoons from Memorial Day to Labor Day. The island has a network of maintained trails through the woods and along the shore, easy and not-so-easy; some can be squishy and some are along bouldery beachfront. The trails are rustic and most are unmarked, so proceed carefully. In the center of the island is a beaver pond. (You'll get a sketchy map on the boat, but you can also get one at the Historical Society.)

Frenchboro is the subject of *Hauling by Hand*, a fascinating, well-researched "biography" published in 1999 by eighth-generation islander Dean Lunt, now a journalist in Portland (see *Suggested Reading*). His website (www.islandportpress.com/frenchboro) has helpful info for visiting the island.

There's a restroom above the Dockside Deli and two others near the museum. If you're captivated by the island, you can rent a harborfront cottage on the property of the Israel B. Lunt House (207/334-2973 or 207/334-2991).

In August, Frenchboro hosts its annual **Lobster Festival** (Lunt & Lunt Lobster Company, 207/334-2922), a mid-day meal comprising of lobster, chicken salad, hot dogs, coleslaw, homemade pies, and more, served rain or shine, with proceeds benefiting a local cause. Islanders and hundreds of visitors gather in the village for the occasion. The Maine State Ferry makes a special run that day.

COMMUNITIES

www.bassharborcruises.com) for its narrated 3.5-hour **lunch cruise to Frenchboro.** The 49-passenger *R. L. Gott,* which Strauss built, departs at 11 A.M. daily during the summer. Kim has been navigating these waters for more than 55 years, and his experience shows not only in his boat handling, but also in his narration. Expect to pick up lots of local heritage and lore about once-thriving and now abandoned granite-quarrying and fishing communities, the sardine industry, and lobstering, and to see seals, cormorants, guillemots, and often eagles, too. The trip allows enough time on Frenchboro for a picnic (or lunch at the summertime deli on the dock) and a short village stroll, then a return through the sprinkling of islands along the 8.3-mile route. Kim also hauls a few traps and explains lobstering. He also earns major points for maneuvering the boat so that passengers on both sides get an up-close view of key sights. It's an excellent, enthralling tour for all ages. Round-trip cost is $27 adults, $17 children 11 and younger. Be sure to make reservations, and if the weather looks iffy, call ahead to confirm. Most of the trip is in sheltered water, but rough seas can put the kibosh on it. Island Cruises also does a two-hour **afternoon nature cruise** among the islands that covers the same topics but spends a bit more time at seal ledges and other spots ($23 adults, $17 kids). On either trip, don't forget to bring binoculars. You'll find the Island Cruises dock by following signs to the Swans Island Ferry and turning right at the sign shortly before the state ferry dock.

SHOPPING

It's fun to poke around **Ravenswood** (McMullen Ave., Bass Harbor, 207/669-4287), a musty shop filled with old books, nautical gifts, model ship kits, and marvelous birds carved on site.

Stop in at **E. L. Higgins** (Bernard Rd., Bernard, 207/244-3983, www.antiquewicker .com). In two one-time classrooms in an 1890s schoolhouse, Edward Higgins has the state's best collection of antique wicker furniture, about 400 pieces at any given time.

Right next door is **Linda Fernandez Handknits** (Bernard Rd., Bernard, 207/244-

Poke around Ravenswood, a fun shop with painted buoys, eclectic antiques, folk art, carvings, and old books.

© TOM NANGLE

7224), with beautiful hand-knit sweaters, mittens, hats, socks, Christmas stockings, and embroidered pillowcases all handcrafted by the talented and extended Hernandez family. The kids' lobster sweaters are especially cute. This is a great place to stock up on mittens for holiday gift giving.

When a psychic told A. Jones more than 30 years ago that she would move to an island, she thought: wrong. Actually, the psychic was right. Continue down Bernard Road then hang a left on Columbia Avenue to find **A. Jones Gallery** (Columbia Ave., Bernard, 207/244-5634). Inside is a double find: artworks in a variety of media and styles and a working studio in the barn; country antiques and folk art finds in the garage.

Potters Lisbeth Faulkner and Edwin Davis can often be seen working in their studio at **Seal Cove Pottery & Gallery** (Kelleytown Rd., Seal Cove, 207/244-3602, www .sealcovepottery.com). In addition to their functional hand-thrown or hand-built pottery, they exhibit Davis's paintings as well as crafts by other island artisans.

ACCOMMODATIONS
Inns and Cottages

When price is no object and you *really* want to be pampered, check into the **Ann's Point Inn & Spa** (79 Anns Point Rd., Bass Harbor, 207/244-9595, www.annspointinn.com, $195–345), an oceanfront inn at the tip of Ann's Point. Each of four rooms has a king-size bed covered in luxurious linens, a gas fireplace, and all the amenities you might expect, including robes and slippers, in-room TV/DVDs, phones, Wi-Fi, CD players, and air-conditioning. Rooms are huge, and all have ocean views. If that's not enough, there's an indoor pool, hot tub, and sauna. Add afternoon hors d'oeuvres and evening sweets. All this is on two acres with 690 feet of shorefront. The inn is open year-round.

On a lower rung of the luxury scale, but also on the water is **Bass Harbor Cottages** (95 Harbor Dr., Rte. 102A, Bass Harbor, 207/244-3460, www.bassharborcottages.com). The sturdy white home has three guest rooms with private baths. Room 2, with an old-fashioned bath, is least expensive. Room 1 has a fireplace, TV, and deck. Room 3 has a fireplace and full kitchen. Rates range $85–150. No breakfast is served. Also on the premises are a number of cottages and suites with a wide range of amenities ($200–300 daily, $1,200–2,000 weekly). The Carriage House has a fireplace, sauna, full kitchen, TV, deck, and balcony; the Pine Cottage has a fireplace, full kitchen, TV, and screened porch. All the Boat House Suites have a full kitchen, TV, and deck; some have a fireplace or balcony. There's a staircase down to a rocky beach.

Camping

A budget-friendly option is the nicely wooded **Quietside Campground and Cabins** (397 Tremont Rd., Rte. 102, Tremont, 207/244-5992, www.quietsidecampground.com, Memorial Day weekend through Labor Day), with 37 wooded sites accommodating tents ($21; platforms provided) and small RVs ($25; up to 28 feet, some with water and 30-amp electric). It also has log camping cabins ($60; with heat, electricity, and a small refrigerator, but no plumbing), rustic cabins ($55; with a propane lantern, gas grill, and screened porch), and a camping cabin ($70; with a microwave, gas fireplace, small refrigerator, and gas grill). There are two bathhouses with free hot showers, one with coin-op laundry. Quiet, well-behaved pets are allowed for $1 per night. The campground is off the beaten track, but the tenting sites are very private and the location ensures quiet.

Just a 10-minute walk from Bass Harbor Light is **Bass Harbor Campground** (342 Harbor Dr., Rte. 102A, Bass Harbor, 207/244-5857 or 800/327-5857, www.bassharbor.com), owned and operated by the Carsey family. The 130-site campground has pull-through sites with electric, water, sewer, and cable TV for RVs as well as plenty of wooded tent sites, some with platforms. Hot showers are free. There's a heated pool, a playground, free Wi-Fi, and a self-service coin-op laundry. Tent sites are $25.

Thurston's Lobster Pound hangs over Bass Harbor.

Sites with utilities range $35–50. Also on site are one- and two-room camping cabins (without bathrooms), with electricity, a small refrigerator, and an outdoor gas grill; bring your own sheets, towels, blankets, dishes, and cooking utensils. These rent for $475–575 per week.

FOOD

If you have a penchant for puns—or can tune them out—head for the family-run **Seafood Ketch Restaurant** (McMullin Ave., Bass Harbor, 207/244-7463, 11 A.M.–9 P.M. late May–mid-Oct.). The corny humor begins with "Please no fishing from dining room windows or the deck" and "What foods these morsels be," and goes up or down from there (depending on your perspective). But there's nothing corny about the seafood roll, an interesting change from the usual lobster or crab roll. There are a few "landlubber delights," but mostly the menu has fresh seafood dishes—including the baked lobster-seafood casserole (a recipe requested by *Gourmet*). Most entrées run $19–24, but sandwiches and lighter fare are available. This is a prime family spot

(with a kids' menu), where the best tables are on the flagstone patio overlooking Bass Harbor. Follow signs for the Swans Island ferry terminal.

Lobster-in-the-Rough

Few restaurants have as idyllic a setting as ◖ **Thurston's Lobster Pound** (Steamboat Wharf Rd., Bernard, 207/244-7600, www .thurstonslobster.com, 11 A.M.–8 P.M. early and late in the season, to 8:30 P.M. in July and Aug.), which overlooks lobster boat–filled Bass Harbor. The screened dining room practically sits in the water. Family-oriented Thurston's also has chowders, sandwiches, and terrific desserts. Beer and wine are available. Be sure to read the directions at the entrance and order before you find a table on one of two levels.

SERVICES

There's a **public restroom** at the Swans Island ferry terminal.

Tremont and Bass Harbor are serviced by Route 7/Southwest Harbor of the **Island Explorer** bus system.

THE LOBSTER EXPERIENCE

No visit to Acadia National Park and the surrounding region can be considered complete without the "real Maine" experience of a "lobsta dinnah" at a lobster wharf/pound/shack. Keep an eye on the weather, pick a sunny day, and head out.

If you're in the area before Memorial Day or after Labor Day, the options are not as great – many such enterprises have a short season, although more and more are staying open at least through September.

There's nowhere to eat lobster within Acadia National Park (unless you're camping and cook it yourself over a campfire), but Mount Desert Island and the surrounding region provide plenty of opportunities. Almost every restaurant, café, bistro, or whatever serves lobster in some form or other. But as you drive, bus, bike, or walk around, watch for the genuine article – the "real" lobster wharf. You want to eat outdoors, at a wooden picnic table, with a knockout view of boats and the sea. (Incidentally, if you're camping, most lobster wharves will boil lobsters for you free or for a small fee. They'll wrap them in newspaper so they stay warm until you get back to your campsite. The best advice is to order them like pizza: Call ahead so they'll be ready when you show up for them.)

At whatever place you choose, the drill is much the same, and the "dinners" are served anytime from 11 A.M. or noon onward (some places close as early as 7 P.M.). First of all, dress very casually so you can manhandle the lobster without messing up decent clothes. If you want beer or wine, call ahead and ask if the place serves it; you may need to bring your own, since many such operations don't have beer/wine licenses, much less liquor licenses. In the evening, carry some insect repellent, in case mosquitoes crash the party. (Some places light citronella candles or dispense Skin-So-Soft to keep the bugs at bay; Mosquito Magnets may soon be doing the job.)

A basic one-pound lobster and go-withs (coleslaw or potato salad, potato chips, and butter for dipping) should run $15-20, based on the seasonal lobster price. Unfortunately, some places use margarine, which doesn't do lobster any favors. Depending on your hunger level – or the length of time since your last lobster – you may want to indulge in a shore dinner (lobster, steamed clams, potato chips, and maybe coleslaw or corn), for which you might have to part with $20 or $25, again depending on the lobster market price. Don't skip dessert; many lobster pounds are known for their homemade pies.

It's not unusual to see lobster-wharf devotees carting picnic baskets with hors d'oeuvres, salads, and baguettes. I've even seen candles and champagne and cloth napkins and bibs. Creativity abounds, but don't stray too far from the main attraction – the crustaceans.

Typically, you'll need to survey a chalkboard or whiteboard menu and step up to a window to order. You'll either give the person your name or get a number. A few places have staff to take your order or deliver your meal (and help you figure out how to eat it), but usually you'll head back to the window when your name or number is called. Don your plastic lobster bib and begin the attack. If you're a neophyte, watch a pro at a nearby table. Some lobster wharves have "how-to" info printed on paper placemats. If you're really concerned (you needn't be), contact the Maine Lobster Promotion Council (382 Harlow St., Bangor 04401, www.mainelobsterpromo.com). The council produces a brochure with detailed instructions. Don't worry about doing it "wrong"; you'll eventually get what you came for, and it'll be an experience to remember.

Here (in alphabetical order) are four great places to experience lobster between the Schoodic Peninsula and Deer Isle. Each is described in more detail in the regional chapters.

- **Bernard (Mount Desert Island):** Thurston's Lobster Pound, 207/244-7600

- **Hancock (between Mount Desert and Schoodic):** Tidal Falls Lobster Pound, 207/422-6457

- **Southwest Harbor (Mount Desert Island):** Beal's Lobster Pier, 207/244-3202

- **Trenton (on the access road to Mount Desert Island):** Trenton Bridge Lobster Pound, 207/667-2977

COMMUNITIES

Islands near Mount Desert

The most popular island day trip destinations from Mount Desert Island are the Cranberry Isles and Swans Island, but Frenchboro has begun seeing a steadier stream of visitors.

Most commercial boats and mailboats for the Cranberries depart from Northeast Harbor, although one line originates in Southwest Harbor (all carry bikes but no cars); state car ferries for Swans Island depart from Bass Harbor, south of Southwest Harbor and part of the town of Tremont.

The Maine State Ferry Service also operates the ferry to Long Island (referred to as Frenchboro, the name of the village on the island) from Bass Harbor, but the schedule requires careful planning for day trips.

◖ CRANBERRY ISLES

The Cranberry Isles, south of Northeast and Seal Harbors, comprise **Great Cranberry, Little Cranberry** (called Islesford), **Sutton,** **Baker,** and **Bear Islands.** Islesford and Baker include property belonging to Acadia National Park. (See *Acadia on Mount Desert Island* for information on a ranger-narrated excursion to Baker Island.)

Bring a bike and explore the narrow, mostly level roads on the two largest islands (Great Cranberry and Islesford), but remember to respect private property. Unless you've asked for (and received) permission, *do not* cut across private land to reach the shore.

The Cranberry name has been attributed to 18th-century loyalist governor Francis Bernard, who received these islands (along with all of Mount Desert) as a king's grant in 1762. Cranberry bogs (now long gone) on the two largest islands evidently caught his attention. Permanent European settlers were here in the 1760s, and there was even steamboat service by the 1820s.

Lobstering and other marine businesses are

Cranberry House, on Great Cranberry, is home to both the island's museum and a café.

© TOM NANGLE

the commercial mainstays, boosted in summer by the various visitor-related pursuits. Artists and writers come for a week, a month, or longer; day-trippers spend time on Great Cranberry and Islesford. According to the 2000 census, the Cranberries have 128 year-rounders (primarily on Great Cranberry and Islesford).

Great Cranberry

Largest of the islands is Great Cranberry, with a year-round population of about 50 souls that swells to around 300 in the summer. You can easily explore this island's highlights in a couple of hours. The Main Road extends the length of the island, about two miles, with a few pleasant viewpoints along the way. It's an easy walk or bicycle ride, with a few gentle hills and very little traffic; do follow the rules of the road, though. If you bring your dog, it must be kept leashed.

As soon as you get off the boat, you'll find the **Cranberry General Store** (207/244-5336), along with the takeout **Seawich Café,** where you can pick up picnic fixings or sandwiches, burgers, and the like, if it's open. Tucked between the store and the shore are public restrooms.

It's about a 15-minute walk to **Cranberry House** (207/244-7800, www.gcihs.org, 10 A.M.–4 P.M., mid-June–mid-Sept.), home to the **Preble-Marr Historical Museum** and **Hitty's Café** (207/244-7845). The volunteer-operated museum is a pleasure to visit, with well-informed staff who radiate enthusiasm. One museum exhibit commemorates *Hitty, Her First 100 Years,* the Newbery Medal–winning novel by Rachel Field, an island summer resident, about a doll. The take-out café serves sandwiches and sweets, and there are tables on the deck. Better yet, get them to go and wander down the mile-long trail cut behind the museum to Whistler Cove. It moseys through an evergreen forest with a green moss floor to a rock beach; do bring bug dope.

About another half-mile up the road is Polly Bunker's **Whale's Rib Gift Shop** (207/244-5153), which carries jewelry by island artisan Lisa Hall as well as a nice selection of other items. Take the left after the gift shop to wander down to the **Cranberry Island Boatyard,** which repairs old boats and also builds new ones.

There are no overnight lodgings other than private rental cottages on the island.

Little Cranberry (Islesford)

The second-largest island is Little Cranberry, locally known as Islesford. (Get a feel for the place by visiting www.islesford.com.) You'll arrive at the newly refurbished Town Dock, one of three adjacent docks (the others are the Fishermen's Wharf and the Islesford Dock).

Just east of the Islesford Dock is the handsome brick **Islesford Historical Museum** (207/288-3338, www.nps.gov/acad, 9 A.M.–noon and 12:30–3:30 P.M. Mon.–Sat. and 10:45 A.M.–noon and 12:30–3:30 P.M. Sun., mid-June–early Sept., free), operated by the National Park Service since 1948. Inside is the collection of William Otis Sawtelle (1874–1939), a summer resident of the island, who purchased the old island market in 1917. Inside he found artifacts belonging to the Hadlock family, which built the shorefront building in 1850. Among his finds were decoys, which he painted blue and placed around the property, including one over the door. That building (which now has public restrooms) became known as the Blue Duck. It's there where he first displayed his expanding collection of local historical materials. In 1926, he began construction of the adjacent current brick-and-slate museum, which is now part of the park. Inside are displayed pieces from Sawtelle's collection as well as other artifacts related to the Cranberry Isles' seafaring heritage.

On the wharf nearest the museum is **The Islesford Dock** (207/244-7494, www.islesford .com/idcbusiid.html, 11 A.M.–3 P.M. Tues.–Sun. and 5–9 P.M. daily, late June–Labor Day), hanging over the water and serving lunch and dinner. Sunday brunch is 10 A.M.–2 P.M. Prices are moderate, food is home-cooked and creative, and views across to Acadia's mountains are incredible. If the weather's good, eat on the

© TOM NANGLE

Big windows and a deck take in the harbor views from the Islesford Dock Restaurant.

small deck. Reservations are wise in midsummer. Water taxis are available for returning to Northeast Harbor after dinner, or, three times each week, the Cranberry Cove Ferry adds evening runs at 7 and 9 P.M.

Also on the dock is **Islesford Pottery** (207/244-9108, www.islesford.com/idcartmb.html), Marian Baker's summertime ceramic studio. A teacher at Maine College of Art in Portland, Marian makes particularly appealing functional pieces, and she carries the work of other potters, too. If you're lucky, she'll have a pot on the wheel. She also sells a handy map of the island ($1, with profits given to charity). Street/road signs are scarce on the island, but the map at least provides orientation.

Also sharing the dock is **Winter's Work** (www.winterswork.com), a tiny, one-room gallery with an eclectic selection of works—and fudge!—by primarily island and Maine artists and authors.

A five-minute walk from the waterfront will bring you to **Islesford Artists** (Mosswood Rd., www.islesfordartists.com), an excellent gallery specializing in local artists' depictions

of local sites (lots of landscapes and seascapes, naturally). Run by Danny and Katy Fernald, the gallery is open daily 10 A.M.–5 P.M. in July and August; weekdays 10 A.M.–4 P.M. or by appointment the rest of the season; and closed in winter. It's several blocks from the harbor, but there's a sign (and Marian Baker's map will get you there). Or just ask—the islanders are always helpful.

On the same road, and also worth a look-see if open, is the **Islesford Historical Society History Room**, part of the library located in Neighborhood House. And check out the garden while here.

Islesford's imaginative postmaster, Joy Sprague, brought the island a bit of postal fame by initiating Maine's busiest stamps-by-mail operation. Many of the other year-round islands' postmasters have now followed suit, aided by the Rockland-based Island Institute, which occasionally publishes an order form in *The Working Waterfront,* its monthly tabloid newspaper. The goal is to save island post offices from extinction; so far, so good.

RALPH STANLEY, NATIONAL TREASURE

Wooden boatbuilding in Maine dates from the construction of the pinnace *Virginia* by English settlers in 1607. Nearly 400 years later, traditional wooden boatbuilding survives, with many boatbuilders concentrated in the Acadia region. Only one has been declared a national treasure.

Boatbuilding for Ralph W. Stanley has been a lifelong pursuit of perfection in wood. "You could say that the fiberglass boat moves on the water, while a wooden boat moves through the water," he says in *Ralph Stanley: Tales of a Maine Boatbuilder*, by Ralph Stanley and Craig Milner (Down East Books, 2004).

Stanley's excellence was recognized in 1999, when the National Endowment for the Arts awarded him a $10,000 National Heritage Fellowship. The award recognizes "lifetime achievement, artistic excellence, and contributions to our nation's traditional arts heritage."

Stanley, who was born in Bar Harbor and grew up and settled in Southwest Harbor, can trace his family roots in the area to the settlement of Little Cranberry Island in 1769. No surprise that seafaring enterprises were his family's calling. As a child, he made wooden toy boats and watched professional boatbuilders at work. After graduating from college, he began his first boat. Over his lifetime, Stanley gained a reputation as a master designer and builder of wooden lobster boats and Friendship sloops, as well as for being a fine fiddler and a good storyteller.

"I've always had strong feelings about my own models, especially the lobster boats. When I design a boat, it's unique. It's mine. There's no other like it. It has to do with the shape, the sheer, the way I put things together, and little things that I do that nobody else does, that nobody else can do," Stanley relates in his book, which is complemented by anecdotes and historical notes.

The Stanley tradition of boatbuilding continues. His daughter Nadine and sons Tim, Edward, and Richard run various aspects of the business. As he notes: "It everybody just stopped building in wood, the art of building a boat would soon be lost." That would be a national tragedy that this national treasure hopes will never happen.

COMMUNITIES

The post office occupies one corner inside **The Islesford Market** (Main St., 207/244-7667), three short blocks up from the Town Dock. Suzie ("Soos") Krasnow holds forth here—giving advice, baking pizza, marketing her attractive silk-screened notecards, and doing whatever else needs to be done. Don't miss the white gingerbread. The recipe was created when the former island hotel ran out of molasses.

On the road behind the market is **Island Girl Seaglass,** a one-room shop in a shack filled with sea-glass jewelry and ornaments and other island souvenir delights.

And if you want to get out and explore the neighboring waters, you have two options. On **Lobster Boat Tours** (207/244-7466 or 207/460-8697, www.islesford.com), Captain Stefanie Alley, a year-round resident, hauls traps, explaining the process and the habitat. The one-hour tours begin at $75, and the boat carries a max of six passengers. Or rent a single or double kayak for $30 per day from Joy Sprague's **Joy of Kayaking** (207/244-4309). Joy only has a few kayaks, so make a reservation if this is something you really want to do.

If you want to stay overnight, Evelyn Boxley operates the **Islesford House B & B** (207/244-9309, $100), with four rooms—two queens, two twins—sharing one bath. Guests have plenty of room to spread out in two living rooms and a back porch. A full breakfast is served. The house is located near the school, but Evelyn will pick you up at the dock so you don't have to schlep luggage.

For **cottage rentals,** see www.islesford.com.

Getting There

Decades-old, family-run **Beal & Bunker** (207/244-3575) provides year-round mailboat/passenger service to the Cranberries from Northeast Harbor. The ferries don't carry cars, but you can take a bike. Or just plan to explore on foot. The summer season, with more frequent trips, runs late June until Labor Day. The first boat departs Northeast Harbor's Municipal Pier at 7:30 A.M. Monday–Saturday; the first Sunday boat is at 10 A.M. The last boat for Northeast Harbor leaves Islesford at 6:30 P.M. and leaves (Great) Cranberry at 6:45 P.M. The boats do a bit of to-ing and fro-ing on the three-island route (including Sutton in summer), so be patient as they make the circuit. It's a people-watching treat. If you just did a round-trip and stayed aboard, the loop would take about 1.5 hours. Round-trip tickets (covering the whole loop, including intra-island if you want to visit both Great Cranberry and Islesford) are $24 adults, $12 kids under 12, and free for kids under three. Bicycles are $7 round-trip. The off-season schedule operates early May through mid-June and early September through mid-October; the winter schedule runs mid-October through April. In winter, the boat company advises phoning ahead on what Mainers quaintly call "weather days."

The **Cranberry Cove Ferry** (Upper Town Dock, Clark Point Rd., Southwest Harbor, 207/244-5882, cell 207/460-1981, www.downeastwindjammer.com), part of Captain Steve Pagels's fleet, operates a summertime service to the Cranberries, mid-May to mid-October, aboard the 47-passenger *Island Queen*. Pagels also owns the *Margaret Todd* in Bar Harbor and the *Bar Harbor Ferry,* connecting Bar Harbor and Winter Harbor. The ferry route begins at the Upper Town Dock (Clark Point Road) in Southwest Harbor, with stops in Manset and Great Cranberry before reaching Islesford an hour later. (Stops at Sutton can be arranged.) In summer (mid-June to mid-September), there are six daily round-trips, with two additional evening trips Tuesdays, Thursdays, and Saturdays. The first departure

from Southwest Harbor is 7 A.M.; the last regular departure from Islesford is 6 P.M. Round-trip fares are $22 adults, $14 children. Bicycles are $6 round-trip. Off-season, call 207/546-2927 to check on the schedule.

Captain John Dwelley (207/244-5724) also operates a water-taxi service to the Cranberries. His six-passenger *Delight* is just that, a comfy launch seating six on wicker chairs. It makes the run from Northeast, Southwest, or Seal Harbor for $55–70 per trip, depending upon time of day, from early June through late September. Reservations are required for trips 6–11 P.M. and 6–8 A.M. Custom cruises are available, including excursions to Baker's Island.

The **MDI Water Taxi,** a converted lobsterboat, makes frequent on-demand trips to the Cranberries. Rates range from $50–75 per trip, varying by time of day. Custom cruises also are available. Call 207/244-7312.

SWANS ISLAND

Six miles off Mount Desert Island lies scenic, roughly 7,000-acre Swans Island (pop. 327), named after Colonel James Swan, who bought it and two dozen other islands as an investment in 1786. (Unfortunately, the island's library, home to its historical society collection, burned to the ground in 2008.) As with the Cranberries, fishing is the year-round way of life here, with lobstering being the primary occupation. In summer, the population practically triples with the arrival of artists, writers, and other seasonal visitors. The island has no campsites, few public restrooms, a tiny motel, and two small, traditional-style B&Bs. Visitors who want to spend more than a day tend to rent cottages by the week.

You'll need either a bicycle or a car to get around on the island, as the ferry comes in on one side and the village center is on the other. Should you choose to bring a car, it's wise to make reservations for the ferry, especially for the return trip. Bicycling is good way to get around, but be forewarned that the roads are narrow, lacking shoulders, and hilly in spots.

If you can be flexible, wait for a clear day,

THE MAINE SEA COAST MISSION

Remote islands and other isolated communities along Maine's rugged coastline may still have a church, but few have a full-time minister; fewer yet have a healthcare provider. Yet these communities aren't entirely shut off from either preaching or medical assistance.

Since 1905, the Maine Sea Coast Mission, a nondenominational, nonprofit organization rooted in a Christian ministry, has offered a lifeline to these communities. The mission, based in Bar Harbor (127 West St., 207/288-5097 or 888/824-7258), serves nearly 2,800 people on eight different islands, including Frenchboro, the Cranberries, Swans, and Isle au Haut, as well as others living in remote coastal locations on the mainland. Its numerous much-needed services include a Christmas program; in-school, after-school, and summer school programs; emergency financial assistance; food assistance; a thrift shop; ministers for island and coastal communities; scholarships; and health services.

Many of these services are delivered via the mission's *Sunbeam V*, a 75-foot diesel boat that has no limitations on when it can travel and few on where it can travel. In winter, it even serves as an icebreaker, clearing harbors and protecting boats from ice damage.

A nurse and a minister usually travel on the *Sunbeam*. The minister may conduct services on the island, or on the boat, which also functions as a gathering place for fellowship, meals, and meetings. The minister also reaches out to those in need, marginalized, or ill, and often helps with island funerals. Onboard telemedicine equipment enables the nurse to provide much-needed healthcare, including screening clinics for diabetes, cholesterol, and prostate and skin cancer; flu and pneumonia vaccines; and tetanus shots.

During your travels in the Acadia region, you might see the *Sunbeam* homeported in Northeast Harbor or on its rounds. If you want to learn more about or support this worthwhile organization, visit www.seacoastmission.org.

---

then pack a picnic and catch the first ferry (7:30 A.M.) from Bass Harbor. At the ferry office in Bass Harbor, request a Swans Island map. Keep an eye on your watch so you don't miss the last ferry (4:30 P.M.) back to Bass Harbor.

The ferry arrives in the northeast corner of the island. Head off down the main road toward Burnt Coat Harbor. (The island has three villages—Atlantic, Minturn, and Swans Island.)

Pedal around to the west side of the harbor and down the peninsula to **Hockamock Head Light** (officially, Burnt Coat Harbor Light). From the ferry landing, Hockamock Head is 4.5 miles. The distinctive square lighthouse, built in 1872 and now automated, sits on a rocky promontory overlooking Burnt Coat Harbor, Harbor Island, lobsterboat traffic, and crashing surf. The keeper's house is unoccupied; the grounds are great for picnics.

If it's hot, ask for directions to one of two prime island swimming spots: **Fine Sand Beach** (saltwater) or **Quarry Pond** (freshwater). Fine Sand Beach is on the west side of Toothacher Cove; you'll have to navigate about a mile of unpaved road to get there, but it's worth the trouble. Be prepared for chilly water, however. Quarry Pond is in Minturn, on the opposite side of Burnt Coat Harbor from the lighthouse. Follow the one-way loop around, and you'll see it on your right as you're rounding the far side of the loop.

Shopping options are few on Swans, but there is one worth noting. If you head left at the end of Ferry Terminal Road, you'll come to **Saturn Press** (463 Atlantic Rd., 207/526-4000), where designer Jane Goodrich and printer James Van Pernis create notecards and papers using antique letterpresses. The shop is usually open Monday through Friday, 9 A.M.–5 P.M., and the informal tours explain the letterpress process (you can usually see them in action) and visit the studios where the designs, based on the company's library of tens of thousands of graphic image ephemera, are created. Afterwards, pick up some notecards in the small shop or at least a catalog. Saturn has few retail outlets, as most of its products are carried by museums and fine paper stores.

A Swans Island summer highlight is the **Sweet Chariot Music Festival,** a three-night midweek extravaganza in early August. Windjammers arrive from Camden and Rockland, enthusiasts show up on their private boats, and the island's Oddfellows Hall is standing-room-only for three evenings of folk singing, storytelling, and impromptu hijinks. In mid-afternoon of the first two days (about 3:30 P.M.), musicians go from boat to boat in Burnt Coat Harbor, entertaining with sea chanteys. Along the route from harbor to concert, enterprising local kids peddle lemonade, homemade brownies, and kitschy craft items. It's all very festive, but definitely a "boat thing," not very convenient for anyone without waterborne transport.

Accommodations

If you want to stay over, don't expect to find a bed on the island during the festival unless you know someone. Other times, there's **The Harbor Watch Motel** (111 Minturn Rd., 207/526-4563 or 800/532-7928, www.swansisland.com). The motel's four rooms (two with kitchen facilities) go for $95–120. Motel rooms are spacious and clean. Two have water views.

Two small B&Bs are also available. **Jeannie's Place** (272 Harbor Rd., 207/526-4116) overlooks Burnt Cove Harbor. Jeannie Joyce has three simple rooms that share one bath (actually the best view is from the bathroom). A full breakfast is included in the $50 rate. She also rents a small, rustic housekeeping cottage that sleeps four for $75 per night; bring your own linens. On the other side of the island, in Atlantic, is **Appletree House B&B & Guesthouse** (49 Scofield La., 207/526-4438, www.appletreehouse.com, $88–110 per day or

$550–770 per week), an 1850s cape on Joyce's Beach, with two guest rooms sharing one bathroom. You can rent either individually or the entire house; both rooms go for $192 per night or $1,100 per week. The pricier Jacob Reed Room has the best view. Rates include breakfast. Note that both B&Bs have very steep and narrow stairs leading to guest rooms and therefore aren't a good choice for young children or the mobility impaired.

Food

Swans has one small, struggling grocery store, **Carrying Place Market** (Minturn Rd., 207/526-4043).

Dining choices are few, but a good stop for day-trippers is the **Island Bake Shop** (73 Ferry Terminal Rd., 207/526-4123, 9 A.M.–2 P.M. Mon.–Sat.). Reasonably priced breakfasts, delicious baked goodies, sandwiches, soups (the seafood chowder earns rave reviews), and salads are all homemade. There are two tiny dining rooms as well as a few tables on the front lawn with harbor views. You'll find it on your left, just after you get off the ferry. Another possibility is **Boathouse Take-Out** (207/526-4201), clinging to a cliffside overlooking the harbor on the way to the lighthouse.

Getting There and Around

Swans Island is a six-mile, 40-minute trip on the state-operated car ferry *Captain Henry Lee.* Between mid-April and late October, the ferry makes five or six round-trips a day, the first from Bass Harbor at 7:30 A.M. (Sunday 9 A.M.) and the last from Swans Island at 4:30 P.M. Other months, the first and last runs are at the same time, but there are only four or five trips. For more information, contact **Maine State Ferry Service** (P.O. Box 114, Bass Harbor, 207/244-3254; 303 Atlantic Rd., Swans Island; 207/526-4273 or daily recorded info at 800/491-4883, www.state.me.us/mdot/opt/ferry/ferry). Round-trip fares are around $16 adults, $7 children 5–11. Bikes are $14 round-trip per adult, $7 per child. Round-trip vehicle fare is $47 May through October. Reservations are accepted only for vehicles (be in line at least 15 minutes before departure, or you'll risk forfeiting your space).

To reach the Bass Harbor ferry terminal on Mount Desert Island, follow the distinctive blue signs, marked Swans Island Ferry, along Routes 102 and 102A.

Southwest Cycle (Main St., Southwest Harbor, 207/244-5856 or 800/649-5856) rents bikes by the day and week and is open all year. It also has ferry schedules and Swans Island maps. (For the early morning ferry, you'll need to pick up bikes the day before; be sure to reserve them if you're doing this in July or August.)

SCHOODIC PENINSULA

Slightly more than 2,366 of Acadia National Park's acres are on the mainland Schoodic Peninsula—the rest are all on islands (including Mount Desert). World-class scenery and the relative lack of congestion, even at the height of summer, make Schoodic a special Acadia destination.

The Schoodic Peninsula is just one of several "fingers" of land that point oceanward as part of eastern Hancock County and western Washington County. Sneak around to the eastern side of Frenchman Bay to see this region from a whole new perspective. One hour from Acadia National Park's visitor center, you'll find Acadia's mountains silhouetted against the sunset, the surf slamming onto Schoodic Point, and the peace of a calmer lifestyle.

As with so much of Acadia's acreage on Mount Desert Island, the Schoodic section became part of the park largely due to the deft diplomacy and perseverance of George B. Dorr. No obstacle ever seemed too daunting to Dorr. In 1928, when the owners objected to donating their land to a national park tagged with the Lafayette name (geopolitics being involved at the time), Dorr even managed to obtain congressional approval for the 1929 name change to Acadia National Park—and Schoodic was part of the deal.

This section of Acadia National Park isn't as overpowering as that on Mount Desert, but it's no less powerful. Even though it's on the mainland, it feels more remote, and the landscape has a raw edge, with too-frequent fog shrouding the stunted and scraggly spruce clinging to its pink granite shores.

© HILARY NANGLE

HIGHLIGHTS

◖ **Schoodic Point:** Remote and raw best describe the tip of the Schoodic Peninsula, where surf crashes against slabs of pink granite (page 134).

◖ **Schoodic Loop:** Drive around the tip of the peninsula if you must, but a better way to see it is on a bicycle (page 134).

◖ **Donnell Pond Public Reserved Land:** A treasure for outdoor enthusiasts, this reserve includes mountains to hike and ponds to paddle and fish, plus sandy beaches and backwoods campsites (page 136).

◖ **Maine Coastal Islands National Wildlife Refuge:** Birds, birds, birds, as well as easy hiking with great views are your rewards for visiting the Petit Manan Division (page 136).

◖ **Schoodic Head Loop:** Although you can drive almost to the summit, it's far more rewarding – and peaceful – to hike it (page 137).

◖ **Hancock and Sullivan Gallery Tour:** Mega-talented artists and artisans are plentiful, and visiting their off-the-beaten-path shops and studios is a perfect way to explore the region, not to mention come home with a great souvenir (page 148).

LOOK FOR ◖ TO FIND RECOMMENDED SIGHTS, ACTIVITIES, DINING, AND LODGING.

While you're this far east, explore a couple other natural treasures: the Petit Manan section of the Maine Coastal Islands National Wildlife Refuge, a spectacular spot for bird-watching; and the Donnell Pond Public Reserved Land, an inland trove of lakes and peaks. Both are beyond any traditional definition of the Acadia region, but they're worth discovering. Better yet, you can loop them together via two scenic byways, one national and one state.

PLANNING YOUR TIME

While most visitors still arrive by car or RV, a new option opened up in the summer of 2003. The propane-powered **Island Explorer** bus service expanded to include a route in this area between late June and Labor Day. It connects with ferry service from Bar Harbor.

Don't limit your explorations to just the park, either. Besides the jaw-dropping scenery, the calling cards for the region are the outdoor recreation opportunities and, believe it or not, shopping. You can easily do your gift shopping for the year at the dozens of artists' and artisans' studios tucked throughout this region.

The biggest attractions in this area are the spectacular vignettes and vistas—of offshore lighthouses, distant mountains, close-in islands, and unchanged villages.

Check out each small and large finger of land: Lamoine, Hancock Point, Sorrento, and Winter Harbor's Grindstone Neck. Circle the Gouldsboro Peninsula, including Prospect Harbor, and detour to Corea. Meander down the Petit Manan peninsula to the **Maine Coastal Islands National Wildlife Refuge.** If you still have enough time, head inland and follow Route 182, a designated Scenic Highway, from Hancock and on to Cherryfield, making it a point to visit the **Donnell Pond Public Reserved**

Land. Accomplish all this and you'll have a fine sense of place.

LOCAL TOWNS
Winter Harbor

Winter Harbor (pop. 988) is known best as the gateway to Schoodic. It shares the area with an old-money, low-profile, Philadelphia-linked summer colony on exclusive Grindstone Neck. Only a few clues hint at the colony's presence, strung along the western side of the harbor. Winter Harbor's summer highlight is the annual Lobster Festival, the second Saturday in August. The gala daylong event includes a parade, live entertainment, games, and more crustaceans than you could ever consume.

Gouldsboro

Gouldsboro (pop. 1,941)—including the not-to-be-missed villages of Birch Harbor, Corea, and Prospect Harbor—earned its own minor fame from Louise Dickinson Rich's 1958 book *The Peninsula,* a tribute to her summers on Corea's Cranberry Point, "a place that has stood still in time." Since 1958, change has crept into Corea, but not so's you'd notice. It's still the same quintessential lobstering community, perfect for photo ops.

Hancock and Sullivan

Between Ellsworth and Gouldsboro is Hancock (pop. 2,147). Venture down the oceanside back roads, and you'll discover an old-timey summer colony at Hancock Point, complete with library, post office, yacht club, and tennis courts. Meander inland, and you'll be rewarded with artisans' studios, especially in Sullivan. Route 1 ties the region together, providing just enough glimpses and vistas of Frenchman Bay.

Sorrento

Tiny Sorrento (pop. 290) isn't really much more than a classic summer colony, and that's all the reason you need for a leisurely drive down the peninsula. It has tennis courts, a yacht club, a nine-hole golf course edging the ocean, and a swimming pool, created in 1913 by damming a cove just above the village. If you fall for the place, try to find a copy of *Sorrento, A Well-Kept Secret,* by Catherine O'Clair Herson, published in 1995 for the town's centennial. It's filled with historical photos and stories.

© HILARY NANGLE

Mosey down to Corea, where most year-rounders make their living on the sea.

Steuben

Continue northeast beyond the Schoodic Peninsula, and you'll arrive in Steuben, on the far side of Gouldsboro Bay. Not that you'll notice; frankly, there's little here to mark its presence on Route 1, and only a small village if you venture off it, although that's changing as the land is carved up by developers (the number of Land For Sale signs is frightening). Only a small sign indicates that the Petit Manan section of the Maine Coastal Islands National Wildlife Refuge awaits those who turn down Pigeon Hill Road.

SCHOODIC PENINSULA

Sights

SCHOODIC SECTION OF ACADIA NATIONAL PARK

The Schoodic section of Acadia National Park has an entirely different feel than the main part of the park on Mount Desert. It's much smaller and less busy and provides fewer recreational opportunities, but it's still magnificent and well worth visiting. There's no official visitor center in this area, so you'll want to stop at the main Acadia Visitor Center on Mount Desert Island, or download Schoodic information before you come.

There's no camping in this section of the park, but private camping and other lodging options are available in the area. There are also no restaurants or other food sources in

LIGHTHOUSES

The best known of the Acadia region's coastal beacons is **Bass Harbor Head Light,** part of Acadia National Park. Perched high on a promontory overlooking the entrance to Bass Harbor, it flashes a distinctive red beacon (automated since 1974). To visit the light, take Route 102 to the bottom (southern end) of Mount Desert Island, then take Route 102A and watch for signs. The setting is spectacular and the grounds are accessible during the daytime. (The house is government property, occupied by the Southwest Harbor Coast Guard commander.) Be sure to descend the stairs toward the shore and view the 26-foot tower upward from there.

Roughly from north to south (strictly speaking, though, it's east to west), here are the other still-operating lighthouses in the Acadia region. All are automated; most are accessible only by boat. None of the light towers are accessible to the public. Four lights in this area – Winter Harbor, Blue Hill, Dyce's Head, and Pumpkin Island – are no longer used as navigational beacons, although their towers still stand.

On a clear day, you can spot **Petit Manan Light** from the tip of Petit Manan Point, on the mainland Petit Manan section of the Maine Coastal Islands National Wildlife Refuge. Built in 1817 and rebuilt in 1855, it rises 119 feet from its base. It's located 3.5 miles offshore, directly south of Milbridge. Some excursion boats cruise by the island, which also is home to puffins.

Prospect Harbor Light, established in 1850, rebuilt in 1891, and automated in 1951, sits on the tip of Prospect Point. It can be viewed across the harbor from Route 186, or you can drive to the gate for a closer look.

Clearly visible (on a clear day, that is) from Acadia's Park Loop Road, **Egg Rock Light** was built in 1875 on bleak, barren Egg Rock, protecting the entrance to Frenchman Bay. The squat square keeper's house, topped by a square light tower, resembles no other Maine lighthouse. The light, now under the aegis of the Petit Manan National Wildlife Refuge, was automated in 1976.

The Cranberry Isles mailboat out of Northeast Harbor passes dramatically sited **Bear Island Light** on its daily rounds. Located on Acadia National Park land at the entrance to Northeast Harbor, the light tower and its keeper's house are privately leased in exchange for upkeep. (There's no public access to the island.) The automated light has been a privately maintained navigational aid since 1989. The present tower was built in 1889.

Baker Island Light, built in 1828 (during John Quincy Adams's presidency) and rebuilt in 1855, is accessible only by boat, and then via a boardwalk. The brick tower rises 43 feet. Most of the 123-acre island, one of the five Cranberry Isles, is part of Acadia National Park. Charles W. Eliot, president of Harvard (1869-1909) and one of the prime movers behind the establishment of the park, shone a small spotlight on Baker Island when he pub-the park, but you won't need to go far for a bite to eat.

To reach the park boundary from Route 1 in Gouldsboro, take Route 186 south to Winter Harbor. Continue through town, heading east, then turn right and continue to the park entrance sign, just before the bridge over Mosquito Harbor.

You can also tour the park using the free **Island Explorer** bus, which circulates through Winter Harbor, around the Schoodic Loop, and on to Prospect Harbor, with stops along the way. It's an efficient and environmentally friendly way to go.

Perhaps one of the best ways to get to know the park is to become involved with the **Friends of Schoodic** (www.friendsofschoodic .org), which supports the park with clean-up projects, trail and building maintenance, and by staffing the visitor information booth at the Schoodic Education and Research Center Gatehouse.

---

lished a sympathetic short memoir of a 19th-century Baker Island farmer and fisherman. Entitled *John Gilley, One of the Forgotten Millions*, and reprinted in 1989 by Bar Harbor's Acadia Press, it's a must-read – a poignant story of a hardscrabble pioneering life.

Eleven miles out to sea from Bar Harbor, **Great Duck Island Light** stands on a 12-acre parcel owned by the College of the Atlantic (Bar Harbor). It serves as a year-round site (the solar-powered Alice Eno Biological Station) for the college's ecology researchers. The rest of the island is owned by the Nature Conservancy, which has estimated that Great Duck sustains about 20 percent of the state's nesting seabirds. In 2002, some 1,000 pairs of herring gulls nested here; others include Leach's storm petrels, black-backed gulls, and black guillemots. The 42-foot granite-and-brick light tower, built in 1890, was automated in 1986. The light is visible only from private boats, and there's no island access.

The College of the Atlantic also conducts research on the minuscule, barren, remote island surrounding **Mount Desert Rock Light,** built in 1847. The college's Allied Whale program, based in the keeper's house (the Edward Mc Blair Marine Research Station), monitors the movements of finback and humpback whales. The tower rises 68 feet; the automated light is solar-powered. Mount Desert Rock is also an automated NOAA weather station, cited daily in marine weather reports. There's no public access to

the island, but whale-watching boats out of Bar Harbor frequently head this way.

Built in 1872, **Burnt Coat Harbor Light** (or Hockamock Head Light), with a distinctive square white tower, protects the entrance to Burnt Coat Harbor on Swans Island, accessible via the Maine State Ferry Service from Bass Harbor on Mount Desert Island. The town-owned light is about five miles from the ferry landing, so a bike comes in handy. Bring a picnic and enjoy it on the lighthouse grounds, with a fabulous view.

Isle au Haut Light, built in 1907 and also known as Robinson Point Light, overlooks the Isle au Haut Thorofare. Access to the island is only by ferry or private boat. The tower itself (not open to the public) is owned by the town of Isle au Haut; the keeper's house is privately owned.

Looking rather lonely without a keeper's house, **Mark Island Light,** also known as Deer Island Thorofare Light, was built in 1857 (the lightkeeper's house burned in 1959). All that remain are the 25-foot square tower and a tiny attached shed. Deer Isle's Island Heritage Trust owns the island, which is accessible only by boat – but *not* during seabird nesting season (typically, April through August).

Another light station without a keeper's house (it was intentionally burned in 1963) is **Eagle Island Light,** in East Penobscot Bay, west of the Deer Isle village of Sunset. Built in 1858, it has a 30-foot granite tower. Plans are in the works to deactivate the light. Access is only by boat.

◖ Schoodic Point

The highlight of this part of the park is Schoodic Point, with vistas that seemingly go all the way to Spain. The point is at the end of a two-way spur off the Schoodic Loop Road. Although crowds gather at the height of summer, especially when the surf is raging, the tiered parking lot, amazingly, seldom fills up. (There are restrooms here, too.) Check local newspapers for the time of high tide and try to arrive here then; the word "awesome" is overused, but it sure describes Schoodic Point's surf performance on the rugged pink granite. The setting sun makes it even more brilliant. This area is open only from 6 A.M. to 10 P.M.

If you've brought children, keep them well back from the water; a rogue wave can sweep them off the rocks all too easily. It *has* happened. Picnics are great here (make sure you bring a litter bag), and so are the tide pools at mid-tide to low tide. Birding is spectacular during spring and fall migrations.

And on the subject of birds, you'll see a sign here: Do Not Feed Gulls or Other Wildlife. Heed it. Even if you *don't* feed the gulls, they can threaten your lunch if you're having a picnic here. They'll swoop down shamelessly and snatch it away before you even realize they've spotted you. From extensive practice with unsuspecting visitors, they're adept at thievery.

◖ Schoodic Loop

The major sights of Acadia's Schoodic section lie along the six-mile one-way road that meanders counterclockwise around the tip of the Schoodic Peninsula. You'll discover official and unofficial picnic areas, the hiking trailheads, offshore lighthouses, and turnouts with scenic vistas. Also named the Park Loop Road, it's best referred to as the Schoodic Loop, to distinguish it from the one on Mount Desert.

The first landmark is **Frazer Point Picnic Area,** with lovely vistas, picnic tables, and handicapped-accessible restrooms. Other spots are fine for picnics, but this is the only official one. If you've brought bikes, leave your car here and do a counterclockwise 12.2-mile loop through the park and back to your car via Birch Harbor and Route 186. It's a fine day trip.

From the picnic area, the road becomes one-way. Unlike on the Park Loop Road on Mount Desert, no parking is allowed in the right lane. There are periodic pullouts, but not many cars

Schoodic Point is renowned for the surf crashing on its pink granite shores.

© HILARY NANGLE

The Schoodic Education and Research Center hopes to eventually reopen and repurpose the National Historic Register mansion on its campus.

can squeeze in. Despite the fact that this is far from the busiest section of Acadia, it can still be frustrating to be unable to find a space in the summer months. The best advice, therefore, is to stay in the area and do this loop early in the morning or later in the afternoon, perhaps in May or June. (The late September and early October foliage is gorgeous, but traffic *does* increase then.) While you're driving, if you see a viewpoint you like (with room to pull off), stop; it's a long way around to return.

From this side of Frenchman Bay, the vistas of Mount Desert's summits are gorgeous, behind islands sprinkled here and there.

Drive 1.6 miles from the picnic area to Raven's Head, a Thunder Hole–type cliff with sheer drops to the churning surf below (no fences, so not a good place for little ones) and fabulous views. The trail is unmarked, but there's a small pullout on the left side of the road opposite it. Be extremely careful here, stay on the path (the environment is very fragile and erosion is a major problem), and stay well away from the cliff's edge.

At 2.2 miles past the picnic area, watch for a narrow, unpaved road on the left, across

from an open beach vista. It winds for a mile (keep left at the fork) up to a tiny parking circle, from which you can follow the trail (signposted "Schoodic trails") to the open ledges on 440-foot Schoodic Head. From the circle, there's already a glimpse of the view, but it gets much better. If you bear right at the fork, you'll come to a grassy parking area with access to the Alder Trail and the Schoodic Head Trail.

Continue on the Schoodic Loop Road, and hang a right onto a short, two-way spur to **Schoodic Point.** Just before it is a small info center, staffed by volunteers and park rangers. It's located on the site of a former top-secret U.S. Navy base that became part of the park in 2002. The campus is now the Schoodic Education and Research Center (locally called by its acronym, SERC); occasional lectures and programs are held here.

From Schoodic Point, return to the Loop Road. Look to your right, and you'll see Little Moose Island, which can be accessed at low tide. Be careful though, and don't get stranded here. Continue to the **Blueberry Hill** parking area (about one mile from the Schoodic Point/Loop Road intersection), a moorlike setting where the low growth allows almost 180-degree views of the bay and islands. There are a few trails in this area—all eventually converging on **Schoodic Head**, the highest point on the peninsula. (Don't confuse this with Schoodic Mountain, which is well north of here.) Across the road and up the road a bit is the trailhead for the 180-foot-high **Anvil** headland.

As you continue along this stretch of road, keep your eyes peeled for eagles, which frequently soar here. There's a nest on the northern end of Rolling Island; you can see it with binoculars from some of the roadside pullouts.

From Blueberry Hill, continue 1.2 miles to a pullout for the East Trail, the shortest and most direct route to Schoodic Head. From here, it's about another mile to the park exit, in Wonsqueak Harbor. It's another two miles to the intersection with Route 186 in Birch Harbor. (If you didn't bring a picnic lunch or dinner, Bunker's Wharf Restaurant is an excellent, if a bit pricey, stop, with views of a working wharf.)

DONNELL POND PUBLIC RESERVED LAND

More than 15,000 acres have been preserved for public access in Donnell Pond Public Reserved Land (Maine Bureau of Parks and Lands, 207/827-1818, www.state.me.us/doc/parks), a huge mountain-and-lake area north and east of Sullivan. Developers had their eyes on this gorgeous real estate in the 1980s, but preservationists fortunately rallied to the cause. Outright purchase of 7,316 of the acres, in the Spring River Lake area, came through the farsighted Land for Maine's Future program. Hikers can climb Schoodic, Black, and Caribou Mountains; paddlers and anglers have Donnell Pond, Tunk Lake, Spring River Lake, Long Pond, Round Pond, and Little Pond, among others. Route 182, an official Scenic Highway, cuts right through the Donnell Pond preserve. The preserve encompasses lakes for boating and fishing, mountains for hiking, and primitive campsites. Hunting is permitted, so take special care during hunting season.

MAINE COASTAL ISLANDS NATIONAL WILDLIFE REFUGE

Restoring and managing colonies of nesting seabirds is the focus of the Maine Coastal Islands National Wildlife Refuge, which spans 150 coastal miles and comprises 49 offshore islands and three mainland parcels totaling more than 8,100 acres. Occupying a 2,166-acre peninsula in Steuben with 10 miles of rocky shoreline (and three offshore islands) is the refuge's outstandingly scenic Petit Manan Point Division (Pigeon Hill Rd., Steuben, 207/546-2124, www.fws.gov/northeast/mainecoastal). The remote location means it sees only about 15,000 visitors a year, most of those likely birders, as more than 250 different birds have been sighted here. Among the other natural highlights here are stands of jack pine, coastal raised peatlands, blueberry barrens, freshwater and saltwater marshes, granite shores, and cobble beaches. When asking directions locally, you'll hear it called "'tit Manan."

The moderately easy, four-mile round-trip Birch Point Trail and easy, 1.5-mile round-trip Hollingsworth or Shore Trail provide splendid views and opportunities to spot wildlife along the shore and in the fields, forests, and marshland. The Hollingsworth Trail, leading you to the shoreline, is the best. This is foggy territory, but on clear days, you can see the 123-foot lighthouse on Petit Manan Island, 2.5 miles offshore (for a closer look at the puffin colony there, book a trip on an excursion boat from Milbridge). The Birch Point Trail heads through blueberry fields to Dyer Bay and loops by the waterfront, with much of the trail passing through woods.

From Route 1, on the east side of Steuben, take Pigeon Hill Road. Six miles down is the first parking lot, for the Birch Point Trail; another half mile takes you to the parking area for the Hollingsworth Trail; space is limited. If you arrive in August, help yourself to blueberries. The refuge is open daily all year, sunrise to sunset; cross-country skiing is permitted in winter.

Recreation

HIKING

A pleasant and short shore path begins and ends at the **Dixon Memorial Rock** and follows the water's edge, rising through the woods and passing by cottages on eastern Grindstone Neck in Winter Harbor. The views are fabulous. To find it, take Beach Street to Club House Lane, proceed across the four-way intersection, then go right on Steamboat Lane, following it to the oval at the end.

◖ Schoodic Head Loop

- Distance: 2.7 miles round-trip

- Duration: varies with route, 1.5–2 hours

- Elevation gain: 440 feet

- Effort: Moderate, some steep sections

- Trailhead: Blueberry Hill parking area, Schoodic Loop

The Schoodic Head Loop comprises three connecting trails, and it can be hiked in either direction. If time is tight, choose just one trail to hike. The clockwise route begins with the easiest terrain and ends with a downhill scramble over a steep and rocky hillside. As one ranger noted, it's tough on the knees and you have to be very careful with your footing in this direction. If you hike it counterclockwise, beginning with the Anvil Trail, you'll get the toughest terrain out of the way first.

You can access the loop at various points, but the most parking is at the Blueberry Hill parking area. The easy one-mile Alder Trail departs from just south of the parking lot entrance and connects through the woods and some marshy areas to the unmarked Ranger Cabin Road; head left for about 50 yards, and watch for the Schoodic Head trail marker.

The moderate Schoodic Head trail climbs for 0.7 mile, beginning in woods and emerging onto ledgy terrain as it nears the summit. The views are expansive and well worth any effort.

The one-mile Anvil Trail descends over moderate terrain with a few steep sections. A highlight here is the Anvil promontory, a rocky knoll. Whichever way you choose to hike, be extremely careful on the Anvil Trail, as the terrain is rugged, with lots of roots and loose rocks.

A fourth trail, the 0.6-mile East Trail, descends from the summit and emerges on the Schoodic Loop Road about one mile beyond the Blueberry Hill parking area. This is the shortest and most direct route to the summit and can be hiked independently or looped in with the other trails.

You can also access this loop from the unmarked Ranger Cabin Road, bearing right at the fork.

Schoodic Mountain

- Distance: 2.4 miles round-trip

- Duration: 2 hours

- Elevation gain: 800 feet

- Effort: Moderately difficult

- Trailhead: Off Rte. 183, Franklin

The hiking isn't easy here, but it isn't technical and the options are many. The interconnecting trail system takes in Schoodic Mountain, Black Mountain, and Caribou Mountain on Donnell Pond Public Reserved Land.

Follow the Schoodic Mountain Loop clockwise, heading westward first. To make a day of it, pack a picnic and take a swimsuit (and don't forget a camera and binoculars for the summit views). On a brilliantly clear day, you'll see Baxter State Park's Katahdin, the peaks of Acadia National Park, and the ocean beyond. And in late July and early August, blueberries are abundant on the summit. For such rewards, this is a popular hike, so don't expect to be alone, especially on fall weekends, when the foliage colors are spectacular.

Trailheads can be accessed by either boat or vehicle. To reach the vehicle-access trailhead for Schoodic Mountain from Route 1 in East Sullivan, drive just over four miles northeast on Route 183 (Tunk Lake Road). Cross the Maine Central Railroad tracks and turn left at the Donnell Pond sign onto an unpaved road (marked as a Jeep track on the USGS map). Go about a quarter mile, then turn left for the parking area and trailhead for Schoodic Mountain, Black Mountain, and Caribou Mountain, and a trail to Schoodic Beach.

Black Mountain

• Distance: 5 miles round-trip

• Duration: 3 hours

• Elevation gain: 800 feet

• Effort: Moderately difficult

• Trailhead: Off Rte. 183, Franklin

The Black Mountain ascent begins easily enough, then climbs steadily through the woods on Donnell Pond Public Reserved Land, easing off a bit before reaching bald ledges. Continue to the true summit by taking the trail past Wizard Pond. Views take in the forested lands and nearby lakes and peaks, and extend out to Acadia's peaks. You can piggyback this hike with Schoodic Mountain, using that trailhead as a base for both climbs. Another possibility is to add Caribou Mountain. That loop exceeds seven miles, making a full day of hiking.

Follow the directions for the Schoodic Mountain trail. If you continue straight, you'll come to another trailhead for Black and Caribou Mountains. Water-access trailheads are at Schoodic Beach and Redman's Beach.

PRESERVES

The very active Frenchman Bay Conservancy (207/422-2328, www.frenchmanbay.org) manages a number of small preserves dotting the region, and most have at least one trail providing access. The Conservancy publishes a free Short Hikes map, available locally, that provides directions to seven of these.

Corea Heath

In 2008, Frenchman Bay Conservancy purchased 600 acres of land known as the Corea Heath. "Heath" is a local word for peatland or bog, and this one is a rare coastal plateau bog, distinguished because it rises above the surrounding landscape. It's a spectacular property, with divergent ecosystems including bogs, ledges, and mixed-wood forest. Natural features include pitcher plants, sphagnum mosses, rare vascular plants, and jack pines. It's a fabulous place for bird-watching, too, and the preserve borders a section of the Maine Coastal Islands National Wildlife Refuge. That summer, volunteers began cutting trails. Check with the conservancy or stop into Chapter Two, in Corea (see *Shopping*) for more info. Trail access is off the Corea Road and parking is limited.

Baker Hill

If you only have half an hour or so and want big rewards for minimal effort, hoof it up Baker Hill, another Frenchman Bay Conservancy property. Trails pass through fir trees and over ledges before a short ascent to an overlook with views over Frenchman Bay, and as far as the Camden Hills on a clear day. To find it from Route 1, take the Punkinville Road, northeast of Route 200 in Sullivan. The parking area is on the left, one-tenth of a mile north of Route 1.

BIKING

The Maine Department of Transportation has mapped and provides info on area bicycle routes. These include the Schoodic Peninsula, with 13- and 29-mile loops, and the Downeast Route/East Coast Greenway Trail, a 140-mile trail stretching from Ellsworth to Calais. PDF maps with tour details are available at www.exploremaine.org/bike/bt_downeast.html, or you can request hard copies by calling 207/624-3250. Do be extremely careful pedaling in this

© HILARY NANGLE

Kayaking is one way to explore the nooks and crannies of Schoodic's shoreline.

region, because, as in much of Maine, shoulders are few and traffic moves swiftly. The best choices for cycling are the **Schoodic Loop** and the quiet roads of **Grindstone Neck.**

If you have a bike, try to pedal the **Schoodic Loop Road** early or late in the day—especially if you're doing a family outing, when everyone tends to cluster together. It's a lovely bike route, but the shoulders on this peninsula are soft and sandy and not great for bikes—so you'll see *Share the Road with Bicycles* signs along the way. Keep to the right and use the road, not the shoulders. Leave your car at the Frazer Point Picnic Area and do a counterclockwise 12.2-mile loop through the park and back to your car via Birch Harbor and Route 186. It's a fine day trip.

SeaScape Kayaking (18 E. Schoodic Dr., Birch Harbor, 207/963-5806, www.seascapekayaking.com) rents bicycles on a 24-hour basis ($20); weekly rates are available.

CANOEING AND KAYAKING

Experienced sea kayakers can explore the coastline throughout this region. Canoeists can paddle the placid waters of Jones Pond on the Schoodic Peninsula. In Donnell Pond Public Reserved Land, the major water bodies are **Donnell Pond** (big enough by most gauges to be called a lake) and **Tunk** and **Spring River Lakes;** all are accessible for boats (even, alas, powerboats).

To reach the boat-launching area for Donnell Pond from Route 1 in Sullivan, take Route 200 north to Route 182. Turn right and go about 1.5 miles to a right turn just before Swan Brook. Turn and go not quite two miles to the put-in; the road is poor in spots but adequate for a regular vehicle. The Narrows, where you'll put in, is lined with summer cottages ("camps" in the Maine vernacular); keep paddling eastward to the more open part of the lake. Continue on Route 182 to find the boat launches for Tunk Lake and Spring River Lake (hand-carry only). Canoeists and kayakers can access Tunk Stream from Spring River Lake.

Still within the preserve boundaries, but farther east, you can put in a canoe at the northern end of Long Pond and paddle southward into adjoining Round Pond. In early August,

Round Mountain, rising a few hundred feet from Long Pond's eastern shore, is a great spot for gathering blueberries and huckleberries. The put-in for Long Pond is on the south side of Route 182 (park well off the road), about two miles east of Tunk Lake.

Well off the beaten path is **Dyer Harbor,** in Steuben. Take the Dyer Bay Road off Route 1, then go left on Pinkham Bay Bridge Road. Just before the bridge is a boat launch for small craft. It's a fine spot to launch a kayak for a coastal paddle in relatively protected waters.

Outfitters and Trips

Paddle around the waters of Schoodic or Flanders Bay with Ed and Cheryl Brackett's **SeaScape Kayaking** (18 E. Schoodic Dr., Birch Harbor, 207/963-5806, www.seascapekayaking.com). Guided three- to four-hour tours are $45 per person, including fortification: homemade blueberry scones for morning trips and blueberry–white chocolate chip cookies in the afternoon. Canoe rental for lake usage is $50 per day; kayaks are $40 double, $30 single.

Master Maine Guides Darrin Kelly and Megan Gahl are committed to sustainability and education—they not only talk the talk, they walk the walk, living off the grid in a yurt surrounded by protected lands. Their enthusiasm and knowledge come through on their trips. **Ardea EcoExpeditions** (242 S. Gouldsboro Rd., Gouldsboro, 207/460-9731, www.ardea-ecoexpeditions.com) offers a wide range of sea kayaking options, from half- and full-day trips to camping or inn-to-inn overnights to research expeditions. A half-day coastal exploration and introduction to sea kayaking is $65; a full day of island hopping is $105, including lunch. Family trips are available ($65 adult, $55 accompanying child), as are instructional trips, a first-light sunrise tour geared to birders, and a sunset tour that can be combined with a lobster bake. Custom overnights begin at $145 per person per day. Ask about "voluntourism" research expeditions, including island inventory and monitoring and seabird surveys. Ardea donates 1 percent of sales to local nonprofits—all the more reason to choose this outfitter.

Antonio Blasi, a Registered Maine Sea Kayak and Recreational Guide, leads guided tours of Frenchman or Taunton Bay and hiking and camping expeditions through **Hancock Point Kayak Tours** (58 Point Rd., Hancock, 207/422-6854, www.hancockpointkayak.com). A three-hour paddle, including all equipment, safety and paddling demonstrations, and usually an island break, is $45. You have a choice of a single or double kayak. Minimum age is 9 for a double, 12 for a single. Overnight kayak camping trips are $150 per person. Antonio also leads overnight backpacking trips for $125 per person, and cross-country skiing and snowshoe tours are available in winter.

If you prefer to do it yourself, rent a canoe or kayak from **Water's Edge Canoe & Kayak Rentals** (222 Franklin Rd., Franklin, 207/460-6350). Canoe rentals are $25 for one day, $65 for three days, or $125 per week; single kayaks are $30, $80, or $150; double kayaks are $40, $100, or $200. Although the location is at the water's edge on Hog Bay, it's tidal, so it's advisable to take the crafts elsewhere; delivery is possible. Credit cards are not accepted.

FISHING

It's no surprise that the Donnell Pond Public Reserved Land is a favorite among anglers. Landlocked salmon can be found in Donnell Pond, Tunk Lake, and Spring River Lake. Lake trout (togue) are fished in Tunk Lake. For brown trout, cast your line in Long Pond.

Open-water season in Hancock County and adjacent Washington County is April 1 to September 30, but after August 16, you must use artificial lures in brooks, rivers, and streams. Check with local wardens for information regarding catch limits and other regulations for specific bodies of water, or call the **Maine Department of Fish and Wildlife** (207/288-8000 or 207/287-8003 for 24-hour recorded information, www.state.me.us/ifw).

Fishing licenses can be purchased at many stores and most town offices. Nonresident freshwater licenses for ages 16 and older are

PUFFINS

The chickadee is the Maine state bird, and the bald eagle is our national emblem, but probably the best-loved bird along the Maine coast is the Atlantic puffin *(Fratercula arctica),* a member of the auk (Alcidae) family. Photographs show an imposing-looking creature with a quizzical mien; amazingly, this larger-than-life seabird is only about 12 inches long. Black-backed and white-chested, the puffin has bright orange legs, "clown makeup" eyes, and a distinctive, rather outlandish red-and-yellow beak. Its diet is fish and shellfish.

Almost nonexistent in this part of the world as recently as the 1970s, the puffin (or "sea parrot") has recovered dramatically thanks to the unstinting efforts of Cornell University ornithologist Stephen Kress and his Project Puffin. Starting with an orphan colony (of two) on remote Matinicus Rock, Kress painstakingly transferred nearly a thousand puffin chicks (also known fondly as "pufflings") from Newfoundland and used artificial nests and decoys to entice the birds to adapt to and reproduce on Eastern Egg Rock in Muscongus Bay.

In 1981, thanks to the assistance and persistence of hundreds of interns and volunteers, and despite the predations of great black-backed gulls, puffins finally were fledged on Eastern Egg, and the rest, as they say, is history. Within 20 years, more than three dozen puffin couples were nesting on Eastern Egg Rock, and still more had established nests on other islands in the area. Kress's methods have received international attention, and his proven techniques have been used to reintroduce bird populations in remote parts of the globe. In 2001, *Down East* magazine singled out Kress to receive its prestigious annual Environmental Award.

HOW AND WHERE TO SEE PUFFINS

Puffin-watching, like whale-watching, involves heading offshore (although you might get lucky and spot them at the tip of the Petit Manan division of the Maine Coastal Islands National Wildlife Refuge), so be prepared with warm clothing, rubber-soled shoes, a hat, sunscreen, binoculars, and, if you're motion-sensitive, appropriate medication. Although cruises depart from Bar Harbor, on Mount Desert Island, if you're willing to venture a bit afield, you'll find three companies dedicated to puffin-watching cruises.

Closest is **Robertson Sea Cruises,** in Milbridge (207/546-3883, cell tel. 207/461-7439, www.robertsonseatours.com, May 15-Oct. 1), which heads to Petit Manan Island, and you view the birds from aboard the boat. Cost for a three-hour tour is $70 adult, $55 ages 12 and younger, with a $200 boat minimum.

Two other companies provide daily up-close-and-personal opportunities for puffin-watching along the Down East Coast – specifically, on Machias Seal Island, home of the state's largest puffin colony. Both operate late May to late August, departing at about 7 A.M. and costing about $100 per person. Weather permitting, you'll be allowed to disembark on the 20-acre island and spy on the roughly 3,000 puffins (at peak) who call it their summer home. Naturalist and skilled skipper Andy Patterson of **Bold Coast Charters** (207/259-4484, www.boldcoast.com) is based in Cutler. Captain John Norton of **Norton of Jonesport** (207/497-5933 or 207/497-2560) is the son of Barna Norton, the veteran of puffin-watching trips, and departs from the waterfront in Jonesport.

ADOPT-A-PUFFIN PROGRAM

Stephen Kress's Project Puffin has devised a clever way to enlist supporters via the Adopt-a-Puffin program. For a $100 donation, you'll receive a certificate of adoption, vital statistics on your adoptee, annual updates, and a T-shirt. How's that for a special gift for the bird lover in your life? For information, visit www.projectpuffin.org.

$53 for the season, $12 for one day (24 hours), $24 for three days (72 hours), $37 for seven days, and $41 for 15 days. Licenses for children ages 12 to 16 are $10. Licenses are not required for saltwater fishing.

SWIMMING

The best freshwater swimming in the area is at **Jones Beach,** a community-owned recreation area on Jones Pond in West Gouldsboro. Here you'll find restrooms, a nice playground, picnic facilities, a boat launch, a swim area with a float, and a small beach. Open sunrise to sunset, the beach is located at the end of Recreation Road, off Route 195, which is 0.3 mile south of Route 1. No unleashed pets are permitted.

Two beach areas on Donnell Pond are also popular for swimming, **Schoodic Beach** and **Redman's Beach,** and both have picnic tables, fire rings, and pit toilets. It's a half-mile hike to Schoodic Beach from the parking lot. Redman's Beach is only accessible by boat. Other pocket beaches are also accessible by boat, and there's a rope swing (use at your own risk) by a roadside pullout for Fox Pond.

A sand beach on a remote freshwater pond is the reward for a quarter-mile hike into the Frenchman Bay Conservancy's **Little Tunk Pond Preserve.** From Route 1 in Sullivan, take Route 183 about five miles, then look for the parking area on your left.

GOLF

Play a nine-hole round at the **Grindstone Neck Golf Course** (Grindstone Ave., Winter Harbor, 207/963-7760, www.grindstonegolf.com, May–Oct.), just for the dynamite scenery and for a glimpse of this exclusive, late-19th-century summer enclave. Established in 1891, the public course attracts a tony crowd; 150-yard markers are cute little birdhouses. Tee times usually aren't needed, but call to make sure.

EXCURSION BOATS

If you want to see this part of the coast from the sea, especially Petit Manan lighthouse and

its puffin colony, then you'll need to venture up to Milbridge. Although not truly part of the Acadia region by any definition, it's the closest port with lighthouse-sighting, bird-watching, or scenic nature cruises. Note: Rates will vary with fuel prices.

Robertson Sea Tours and Adventures

Captain Jaime Robertson's Robertson Sea Tours and Adventures (Milbridge Marina, Fickett's Point Rd., 207/546-3883 or 207/461-7439, www.robertsonseatours.com, May 15–Oct. 1) offers a puffin and seabird cruise to Petit Manan Island, a scenic island cruise, a lobstering cruise, and others from Milbridge aboard the *Mairi Leigh,* a classic Maine lobster boat. The puffin and seabird cruise lasts three hours and is $70 for adults, $55 for kids 12 and younger, with a $200 boat minimum. The island cruise ($60 for adults, $45 for kids, $150 boat minimum) lasts 2–2.5 hours, passes seven islands, and highlights the region's aquaculture industry. The lobstering cruise lasts 1.5–2 hours and costs $50 per adult, $30 per kid, with an $100 boat minimum. An option includes a lobster lunch ($75 adults, $50 kids, boat minimum $200), complete with a steamed lobster served aboard. All cruises depart from the Milbridge Marina and require reservations.

Downeast Coastal Cruises

Captains Harry "Buzzy" and Esther Shinn's Downeast Coastal Cruises (207/546-7720, cell tel. 207/598-7740, www.downeastcoastalcruises.com) depart from the Milbridge Landing aboard the comfortable *Alyce K.* for island, lighthouse, puffin, sunset, lobster feast (complete with meal), and even Bar Harbor cruises. Each lasts 2–4 hours and costs $45–75 per adult, $35–65 per child; boat minimums apply. Or create your own adventure with a half-day or full-day charter. Both Shinns have seawater flowing through their veins.

Entertainment and Events

PIERRE MONTEUX SCHOOL

The Pierre Monteux School for Conductors and Orchestra Musicians (Rte. 1, Hancock, 207/422-3280, www.monteuxschool.org), a prestigious summer program founded in 1943, has achieved international renown for training dozens of American and international classical musicians. It presents two well-attended concert series starting in late June and running through July. The Wednesday series (7:30 P.M., $10 adults, $5 students) features chamber music; the Sunday concerts (5 P.M., $15 adults, $5 students) feature symphonies. An annual free children's concert usually is held on a Monday (1 P.M.) in early to mid-July. All concerts are held in the school's Forest Studio. Note that both Chipper's and Le Domaine restaurants are minutes from the school, so it's easy to combine a concert with a nice dinner.

SCHOODIC ARTS FOR ALL

Concerts, art classes, coffeehouses, workshops, and related activities are presented year-round by the energetic Schoodic Arts for All (207/963-2569, www.schoodicarts.org), a volunteer organization. Many activities are held at historic Hammond Hall, in downtown Winter Harbor. A summer series presents monthly concerts from May through October on Friday evenings.

The **Schoodic Arts Festival** takes place over two weeks in early August and is jam-packed with daily workshops and nightly performances for all ages. Call for a schedule, and register early for any program that you don't want to miss.

OCEANSIDE INNSTITUTE

Seeking to add more vibrancy and diversity to the peninsula's entertainment offerings and to indulge their own interests in music and the sciences, the owners of Oceanside Meadows Inn created the Innstitute for Arts and Sciences (Rte. 195, Corea Rd., Prospect Harbor,

207/963-5557, www.oceaninn.com), which presents a series of Thursday night events from late June to late September, with a break during the Schoodic Arts Festival. The wide-ranging calendar includes lectures and concerts as well as art shows. Some are free; others are $10 in advance or $12 at the door.

SERC

Acadia Partners for Science and Learning (P.O. Box 277, Winter Harbor 04693, 207/288-1326, www.acadiapartners.org) is working with Acadia National Park to create a scientific research center at **Schoodic Education and Research Center** (www.nps.gov/acad/serc .htm) on the old Navy base on Schoodic Point, locally called SERC. In 2007, it launched a biennial international sculpture symposium, with the aim of creating granite sculptures to place within coastal communities throughout the region. A lecture series, presented in Moore Auditorium every second Saturday evening year-round (and more often in summer), features speakers, usually researchers or nationally known experts, addressing environmental topics related to the park and its surroundings.

EAGLE HILL SUMMER LECTURES

The Humboldt Field Research Institute (59 Eagle Hill Rd., Steuben, 207/546-2821, www .eaglehill.us), dedicated to natural history science, sponsors various opportunities to meet and mingle with scientists and others. If you're especially interested in natural history and the arts, the institute offers longer programs, too. The institute is located four miles off Route 1. Take Dyer Bay Road off Route 1, bearing left at the fork onto Mogador Road, for a total of 3.6 miles, then left on Schooner Point Road, then right on Eagle Hill Road. Programs take place in the Dining Hall lecture room.

The institute began an artist-in-residence program in 2005. At least once during

EDUCATING FOR THE FUTURE

In 2002, the U.S. Naval Station on Schoodic Point closed, leaving behind a 100-acre campus that was a self-supporting community, with housing, recreational facilities, classrooms, food service, office buildings, and a Norman Provincial–style mansion that's listed on the National Register of Historic Places. Enter the Schoodic Education and Research Center (www.nps.gov/acad/serc.htm), known by its acronym, SERC, which is managed by Acadia Partners for Science and Learning (207/288-1327, www.acadiapartners.org).

SERC's mission is to promote the understanding, protection, and conservation of the park's natural and cultural resources and to advance related research. To accomplish that, says Dennis R. O'Brien, executive director for Acadia Partners, "we need to know what's in the park; you can't protect what you do not know to exist."

To that end, Acadia Partners is conducting "bio blitzes," which research the park's flora and fauna in minute detail. In 2007, more than 100 specialists and volunteers participated in a blitz to catalog spiders. O'Brien says, "they found 60 species that had not been previously identified as being in the park, including eight that hadn't been identified as being in the state." Other blitzes have identified true bugs, flies, beetles, moths and butterflies, and ants.

SERC sponsors an Artist-in-Residence program as well as a biennial Sculpture Symposium, in odd-numbered years, that draws sculptors from around the globe. Visitors can watch the sculptors carve their works. When completed, the sculptures are displayed in towns throughout the Acadia region.

A core part of SERC's mission is education. "We have very high aspirations," O'Brien says. "We're creating a world-class science and education center." That includes a 124-seat auditorium for presentations, some of which are open to the public.

Acadia Partners is offering a number of education and research programs in science and math aimed not only at scientists and researchers, but also students and teachers. These include professional development for math and science teachers, summer scholarship programs for math and science teachers, advanced placement summer institutes for teachers, research fellowships, and fellowships for scientists and educators.

On the local level, Acadia Partners is reaching out to schools with hands-on science programs. "We want to change the way science is taught," O'Brien asserts. Acadia Partners is doing that by getting kids out of the classroom and into the field. "Our goal is to bring ninety percent of middle-school kids within an hour-and-a-half's drive from here for a three-day ranger-led program," says O'Brien, noting that this not only educates the kids in real science and nature, but it also engages them in the outside world. That's another goal, O'Brien adds: "We must prepare the next generation of stewards for the park."

the season, the resident artist discusses his or her experiences in a scheduled talk. Call for details.

Thursday Lectures

The Thursday Evening Lecture Series presents guest lecturers and scholars on wide-ranging topics related to natural history. In past years, these have included "Diversity of Peatmosses," "The Enchanted Forest: Lichens and Mosses in Maine's Landscape," and "Watercolor Landscape Painting in America." Lectures begin at 7:30 P.M. on most Thursdays from mid-July to early October. Admission is free.

Panorama Lectures

This series of free 1.5-hour presentations, focusing on both natural history sciences and the cultural history of nature, take place on Saturdays at 5 P.M. Each is preceded by a free one-hour social in the lounge and followed by a buffet-style, three-course dinner ($25, reservations required 24 hours in advance), during which attendees can mingle and chat with the speaker. Past topics have included "The Nature of Zen Landscape," "Maine Poets and the Natural World: A Different Lens," and "Shakespearean Plants."

FARMSTEAD BARN
During July, **Hancock County Friends of the Arts** (Rte. 1, East Sullivan, 207/422-3615, www.hcfafarmsteadbarn.org) presents a free entertainment series for children. The weekly shows might include juggling, magic, mime, comedy, or music. All are presented in a barn that Ginia Davis Wexler, a former singer, and her husband, Morris, turned into a theater in the late 1960s for just this purpose. The funky interior is decorated with mismatched chairs, Mexican flying creatures, Chinese lanterns, posters, paintings, and other touches. Two shows are presented. Admission is free, but donations are much appreciated. The barn is three miles south of the Gouldsboro Post Office.

WINTER HARBOR LOBSTER FESTIVAL
Winter Harbor's biggest wingding is the annual Lobster Festival, on the second Saturday in August. The gala daylong event includes a parade, live entertainment, lobster boat races (a serious competition, with 13 classes determined by size and power), a crafts fair, games, and lots and lots of crustaceans. For more information, visit www.acadia-schoodic.org.

Shopping

ANTIQUES
Browsers, dreamers, and collectors are welcome at **Art & Old Things** (70 Taunton Dr., Sullivan, 207/422-3551), a one-stop antiques and collectibles shop, art gallery, and sculpture garden that's just plain fun to visit. The eclectic gallery features the work of Joe Martell and other regional artists. The shop is filled with antiques, junktiques, shabby chic furniture, decorative items, home accents, and architectural pieces; the garden is adorned with granite and marble sculptures and unique functional artwork. The shop is just 500 yards off Route 1, just beyond Gazebo Park.

Winter Harbor Antiques and Works of Hand (424-426 Main St., Winter Harbor, 207/963-2547) is a double treat. Antiques fill one building and works by local craftspeople and artists fill the other. It's located across from Hammond Hall.

Here's a nifty place: **Chapter Two** (611 Corea Rd., Corea, 207/963-7269) is home to the Corea Rug Hooking company and Accumulated Books Gallery. Spread out in three buildings are a nice selection of used and antiquarian books, locally made crafts, and Rosemary's hand-hooked rugs. Sip on tea or coffee while browsing. Yarn, rug-hooking supplies, and lessons are available.

Ever seen a palmara, durian jack, pangium edule, or dompaum? Even know what they are? **Coastal Antiques** (Rte. 186, Prospect Harbor, 207/963-5546) has the original nut collection from Perry's Nut House in Belfast, which pulled in tourists from around the globe until its demise. Some specimens are amazing to see. The shop, which also sells antiques, shares a building with DeMarco Realty at the intersection with the Corea Road/Route 195.

Need a good read? Duck into **Scottie's Bookhouse** (209 Rte. 1, Hancock, 207/667-6834) and choose from a wide-ranging selection of about 35,000 used books.

FOOD AND WINE
German and Italian presses, Portuguese corks, and Maine fruit all contribute to the creation of Bob and Kathe Bartlett's award-winning dinner and dessert wines: apple, pear, blueberry, raspberry, blackberry, strawberry, peach, mead, and loganberry. Not ones to rest on their many laurels, in 2008 the Bartletts introduced two grape wines, a sangiovese/blueberry and a zinfandel/blueberry. Founded in 1982,

SCHOODIC PENINSULA

© HILARY NANGLE

Fruit wines are the specialty at the Bartlett Maine Estate Winery.

Bartlett Maine Estate Winery (175 Chicken Mill Pond Rd., Gouldsboro, 207/546-2408, 10 A.M.–5 P.M. Mon.–Sat. Memorial Day to Columbus Day, or by appointment off-season) produces more than 20,000 gallons annually in a handsome wood-and-stone building designed by the Bartletts. No tours, but you're welcome to sample the wines, and you can buy single bottles and gift packages. Reserve wines and others of limited vintage are sold only on premises. Bartlett's is a half mile south of Route 1 in Gouldsboro.

Organic fruit and honey wines are produced at family-operated **Shalom Orchard Organic Winery and Bed and Breakfast** (158 Eastbrook Rd., Franklin, 207/565-2312, www.shalomorchard.com). The certified-organic farm is well off the beaten path but worth a visit not only for the wines, but also for yarns, pelts, fleece, and especially the views of Frenchman Bay from the hilltop orchard. The farm also has two simple guest rooms, sharing one bath and kitchenette. A full farm breakfast is included in the $55–65 rate. Pets

and kids are welcome. To find the farm, take Route 182 to Route 200/Eastbrook Road, and go 1.6 miles.

This area has two excellent smoke-houses. Defying its name, **Sullivan Harbor Smokehouse** (Rte. 1, Hancock, 207/422-3735 or 800/422-4014, www.sullivanharborfarm .com) has moved to spacious, modern new digs in Hancock. Big interior windows allow visitors to see into the production facility and watch the action. Among the offerings are Scottish-style smoked salmon, gravlax, smoked scallops, smoked trout, smoked Arctic char, smoked salmon pâté, and more.

The newer **Grindstone Neck of Maine** (311 Newman St., Rte. 186, just north of downtown Winter Harbor, 207/963-7347 or 866/831-8734, www.grindstoneneck.com) also earns high marks for its smoked salmon, shellfish, spreads, and pâtés, all made without preservatives or artificial ingredients. Also available are fresh fish, wine, and frozen foods for campers. The best seller is a can of Road Kill Stew; go figure.

Cindy and Bill Thayer's enthusiasm is contagious as they explain their prolific 150-acre certified-organic farm—home to hairy Scotch Highland cattle, turkeys, sheep, pigs, chickens, and border collies. At **Darthia Farm** (W. Bay Rd., Rte. 186, Gouldsboro, 207/963-7771, 207/963-2770, or 800/285-6234, www .darthiafarm.com), check out Hattie's Shed for Cindy's outstanding ikat weavings and work by half a dozen other craftspeople. The Farm Store (8 A.M.–5 P.M. Mon.–Fri., until noon Sat. June–Sept.) sells fresh produce as well as herbal salves and vinegars, handspun hand-dyed yarn, and other products. Sleigh rides are available in the fall and winter.

Norwegian Fjord horses do the work at **Mandala Farm** (46 Young's Farm Rd., Gouldsboro, 207/963-2984, www.mandala-farm.com), an organic farm off Route 186. The self-serve farm store carries produce and meats. Now here's a unique experience: If you're intrigued by the horses, you can take a driving lesson, no previous experience necessary. Individual lessons for one or two are $35 per hour; a minimum of two to three hours is recommended. A two-day package, with four hours of lessons daily and the opportunity to drive multiple horses and vehicles, is $240.

GENERAL STORE

You can find just about anything at the **Winter Harbor 5 & 10** (349 Main St., Winter Harbor, 207/963-7927, www.winterharbor5and10 .com). It's the genuine article, an old-fashioned five-and-dime that's somehow still surviving in the age of Wal-Mart.

ARTS AND CRAFTS GALLERIES

Art and artisan studios and galleries are numerous, and it's easy to while away a day browsing and buying. Hours and days of operation vary and often are subject to whim; it's best to call first if you really want to visit a gallery. Begin by picking up copies of the *Artist Studio Tour Map*, which details and provides directions to about a dozen galleries in the Hancock area, and the *Schoodic Peninsula* brochure, which notes galleries and shops on the peninsula. Both are widely available and free.

Schoodic Peninsula

Galleries dot the Schoodic Peninsula. To find these, loop down to Winter Harbor, then back up on Route 186.

Architectural stoneware, with a specialty in hand-formed bathroom sinks, is the drawing card at Dan Weaver's **Maine Kiln Works** (115 S. Gouldsboro Rd./Hwy. 186, Gouldsboro, 207/963-5819, www.waterstonesink.com), but you'll also find functional pottery in the shop. You might also see Dan Weaver at work on the wheel in the back room. Be careful when arriving or departing; the shop is on a killer corner and traffic seems to zoom by.

Every piece handcrafted at **Gypsy Moose Glass Studio** (20 Williamsbrook Rd., South Gouldsboro, 207/963-2674) is made from a single glass rod, which means no two are alike. You'll find glass beads, fused-glass earrings, swan weather predictors, and much more at this working studio just off Route 186.

© TOM NANGLE

Art galleries pepper the Schoodic Peninsula and surrounding towns.

If you're lucky, you might catch Susan Dickson-Smith throwing a pot at **Stave Island Gallery/Proper Clay Stoneware** (Rte. 186, South Gouldsboro, 207/963-2040, www .properclay.com). Her small gallery features her pottery as well as works by other Maine artisans.

An old post office is the new location for **Lee Art Glass** (679 S. Gouldsboro Rd./Rte. 196, Gouldsboro, 207/963-7280). Although Rod Lee has died, his works live on, thanks to Wayne Tucker and Sheldon R. Bickford, who purchased the business after training with Lee. The fused-glass tableware is created by taking two pieces of window glass and firing them on terra cotta or bisque molds at 1,500°F. What makes the end result so appealing are the colors and the patterns—crocheted doilies or stencils—impressed into the glass. The almost-magical results are beautiful and delicate-looking, yet functional.

Visiting the **U.S. Bells Foundry & Watering Cove Pottery** (56 West Bay Rd., Rte. 186,

Prospect Harbor, 207/963-7184, www.usbells .com) is a treat for the ears, as browsers try out the many varieties of cast-bronze bells made in the adjacent foundry by Richard Fisher. If you're lucky, he may have time to explain the process—particularly intriguing for children, and a distraction from their instinctive urge to test every bell in the shop. The store also carries quilts by Dick's wife, Cindy, and wood-fired stoneware and porcelain by their daughter-in-law Liza Fisher, as well as works by other area artisans. U.S. Bells is a quarter mile up the hill from Prospect Harbor's post office.

ℂ Hancock and Sullivan Gallery Tour

Take the Point Road 2.5 miles to find Russell and Akemi Wray's **Raven Tree Gallery** (536 Point Rd., Hancock, 207/422-8273, www .raventreegallery.com). Russell specializes in wood carvings, bronzes, prints, and jewelry; Akemi crafts pottery.

Return to Route 1 and take Eastside Road, just before the Hancock-Sullivan Bridge, and drive 1.5 miles south to the Wray family's **Gull Rock Pottery** (325 Eastside Rd., Hancock, 207/422-3990). Torj and Kurt Wray (and daughter-in-law Akemi, of Raven Tree Gallery) craft wheel-thrown, hand-painted, dishwasher-safe pottery decorated with cobalt blue and white Japanese-style motifs.

Cross the Hancock-Sullivan Bridge, then take your first left off Route 1, onto Taunton Drive, to find the next two galleries. Drawing from her experiences as an oil painter and from her life in Japan, Peg McAloon creates masterful one-of-a-kind quilts, vests and jackets, hand-dyed silk scarves, purses, and wall hangings at **Wildfire Run Quilt Boutique** (148 Taunton Dr., Sullivan, 207/422-3935, www .maineus.com/wildfirerun).

Bet you can't keep from smiling at the whimsical animal sculptures and fun furniture of talented sculptor/painter Philip Barter. His work is the cornerstone of the eclectic **Barter Family Gallery** (Shore Rd., Sullivan, 207/422-3190, www.barterfamilygallery.com). But there's more: Barter's wife and seven children,

especially son Matthew, along with son-in-law Brian Emerson, have put their considerable skills to work producing hooked and braided rugs, jewelry, and other craft items. The gallery is 2.5 miles off Route 1.

Return to Route 1, then head north on Route 200, to find the next three galleries. Artist Paul Breeden, best known for the remarkable illustrations, calligraphy, and maps he's done for *National Geographic,* Time-Life Books, and other national and international publications, displays and sells his paintings at the **Spring Woods Gallery and Willowbrook Garden** (40A Willowbrook La., Sullivan, 207/422-3007, www.springwoodsgallery.com or www.willowbrookgarden.com). Also filling the handsome modern gallery space are paintings by Ann Breeden and metal sculptures and silk scarves by the talented Breeden offspring. Be sure to allow time to meander through the sculpture garden, where there's even a playhouse for kids.

Hand-woven textiles are the specialty at **Moosetrack Studio** (388 Bert Gray Rd./Rte. 200, Sullivan, 207/422-9017, www.moosetrackhandweaving.com), where the selections range from hand-woven area rugs to shawls of merino wool and silk. Camilla Stege has been weaving since 1969, and her work reflects her experience and expertise. The gallery is 1.8 miles north of Route 1.

Overlooking Hog Bay, 3.6 miles north of Route 1, Charles and Susanne Grosjean have been the key players at **Hog Bay Pottery** (245 Hog Bay Rd., Rte. 200, Franklin, 207/565-2282, www.hogbay.com) since 1974. Inside the casual, laid-back showroom are Charles's functional, nature-themed pottery and Susanne's stunning hand-woven wool rugs.

Nancy Glista's distinctive sterling silver jewelry mixes spirals and spheres accented with semiprecious stones. Her studio, **Glista Jewelry** (5 Shipyard Point Rd., Hancock, 207/565-3302, www.glistajewelry.com), is a bit off the beaten path. To find it, continue north on Route 200 until it meets with Route 182, then watch for signs on the left. Do make an appointment.

Steuben

Arthur Smith (Rogers Point Rd., Steuben, 207/546-3462) is the real thing when it comes to chainsaw carvings. He's an extremely talented folk artist who looks at a piece of wood and sees an animal in it. His carvings of great blue herons, eagles, wolves, porcupines, flamingoes, and other creatures are incredibly detailed, and his wife, Marie, paints them in lifelike colors. Don't expect a fancy studio; much of the work can be viewed roadside.

Also in Steuben, but on the other end of the spectrum, is **Ray Carbone** (460 Pigeon Hill Rd., Steuben, 207/546-2170), whose masterful wood, stone, and bronze sculptures and fine furniture are definitely worth stopping to see, if not to buy. Don't miss the granite sculptures and birdbaths in the garden.

In the barn of Steuben's second-oldest house, the historical Shaw farm, is **The Shaw Place Antiques** (Village Loop, 207/546-2330), where Jan Whelan sells antiques, treasures, and her magnificent handmade sweaters, made using only the highest-quality yarns. Whelan delight in telling visitors the history of the house and the area, and often weaves in her own heritage—she believes knitting is in her blood, as her 15th-century ancestors were British wool merchants. Check out the guestbook: Shoppers have included Robert Redford and Tom Selleck.

Accommodations

There are no lodgings in the Schoodic section of the park, but within less than a half hour of the Schoodic parkland, you'll have your choice of an impressive range of places to sleep—from an elegant French-style country inn with a fantastic restaurant to a rustic campground with lovely wilderness sites.

INNS

Buffered from the highway by a tall hedge, **Le Domaine** (1513 Rte. 1, Hancock, 207/422-3395 or 800/554-8498, www.ledomaine.com) has gained a five-star reputation for its restaurant, founded in 1946—long before fine dining had cachet here. But that's only part of the story. Above the restaurant is a charming, five-room French country inn. The 80-acre inn property, nine miles east of Ellsworth, is virtual Provence, an oasis transplanted magically to Maine. On the garden-view balconies, or on the lawn out back, you're oblivious to the traffic whizzing by. Better yet, follow the lovely wooded trail to a quiet pond. Three guest rooms ($285, including breakfast and dinner; $200 B&B) and two suites ($370 modified American plan, $285 B&B) all are named after locales in Provence. Continental breakfast, usually including freshly made croissants and jams, can be served in your room or in the dining room. Alert the inn if you'll be arriving after 5:30 P.M., when the staff has to focus on dinner. The ultra-French restaurant is open to the public 6–9 P.M. Tuesday–Sunday. Reservations are essential, especially in July and August. Le Domaine's season is mid-June to early November.

Follow Hancock Point Road 4.8 miles south of Route 1 to the three-story, gray-blue **Crocker House Country Inn** (967 Point Rd., Hancock, 207/422-6806, www.crockerhouse .com, $110–165), Rich and Liz Malaby's antidote to Bar Harbor's summer traffic. Built as a summer hotel in 1884, the inn underwent rehabbing a century later, but it retains a decidedly old-fashioned air, although Wi-Fi is now available. Breakfast is included. Guests can relax in the common room or reserve spa time in the carriage house. One kayak and a few bicycles are available. Nearby are clay tennis courts, quiet walking routes past Hancock Point's elegant seaside "cottages," and a unique octagonal public library. The Malabys will pack picnic lunches (extra charge) for day trips to Campobello Island, Acadia, or Lamoine State

Park. If you're arriving by boat, request a mooring. The inn's dining room is a draw in itself.

BED-AND-BREAKFASTS
Schoodic Peninsula

Overlooking the Gouldsboro Peninsula's only sandy saltwater beach, **Oceanside Meadows Inn** (Rte. 195, Corea Rd., Prospect Harbor, 207/963-5557, www.oceaninn.com, $149–209, May–late Oct.) is a jewel of a place on 200 acres with fabulous gardens, wildlife habitat, and walking trails. The elegant 1860s Captain's House has seven attractive rooms, and the 1820 Shaw farmhouse next door has another seven. Each room has a copy of Louise Dickinson Rich's *The Peninsula*—a thoughtful touch. Breakfast is an impressive four-course event, usually featuring herbs and flowers from the inn's gardens. Energetic husband-and-wife team of Ben Walter and Sonja Sundaram seem to have thought of everything—hot drinks available all day, a guest fridge, beach toys, even detailed guides to the property's trails

and habitats (great for entertaining kids). As if all that weren't enough, Sonja and Ben have totally restored the 1820 timber-frame barn out back—creating the **Oceanside Meadows Innstitute for the Arts and Sciences.** Local art hangs on the walls, and, from June to September, the 125-seat barn has a full schedule of classical concerts and lectures on natural history, Native American traditions, and more, usually on Thursday nights. Some are free, some require tickets; all require reservations. The inn's website is also a phenomenal resource on area activities. Oceanside Meadows is six miles off Route 1.

Watch lobster boats unload their catch at the dock opposite **Elsa's Inn on the Harbor** (179 Main St., Prospect Harbor, 207/963-7571, www.elsasinn.com, $115–165). Jeffrey and Cynthia Alley; their daughter, Megan; her husband, Glenn Moshier; and grandsons Andrew and Emmett have turned Jeff's mother Elsa's home into a warm and welcoming inn. The Alley family roots in the area go back more

Oceanside Meadows Inn sits on 200-plus acres, stretching from a sand beach through forests to a salt bay.

© TOM NANGLE

than 10 generations, so you're guaranteed to receive solid information on where to go and what to do. Every room has an ocean view, and Megan, an experienced innkeeper whose career included positions at Ritz-Carlton and luxury boutique hotels, pampers guests with sumptuous linens, down duvets, terry robes, Wi-Fi, and a hearty hot breakfast. After a day exploring, settle into a rocker on the veranda and gaze over the boat-filled harbor out to Prospect Harbor Light. And afterward? Well, perhaps a lobster bake. Upon request, Megan's dad will bring over some fresh lobster and Megan will prepare a complete lobster dinner—corn on the cob, coleslaw, homemade rolls, and a seasonal dessert, all for about $25 per person, depending upon market rates.

Set well back from Route 1, **Acadia View Bed and Breakfast** (175 Rte. 1, Gouldsboro, 207/963-7457 or 866/963-7457, www.acadia-view.com, $139–169) is built on a bluff with views across Frenchman Bay to the peaks of Mount Desert and a path down to the shorefront. Pat and Jim Close built the oceanfront house as a B&B, opening it in 2005. The building may be new, but it's filled with antique treasures from the Closes' former life in Connecticut. Each of the four guest rooms has a private deck. The Route 1 location, while next to nothing, is convenient for everything.

Off the beaten path is Bob Travers and Barry Canner's **Black Duck Inn on Corea Harbor** (Crowley Island Rd., Corea, 207/963-2689, www.blackduck.com, $140–200, May–mid-Oct.), literally the end of the line on the Gouldsboro Peninsula. Set on 12 acres in this timeless fishing village, the B&B has four handsomely decorated rooms and plenty of common space. Across the way, perched on the harbor's edge, are two little seasonal cottages, one rented by the day (three-night minimum) and one by the week. The inn and Corea are geared to wanderers, readers, and anyone seeking serenity (who isn't?). Rocky outcrops dot the property and a nature trail meanders to a millpond; in early August, the blueberries are ready. If the fog socks in, the large parlor has comfortable chairs and loads of books.

Something of a categorical anomaly, **The Bluff House Inn** (Rte. 186, Gouldsboro, 207/963-7805, www.bluffinn.com, $65–130) is part motel, part hotel, part B&B—a seemingly successful mix in a contemporary building overlooking Frenchman Bay, on the west side of the Gouldsboro Peninsula. Verandas wrap around the first and second floors, so bring binoculars for osprey and bald eagle sightings. Pine walls and flooring give a lodge feeling to the open first floor. Settle by the stone fireplace or grab a seat by the window. Breakfast, a generous continental with excellent baked goodies, is served here. On Saturday nights, a lobster bake is served ($25). The eight second-floor rooms are decorated "country" fashion, with quilts on the very comfortable beds. (In hot weather, request a corner room.) Also available is a two-bedroom housekeeping apartment ($150 per day or $875 per week) built above a garage. The inn is open all year; pet-friendly rooms are available.

Hancock, Sullivan, and Sorrento

About 12 miles east of Ellsworth is the **Island View Inn** (12 Miramar Ave., Sullivan, 207/422-3031, www.maineus.com/islandview, $145–165, late May–mid-Oct.); its name is the height of understatement. Out front are the peaks of Mount Desert, a remarkable panorama. Four of the seven rooms (all with decks) capture the view from this updated 1889 summer home run by Evelyn Joost and her daughter Sarah. The inn evokes the easy elegance of days gone by. Many of the furnishings are original. The Island View has a private beach, but the water is terminally chilly. Sailing excursions are available by reservation on the inn's Rhodes 18 sloop. Guests have free use of a canoe and a dinghy. Pets and kids over six are welcome.

Machias-native Dottie Mace operated a B&B in Virginia before returning to Maine to open **Taunton River Bed & Breakfast** (19 Taunton Dr., Sullivan, 207/422-2070, www.tauntonriverbandb.com, $125–150) in a 19th-century farmhouse with river views. Rooms are carefully decorated; they're warm and inviting, formal without being stuffy. Two of the three bedrooms share a bath. It would be easy to spend the day just sitting on the porch swing, but it's an easy pedal or drive to local art galleries, and the Tidal Falls Lobster Pound is within walking distance. The inn is just a stone's throw off Route 1, so traffic noise might bother the noise sensitive.

Sustainable living is the focus of Karen and Ed Curtis's peaceful **(Three Pines Bed and Breakfast** (274 East Side Rd., Hancock, 207/460-7595, www.threepinesbandb.com, $100–125, year-round), fronting on Sullivan Harbor, just below the Reversing Falls. Their quiet, off-the-grid, 40-acre oceanfront organic farm faces Sullivan Harbor and is home to a llama, rare-breed chickens and sheep, ducks, and bees, as well as a large organic garden, berry bushes, an orchard, and greenhouses. Photovoltaics provide electricity; appliances are primarily propane-powered; satellite technology operates the phone, TV, and Internet systems. Two inviting guest rooms have private entrances and water views. A full vegetarian breakfast (with fresh eggs from the farm available) is served. Bicycles and a canoe are available. You can walk or pedal along an abandoned railway line down to the point or up to the lobster pound, and you can launch a canoe or kayak from the back—or is it the front?—yard. Children are welcome; pets are a possibility; open year-round.

Innkeeper Carolyn Bucklin is determined to create the perfect B&B experience at **Cottage by the Sea** (38 Kilkenny Cove, Hancock, 207/422-6783, www.cottagebytheseamaine .com, $145–165, June 1–mid-Oct.). Top-quality linens, fully equipped rooms (satellite TV, irons and ironing boards, hair dryers, telephones), evening turndown service, and air-conditioning make it hard to tear yourself away from the oceanfront inn. Three rooms are available, one with a view of Kilkenny Cove. Breakfast is a multicourse affair; afternoon refreshments are served. No pets, as there is a resident dog.

Sorrento is such a low-key place that lots of people don't realize it has a B&B, an ultracasual homestay-style one at that. **Bass Cove Farm Bed and Breakfast** (312 Eastside Rd., Rte. 185, Sorrento, 207/422-3564, www .basscovefarm.com, $70–110) was opened in 1992 by spinner/weaver/gardener/editor Mary Ann Solet and her husband, Michael Tansey, a group-home supervisor whose résumé also includes the Harry S. Truman Manure Pitchoff Championship at the annual Common Ground Country Fair. The 1840s-era farmhouse uses solar-heated water; the cleaning is done with nontoxic products. Mary Ann can rattle off dozens of ideas for exploring the area, particularly in the craft department, and she raids her extensive vegetable garden daily to produce a hearty, healthful breakfast. Guest rooms have quilt-covered beds and other homey touches— some share baths. A second-floor apartment sleeps four and has a kitchen and living room.

MOTELS AND COTTAGES
Schoodic Peninsula

Next to their Black Duck Inn, Barry Canner and Bob Travers operate **Black Duck Properties** (Crowley Island Rd., Corea, 207/963-2689 or 877/963-2689, www.black-duck.com), handling both home sales and seasonal rentals. Corea is the primary focus, with harborfront cottages a specialty, but they can suggest suitable spots in Winter Harbor, Gouldsboro, and Prospect Harbor. Most of the rentals forbid smoking. Weekly rental range is $900–1,600.

Roger and Pearl Barto, whose family roots in this region go back five generations, have four rental accommodations on their Henry's Cove oceanfront property, **Main Stay Cottages** (66 Sargent St., Winter Harbor, 207/963-2601, www.awa-web.com/stayinn, $90–115). Most unusual is the small, one-bedroom Boat House, which has stood since the 1880s. It hangs over the harbor, with views to Mark Island Light, and you can hear the water gurgling below you at high tide. Other options include a very comfortable efficiency cottage, a one-bedroom cottage, a second-floor suite with a private entrance, and a four-bedroom house ($250 per night). All have big decks and fabulous views over the lobsterboat-filled harbor; watch for the eagles that frequently soar overhead. Main Stay is on the Island Explorer bus route and just a short walk from where the Bar Harbor Ferry docks.

Also rustic and in need of serious attention, but charming in a sweet, old-fashioned way are **Albee's Cottages** (Rte. 186, Prospect Harbor, 207/963-2336 or 800/963-2336, www.theshorehouse.com, $69–106 per night or $455–715 per week, May–mid-Oct.), a cluster of 10 somewhat ramshackle cottages, decorated with braided rugs, fresh flowers, and other homey touches. Two things make this place special: the waterfront location—and it's truly waterfront; many of the cottages are just a couple of feet from the high-tide mark—and the management. Owner Richard Rieth goes out of his way to make guests feel welcome. Pick up lobsters and say what time you want dinner, and they'll be cooked and delivered to your cottage. Richard sometimes brings home-baked sweets and other treats to cottages when he has the time and inclination. He's slowly fixing up the simple cottages, first tackling much-needed new roofs and exterior painting. After that, he'll begin on the interiors. In peak season, cottages rent on a Saturday-to-Saturday basis, but shorter rentals are often available. Dogs are welcome.

Sullivan

Set back from the highway 12 miles east of Ellsworth, **Sullivan Harbor Farm** (Rte. 1, Sullivan, 207/422-3735 or 800/422-4014, www.sullivanharborfarm.com) is a beautifully sited property with spectacular sea and mountain views. (The word "farm" is a bit misleading—it's a long way from agriculture.) Across Route 1 from a quiet cove, the driveway curves through two giant outcrops higher than a car—great lookout points for watching the passing scene. Three whimsically named cottages are available by the week ($975–1,700, with three-night stays possible after Labor Day). The two-bedroom Cupcake cottage and three-bedroom Guzzle have phones and cable TV; one-bedroom Milo does not (bring a cell phone and you're all set, or use the phone in the main house). All are comfortably

and attractively outfitted (there are views of Frenchman Bay from Guzzle and Cupcake). Ask owner Joel Frantzman to steer you toward his favorite ponds and hiking trails—he'll even lend you a canoe or kayak. Or just hang out in the peaceful backyard or visit the spotless **Sullivan Harbor Smokehouse** and ship your pals some fantastic cold-smoked salmon (they also do hot-smoked salmon, not to mention fabulous salmon pâté). Sullivan Harbor's product has become the salmon du jour for some of the biggest-name restaurants and high-end provisioners in New England and beyond.

The closer you get to the water's edge, the better the accommodations are at **Flander's Bay Cabins** (22 Harbor View Dr./Rte. 1, Sullivan, 207/422-6408, www.acadia.net/flandersbay). Skip the overnight cabins; the two- and three-bedroom cabins ($550–675 per week) are nicer. Even better is a three-bedroom chalet ($950). Best is the oceanfront three- to four-bedroom house ($1,800). There's on-site access for kayaks and canoes as well as fishing and swimming. This property is adjacent to and run by the same family as Mountainview Campground.

CAMPING
Schoodic Peninsula

On a wooded finger of land projecting eastward from the Schoodic Peninsula, **◖ Ocean Wood Campground** (Birch Harbor, 207/963-7194, early May–late Oct.) gets kudos for eco-sensitivity, noise control, and 17 fantastic wilderness sites, most on the ocean. Don't expect frills; nature provides the entertainment. The 70 campsites (20 with hookups) are $20–43, depending on location and services. Pets (leashed) and visitors are allowed at regular sites, but not at the wilderness ones. No credit cards are accepted; free hot showers are available. The meticulously maintained campground is a terrific base for exploring the Schoodic section of Acadia National Park. (Note, however, that the campground is at the *end* of the one-way Schoodic Loop Road. It's no problem hiking back into the park area the wrong way, but if you're driving or biking, you'll need to go around, about five miles, via Route 186, to do the loop.)

Sullivan

Sites at **Mountainview Campground** (22 Harbor View Dr./Rte. 1, Sullivan, 207/422-6408, www.acadia.net/flandersbay, May–Oct., $24–36) are spread throughout an oceanfront field, so there's not a lot of privacy here. The best sites edge the Frenchman Bay shorefront and are reserved for tents and small campers using 20-amp service. Other sites can accommodate full hookups with 30- to 50-amp service. Hot showers are free, and if you stay six days, your seventh day is free. There's also an antiques shop on the premises.

Donnell Pond Public Reserved Land

A handful of authorized, primitive camp-sites can be found on Tunk Lake (at the area's southwestern corner) and Donnell Pond (at Schoodic Beach and Redman's Beach), all accessible by foot or boat. Each has a table, a fire ring, and a nearby pit toilet. Many of the sites are lakefront. All are first-come, first-served (no fees or permits required) and are snapped up quickly on midsummer weekends. You can camp elsewhere within the unit, excepting Day Use areas, but fires are not permitted on unauthorized sites.

Steuben

Since 1958, the Ayr family has opened its quiet, well-off-the-beaten-path property on Joy Cove to campers. With a convenient location 15 minutes from Petit Manan National Wildlife Refuge and 20 minutes from Schoodic Point, **Mainayr Campground** (321 Village Rd., Steuben, 207/542-2690, www.mainayr.com, late May–mid-Oct., $25–30) has 35 tenting and RV sites (five with full hookups). Also on the premises are a playground, a laundry, a beach for tidal swimming, clamming flats, a grassy launch area for kayaks and canoes, a camp store, berries for picking, and fresh lobsters. If that's not enough, David Ayr enjoys regaling campers with stories.

Food

LOCAL FLAVORS

There's no food in the park's Schoodic section, so if you're planning a picnic, you'll need to stock up along the way—in Winter Harbor or Prospect Harbor—if you haven't done so earlier.

Make a point to attend one of the many **public suppers** held throughout the summer in this area and in so many other rural corners of Maine. Typically benefiting a worthy cause, these usually feature beans or spaghetti or the serendipity of potluck. Everyone saves room for the homemade pies. Notices of such suppers are usually posted on public bulletin boards in country stores and in libraries, on signs in front of churches, and at other places people gather. Local newspapers also often detail such events.

Schoodic Peninsula

Pick up veggies, meats, eggs, cheeses, and handcrafted fiber products as well as jams, preserves, and baked goods at the **Winter Harbor Farmers Market** (parking lot at the corner of Newman St. and Rte. 186, Winter Harbor, 9 A.M.–noon Tues. late June–early Sept.).

Once a true old-fashioned country store with a classic traditional soda fountain and penny candy, Gerrish's Store has undergone many changes in recent years. Its latest incarnation is as **Two Sisters** (352 Main St., Winter Harbor, 207/963-2727, 4:30 A.M.–3:30 P.M. Mon.–Sat. and 7 A.M.–2 P.M. Sun., fewer hours off season), a full bakery and Internet café. Breakfast, lunch, Gifford's ice cream, coffee and tea, and sweets are available at quite reasonable prices. Kathryn Baltef, who had previous experience operating a bakery in Georgia, operates it with daughter Alyssa Rider.

Shoot pool, watch the game on TV, play horseshoes, sip a cold drink, and savor a burger at **Nautica Pub** (East Schoodic Dr., at the intersection with Rte. 186, Birch Harbor, 207/963-7916). It opens at 11 A.M. Monday–Friday, at noon on Saturday and Sunday.

Hancock, Sullivan, and Franklin

Delicious soups and sandwiches, baked goods, and a nice selection of prepared foods are available at **Mano's Market** (1517 Rte. 1, Hancock, 207/422-6500, 9 A.M.–6 P.M. Tues.–Fri., 10 A.M.–4 P.M. Sat.), a small market that also sells some wines and artisan cheeses. If you have cooking facilities at your accommodations, you can't miss with the prepared foods selection. The crab cakes and spit-roasted chicken are both fabulous. A nice selection of sandwiches is offered—ask for one on the housemade focaccia bread; soups are usually available, too. There are tables on the back deck.

Craving curry? Call in your order 24 hours in advance, and **Tandoor Downeast** (119 Eastbrook Rd., Franklin, 207/565-3598, www.tandoordowneast.com, 5–8 P.M. Mon.–Fri., 1–8 P.M. weekends) will prepare authentic Indian cuisine for you to take away. Chef Gunjan Gilbert's menu is extensive, and prices are reasonable, with most choices $6–8. Or take your chances and simply stop by and choose from whatever's available. If you have a cottage, in-house preparation—they come and cook in your kitchen—is available. A selection is usually also available at the Winter Harbor Farmers Market.

From India, step into Italy at Buzzy Gioia's **Maple Knoll Pizza** (132 Blackswoods Rd./Rte. 182, Franklin, 207/565-2068, www.franklinmaine.net, 2–9 P.M. Wed.–Sun.), on the eastern edge of "intown" Franklin. Buzzy draws on his Italian heritage—his parents came from the Old Country—to craft authentic pizzas, submarine sandwiches, and calzones. Try the white scallop and bacon pizza.

Take Route 182 to Route 200/Eastbrook Road, and go 1.6 miles to family-operated

Shalom Orchard Organic Winery and Bed and Breakfast (158 Eastbrook Rd., Franklin, 207/565-2312, www.shalomorchard.com). The certified-organic farm is well off the beaten path, but worth a visit for its organic fruit and wines, as well as for its yarns, pelts, fleece, and especially the views of Frenchman Bay from the hilltop.

Steuben

Cinnamon doughnut muffins, chocolate-pecan cookies, multigrain breads, and English muffins are just a few of the reason to dip off Route 1 to **Wildflour Bakery** (314 Village Rd., Steuben, 207/546-0978, 8 A.M.–noon Sat.), the tiny bakery where auto-mechanic-turned-baker Rich Chevalier turns out hearty, creative breads and sweets. It's a great spot to catch the local gossip, too. The schedule can vary; call for current days and hours of operation.

At the end of a long driveway winding through the woods in the back of beyond is **Painted Pepper Farm** (Good's Point Rd., Steuben, 207/546-9777, www.paintedpepperfarm.com), an organic farm operated by Lisa Reilich and Jordan Godino and their children. At the self-serve farm store you can purchase their maple syrup (you pass the sugar house on the drive), granola, preserves, applesauces, and, for a real treat, their yogurts, gelatos (the lemon zest is to die for), and cheese produced from their herd of Nigerian goats. From Route 1, take the Dyers Bay Road three miles to Good's Point Road. The farm is on the right. It's open daily, except Thursday and Sunday, from 10 A.M.–4 P.M., but it's wise to call before making a special trip.

FAMILY FARE
Schoodic Peninsula

The best place for grub and gossip in Winter Harbor is **Chase's Restaurant** (193 Main St., Winter Harbor, 207/963-7171, 7 A.M.–8 P.M., to 2 P.M. Sun.), a seasoned, no-frills booth-and-counter operation that turns out first-rate fish chowder, fries, onion rings, wraps, home-style dinners, and downright cheap breakfasts.

In "downtown" Prospect Harbor, the

Downeast Deli (at the corner of Rtes. 186 and 195, Prospect Harbor, 207/963-2700, 11 A.M.–7 P.M. Sun.–Tues., 10 A.M.–8 P.M. Wed.–Sat.) will fix you right up with plenty of sandwich choices: hot or cold hoagies, deli-style sandwiches, and good pizza with a wide array of mix-and-match choices. The biggest seller is the homemade ice cream sandwich.

Hancock and Sullivan

Don't be put off by the lobster "sculpture" outside Ruth & Wimpy's Kitchen (792 Rte. 1, Hancock, 207/422-3723, www.ruthand-wimpys.com, 11 A.M.–9 P.M. daily Apr.–Dec.); you'll probably see a crowd as well. This family-fare standby serves hefty sandwiches, lobster prepared 30 ways, pizza, pasta, and steak. Prices begin at less than $3 for a cheeseburger and climb to about $25 for a twin-tail lobster dinner. Locals praise the lobster roll as the cheapest and best around. Antique license plates and collections of miniature cars and trucks accent the interior. It's five miles

Craving lobster? Ruth & Wimpy's is a road food classic serving it about two dozen ways.

east of Ellsworth, close to the Hancock Point turnoff.

Here's a surprise: You can't get much farther from Mexico than coastal Maine and still be in the States, but The Mexican Restaurant (1166 Rte. 1, Hancock, 207/422-3723, 11 A.M.–8 P.M. daily) has earned a reputation for being a hot spot for authentic Mexican and Central American fare. Originally in Harrington, where it catered to the region's migrant blueberry pickers, this multi-generation family operation now shares a huge log building with a motorcycle shop. Everything's made on the premises, even the tortilla chips. The interior is bright and cheerful, and there also are tables on the porch and a few picnic tables on the lawn. Almost everything on the menu is $3–8, and the choices are plentiful.

Good food served by friendly folks is what pulls the locals into ◖ Chester Pike's Galley (2236 Rte. 1, Sullivan, 207/422-8200, 6 A.M.–2 P.M. Mon.–Sat., opens at 7 A.M. Sun., also 4:30–8:30 P.M. Fri. and Sat.). The prices are low, the portions big. If you're on a diet, don't even *look* at the glass case filled with fresh-baked pies, cakes, and cookies. Go early if you want to snag one of the homemade doughnuts (and order dessert first). It's also open Friday nights for a fish fry with free seconds, and Saturday nights for prime rib.

Two walls of windows frame the Taunton River, looking downriver toward the Reversing Falls, from The Galley by the Bridge (1715 Rte. 1, Sullivan, 207/422-2059, 11 A.M.–9 P.M. Tues.–Sat., 2–8 P.M. Sun.). Expect good home cookin' and big portions at small prices for fried foods, pizza, and calzones, as well as a kiddo menu and ice cream.

Steuben and Milbridge

If you're heading out to Petit Manan National Wildlife Refuge, trust me on this. Ignore the exterior and venture into Country Charm (336 Pigeon Hill Rd., Steuben, 207/546-3763, 5:30 A.M.–8 P.M., until 7 P.M. Sun.). The fried fish is fabulously fresh, crispy, light, and cheap, even by local standards. You easily can get out of here for less than $10 per person, far less if you're on a tight budget. The original dining room has, well, country charm (sit here if you want to listen in on the local gossip); the newer ones (added when a real kitchen replaced the original blue trailer) are purely functional. Hungry? Order the Charm Special: two eggs, bacon, sausages, pancakes, toast, and coffee all for a whopping $5; omelets begin at $2.74.

In Milbridge, the best choice is **44 Degrees North** (17 Main St., Milbridge, 207/546-4440, www.44-degrees-north.com, 11 A.M.–8 P.M., Fri.–Sat. to 9 P.M.). The front room is family oriented, with booths, tables, and cheerful decor. The back room doubles as a bar and has a big-screen TV. Expect good home cooking, with a few surprises, and, as is usually the case in this part of Maine, mouthwatering desserts. Prices top out at $15 for prime rib, served Friday and Saturday nights, baby back ribs, or the house specialty, seafood lasagna. The pub side opens daily at 11 A.M. and stays open through last call.

CASUAL DINING
Schoodic Peninsula
Make it a point to find **Bunkers Wharf** (260 E. Schoodic Dr., Birch Harbor, 207/963-2244, 11:30 A.M.–10 P.M. daily, open seasonally), just one mile from the end of the Schoodic Loop. The dining room overlooks a working wharf, and there's a big stone fireplace to ward off the chill on inclement days. Crisp white linens and fresh flowers add a formal touch in the dining room, yet the feeling is unpretentious. You can also dine in the pub or on a patio that's practically in the harbor. The only drawback is that dinners are pricey: entrées are $18 and up.

The Fisherman's Inn (7 Newman St., Rte. 186, Winter Harbor, 207/963-5585, 5–9 P.M. daily late May–mid-Oct.) has been an institution in these parts since 1947. Kathy Johnson runs the front of the house; her husband, Carl, is the master in the kitchen. He's also the brains behind Grindstone Neck of Maine, the smoked seafood operation just up the road, and diners are welcomed with a sample of smoked salmon spread and a cheese spread. That's followed up with Carl's focaccia bread and the house

dipping sauce, a tasty blend of romano cheese, fresh garlic, red pepper, and parsley with olive oil. And that all comes before any appetizers. Seafood is the specialty here, and there's a good chance that the guy at the neighboring booth caught your lobster or fish. Asian influences are evident, too. Entrée range is $14–25, although some dishes can top that given seasonal market rates.

Hancock
It's easy to miss **Chipper's** (Rte. 1, Hancock, 207/422-8238, 5–9 P.M., closed Sun.–Mon.), a simple Cape-style building *hard by* Route 1 (that's "very close to" Route 1 in Maine lingo), but that would be a mistake. Chip definitely knows his way around the kitchen. The wide-ranging menu includes rack of lamb and even chateaubriand, but the emphasis is on seafood; the crab cakes earn their rave reviews. Meals include a sampling of tasty haddock chowder and a salad, but save room for the homemade ice cream for dessert. Entrées are in the $16–30 range, but some appetizer/salad combo options provide budget options.

FINE DINING
Hancock
The ultra-French restaurant **⟨ Le Domaine** (1515 Rte. 1, Hancock, 207/422-3395 or 800/544-8498, www.ledomaine.com, 6–9 P.M. Tues.–Sun. mid-June–early Nov. and 11 A.M.–2 P.M. Sun. mid-June–early Sept.) has gained a five-star reputation. Although ownership changed in 2005, the same crew is in the kitchen and the menu remains *très* French. The restaurant is equally renowned for its 5,000-bottle wine cellar and lovely Provençal decor. Reservations are essential, especially in July and August. Opt for the five-course fixed-price menu for $35; otherwise the tab may dent your budget (entrées $22–31), but stack that up against plane fare to France.

The unpretentious dining rooms at the **Crocker House Country Inn** (967 Point Rd., Hancock Point, 207/422-6806, www.crockerhouse.com, 5:30–9 P.M.) provide a setting for well-prepared Continental fare with flair, crafted from fresh and local ingredients (entrées $22–32), and Sunday brunch (11 A.M.–2 P.M.); reservations are essential as this is one of the area's most consistent and popular dining spots. The dining room is open daily May 1–October 31 and Friday–Sunday in April, November, and December.

LOBSTER-IN-THE-ROUGH
Hancock

Thank the Ellsworth-based Frenchman Bay Conservancy for buying the four-acre **Tidal Falls Preserve** (off Eastside Rd., Hancock), overlooking Frenchman Bay's only reversing falls (roiling water when the tide turns), and opening it to public access. When a half-century-old lobster pound went on the market a few years ago, the conservancy hastened into action, raised more than half a million dollars,

and bought the property. Today, a dozen picnic tables on the lawn overlook the falls, and seals often haul out on nearby ledges. There's also a screened-in dining pavilion. It's an idyllic spot. (**Tidal Falls Lobster Pound** (207/422-6457, 3–8:30 P.M. Mon.–Wed. and 11 A.M.–8:30 P.M. Thurs.–Sun. late May–early Sept.) leases the site. Come for the lobster (pricey for a lobster shack, but the view makes up for it), but there also are fried foods and even a few barbecue items (BYOB). Every Friday night is a fish fry, with free seconds, and Monday nights have live entertainment. Order at the window and then grab a seat. Eastside Road is off Route 1 (on your right, if you're heading north), just south of the Hancock–Sullivan bridge; follow it one mile and look for a sign on your left. Follow the gravel road to the end.

Information and Services

ACADIA NATIONAL PARK

Information about Acadia National Park on the Schoodic Peninsula is available on Mount Desert Island at the park's **Hulls Cove Visitor Center** and at the **Thompson Island Visitor Center,** at the head of the island.

To plan ahead, see the Acadia website (www.nps.gov/acad/), where you can download a Schoodic map. To see the Island Explorer bus schedule for Schoodic, as well as all of Mount Desert Island, log on to www.explore-acadia.com. The Bar Harbor Ferry schedule is at www.barharborferry.com.

REGIONAL INFORMATION

For advance information about eastern Hancock County, contact the **Schoodic Peninsula Chamber of Commerce** (P.O. Box 381, Winter Harbor 04693, 207/963-7658, www.acadia-schoodic.org) and request its handy map and brochure, revised annually.

Another source for advance information is **Downeast & Acadia Regional Tourism** (394

S. Gouldsboro Rd., Gouldsboro, 207/963-7283 or 800/231-3008, www.downeastacadia.com).

The nearest convenient information center is run by the **Ellsworth Area Chamber of Commerce** (P.O. Box 267, Ellsworth 04605, 207/667-5584, www.ellsworthchamber.org), on the Route 1/3 commercial strip, close to where the highway forks toward Mount Desert Island and eastern Hancock County. It's open daily in July and August; Monday–Saturday from mid-June to mid-September; and weekdays 9 A.M.–4:30 P.M. the rest of the year.

For information on the National and Maine Scenic Byways in this region, visit www.byways.org or www.exploremaine.org/byways/.

LIBRARIES

Check out **Dorcas Library** (Rte. 186, Prospect Harbor, 207/963-4027, www.dorcas.lib.me.us) or **Winter Harbor Public Library** (18 Chapel La., Winter Harbor, 207/963-7556,

© TOM NANGLE

Check the bulletin boards at Hancock's octagonal library for local doings.

www.winterharbor.lib.me.us), in the 1888 beach stone and fieldstone Channing Chapel.

The inviting octagonal **Hancock Point Library** (Hancock Point Rd., Hancock Point, 207/422-6400, summer only, call for hours) was formed in 1899. More than a library, it's a center for village activities. Check the bulletin boards by the entrance to find out what's happening when.

GETTING AROUND

Although you can get here by passenger ferry from Bar Harbor or bus from Ellsworth, you'll need a car to explore beyond the part of the Schoodic Peninsula that's served by the Island Explorer bus.

By Car

To reach the Schoodic Region from Ellsworth, continue north on Route 1 from where it splits with Route 3. Stay on Route 1 for about 16 miles (through Hancock and Sullivan) until you reach Gouldsboro. From Route 1 in Gouldsboro, the park entrance is eight miles.

Take Route 186 south to Winter Harbor. Continue through town, heading east, then turn right onto Moore Road and continue to the park entrance sign, just before the stone-lined causeway over Mosquito Harbor.

To reach the park boundary from Bar Harbor, take Route 3 northward to the head of Mount Desert Island, then across Mount Desert Narrows to Trenton. The usual route is to continue to a congested intersection at the edge of Ellsworth, where you'll pick up Route 1 North (turn right) and continue as above. But you can avoid some of the traffic congestion on Route 3 in Trenton by ducking east via Route 204 toward Lamoine and its state park and then back up to Route 1 via the Mud Creek Road.

By Passenger Ferry

The **Bar Harbor Ferry** (207/288-2984, www.barharborferry.com, round-trip $29.50 per adult, $19.50 per child, $6 per bike), owned by Captain Steve Pagels (who also operates the four-masted schooner *Margaret Todd*

SCENIC BYWAYS

This region boasts not one, but two designated scenic byways, the **Schoodic National Scenic Byway,** which wraps around the peninsula, and the **Blackwoods Scenic Byway** (formerly the State Route 182 Scenic Byway), an inland blue highway cutting through the Donnell Pond Public Reserved Lands. If time permits, drive at least one of these two routes. Ideally, you'd do both, because the scenery differs greatly. Best idea yet: Connect the two via Route 1, creating a route that includes lakes and forests, mountains and fields, ocean and rocky coast. If you only have one day to explore this region, this takes in the best of it. In early to mid-October, when the foliage is at its peak, the vistas are especially stunning.

The 29-mile Schoodic National Scenic Byway stretches from Sullivan on Route 1 to Gouldsboro and then southward on Route 186 and around the Schoodic Peninsula, ending in Prospect Harbor. A detailed guide is available online at www .schoodicbyway.org. Other information is available at www.byways.org.

The 12.5-mile Blackwoods Scenic Byway meanders along State Route 182 inland of Route 1, from Franklin to Cherryfield, edging lakes and passing through small villages. You'll find access to trailheads and boat launches at Donnell Pond and Tunk Lake. Although Cherryfield is beyond the Schoodic region, it's a beautiful town to visit, filled with stately Victorian homes, and it's also the self-proclaimed wild blueberry capital of the world. Maps and information are available from www.exploremaine.com.

and ferry service to the Cranberry Isles), makes at least five trips daily from late June to late September with his Bar Harbor–to–Winter Harbor passenger-only ferry. You can board it with a bike in Bar Harbor (at the Bar Harbor Inn Pier), disembark in Winter Harbor (behind Winter Harbor Marine, on Sargent St.), pedal the short distance to Schoodic, then bike the Schoodic Loop Road, and return later to Bar Harbor on the ferry (last boat is 5 P.M.; 3 P.M. after Sept. 1). The free **Island Explorer** bus meets the ferry, late June to mid-October, on either end.

Since the ferry's summer schedule is coordinated with the Island Explorer bus's summertime Schoodic route, you can board the ferry in Bar Harbor, pick up the bus at the dock in Winter Harbor, and be shuttled along the Schoodic Loop. Stop where you like for a picnic, then board a later bus. Take the last bus back to the ferry and return to Bar Harbor. A super car-free excursion!

By Bus

The free **Island Explorer** covers the lower part of the peninsula, from Winter Harbor through Prospect Harbor, on its hourly route.

BLUE HILL PENINSULA

Once dubbed "The Fertile Crescent," the Blue Hill Peninsula harbors an unusually high concentration of artisans, musicians, and active retirees juxtaposed with top-flight wooden boat builders, lobstermen, and umpteenth-generation Mainers. Perhaps surprisingly, the mix seems to work.

The peninsula dangles into Penobscot Bay, anchored by the towns of Bucksport to the west and Ellsworth to the east and tethered via bridge to Deer Isle at its tip. It comprises several enclaves with markedly distinctive personalities—artsy Blue Hill, historic Castine, quiet Orland, boaty Brooklin, rural Brooksville, and sedate Sedgwick—all stitched together by a network of narrow, winding country highways and byways. Thanks to the mapmaker-challenging coastline and a handful of freshwater ponds and rivers, there's a view of water around nearly every bend.

You can watch the sun set from atop Blue Hill Mountain; tour the home of the fascinating Jonathan Fisher; stroll through the village of Castine (charming verging on precious), whose streets are lined with dowager-like homes; visit *WoodenBoat* magazine's world headquarters in tiny Brooklin, the self-proclaimed wooden boat–building capital of the world; and browse top-notch studios and galleries salted throughout the peninsula. Mosey over to Cape Rosier (which is—if possible—even more off the beaten path), and visit the homestead of back-to-the-landers Helen and Scott Nearing, the nearby Four Season Farm (where organic guru Eliot Coleman sets the trend), and hike the underutilized trails of the

© HILARY NANGLE

HIGHLIGHTS

◖ Fort Knox: A good restoration, frequent events, and secret passages to explore make this late-19th-century fort one of Maine's best (page 164).

◖ Penobscot Narrows Bridge and Observatory: On a clear day, the views from the 447-foot-high tower, one of only three bridge observatories in the world, extend from Mt. Katahdin to Cadillac Mountain (page 165).

◖ Parson Fisher House: More than just another historic house, the Parson Fisher House is a remarkable testimony to one man's ingenuity (page 170).

◖ Blue Hill Mountain Trail: It's a relatively easy hike for fabulous 360-degree views from the summit of Blue Hill Mountain (page 171).

◖ Four Season Farm: Internationally renowned organic gardeners Eliot Coleman and Barbara Damrosch have reopened their fabulous farmstand and farm (page 179).

◖ Holbrook Island Sanctuary State Park: Varied hiking trails and great birding are the rewards for finding this off-the-beaten-path preserve (page 180).

◖ Flash in the Pans Community Steel Band: Close your eyes, and you might think you're on a Caribbean island, rather than in Maine, when you hear this phenomenal steel-pan band (page 181).

◖ Castine Historic Tour: A turbulent history detailed on signs throughout town makes Castine an irresistible place to tour on foot or by bike (page 186).

◖ Sea Kayaking: Hook up with "Kayak Karen" in Castine for a tour (page 188).

LOOK FOR ◖ TO FIND RECOMMENDED SIGHTS, ACTIVITIES, DINING, AND LODGING.

Holbrook Island Sanctuary. Venture a bit inland of Route 1, and you'll find lovely lakes for paddling and swimming and another hill to hike.

The peninsula is home to some of Maine's finest traditional inns and lodges and a surprising number of excellent restaurants.

PLANNING YOUR TIME

It's a stretch to consider **Bucksport** as part of the Blue Hill Peninsula, let alone include it in the Acadia region, but it is the gateway to it all, and the area has some sights worth a look-see, a nice riverfront walkway, and reasonably priced accommodations and campsites. Route 1 east of Bucksport leads to Orland, whose idyllic setting on the banks of the Narramissic River makes it a magnet for shutterbugs. It's also the site of a unique service organization called H.O.M.E. (Homeworkers Organized for More Employment). East Orland (officially part of Orland) claims the Craig Brook

© AVALON TRAVEL

National Fish Hatchery and Great Pond Mountain (you can't miss it, jutting from the landscape on the left as you drive east on Route 1).

Twelve miles south of Route 1 is the hub of the peninsula, **Blue Hill** (pop. 2,390), exuding charm from its handsome old homes to its waterfront setting to the shops, restaurants, and galleries that boost its appeal.

The towns of **Brooklin, Brooksville,** and **Sedgwick,** near the bottom of the Blue Hill Peninsula, offer hiking, kayaking, and sailing;

historic homes; unique shops and galleries; and accommodations.

If you're staying in Blue Hill—or even Bar Harbor—spend a day in **Castine,** a National Historic Register enclave that many people never find. What visitors discover is a year-round community with a busy waterfront, an easy-to-conquer layout, a handful of traditional inns and boutiques, wooded trails on the outskirts of town, an astonishing collection of splendid Georgian and Federalist architecture, and water views nearly every which way you turn.

Bucksport Area

The new Penobscot Narrows Bridge provides an elegant entry to Bucksport, a longtime rough-and-ready river port and papermaking town that's slowly gentrifying. Bucksport is no upstart. Native Americans first gravitated to these Penobscot River shores in summer, finding here a rich source of salmon for food and grasses for basket making. In 1764, the area was officially settled by Colonel Jonathan Buck, a Massachusetts Bay Colony surveyor who modestly named it "Buckstown" and organized a booming shipping business here. His remains are interred in a local cemetery, where his tombstone bears the distinct outline of a woman's leg; this is allegedly the result of a curse by a witch Buck ordered executed, but in fact it's probably a flaw in the granite. Most townsfolk prefer not to discuss the matter, but the myth refuses to die—and it has immortalized a man whose name might otherwise have been consigned to musty history books. (The monument is across Route 1 from the Hannaford supermarket, on the corner of Hinks Street.)

Papermaking came to Bucksport in 1930, and a huge mill on Indian Point still dominates the riverfront.

Just south of Bucksport, at the bend in the Penobscot River, Verona Island is best known as the mile-long link between Prospect and Bucksport. Just before you cross the bridge

from Verona to Bucksport, hang a left, then a quick right to a small municipal park with a boat launch and broad views of Bucksport Harbor (and the paper mill). In the Buck Memorial Library is a scale model of Admiral Robert Peary's Arctic exploration vessel, the *Roosevelt,* built on this site.

SIGHTS
◖ Fort Knox
Looming over Bucksport Harbor, the *other* Fort Knox (Rte. 174, Prospect, 207/469-7719, http://fortknox.maineguide.com, 9 A.M.–sunset May 1–Nov. 1, $3 adults, $1 ages 5–11) is a 125-acre state historic site, just off Route 1. Named for Major General Henry Knox, George Washington's first secretary of war, the sprawling granite fort was begun in 1844. Built to protect the upper Penobscot River from attack, it was never finished and never saw battle. Still, it was, as guide Kathy Williamson says: "very well thought out and planned, and that may have been its best defense." Begin your visit at the Visitor and Education Center, operated by the Friends of Fort Knox, a nonprofit group that has partnered with the state to preserve and interpret the fort. Guided tours are available Memorial Day–Labor Day, and well worth it, as guides point out some of the fort's distinguishing features, including two complete Rodman cannons. In 2004, restoration of the

Fort Knox Officers' Quarters was completed. Wear rubberized shoes and bring a flashlight to explore the underground passages; you can set the kids loose. The fort hosts Civil War reenactments several times a summer (check with the Bucksport Bay Area Chamber of Commerce). The Halloween Fright at the Fort is a ghoulish event for the brave. The grounds are accessible all year. Bring a picnic; views over the river to Bucksport are fabulous.

Penobscot Narrows Bridge and Observatory

Do not miss the Penobscot Narrows Bridge and Observatory (9 A.M.–5 P.M., to 7 P.M. July and Aug., $5 adults, $3 ages 5–11, includes fort admission, open late May–Nov. 1), accessible via Fort Knox. The observatory, 447 feet or 42 stories high, caps the west tower of the bridge spanning the Penobscot River. It's one of only three such structures in the world and the only one in the Western Hemisphere. You'll zip up in an elevator, and when the doors

© HILARY NANGLE

An observatory caps one tower of the new Penobscot Narrows Bridge.

open, you're facing a wall of glass (yes, it's a bit of a shocker, and downright terrifying for anyone with a serious fear of heights). Ascend two more flights (elevator available), and you're in the glass-walled observatory; the views on a clear day extend from Mt. Katahdin to Mount Desert Island. Even when it's hazy, it's still a neat experience.

Alamo Theatre

Phoenixlike, the 1916 Alamo Theatre (85 Main St., Bucksport, 207/469-0924 or 800/639-1636, event line 207/469-6910, www.alamotheatre .org) has been retrofitted for a new life—focusing on films about New England produced and/or revived by the unique Northeast Historic Film (NHF), which is headquartered here. Stop in, survey the restoration, visit the displays (donation requested), and browse the Alamo Theatre Store for antique postcards, T-shirts, toys, and reasonably priced videos on ice harvesting, lumberjacks, maple sugaring, and other traditional New England topics. One-half mile west of Route 1, it's open 9 A.M.–4 P.M. weekdays all year. The Alamo has also become an active cinema, screening classic and current films regularly in the 120-seat theater, usually on weekends. Each summer there's also a silent film festival.

Homeworkers Organized for More Employment (H.O.M.E.)

Adjacent to the flashing light on Route 1 in Orland, H.O.M.E. is tough to categorize. Linked with the international Emmaus Movement founded by a French priest, H.O.M.E. was started in 1970 by Lucy Poulin, still the guiding force, and two nuns at a nearby convent. The quasi-religious organization shelters refugees and the homeless, operates a soup kitchen and a car-repair service, runs a day-care center, and teaches work skills in a variety of hands-on cooperative programs. Seventy percent of its income comes from sales of crafts, produce, and services. At the Route 1 store (at the corner of Upper Falls Rd.; open 9 A.M.–4:30 P.M. daily), you can buy handmade quilts, organic produce, maple syrup, and jams—and support a worth-while effort. While you're here, tour the crafts workshops on the property. To volunteer time in the workshops, store, or learning center, write to P.O. Box 10, Orland 04472, or call 207/469-7961.

Historical Society Museums

If you're a fan of small museums pertaining to local history and genealogy, poke your head into the **Bucksport Historical Society Museum** (92 Main St., Bucksport, 1–4 P.M. Wed.–Fri. and 2–5 P.M. Sat.), housed in an 1874 railway station between Main Street and the waterfront, or the **Orland Historical Society Museum** (Castine Rd., Orland, 207/469-3186, 2–4 P.M. Wed. and Sat. July–Sept.), in the early 19th-century Narramissic Grange building next to the Orland Market.

RECREATION

Hiking

GREAT POND MOUNTAIN TRAIL

- Distance: 1.8 miles round-trip

- Duration: 2 hours

- Elevation gain: 500 feet

- Effort: Easy to moderate

- Trailhead: 1 mile north of Craig Brook National Fish Hatchery on Hatchery Rd., East Orland

Great Pond Mountain's biggest asset is its 1,038-foot summit, with 360-degree views and lots of space for panoramic picnics. On a clear day, Baxter State Park's Katahdin is visible from Great Pond Mountain's north side. In fall, watch for migrating hawks. Access to the mountain is via gated private property beginning about a mile north of the hatchery parking area. Roadside parking is available near the trailhead, but during fall foliage season, you may need to park at the hatchery. Pick up a brochure from the box at the trailhead, stay on the trail, and respect the surrounding private property. The **Great Pond Mountain**

Conservation Trust (207/469-6772, www .greatpondtrust.org) acts as conscientious local steward for Great Pond Mountain and surrounding wild lands. It also hosts hikes and other activities.

Great Pond Mountain Wildlands

Encompassing two parcels of land and nearly 4,300 acres, the Great Pond Wildlands is a jewel. Acquired by the **Great Pond Mountain Conservation Trust** (207/469-6772, www .greatpondtrust.org) in 2005 after a decade of negotiation, the Wildlands is divided into two areas. The larger parcel totals 3,420 acres and surrounds Hothole Valley, including Hothole Brook, prized for its trout, and shoreline on Hothole Pond. The smaller, 875-acre tract includes two miles of frontage on the Dead River (not to be confused with the Dead River of rafting fame in northwestern Maine) and reaches up Great Pond Mountain and down to the ominously named Hell Bottom Swamp. The land is rich with wildlife: black bear, moose, bobcat, and deer, just to name a few species, plus with the pond, swamp, and river, it's ideal for bird-watching. With 14 miles of woods roads lacing the land, it's prime territory for walking, mountain biking, and snowshoeing, and the waterways invite fishing and paddling. Avoid the area during hunting season. Snowmobiling is permitted; ATVs are banned. Access to the Dead River tract is from the Craig Brook National Fish Hatchery; follow Don Fish Road to the Dead River Gate and Dead River Trail. The South Gate to Hothole Pond Tract is on Route 1, just southwest of Route 176. You can drive in along Valley Road about 2.5 miles to a parking area.

Craig Brook National Fish Hatchery

For a day of hiking, picnicking, swimming, canoeing, and a bit of natural history, pack a lunch and head for 135-acre Craig Brook National Fish Hatchery (306 Hatchery Rd., East Orland, 207/469-2803), on Alamoosook Lake. Turn off Route 1 six miles east of

Bucksport and continue 1.4 miles north to the parking area just above the visitors center. The visitors center (open 8:30 A.M.–3:30 P.M. weekdays, 8 A.M.–3:30 P.M. Sat. and Sun. in summer, free) offers interactive displays on Atlantic salmon (don't miss the downstairs viewing area), maps, and a restroom. The grounds are accessible all year, 6 A.M. to sunset daily. Established in 1889, the U.S. Fish and Wildlife Service hatchery raises sea-run Atlantic salmon for stocking six Maine rivers. Each river has a different strain, so they're kept separate. The birch-lined shorefront has picnic tables, a boat-launching ramp, an Atlantic salmon display pool, additional parking, and a spectacular cross-lake view. Watch for eagles, osprey, and loons. Also on the premises is the small **Atlantic Salmon Museum** (open noon–3 P.M. Thurs., Sat., and Sun. or by arrangement with the hatchery), housed in a circa-1896 ice house and a new addition, and operated by the Friends of Craig Brook. Inside are salmon and fly-fishing artifacts and memorabilia. Hiking options include two to three miles of nature trails through old-growth woods between Alamoosook and Craig Ponds and an easy-to-moderate two-hour (round-trip) hike up Great Pond Mountain.

Waterfront Walk

Stroll the walkway edging the restored Bucksport waterfront for nearly a mile. Along the way are historical markers, picnic tables, a gazebo, a restroom, and expansive views of the harbor and Fort Knox.

Canoeing

If you've brought a canoe, **Silver Lake,** just two miles north of downtown Bucksport, is a beautiful place for a paddle. There's no development along its shores, and the birding is excellent. No swimming ($500 fine); this is Bucksport's reservoir. To get to the public launch, take Route 15 north off Route 1 after crossing the Verona-Bucksport Bridge. Go 0.5 mile and turn right on McDonald Road, which

becomes Silver Lake Road, and follow it 2.1 miles to the launch site.

River Cruise

See Fort Knox and the bridges from the water and learn about the region's history and lore on a narrated trip aboard *Lil' Toot* with **Bucksport Harbor Tours** (96 Main St., Bucksport, 207/469-7498, www.littletoottours .com). Wildlife sightings, including osprey, eagles, and seals, are a possibility. The 75-minute tours depart from the Bucksport Town Dock four times on Friday, Saturday, and most Sundays in July and August, with fewer trips in the spring and fall, but call, as the schedule varies year to year. An evening cruise lasts two hours. Buy tickets, $15–20 adult, $7.50–10 ages 16 and under, at **Bittersweet Gift Shop** (81 Main St., Bucksport).

Golf

Bucksport Golf Club (Duck Cove Rd., Route 46, Bucksport, 1.5 miles north of Rte. 1, 207/469-7612, mid-Apr.–Sept.) prides itself on having Maine's longest nine-hole course. Greens fees are moderate; facilities include a pro shop, a snack bar, a driving range, and carts.

SHOPPING

You'll find a smattering of antique and curiosity shops dotting Route 1. Just south of Route 1 is **Wild Blueberry Patch Gift Shop** (Allen's Wild Maine Blueberries, Rte. 15, Orland, 207/469-7060), a tiny blue cottage next to the Allen family's blueberry processing building. Stop in for fresh, canned, frozen, or dried wild Maine blueberries and all manner of blueberry merchandise, from baking mixes to T-shirts.

ACCOMMODATIONS
Inns and Bed-and-Breakfasts

The most attractive B&B in this area is the 1820 **The Orland House** (10 Narramissic Dr., Orland, 207/469-1144, www.orlandhousebb .com, $85–105). Alvion and Cindi Kimball's elegant, yet comfortable, Greek Revival home overlooks the Narramissic River. It's been beautifully restored, preserving the architectural details but adding plenty of creature comforts. Cindi heads the local chamber of commerce, so she's a wealth of info.

Location, location, location. If only the six simple rooms at the old-timey **Alamoosook Lakeside Inn** (off Rte. 1, Orland, 207/469-6393 or 866/459-6393, www.alamoosooklakesideinn.com, $125) actually overlooked the lake, then it would be the perfect rustic lakeside lodge. The property is gorgeous, and the location well-suited for exploring the area, but the rooms are so-so, with tiny bathrooms. All have windows and doors opening onto a long sunporch overlooking the lake. Now the upside: The lodge has a quarter mile of lake front. Alamoosook is great for wildlife-watching and fishing, especially for bass, trout, salmon, and pickerel, and guests have access to canoes and kayaks. Paddle across the lake to the fish hatchery for a hike up Great Pond Mountain. You can even hire a guide for a four-hour fishing trip ($200 for two). If the weather doesn't cooperate, retreat to the basement rec room, with games, a fireplace, a library, and even a kitchenette. A full breakfast is served; free Wi-Fi. It's open year-round.

Motels

In downtown Bucksport, the award for best view goes to the **Fort Knox Inn** (64 Main St., Bucksport, 207/469-3113 or 800/528-1234, $99–159), a four-story Best Western motel nudged right up to the harbor's edge. Forty modern rooms have phones, air-conditioning, free Wi-Fi, and cable-satellite TV. Be sure to request a water view, or you'll be facing a parking lot.

Camping

The rivers, lakes, and ponds between Bucksport and Ellsworth make the area especially appealing for camping, and sites tend to be cheaper than in the Bar Harbor area. During July and August, especially on weekends, reservations are wise.

Six miles east of Bucksport, across from Craig Pond Road, is Back Ridge Road, leading to **Balsam Cove Campground** (286 Back Ridge Rd., East Orland, 207/469-7771 or 800/469-7771, www.balsamcove.com, $20–39). From Route 1, take Back Ridge Road 1.5 miles to the left turn for the campground, on the shores of 10-mile-long Toddy Pond. Facilities on the 50 acres include 60 wooded waterfront or water-view tent and RV sites, a one-room rental cabin ($52–65), on-site rental trailers ($65–80), a dump station, a store, laundry, free showers, boat rentals, and freshwater swimming. Open late May to late September. Dogs are welcome on camping sites for $2 per day.

The same season holds for 10-acre **Whispering Pines Campground** (Rte. 1, East Orland, 207/469-3443, www.campmaine.com/whisperingpines/, $34 for two people, $2 per child over age 7), also on Toddy Pond, but with access directly from Route 1. Facilities include 50 tent and RV sites (request one close to the pond), free use of canoes and rowboats, freshwater swimming, a playground, free showers, and a recreation hall. Whispering Pines is 6.5 miles east of Bucksport.

FOOD

MacLeod's (Main St., Bucksport, 207/469-3963, 11:30 A.M.–2 P.M. Tues.–Sat. and 5–9 P.M. Tues.–Sun.) is Bucksport's most popular and enduring restaurant. Some tables in the pleasant dining room have glimpses of the river and Fort Knox. The wide-ranging menu has choices for all tastes and budgets. Reservations are wise for Saturday dinner.

On Verona Island, just before you cross the bridge to Bucksport (if you're heading north), is **Kravings Bakery and Restaurant** (42 Rte. 1, Verona, 207/469-9900, 11:30 A.M.–close Tues.–Sun.), a casual restaurant with seating indoors and on an outdoor patio. The interior is pleasant, homey, and accented with knickknacks. Outside, you're subject to the roar of traffic on Route 1. Additions to the regular menu vary nightly, alternating between New England (Thursday), Mexican (Wednesday and Saturday), and Italian (Tuesday and Friday) fare, all at very reasonable prices. Fajitas and nachos are big hits during lunch, but the sandwiches are excellent, too. And then there are the whoopie pies and other baked treats.

In what passes as downtown Orland (hint: don't blink), **Orland Market and Pizza** (Rte. 175/91 Castine Rd., Orland, 207/469-9999, 7 A.M.–9 P.M.) is a delight. Established in 1860, the old-fashioned country store has a little of this and a bit of that along with breakfast sandwiches, hot and cold sandwiches, grilled foods, salad, and all kinds of pizza. Call or drop by to find out the day's homemade specials, perhaps lasagna or spaghetti and meatballs. Smoked ribs are the specialty every other Thursday, weather permitting.

INFORMATION AND SERVICES

The **Bucksport Bay Area Chamber of Commerce** (52 Main St., Bucksport, 207/469-6818, www.bucksportchamber.org) is right next to the municipal office in downtown Bucksport. Office hours are 9 A.M.–5 P.M. Mon.–Fri., but the side door is always open for access to an extensive array of brochures, newspapers, and other publications, plus bulletin board notices. The local *Enterprise* newspaper and the Bucksport Chamber of Commerce produce a very helpful annual, *The Guide,* covering Bucksport, Orland, and Verona Island. Be sure to request a copy.

Public Restrooms

In Bucksport, public restrooms next to the town dock (behind the Bucksport Historical Society) are open spring, summer, and fall. Restrooms are open year-round in the Gateway Mobil gas station (at the Route 1 traffic light next to the Bucksport bridge) and in the Bucksport Municipal Office (weekdays) on Main Street.

Blue Hill

Eons back, Native American summer folk gave the name Awanadjo (Small Hazy Mountain) to the mini-mountain that looms over the town of Blue Hill and draws the eye for miles around. The first permanent settlers arrived after the French and Indian War, in the late 18th century, and established mills and shipyards. More than 100 ships were built here between Blue Hill's incorporation, in 1789, and 1882, bringing prosperity to the entire peninsula.

Critical to the town's early expansion was its first clergyman, Jonathan Fisher, a remarkable fellow who's been likened to Leonardo da Vinci. In 1803 Fisher founded Blue Hill Academy (the predecessor of today's George Stevens Academy), then he built his home (now a museum), and eventually he left an immense legacy of inventions, paintings, engravings, and poetry.

Throughout the 19th century and into the 20th, Blue Hill's granite industry boomed, reaching its peak in the 1880s. Scratch the Brooklyn Bridge and the New York Stock Exchange and you'll find granite from Blue Hill's quarries. Around 1879, the discovery of gold and silver brought a flurry of interest, but little came of it. Copper was also found here, but quantities of it, too, were limited.

At the height of the town's industrial prosperity, tourism took hold, attracting steamboat-borne summer boarders. Many succumbed to the scenery, bought land, and built waterfront summer homes. Thank these summer folk and their offspring for the fact that music has long been a big deal in Blue Hill. The Kneisel Hall

© TOM NANGLE

The town of Blue Hill edges pretty Blue Hill Bay.

Chamber Music School, established in the late 19th century, continues to rank high among the nation's summer music colonies. New York City's Blue Hill Troupe, devoted to Gilbert and Sullivan operettas, was named for the longtime summer home of the troupe's founders.

SIGHTS
◖ Parson Fisher House
Named for a brilliant Renaissance man who arrived in Blue Hill in 1794, the Parson Fisher House (Rte. 15/176, 44 Mines Rd., Blue Hill, 207/374-2459, www.jonathanfisherhouse.org, 1–4 P.M. Thurs.–Sat. early July–mid-Sept., $5) immerses visitors in period furnishings and Jonathan Fisher lore. And Fisher's feats are breathtaking: He was a Harvard-educated preacher who also managed to be an accomplished painter, poet, mathematician, naturalist, linguist, inventor, cabinetmaker, farmer, architect, and printmaker. In his spare time, he fathered nine children. Fisher also pitched in to help build the yellow house on Tenney Hill, which served as the Congregational Church parsonage. Now it contains intriguing items

created by Fisher, memorabilia that volunteer tour guides delight in explaining, including a camera obscura. Don't miss it.

Historic Houses
A few of Blue Hill's elegant houses have been converted to museums, inns, restaurants, and even some offices and shops, so you can see them from the inside out. To appreciate the private residences, you'll want to walk, bike, or drive around town.

In downtown Blue Hill, a few steps off Main Street, stands the **Holt House** (3 Water St., Blue Hill, 207/326-8250, www.bluehillhistory .org, 1–4 P.M. Tues. and Fri. and 11 A.M.–2 P.M. Sat. July–mid-Sept., $3 adults, free for children 12 and under), home of the Blue Hill Historical Society. Built in 1815 by Jeremiah Holt, the Federal-style building contains restored stenciling, period decor, and masses of memorabilia contributed by local residents. In the carriage house are even more goodies, including old tools, a sleigh, carriages, and so forth.

Walk or drive up Union Street (Route 177), past George Stevens Academy, and wander **The**

Old Cemetery, established in 1794. If gnarled trees and ancient headstones intrigue you, there aren't many good-sized Maine cemeteries older than this one.

Bagaduce Music Lending Library

At the foot of Greene's Hill in Blue Hill is one of Maine's more unusual institutions, a library where you can borrow by mail or in person from a collection of more than one million scores and pieces of sheet music (3 Music Library La., Rte. 172, Blue Hill, 207/374-5454, www.bagaducemusic.org, 10 A.M.–3 P.M. Mon.–Fri. or by appointment). Somehow this seems so appropriate for a community that's a magnet for music lovers. Annual membership is $10 ($5 for students). The library publishes catalogs of its holdings or browse online; fees range $1–4 per piece.

Scenic Routes

Parker Point Road (turn off Route 15 at the Blue Hill Library) takes you from Blue Hill to Blue Hill Falls the back way, with vistas en route toward Acadia National Park. For other great views, drive the length of **Newbury Neck,** in nearby Surry, or head west on Route 15/176 toward Sedgwick, Brooksville, and beyond.

RECREATION
Hiking
◖ BLUE HILL MOUNTAIN TRAIL

- Distance: 2 miles round-trip

- Duration: 1.5–2 hours

- Elevation gain: 500 feet

- Effort: Easy to moderate

- Trailhead: Mountain Road, off Route 15 (Pleasant St., Blue Hill)

Mountain seems like a fancy label for a 943-footer, yet Blue Hill stands alone, visible from Camden and even beyond. On a clear day, head for the summit and take in the wraparound view encompassing Penobscot Bay, the hills of Mount Desert, and the Camden Hills. Climb the fire tower and you'll see even more. In mid-June, the lupines along the way are breathtaking; in fall, the colors are spectacular—with reddened blueberry barrens added to the variegated foliage. Go early in the day; it's a popular hike. A short loop on the lower slopes takes only half an hour. Take Route 15 (Pleasant Street) to Mountain Road. Turn right and go 0.8 mile to the trailhead (on the left) and the small parking area (on the right). You can also walk (uphill) the mile from the village. The trail can be squishy, especially in the wooded sections, so you'll want rubberized or waterproof shoes or boots.

Blue Hill Heritage Trust

This fine organization (258 Mountain Rd., Blue Hill, 207/374-5118, www.bhht.org, 9 A.M.–5 P.M. Mon.–Fri.) works hard at preserving the region's landscape. It also presents a **Walks and Talks series,** with offerings such as kayaking by preservation land along Eggemoggin Reach, a full moon hike up Blue Hill Mountain, and walks through other trust properties, such as 800-acre Kingdom Woods Conservation Preserve and Cooper Farm at Caterpillar Hill. Many include talks by knowledgeable folks on complementary topics. Check the website, call, or stop by to see what's up when you're in town.

Blue Hill Town Park

At the end of Water Street is a small park with a terrific view. It has a small pebble beach, picnic tables, and a creative playground. Pick up picnic fixings at Blue Hill Hearth or the Blue Hill Co-op and bring it all here.

MERI Center

A great way to raise kids' environmental consciousness is to enroll them in summer activities sponsored by the MERI Center for Marine Studies (55 Main St., Blue Hill, 207/374-2135, www.meriresearch.org). MERI (the Marine Environmental Research Institute), a nonprofit marine-ecology organization, schedules **island excursions** and **"eco-cruises"** geared to different age groups

($20–60); cruises are limited to 12 passengers. The MERI Center has a touch tank, a marine lending library, and exhibit space. On Fridays at 10 A.M. it hosts a story hour for preschoolers that concludes with a craft program. There's also a Thursday evening Ocean Environment lecture series, offered once or twice monthly. During fall, winter, and spring, MERI offers a Friday evening movie night, with refreshments, during which it screens marine-related films. It's free, but a $3 donation is appreciated. MERI is open Monday–Saturday all year.

Blue Hill Falls

A favorite spot for *experienced* kayakers and canoeists is Blue Hill Falls, which churns with white water when the tide turns. Check for times of high and low tide. Roadside parking is illegal, but the law is too often ignored. The Route 175 bridge is narrow, and cars often stop suddenly as they come over the hill, so be particularly cautious here.

Unless you own a boat or know a member of the Kollegewidgwok Yacht Club in East Blue Hill (207/374-5581), there's no sailing out of Blue Hill. If you're trailing a boat, use the public boat launch down on the harbor. *Kollegewidgwok,* incidentally, is a Penobscot Indian word meaning "blue hill on shining green water."

Outfitters

The Activity Shop (61 Ellsworth Rd., Blue Hill, 207/374-3600, www.theactivityshop .com) rents bicycles for $35 per week and Old Town canoes and kayaks at rates beginning at $135 per week. Daily rentals are possible if the equipment isn't all rented. Rates include delivery within a reasonable area.

Anna and Barry Snow's **Rocky Coast Outfitters** (Grindleville Rd., Blue Hill, 207/374-8866, rockycoastoutfitters@verizon. net) rents bikes ($75) and canoes and kayaks ($135 single, $155 tandem) by the week. Delivery is free.

ENTERTAINMENT AND EVENTS

Variety and serendipity are the keys here. Check local calendar listings and tune in to radio station **WERU** (89.9 and 102.9 FM, www.weru .org), the peninsula's own community radio; there might be announcements of concerts by resident pianist Paul Sullivan or the Bagaduce Chorale, maybe a contra dance or a tropical treat from Carl Chase's Atlantic Clarion Steel Band or Flash in the Pans Community Band, perhaps a production by the New Surry Theatre, or lectures and readings at the library. The George Stevens Academy (www.georgestevensacademy .org) also presents a free summer lecture series.

Music

Since 1922, chamber-music students have been spending summers perfecting their skills and demonstrating their prowess at the **Kneisel Hall Chamber Music School** (Pleasant St., Rte. 15, Blue Hill, 207/374-2811, www.kneisel .org). Faculty concerts run Friday evenings at 8:15 P.M. and Sunday afternoons at 4 P.M. late June to late August. The concert schedule is published in the spring, and reserved-seating tickets ($30 inside, $20 on the veranda outside; nonrefundable) can be ordered by phone. There is also unreserved tent seating ($10) for the Friday evening and Sunday afternoon concerts. Other opportunities to hear the students and faculty exist, including young artist concerts, children's concerts, open rehearsals, and more. Check the website for details. Kneisel Hall is about a half mile from the center of town.

Chamber music continues in winter thanks to the volunteer **Blue Hill Concert Association** (P.O. Box 140, Blue Hill 04614). Five concerts are performed between January and March at the Blue Hill Congregational Church, a handsome, traditional New England spired edifice on Main Street.

During the summer months, the **Vanderkay Summer Music Series** (207/374-2891) brings a variety of sounds, from folk to jazz, to the Blue Hill Congregational Church.

Fairs and Festivals

WERU's annual **Full Circle Fair** takes place at the Blue Hill Fairgrounds (Rte. 172, north of downtown Blue Hill). Expect world music, good food, crafts, and socially and environmentally progressive talks.

On Labor Day weekend, the **Blue Hill Fair** (Blue Hill Fairgrounds, Rte. 172, Blue Hill, 207/374-9976) is one of the state's best agricultural fairs. Besides the food booths (good-for-you fare competes with fried dough), a carnival, fireworks, sheepdog trials, and live musical entertainment, you can check out the blue-ribbon winners for finest quilt, beefiest bull, or largest squash.

SHOPPING

Boutiques, antiques, galleries, and even two downtown bookstores make shopping a pleasure in Blue Hill, especially if you're looking for the unusual. (See the sidebar *Gallery Hopping in Blue Hill.*)

Antiques

Blue Hill Antiques (8 Water St., Blue Hill, 207/374-2199 or 207/326-4973) specializes in 18th- and 19th-century French and American furniture, attracting a high-end clientele. The same patrons seek out neighboring Brad Emerson's **Emerson Antiques** (33 Water St., Blue Hill, 207/374-5140), concentrating on early Americana, such as hooked rugs and ship models.

Books

Blue Hill's literate population manages to support two full-service, year-round, independent bookstores. The selection is excellent at **Blue Hill Books** (26 Pleasant St., Rte. 15, Blue Hill, 207/374-5632, www.bluehillbooks.com), thanks to knowledgeable owners Nick Sichterman and Mariah Hughs. The store organizes an "authors series" during the summer.

Around the corner, ever-helpful Bonnie Myers provides free advice on the region with a money-back guarantee at **North Light Books** (58 Main St., Blue Hill, 207/374-5422). It's a delight to browse, the children's book selection is terrific, and out back is Blue Hill Hearth, with all sorts of treats.

Eclectic Shops

In downtown Blue Hill is Peter Stremlau's **New Cargoes** (49 Main St., Blue Hill, 207/374-3733, www.newcargoes.com), following somewhat in the Pier One/Crate & Barrel tradition and offering furniture, linens, notecards, candles, and on and on. The shop name is apt—new things arrive on a regular basis. Bet you can't walk out of here empty-handed.

Wine

Blue Hill Wine Shop (138 Main St., Blue Hill, 207/374-2161), tucked into a converted horse barn, carries more than 800 wines, plus teas, coffees, and blended tobaccos and unusual pipes for diehard, upscale smokers. Monthly wine tastings (2–5 P.M., last Saturday of the month) are always an adventure.

ACCOMMODATIONS
Inns and Bed-and-Breakfasts

On a quiet side street close to town, **☕ The Blue Hill Inn** (40 Union St., Rte. 177, Blue Hill, 207/374-2844 or 800/826-7415, www .bluehillinn.com, $155–205, mid-May–late Oct.) has been welcoming guests since 1840. If you're trying to imagine a classic country inn, this would be it. It came into new hands midsummer 2007, but new owner Sarah Pebworth planned few changes—still, it's wise to inquire about particulars. Stay here if you enjoy antiques, warm hospitality, and classic New England inns; don't stay if you're on a tight budget or have small children. Ten rooms and a suite, all with air-conditioning, boast real chandeliers, four-posters, down comforters, fancy linens, and braided and Oriental rugs; three have wood-burning fireplaces. The third-floor garret suite is ideal for families with well-behaved children; a first-floor room

GALLERY HOPPING IN BLUE HILL

Perhaps it's Blue Hill's location near the renowned Haystack Mountain School of Crafts. Perhaps it's the way the light plays off the rolling countryside and onto the twisting coastline. Perhaps it's the inspirational landscape. Whatever the reason, numerous artists and artisans call Blue Hill home, and top-notch galleries are abundant.

Judith Leighton knows contemporary art, and her **Leighton Gallery** (24 Parker Point Rd., Blue Hill, 207/374-5001, www.leightongallery.com) is a real treat. The airy two-story-plus-basement space, in a converted barn on the Parker Point Road, is filled with a great selection. Be sure to visit the equally spectacular and extremely peaceful backyard sculpture garden. The **Liros Gallery** (14 Parker Point Rd., Blue Hill, 207/374-5370 or 800/287-5370, www.lirosgallery.com) has been dealing in Russian icons since the mid-1960s. Prices are high, but the icons are fascinating. The gallery also carries Currier & Ives prints, antique maps, and 19th-century British and American paintings. From here, it's a short walk to **Blue Hill Bay Gallery** (Main St., Blue Hill, 207/374-5773, www.bluehillbaygallery.com), which represents contemporary artists in various media.

Don't miss **Jud Hartmann** (79 Main St., at Rte. 15, Blue Hill, 207/374-991, www.judhartmanngallery.com). The spacious, well-lit, in-town gallery carries Hartmann's limited-edition bronze sculptures of the Woodland Tribes of the Northeast. Hartmann often can be seen working on his next model in the gallery – a real treat. He's a wealth of information about his subjects, and he loves sharing the mesmerizing stories he's uncovered during his meticulous research.

Also on Main Street are two other fun, artsy gallery-shops. **Handworks Gallery** (48 Main St., Blue Hill, 207/374-5613, www.handworksgallery.org) sells a range of fun, funky, utilitarian and fine-art crafts by more than 50 Maine artists and craftspeople, including jewelry, furniture, rugs, wall hangings, and clothing. Browse **North Country Textiles** (Main St., Blue Hill, 207/374-2715, www.northcountrytextiles.com) for fine hand-woven throws, rugs, clothing, and table linens, as well as other fine crafts.

Pottery is abundant in Blue Hill. **Rackliffe Pottery** (Rte. 172, Blue Hill, 207/374-2297 or 888/631-3321, www.rackliffepottery.com), noted for its vivid blue wares, also makes its own glazes and has been producing lead-free pottery since 1969.

About two miles from downtown is another don't-miss. **Mark Bell Pottery** (Rte. 15, Blue Hill, 207/374-5881), in a tiny building signaled only by a small roadside sign, is the home of exquisite, award-winning porcelain by the eponymous potter. It's easy to understand why his wares were displayed at the Smithsonian Institution's Craft Fair as well as at other juried shows across the country. The delicacy of each vase, bowl, or piece is astonishing, and the glazes are gorgeous. Twice each summer he has kiln openings – must-go events for collectors and fans. Call for details.

Richard Taylor fires his functional and decorative stoneware in wood-fired kilns at **Richard Taylor Ceramics** (Rte. 15, Sedgwick, 207/359-2374, www.taylorpots.com), located four miles south of Blue Hill.

is wheelchair-accessible. Rear rooms overlook the extensive cutting garden, with chairs and a hammock. The library, dominated by a Persian chandelier, has masses of local information. Refreshments are available all day; superb hors d'oeuvres are served 6–7 P.M. in two elegant parlors or the garden. Off-season, two adjacent suite in the elegant Cape House

are available for $175. Sarah will arrange for Kneisel Hall tickets, kayak rentals, cruises, massages, and more.

What's old is new at **Barncastle** (125 South St., Blue Hill, 207/374-2330, www.barncastlehotel.com, $125–175), a late-19th-century Shingle-style cottage that's listed on the National Register of Historic Places. It opens to a two-story foyer with a split stairway and balcony. Rooms and suites open off the balcony, and all are spacious and minimally decorated and have contemporary accents, including flat-screen TVs, Wi-Fi, a fridge, and a microwave. Rates include a continental breakfast. Downstairs is a tavern, serving pizza, salads, and sandwiches.

Two miles north of town, at Marcia and Jim Schatz's **Blue Hill Farm Country Inn** (Rte. 15, Blue Hill, 207/374-5126, www.bluehillfarminn.com, $95–115), a huge refurbished barn serves as the gathering spot for guests. If the weather is lousy, you can plop down in front of the oversize woodstove and start in on cribbage or other games. Antique sleigh-runner banisters lead to the barn's seven second-floor rooms—all with private baths, skylights, hooked rugs, and quilts. A wing of the farmhouse has seven more rooms with shared baths and more quilts. Breakfast is generous continental. During the summer, visiting jazz or classical musicians sometimes entertain in the barn, but it all eases off early. On the inn's 48 acres are well-cleared nature trails, an 18th-century cellar hole, and a duck pond. The inn is open year-round.

Seasonal Rentals

Weekly rentals (or longer) can pay off if you have a large family or are planning a group vacation. The Blue Hill Peninsula has lots of rental cottages, camps, and houses, but the trick is to plan well ahead. This is a popular area in summer, and many renters sign up for the following year before they leave town. For information, contact Sandy Douvarjo of **Peninsula Property Rentals** (15 Main St., Blue Hill, 207/374-2428, www.peninsulapropertyrentals.com).

FOOD
Local Flavors

Picnic fare and pizza are available at **Merrill & Hinckley** (11 Union St., Blue Hill, 207/374-2821, 6 A.M.–9 P.M. Mon.–Fri., 7 A.M.–9 P.M. Sat., 8 A.M.–8 P.M. Sun.), a quirky, 150-year-old, family-owned grocery and general store.

The **Blue Hill Co-op and Café** (4 Ellsworth Rd., Rte. 172, Blue Hill, 207/374-2165, cafe 207/374-8999, 8 A.M.–7 P.M. Mon.–Fri., to 6 P.M. Sat., 9 A.M.–5 P.M. Sun.) sells organic and hydroponic produce and grains, cheeses, organic coffee, and more. Breads are terrific here. Breakfast items, sandwiches, salads, and soups—many with ethnic flavors—are available in the café, and there's a seating area. The staff will pack it all up for a picnic, too.

Tucked behind North Light Books is **Blue Hill Hearth** (58 Main St., Blue Hill, 207/610-9090, 8 A.M.–7 P.M. Mon.–Fri., to 6 P.M. Sat., 10 A.M.–4 P.M. Sun.), operated by the former owner of Pain de Famille. The breads are outstanding, but you can also pick up ready-made sandwiches, soups, and irresistible baked goods. Vegan options are available and these are made using completely separate utensils.

Local gardeners, farmers, and craftspeople peddle their wares at the **Blue Hill Farmers Market** (9–11:30 A.M. Sat.) It's a particularly enduring market, well worth a visit. Demonstrations by area chefs and artists are often on the agenda. The major effort is late June through September at the Blue Hill Fairgrounds (Rte. 172, just north of downtown).

Here's a double hit: **Bird Watcher's Store & Cafe** (37 Water St., Blue Hill, 207/374-3740, 9:30 A.M.–5:30 P.M. Mon.–Sat., to 2 P.M. Sun.). Half the store is a café, serving baked goods, soups, salads, and sandwiches; the other half is a store catering to birders. There are a few tables inside, others are on the waterview deck, or just take it down the street to the park. It's all inexpensive.

Another possibility for a no-frills, inexpensive breakfast or lunch is **The Pantry** (27 Water St., 207/374-2229, 7:20 A.M.–2 P.M. Mon.–Fri., 8 A.M.–2 P.M. Sat. and Sun.). The homemade chowder earns raves.

Family Friendly

The first choice for families or anyone looking for a casual but very good meal is **The Blue Moose** (50 Main St., Blue Hill, 207/374-3274, www.thebluemooserestaurant.com,

10 A.M.–3 P.M. and 5–9 P.M. Mon.–Thurs., 10 A.M.–9:30 P.M. Fri., 7:30 A.M.–3 P.M. and 5–9:30 P.M. Sat., to 9 P.M. Sun.), which has a wide-ranging menu and welcomes kids. Most choices are in the $8–12 range. Kids'/small appetite menu ranges $3–5. It's open daily for breakfast, lunch, and dinner.

Very popular with local folks is **Marlintini's Grill** (83 Mines Rd., Blue Hill, 207/374-2500, 11:30 A.M.–9 P.M. daily, bar stays open until 1 A.M.). Inside, half is a sports bar, the other half a restaurant. You can sit in either, but the bar side can get raucous. Best bet: the screened-in porch. Expect burgers, salads, sandwiches, fried foods, and a kids' menu. The portions are big; the service is good; the food is reliable.

Just south of town is **Barncastle** (125 South St., Blue Hill, 207/374-2300, www.barncastle-hotel.com, 11:30 A.M.–8 P.M. daily), serving a creative selection of wood-fired pizzas as well as sandwiches, subs, paninis, calzones, and salads in a lovely Shingle-style cottage. There are vegetarian and vegan options. Most choices are less than $10. Expect to wait for a table; this is one popular spot.

Fine Dining

Here's a double header: ☾ **Arborvine** and **The Vinery** (Main St., Blue Hill, www .arborvine.com). For a light lunch or dinner, head to The Vinery (207/374-2441, 5:30–9 P.M. Wed.–Sun.), a piano and wine bar bistro in a beautifully renovated barn, with live music. Entrées are $7–14. If you're up for something fancier, make reservations at the Arborvine (207/374-2119, 5:30–9 P.M. Tues.–Sun. summer, Fri.–Sun. winter), a conscientiously renovated two-century-old Cape-style house with four dining areas, each with a different feel and understated decor. Most entrées are in the $25–30 range. The wine list is small but select. Chef/owner John Hikade and his wife, Beth, operate both establishments.

Anneliese Riggall brought new life to the historic old forge building that hangs over the river downtown, reopening it as ☾ **The Wescott Forge** (66 Main St., Blue Hill, 207/374-9909, www.thewescottforge.com,

11:30 A.M.–2:30 P.M. and 5:30–9 P.M. Wed.–Sat.). The menu changes weekly but might include entrées such as seaweed-seared yellowfin tuna and Moroccan chickpea stew. Most run $16–25. The upstairs is a casual lounge; the downstairs has an easy elegance, all highlighted by beautiful forged accent pieces (check out the stairway railing). Request a table on the porch, and you'll be serenaded by the water rushing (or, during dry spells, at least attempting to gurgle) underneath as you dine.

Seafood

For lobster, fried fish, and the area's best lobster roll, head to **The Fish Net** (Main St., Blue Hill, 207/374-5240, 11 A.M.–8 P.M. Mon.–Thurs., until 9 P.M. Fri. and Sat.), an inexpensive, mostly take-out joint on the eastern end of town. Dine outdoors on picnic tables or inside.

It's not easy to find **Perry's Lobster Shack** (1076 Newbury Neck Rd., Surry, 207/667-1955, 11 A.M.–7 P.M. daily), but for a no-frills,

The Wescott Forge restaurant hangs over a stream.

true lobster shack experience, make the effort. Expect lobster, rolls, corn, chips, mussels, and clams and a few picnic tables on the water's edge. Do call first.

INFORMATION AND SERVICES
Information
The **Blue Hill Peninsula Chamber of Commerce** (15 Main St., Box 520, Blue Hill 04614, 207/374-3242, www.bluehillpeninsula.org) is stocked with brochures, menus, and other information on Blue Hill and the surrounding area. You can also find information (although some is outdated) at www

.bluehillme.com. One interesting feature on this site is a section on wildlife sightings.

At the **Blue Hill Public Library** (5 Parker Point Rd., 207/374-5515, www.bluehill.lib.me.us, Mon., Tues., Wed., and Fri. 10 A.M.–6 P.M., Thurs. 10 A.M.–8 P.M., Sat. 10 A.M.–2 P.M.), ask to see the suit of armor, which *may* have belonged to Magellan. The library also sponsors a summer lecture series.

Public Restrooms
Public buildings with restrooms are the Blue Hill Town Hall (Main St.), Blue Hill Public Library (Main St.), and Blue Hill Memorial Hospital (Water St.).

Brooklin, Brooksville, and Sedgwick

Nestled near the bottom of the Blue Hill Peninsula and surrounded by Castine, Blue Hill, and Deer Isle, are the often-missed towns Brooklin, Brooksville, and Sedgwick. This area offers superb hiking, kayaking, and sailing, plus historic homes and unique shops, studios, lodgings, and personalities.

The best-known town is Brooklin (pop. 841), thanks to two magazines: *The New Yorker* and *WoodenBoat*. Wordsmiths extraordinaire E. B. and Katharine White "dropped out" to Brooklin in the 1930s and forever afterward dispatched their splendid material for *The New Yorker* from here. (The Whites' former home, a handsome colonial not open to the public, is on Route 175 in North Brooklin, 6.5 miles from the Blue Hill Falls bridge.) In 1977, *WoodenBoat* magazine moved its headquarters to Brooklin, where its 60-acre shoreside estate attracts builders and dreamers from all over the globe.

Nearby Brooksville (pop. 911) drew the late Helen and Scott Nearing, whose *Living the Good Life* made them role models for back-to-the-landers. Their compound now verges on "must-see" status. Buck's Harbor, a section of Brooksville, is the setting for *One Morning*

in Maine, one of Robert McCloskey's beloved children's books.

The oldest of the three towns is Sedgwick (pop. 1,175; incorporated in 1789), which once included all of Brooklin and part of Brooksville. Now wedged *between* Brooklin and Brooksville, it includes the hamlet of Sargentville, the Caterpillar Hill scenic overlook, and a well-preserved complex of historic buildings. The influx of pilgrims continues in this area—many of them artist wannabes bent on capturing the spirit that has proved so enticing to creative types.

SIGHTS
WoodenBoat Publications
On Naskeag Point Road, off Route 175 1.2 miles from downtown Brooklin, a small sign marks the turn to the world headquarters of the WoodenBoat empire (Naskeag Point Rd., Brooklin, 207/359-4651, www.woodenboat.com). Buy magazines, books, clothing, and all manner of nautical merchandise at the handsome new store (www.woodenboatstore.com), stroll the grounds, or sign up for one of the dozens of one- and two-week spring, summer, and fall courses in seamanship, navigation,

Shop for all things wooden-boat-related at the WoodenBoat School's shop.

boatbuilding, sailmaking, marine carving, and more. Special courses are geared to kids, women, pros, and all-thumbs neophytes; the camaraderie is legendary, and so is the cuisine. Tuition varies by course and duration. School visiting hours are 8 A.M.–5 P.M. Monday–Saturday June–October.

Historic Sights

The **East Penobscot Bay Blue Hill Peninsula History Tour** (www.eastpenobscothistory.org), a brochure available both online and locally, provides information on nine local history museums.

Now used as the museum and headquarters of the Sedgwick-Brooklin Historical Society, the 1795 **Reverend Daniel Merrill House** (Rte. 172, Sedgwick, 207/359-8958, 2–4 P.M. Sun. in July and Aug., or by appointment, donations welcomed) was the parsonage for Sedgwick's first permanent minister. Inside the house are period furnishings, old photos, toys, and tools; a few steps away are a restored 1874 schoolhouse, an 1821 cattle pound (for corralling

wandering bovines), and a hearse barn. Pick up a brochure during open hours and guide yourself around the buildings and grounds. The **Sedgwick Historic District,** crowning Town House Hill, comprises the Merrill House and its outbuildings, plus the imposing 1794 Town House and the 23-acre Rural Cemetery (the oldest headstone dates from 1798) across Route 172.

The **Brooksville Historical Society Museum** (Rte. 176, Brooksville, 207/326-8987, 1–4 P.M. Wed. and Sun.) houses a collection of nautical doodads, farming implements, blacksmith tools, and quilts in a converted boathouse. The museum also plans to open a Farmhouse Museum.

The Good Life Center

Forest Farm, home of the late Helen and Scott Nearing, is now the site of The Good Life Center (372 Harborside Rd., Harborside, 207/326-8211, www.goodlife.org). Advocates of simple living and authors of 10 books on the subject, the Nearings created a trust to perpetuate their farm and philosophy. Resident

E. B. WHITE: SOME WRITER

Every child since the mid-1940s has heard of E. B. White – author of the memorable *Stuart Little, Charlotte's Web,* and *Trumpet of the Swan* – and every college kid for decades has been reminded to consult his copy of *The Elements of Style.* But how many realize that White and his wife, Katharine, were living not in the Big City but in the hamlet of North Brooklin, Maine? It was Brooklin that inspired Charlotte and Wilbur and Stuart, and it was Brooklin where the Whites lived very full creative lives.

Abandoning their desks at *The New Yorker* in 1938, Elwyn Brooks White and Katharine S. White bought an idyllic saltwater farm on the Blue Hill Peninsula and moved here with their young son, Joel, who became a noted naval architect and yacht builder in Brooklin before his untimely death in 1997. Andy (as E. B. had been dubbed since his college days at Cornell) produced 20 books, countless essays and letters to editors, and hundreds (maybe thousands?) of "newsbreaks" – those wry clipping-and-commentary items sprinkled through each issue of *The New Yorker.* Katharine continued wielding her pencil as the magazine's standout children's-book editor, donating many of her review copies to Brooklin's Friend Memorial Library, one of her favorite causes. (The library also has two original Garth Williams drawings from *Stuart Little,* courtesy of E. B., and a lovely garden dedicated to the Whites.) Katharine's book, *Onward and Upward in the Garden,* a collection of her *New Yorker* gardening pieces, was published in 1979, two years after her death.

Later in life, E. B. sagely addressed the young readers of his three award-winning children's books: "Are my stories true, you ask? No, they are imaginary tales, containing fantastic characters and events. In real life, a family doesn't have a child who looks like a mouse; in real life, a spider doesn't spin words in her web. In real life, a swan doesn't blow a trumpet. But real life is only one kind of life – there is also the life of the imagination. And although my stories are imaginary, I like to think that there is some truth in them, too – truth about the way people and animals feel and think and act."

E. B. White died on October 1, 1985, at the age of 86. He and Katharine and Joel left large footprints on this earth, but perhaps nowhere more so than in Brooklin.

---

stewards lead tours 1–5 P.M. Thursday–Tuesday in July and August (Thurs.–Mon. the rest of the year, but call ahead); suggested donation is $5. Copies of Nearing books are available for purchase. From mid-June to mid-September, Monday night meetings (7 P.M.) feature free programs by gardeners, philosophers, musicians, and other guest speakers; call for details and locations. Occasional work parties, workshops, and conferences are also on the center's schedule. The farm is on Harborside Road, just before it turns to dirt. From Route 176 in Brooksville, take Cape Rosier Road and go 8 miles, passing Holbrook Island Sanctuary. At the Grange Hall, turn right and follow it 1.9 miles to the end. Turn left onto Harborside Road and continue 1.8 miles to Forest Farm, across from Orr Cove.

◀ Four Season Farm

About a mile from the Nearings' place is Four Season Farm (609 Weir Cove Rd., Harborside, 207/326-4455, www.fourseasonfarm.com, 1–5 P.M. Mon.–Sat.), the lush organic farm owned and operated by internationally renowned gardeners Eliot Coleman and Barbara Damrosch. Both have written numerous books and articles and starred in TV gardening shows. Coleman is a driving force behind the use of the word "authentic" to mean "beyond organic," demonstrating a commitment to food that is local, fresh, ripe, clean, safe, and nourishing. He's also successfully pioneered a "winter harvest," developing environmentally sound and economically viable systems for extending fresh vegetable production from October through May in cold-weather climates. After

BLUE HILL PENINSULA

26 years, Coleman and Damrosch reopened their farm to the public in 2005. It's a treat for the eyes as well as the taste buds—you've never seen such gorgeous produce. New in 2008 was a gallery featuring works by Cape Rosier artists. To find the farm, continue past The Good Life Center and look for a sign on the left.

Scenic Routes

No one seems to know how **Caterpillar Hill** got its name, but its reputation comes from a panoramic vista of water, hills, and blueberry barrens—with a couple of convenient picnic tables where you can stop for lunch, photos, or a ringside view of sunset and fall foliage. From the 350-foot elevation, the views take in Walker Pond, Eggemoggin Reach, Deer Isle, Swans Island, and even the Camden Hills. The signposted rest area is on Route 175/15, between Brooksville and Sargentville, next to a small gift shop; watch out for the blind curve when you pull off the road. If you want to explore on foot, the one-mile Cooper Farm Trail loops through the blueberry barrens and woods. From the scenic overlook, walk down to and out Cooper Farm Road to the trailhead. Between Sargentville and Sedgwick, Route 175 offers nonstop views of Eggemoggin Reach, with shore access to the Benjamin River just before you reach Sedgwick village.

Two other scenic routes are **Naskeag Point,** in Brooklin, and **Cape Rosier,** the westernmost arm of the town of Brooksville. Naskeag Point Road begins off Route 175 in "downtown" Brooklin, heads down the peninsula for 3.7 miles past the entrance to WoodenBoat Publications, and ends at a small shingle beach (limited parking) on Eggemoggin Reach. Here you'll find picnic tables, a boat launch, a seasonal toilet, and a marker commemorating the 1778 Battle of Naskeag, when British sailors came ashore from the sloop *Gage,* burned several buildings, and were run off by a ragtag band of local settlers. Cape Rosier's roads are poorly marked, perhaps deliberately, so keep your DeLorme atlas handy. The Cape Rosier loop takes in Holbrook Island Sanctuary, Goose Falls, the hamlet of Harborside, and plenty of water and island views. Note that some roads are unpaved, but they usually are well maintained.

RECREATION
(Holbrook Island Sanctuary State Park

In the early 1970s, farsighted benefactor Anita Harris donated to the state 1,230 acres in Brooksville that would become the Holbrook Island Sanctuary (207/326-4012, www.state.me.us/doc/parks, free). From Route 176, between West Brooksville and South Brooksville, head west on Cape Rosier Road, following brown-and-white signs for the sanctuary. Trail maps and bird checklists are available in boxes at trailheads or at park headquarters. The easy Backshore Trail (about 30 minutes) starts from a parking lot on Indian Bar Road, or go back a mile and climb the steepish Summit Trail (trailhead on main park road) to **Backwoods Mountain** for the best vistas. Other trails include the 1.1-mile easy Beaver Flowage trail, which circles around a beaver flowage; parking along the main park road is available at trailheads on either end. Other attractions include shorefront picnic tables and grills, four old cemeteries, and super birding during spring and fall migrations. Leashed pets are allowed, but no bikes on the trails and no camping. The park is officially open May 15–October 15, but the access road and parking areas are plowed for cross-country skiers.

Or you can take a picnic to the **Bagaduce Ferry Landing,** in West Brooksville off Route 176, where there are picnic tables and cross-river vistas toward Castine.

A small, relatively little-known beach is Brooklin's **Pooduck Beach.** From the Brooklin General Store (on Route 175), take Naskeag Point Road about half a mile, watching for the Pooduck Road sign on the right. Drive to the end. You can also launch a sea kayak into Eggemoggin Reach here.

Biking

Bicycling in this area is hazardous. Roads here are particularly narrow and winding, with poor shoulders. If you're determined to pedal, consider either the Naskeag Scenic Route or around Cape Rosier, where traffic is light.

Sailing

Ensign-class Antares day sailboats are available for rental at **Buck's Harbor Marine** (on the dock, South Brooksville, 207/326-8839, www.bucksharbor.com). The full-keel boats rent for $135 per day. Buck's Harbor also charters bareboat sail and power yachts to qualified skippers.

EXCURSION BOATS

Captain LeCain Smith sails *Perelandra* (Buck's Harbor, 207/326-4279), a 44-foot steel-hulled ketch, in the waters of Penobscot Bay. Rates begin at $40 per person for a two-hour trip and increase to $60 per person for a four-hour sail. The boat holds a maximum of six passengers.

Sail on a Maine windjammer with Captain Bill Brown on the **Summertime** (207/326-8485 or 800/562-8290, www.schoonersummertime .com), which sails from various locations on the peninsula, including Brooksville, Sedgwick, and Stonington in spring and fall. Six-hour sails are $40 per adult, $20 per child younger than 12; three-hour sails are $18 and $9. The schooner takes a maximum of 20 guests.

Charter a day sail through Jericho and Penobscot Bays with Captain Bruce Fowler aboard the *Emily Marshall*, a 35-foot gaff-headed yawl, with **Brooklin Charters** (207/359-2384, www.brooklincharters.com). A four- to six-hour day sail costs $350, and the boat can hold up to six passengers. The rate includes a light snack and soft drinks, but you'll need to bring your own lunch. An overnight charter is $850, including meals and snacks.

ENTERTAINMENT AND EVENTS

◖ Flash in the Pans Community Steel Band

If you're a fan of steel-band music, check to see where and when Carl Chase's Flash in the Pans Community Steel Band (207/374-2172,

www.peninsulapan.org) is performing. It usually performs somewhere on the peninsula on Monday nights (7:30–9 P.M.) mid-June–early September. The musicians aren't professionals, but you'd never know it. Local papers carry the summer schedule for the nearly three-dozen-member band, which performs in various area locales and deserves its devoted following. Admission is usually a small donation to benefit a local cause. It's worth every penny to join the fun.

Eggemoggin Reach Regatta

Wooden boats are big attractions hereabouts, so when a huge fleet sails in for this regatta (usually the first Saturday in August, but the schedule can change), crowds gather. Don't miss the parade of wooden boats. The best locale for watching the regatta itself is on or near the bridge to Deer Isle or near the Eggemoggin Landing grounds on Little Deer Isle. For details, see www.erregatta.com.

SHOPPING

Most of these businesses are small, owner-operated shops, which means they're often catch-as-catch-can. If you want to be sure they're open, call ahead.

Antiques

When you need a slate sink, a clawfoot tub, brass fixtures, or a Palladian window, **Architectural Antiquities** (52 Indian Point La., Harborside, 207/326-4938, www.arch-antiquities.com), on Cape Rosier, is just the ticket—a restorer's delight. Prices are reasonable, and they'll ship your purchases. Open all year by appointment; ask for directions when you call. Antiques dating from the Federal period through the turn of the 20th century are the specialties at **Sedgwick Antiques** (Rte. 172, Sedgwick, 207/359-8834). Early furniture, handmade furniture, and a full range of country accessories and antiques can be found at **Thomas Hinchcliffe Antiques** (Cradle Knolls La., off Rte. 176, West Sedgwick, 207/326-9411). Painted country furniture, decoys, and unusual nautical items are specialties at **Old Cove Antiques** (Rte. 15, Reach Rd., Sargentville, 207/359-2031 or 207/359-8585), a weathered-gray shop across from the Eggemoggin Country Store.

Artists' and Artisans' Galleries

Small studio-galleries pepper Route 175 (Reach Road) in Sedgwick and Brooklin; most are marked only by small signs, so watch carefully. First up is **Eggemoggin Textile Studio** (off Rte. 175/Reach Rd., Sedgwick, 207/359-5083, www.chrisleithstudio.com), where the incredibly gifted Christine Leith weaves scarves, wraps, hangings, and pillows with hand-dyed silk and wool; the colors are magnificent. You might catch her at work on the big loom in her studio shop, a real treat.

Continue along the road to find **Reach Road Gallery** (Reach Rd., Sedgwick, 207/359-8803), where Holly Meade sells her detailed woodblock prints, as well as prints from the children's books she's illustrated.

Only a few doors down is **Mermaid Woolens** (Reach Rd., Sedgwick, 207/359-2747), source of Elizabeth Coakley's wildly colorful hand-knit vests, socks, and sweaters. They're pricey but worth every nickel. She also does seascape paintings. She's a clever woman.

Continue over to Brooklin, where Virginia G. Sarsfield handcrafts paper products, including custom lampshades, calligraphy papers, books, and lamps at **Hand Papers** (Rte. 175 at Center Harbor Rd., Brooklin, 207/359-8345, www.handmadepapersonline.com).

Just a bit farther is **Naskeag Gallery** (Rte. 175, Brooklin, 207/359-4619), where talented glass artist Sihaya Hopkins has a studio gallery.

In Brooksville, more treasures await on Route 176. You'll need to watch carefully for the sign marking the long drive to **Paul Heroux and Scott Goldberg Pottery** (2032 Coastal Rd./Rte. 176, Brooksville, 207/326-9062). The small gallery is a must for pottery fans.

Continue southwest on 176 and watch closely for signs for **Bagaduce Forge** (140 Ferry Rd., Brooksville, 207/326-9676); this isn't easy to find. Joseph Meltreder is both blacksmith and

farrier, and his small forge, with big views, is the real thing.

Books

Here's a find for book lovers: In a tiny building behind Sedgwick Antiques is Bill Henderson's **Pushcart Press Bookstore** (Rte. 172, Sedgwick, 207/359-2427), billed as "the world's smallest bookstore." It's a trove of literary fiction, both used (paperbacks $2, hardbacks $5) and new, including editions of the *Pushcart Prize: Best of the Small Presses* annual series.

Wine and Gifts

Three varieties of English-style hard cider are specialties at **The Sow's Ear Winery** (Rte. 176 at Herrick Rd., Brooksville, 207/326-4649), a minuscule operation in a funky, gray-shingled building. Winemaker Tom Hoey also produces sulfite-free blueberry, chokecherry, and rhubarb wines; he'll let you sample them all. Ask to see his cellar, where everything happens. No credit cards accepted.

Nautical books, T-shirts, gifts, food (including homemade bread and key lime pie), and boat gear line the walls and shelves of the shop at **Buck's Harbor Marine** (on the dock, South Brooksville, 207/326-8839, www.bucksharbor.com).

If you're looping around Cape Rosier, stop by **Olde Crows Cottage** (23 Harborside Rd., Harborside, 207/326-0500, www.oldecrowscottage.com) for a well-chosen selection of gifts, holiday items, sweets, home-baked treats, and tea and coffee.

ACCOMMODATIONS
Bed-and-Breakfasts

A few steps up from the half-mile-long shorefront at the Oakland House Seaside Resort's cottage colony is **Shore Oaks Seaside Inn** (435 Herrick Rd., Brooksville, 207/359-8521 or 800/359-7352, www.oaklandhouse.com/inn.html), a handsome, green-trimmed 1907 stone mansion carefully restored to its Arts-and-Crafts heritage. No in-room phones, no TV, no noise; just peaceful bliss. Hang out for too long in the common rooms or the veranda

© TOM NANGLE

The gazebo-capped dock in front of Shore Oaks is a pleasant place to while away the hours.

rockers and you might never leave; this place is magical and restorative. Ten first-, second-, and third-floor rooms (seven with private baths) top out at $125–320 for a double, $95–170 for a single, plus service charge, including breakfast; for an additional $25 per person (a steal!), include a four-course dinner. Shoulder-season rates (May and late Oct.) are less expensive but still include breakfast.

In 2005, Joe Moore turned an 1874 mansard-roofed Victorian in what passes as downtown Brooklin into the **Dragonflye Inn** (Naskeag Point Rd., Brooklin, 207/359-808, www.dragonflyeinn.com, $145). It's a casual put-your-feet-up kind of place, with a special invitation issued to WoodenBoat school students, gallery fans (lots of work by local artisans), and kayakers. Moore's goal is sustainability: Towels and linens are made from organic cotton; soaps and shampoos are local and all natural; cleaning products are all natural, biodegradable, and earth friendly. Plans call for the roof to be replaced with faux slate comprising recycled auto tires and recycled bottle

insulation and power generated on-site from the sun or the wind. Breakfast is light continental. Wi-Fi is available. Bicycles are provided for guests. Kayak trips can be arranged, including local shuttles.

Best known for its restaurant and pub, **The Brooklin Inn** (Rte. 175, Brooklin, 207/359-2777, www.brooklininn.com, $105–135 with breakfast; add $10 for a one-night stay) also has five comfortable bedrooms; two sharing a bath. It's open year-round.

Cottages

The two operations in this category feel much like informal family compounds—where you quickly become an adoptee. These are extremely popular spots, where successive generations of hosts have catered to successive generations of visitors, and reservations are usually essential for July and August. Many guests book for the following year before they leave. We're not talking fancy; the cottages are old-shoe rustic, of varying sizes and decor. Most of the cottages have cooking facilities, although both colonies include breakfast and dinner in July and August. Both have hiking trails, playgrounds, rowboats, and East Penobscot Bay on the doorstep.

Jim and Sally Littlefield are the enthusiastic fourth-generation hosts at ⟨⟨ **Oakland House Seaside Resort** (435 Herrick Rd., Brooksville, 207/359-8521 or 800/359-7352, www.oaklandhouse.com), a sprawling 50-acre complex of 15 wooded and waterfront cottages, as well as Shore Oaks Seaside Inn. Much of this land, now threaded with hiking trails, was part of the original king's grant to Jim's ancestors, way back in 1765. The Homestead, where meals are served, dates from 1767. Jim is the eighth generation on the property. Weekly rates for a two-person cottage vary by date, but begin around $595 and top off about $1,540, plus service charge, including full breakfast and four-course dinner; lower rates for children. Thursday is lobster picnic night on the beach. The biggest bargains are early May–mid-June and September–October, when meals and housekeeping aren't included. Rowboats are free for guests' use in season, and the staff organizes other boat excursions on request. Also ask about artist workshops—what a perfect location! And wait till you see the gorgeous gardens—enough to warrant a full-time gardener. Two cottages (Lone Pine and Boathouse) are winterized and available all year; the other cottages are closed in winter. Call to ask about last-minute specials and short-term getaway packages.

The fourth generation manages the **Hiram Blake Camp** (220 Weir Cove Rd., Harborside, 207/326-4951, www.hiramblake.com, Memorial Day–late Sept.), but other generations pitch in and help with gardening, lobstering, maintenance, and kibitzing. Thirteen cottages and a duplex line the shore of this 100-acre property, which has been in family hands since before the Revolutionary War. The camp itself dates from 1916. Don't bother bringing reading matter: The dining room has ingenious ceiling niches lined with countless books. Guests also have the use of rowboats. The rate includes home-cooked breakfasts and dinners served family style; lobster is always available at an additional charge. Much of the fare is grown in the expansive gardens. Other facilities include a dock, a recreation room, a pebble beach, and an outdoor chapel. There's a one-week minimum (beginning Sat. or Sun.) in July and August, when cottages go for $600–2,850 a week (including breakfast, dinner, and linens). Off-season rates (no meals or linens, but cottages have cooking facilities) are $630–895 a week. The best chances for getting a reservation are in June and September. Dogs are welcome. No credit cards accepted.

FOOD
Cooking Classes
In summer, chef Terence Janericco (42 Fayette St., Boston, 617/426-7458, or, after July 1, Box 226, Herrick Bay, Brooklin, 207/359-2068, www.terencejanericcocookingclasses.com), author of a dozen cookbooks, moves his cooking school from Boston to Brooklin.

The demonstration-only, three-hour classes are $70 per person, which includes dining on the foods prepared.

Local Flavors
Competition is stiff for lunchtime seats at the **Morning Moon Café** (junction of Rte. 175 and Naskeag Point Rd., Brooklin, 207/359-2373, 7 A.M.–2 P.M. Thurs.–Sun.), mostly because WoodenBoat staffers consider it an annex to their offices. "The Moon" is a friendly hangout for coffee, pizza, or great sandwiches and salads—or order to go.

Across the street from the Morning Moon Café, the **Brooklin General Store** (1 Reach Rd., junction of Rte. 175 and Naskeag Point Rd., Brooklin, 207/359-8817, 5 A.M.–7 P.M. Mon.–Sat. and 7 A.M.–5 P.M. Sun.), vintage 1872, carries groceries, beer and wine, newspapers, take-out sandwiches, and local chatter.

In North Brooksville, where Route 175/176 crosses the Bagaduce River, stands the **Bagaduce Lunch,** named an "American Classic" by the James Beard Foundation in 2008. Owners Judy and Mike Astbury buy local fish and clams. Check the tide calendar and go when the tide is changing; order a clam roll or a hamburger, settle in at a picnic table, and watch the reversing falls. If you're lucky, you might sight an eagle, osprey, or seal. The food is so-so, but the setting is tops. The popular takeout stand (outdoor tables only) is open 11 A.M.–7 or 8 P.M. daily, but closes at 3 P.M. Wednesday from early May to mid-September.

Lunch is the specialty at **Buck's Harbor Market** (Rte. 176, South Brooksville, 207/326-8683, 7 A.M.–7 P.M. Mon.–Fri., 8 A.M.–7:30 P.M. Sat., 8 A.M.–6 P.M. Sun. all year), a low-key, marginally yuppified general store popular with yachties in summer.

Ethnic Fare
Okay, I know it's hard to believe, but **El El Frijoles** (41 Caterpillar Rd./Rte. 15, Sargentville, 207/359-2486, www.elelfrijoles.com, 11 A.M.–8 P.M. Wed.–Sun.) gets good marks for its California-style empanadas,

burritos, and tacos. It's a small, somewhat funky, mostly take-out operation with a few seats inside and out. It's housed in a barn behind Coast to Coast Fine Arts.

Casual Dining

Behind the Buck's Harbor Market is **Buck's Restaurant** (6 Cornfield Hill Rd., Brooksville, 207/326-8688, 5:30–8:30 P.M. daily, $10–24), an outpost of fiery colors calmed down by white tablecloths. Respected chefs Jonathan Chase and Nancy McMillan create comfort foods with a dash of creativity. Choices range from burgers to grilled veal chop.

Country Inn Dining

An 1865 farmstead is the setting for the **Rusticator Restaurant** at the Oakland House Seaside Resort (435 Herrick Rd., Brooksville, 207/359-8521), open to the public by reservation from mid-June to mid-September for its daily breakfast buffet, Sunday brunch, Thursday night shorefront lobster picnic, and superb dinners, with two seatings nightly. In 2008, Oakland House partnered with Richard Hansen, of Cleonice, an Ellsworth restaurant with a stellar reputation, and the results are even better than anyone expected. The menu here emphasizes food "of the place and of the time," which means local foods rooted in tradition. It may sound dowdy, but it's not; the fare is fresh, fabulous, and quite creative. Entrée range is $19–27. The dining rooms are in the property's original farmstead, which dates from 1865. At dinner, families dine in a separate room from couples, keeping everyone happy. Reservations are a good idea, but if it's full or you're arriving between seatings, ask about The Coop, a back-of-the-house shared table. Oh, and if lavender custard is on the menu for dessert, order it!

All the meat and produce is organic and most is sourced locally at **The Brooklin Inn** (Rte. 175, Brooklin, 207/359-2777, www.brooklininn.com, 5:30–9 P.M. daily). The chef tries to know "who raised, grew, picked, or caught all the food," and all the fish are wild, free swimming, and locally caught. Entrées are $18–32; a children's menu is available. Downstairs an **Irish pub** (5:30–10 P.M. daily) serves burgers, Guinness stew, pizza, and, on Fridays, all the fresh baked haddock you can eat for $10.

The chef seems to change annually at **The Lookout** (455 Flye Point Rd., off Rte. 175, North Brooklin, 207/359-2188, www.thelookoutinn.biz, 5:30–8 P.M. Mon.–Fri. and most Sat.). The inn and restaurant, at the tip of Flye Point, have a knockout view of Herrick Bay (as long as there's no fog). It's been owned and operated by Flye family descendants for more than 110 years (judging from the look of the place, little has changed in that period); ask about its current reputation.

INFORMATION AND SERVICES

The best source of information about the region is the **Blue Hill Peninsula Chamber of Commerce** (15 Main St., Blue Hill, 207/374-3242, www.bluehillpeninsula.org). Another possibility, although sorely outdated when I checked, is the website of the **East Penobscot Bay Association** (www.penobscotbay.com). Request a copy of its handy flyer/map. Once you've landed on Route 172 or 175, pop into one of the small roadside convenience stores and start asking questions. The clerks—often the owners—know it all cold, and these markets always have a fair share of local color. Of course, they won't object if you also buy something while you're there.

Libraries

The public libraries in this area are small and welcoming, but hours are limited. **Friends Memorial Library** (Rte. 175, Brooklin, 207/359-2276) has a lovely Circle of Friends Garden, with benches and a brick patio. It's dedicated to the memory of longtime Brooklin residents E. B. and Katharine White. Also check out **Free Public Library** (1 Town House Rd., Rte. 176, Brooksville, 207/326-4560) and Sedgwick Village Library (Main St., Sedgwick, 207/359-2177). Most have Wi-Fi and restrooms.

BLUE HILL PENINSULA

Castine

Castine (pop. 1,343) is a gem—a serene New England village with a tumultuous past. It's on the tip of a cape, surrounded by water on three sides, including the entrance to the Penobscot River, which made it a strategic defense point. Once beset by geopolitical squabbles, saluting the flags of three different nations (France, Britain, and Holland), its only crises now are local political skirmishes. This is an unusual community, a National Historic Register enclave that many people never find. The town celebrated its bicentennial in 1996. If you're staying in Blue Hill or even Bar Harbor, spend a day here. Or bunk here and use Castine as a base for exploring here and beyond. Either way, you won't regret it.

Originally known as Fort Pentagoet, Castine received its current name courtesy of Jean-Vincent d'Abbadie, Baron de St.-Castin. A young French nobleman manqué who married a Wabanaki princess named Pidiwamiska, d'Abbadie ran the town in the second half of the 17th century and eventually returned to France.

A century later, in 1779, occupying British troops and their reinforcements scared off potential American seaborne attackers (including Colonel Paul Revere), who turned tail up the Penobscot River and ended up scuttling their more than 40-vessel fleet—a humiliation known as the Penobscot Expedition and still regarded as one of America's worst naval defeats.

When the boundaries of Maine were finally set in 1820, with the St. Croix River marking the east rather than the Penobscot River, the last British Loyalists departed, some floating their homes north to St. Andrews, in New Brunswick, Canada, where they can still be seen today. For a while, peace and prosperity became the bywords for Castine—with lively commerce in fish and salt—but it all collapsed during the California Gold Rush and the Civil War trade embargo, leaving the town down on its luck.

Today a major presence is Maine Maritime Academy, yet Castine remains the quietest imaginable college town. Students in search of a party school won't find it here; naval engineering is serious business.

Of the many historic landmarks scattered around town, one of the most intriguing must be the sign on "Wind Mill Hill," at the junction of Route 166 and State Street:

> On Hatch's Hill there stands a mill. Old Higgins he doth tend it. And every time he grinds a grist, he has to stop and mend it.

In smaller print, just below the rhyme, comes the drama:

> Here two British soldiers were shot for desertion.

Castine indeed has quite a history.

SIGHTS
Castine Historic Tour

To appreciate Castine fully, you need to arm yourself with the Castine Merchants Association's visitors brochure/map (all businesses and lodgings in town have copies) and follow the numbers on bike or on foot. With no stops, walking the route takes less than an hour, but you'll want to read dozens of historical plaques, peek into public buildings, shoot some photos, and perhaps even do some shopping.

Highlights of the tour include the late-18th-century **John Perkins House,** moved to Perkins Street from Court Street in 1969 and restored with period furnishings. It's open in July and August for guided tours (2–5 P.M. Sun. and Wed.; admission $5).

Next door, **The Wilson Museum** (107 Perkins St., Castine, 207/326-8545, www.wilsonmuseum.org, 2–5 P.M. Tues.–Sun. late May–late Sept., free), founded in 1921, contains an intriguingly eclectic two-story collection of prehistoric artifacts, ship models, dioramas, baskets, tools, and minerals assembled over a lifetime by John Howard Wilson, a geologist/anthropologist who first visited Castine in 1891 (and died in 1936). Among the exhibits are Balinese masks, ancient oil lamps, cuneiform tablets, Zulu artifacts, pre-Inca pottery, and assorted local findings. Don't miss this, even though it's a bit musty—that is changing thanks to a recent multi-million-dollar bequest. (The only comparable Maine institutions are the Nylander Museum, in Caribou, and the L. C. Bates Museum, in Hinckley.)

Open the same days and hours as the Perkins House are the **Blacksmith Shop,** where a smith does demonstrations, and the **Hearse House,** containing Castine's 19th-century winter and summer funeral vehicles. Both are free admission. The **Castine Scientific Society** (P.O. Box 196, Castine 04421), a private foundation, operates the five-building complex (the fifth being the Doudiet House, where the administrative offices are located).

At the end of Battle Avenue stands the 19th-century **Dyce's Head Lighthouse,** no longer operating; the keeper's house is owned by the town. Alongside it is a public path (signposted; pass at your own risk) leading via a wooden staircase to a tiny patch of rocky shoreline and the beacon that has replaced the lighthouse.

The highest point in town is **Fort George State Park,** site of a 1779 British fortification. Nowadays, little remains except grassy earthworks, but there are interpretive displays and picnic tables.

Main Street, descending toward the water, is a feast for historic architecture fans. Artist Fitz Hugh Lane and author Mary McCarthy once lived in elegant houses along the elm-lined street (neither building is open to the public). On Court Street between Main and Green stands turn-of-the-20th-century **Emerson Hall,** site of Castine's municipal offices. Since Castine has no official information booth, you may need to duck in here (it's open weekdays) for answers to questions.

Across Court Street, **Witherle Memorial Library,** a handsome early-19th-century building on the site of the 18th-century town jail, looks out on the Town Common. Also facing

MAINE MARITIME ACADEMY

The state's only merchant-marine college (and one of only seven in the nation) occupies 35 acres in the middle of Castine. Founded in 1941, the academy awards undergraduate and graduate degrees in such areas as marine engineering, ocean studies, and marina management, preparing a student body of about 750 men and women for careers as ship captains, naval architects, and marine engineers.

The academy owns a fleet of 60 vessels, including the historic research schooner *Bowdoin,* flagship of Arctic explorer Admiral Donald MacMillan, and the 499-foot training vessel *State of Maine,* berthed down the hill at the waterfront. In 1996 and 1997, the *State of Maine,* formerly the U.S. Navy hydrographic survey ship *Tanner,* underwent a $12 million conversion for use by the academy. It is still subject to deployment, and, in 2005, the school had to quickly find alternative beds for students using the ship as a dormitory when it was called into service in support of rescue and rebuilding efforts after Hurricane Katrina in New Orleans. Midshipmen conduct free 30-minute tours of the vessel on weekdays in summer (about mid-July to late August). The schedule is posted at the dock, or call 207-326-4311 to check; photo ID is required.

Weekday tours of the campus can be arranged through the admissions office (207/326-2206 or 800/227-8465 outside Maine, www.mainemaritime.edu). Campus highlights include the three-story Nutting Memorial Library, in Platz Hall (open daily during the school year, weekdays in summer and during vacations); the Henry A. Scheel Room, a cozy oasis in Leavitt Hall containing memorabilia from late naval architect Henry Scheel and his wife, Jeanne; and the well-stocked bookstore (Curtis Hall, 207/326-9333, 8 A.M.-3 P.M. Mon.-Fri.).

© TOM NANGLE

The Abbott School is now home to the very active Castine Historical Society.

the Common are the Adams and Abbott Schools, the former still an elementary school. The **Abbott School** (10 A.M.–4 P.M. Tues.–Sat. and 1–4 P.M. Sun. July–Labor Day, reduced schedule spring and fall, free but donations welcome), built in 1859, has been carefully restored for use as a museum and headquarters for the **Castine Historical Society** (207/326-4118, www.castinehistoricalsociety.org). A big draw at the volunteer-run museum is the 24-foot-long Bicentennial Quilt, assembled for Castine's 200th anniversary in 1996. The historical society, founded in 1966, organizes lectures, exhibits, and special events (some free) in various places around town.

On the outskirts of town, across the narrow neck between Wadsworth Cove and Hatch's Cove, stretches a rather overgrown canal (signposted "British Canal") scooped out by the occupying British during the War of 1812. Effectively severing land access to the town of Castine, the Brits thus raised havoc, collected local revenues for eight months, then departed for Halifax with enough funds to establish Dalhousie College (now Dalhousie University). Wear waterproof boots to walk the canal route; the best time to go is at low tide.

If a waterfront picnic sounds appealing, buy the fixings at Bah's Bakehouse and settle in on the grassy earthworks along the harborfront at **Fort Madison,** site of an 1808 garrison (then Fort Porter) near the corner of Perkins and Madockawando Streets. The views from here are fabulous, and it's accessible all year. A set of stairs leads down to the rocky waterfront.

RECREATION
Witherle Woods

This 152-acre preserve, owned by Maine Coast Heritage Trust (maps available via email from info@mcht.org), is a popular walking area with a maze of trails and old woods roads leading to the water. Many Revolutionary War–era relics have been found here; if you see any, do *not* remove them. Access to the preserve is via a shaded old woods road on Battle Avenue, located between the water district property (at the end of the wire fence) and The Manor's exit driveway and diagonally across from La Tour Street.

🛶 Sea Kayaking

Castine Kayak Adventures (15 Sea St., Castine, 207/326-9045, www.castinekayak .com), based at Dennett's Wharf, is spearheaded by Master Maine Sea Kayak Guide Karen Francoeur. Known locally as "Kayak Karen," she's particularly adept with beginners, delivering wise advice from start to end. All skill levels are accommodated. Three-hour half-day trips are $55; six-hour full-day tours are around $110 including lunch. Two-hour sunset tours are $40. Friday nights, there are special two-hour phosphorescence tours, under the stars (weather permitting), for $55 per person; full-moon and meteor-shower paddles are also offered. Longer trips are available for $125 per day. If you have your own boats, call Karen for advice; she knows these waters. She

Plan a picnic at Fort Madison, which dates from the early 1800s.

also offers instruction for all levels as well as a Maine Sea Kayak Guide course.

Swimming

Backshore Beach, a crescent of sand and gravel on Wadsworth Cove Road (turn off Battle Avenue at the Castine Golf Club), is a favorite saltwater swimming spot, with views across the bay to Stockton Springs. Be forewarned, though, that ocean swimming in this part of Maine is not for the timid. The best time to try it is on the incoming tide, after the sun has had time to heat up the mud. At mid- to high tide, it's also the best place to put in a sea kayak. Park along the road.

Golf and Tennis

The **Castine Golf Club** (200 Battle Ave., Castine, 207/326-8844, www.castinegolf-club.com) dates to 1897, when the first hole required a drive from a 30-step-high mound. Redesigned in 1921 by Willie Park Jr., the nine-hole course is open May 15 to October 15. Starting times are seldom required, and greens fees are $20 for 9 holes, $35 for 18. The club also has four Har-Tru tennis courts; for court

reservations ($30/hour adult, $15/hour junior), call 207/326-9348.

HARBOR TOUR

Several times weekly, Captain Melissa Terry's **Belfast Bay Cruises** (207/322-5530, www .belfastbaycruises.com, $13 adult, $6 ages 5–15) offers a one-hour Castine Harbor Tour aboard the *Good Return,* passing by Dyce's Head Lighthouse and Holbrook and Nautilus Islands.

ENTERTAINMENT AND EVENTS

Possibilities for live music include **Dennett's Wharf** (15 Sea St., Castine, 207/326-9045), where some performances require a ticket, and **The Reef** (on the wharf, tucked underneath the bank facing the parking area and harbor).

The Castine Town Band often performs free concerts on the Common. Check www.castine .org for its schedule.

The community-based **Castine Arts Association** (www.castinearts.org) presents concerts, exhibits, workshops, and other performances at various locations around town each summer.

The Wilson Museum (107 Perkins St.,

207/326-8545, www.wilsonmuseum.org) frequently schedules concerts, lectures, and demonstrations.

Celebrate Castine (www.celebratecastine .com) is a town-wide event in mid-July.

SHOPPING

Shopping isn't Castine's strong point, unless you're shopping for real estate.

Antiques, Gifts, and Galleries

Tucked into the back of the 1796 Parson Mason House, one of Castine's oldest residences, **Leila Day Antiques** (53 Main St., Castine, 207/326-8786, www.leiladayantiques.com) is a must for anyone in the market for folk art, period furniture, quilts, and unusual contemporary Shard pottery (from Dover-Foxcroft). Access is via a lovely, flower-lined walkway.

Traditional American craftwork is sold at **Castine Historical Handworks** (9 Main St., Castine, 207/326-4460, www.castinehistoricalhandworks.com). Among the selections are pottery, textiles, and folk art.

Oil paintings by local artists Joshua and Susan Adam are on view at **Adam Gallery** (140 Battle Ave., Castine, 207/326-8272, www .adamgalleryonline.com).

Women's clothing and jewelry are the specialties at **SaraSara's** (1 Main St., Castine, under the bank, 207/326-4442), a branch of Sara Billings's popular Blue Hill shop.

Books

Driving toward Castine on Route 166, watch on your right for a small sign for **Dolphin Books and Prints** (314 Castine Rd., Castine, 207/326-0888, www.dolphin-book.com), where Pete and Liz Ballou have set up their antiquarian business with more than 10,000 books, as well as framed prints and art.

In downtown Castine, a block up from the waterfront, **The Compass Rose Bookstore and Café** (3 Main St., 207/326-9366 or 800/698-9366, www.compassrosebooks .com) carries an ever-expanding selection of new books, cards, games, and prints chosen by owner Sharon Biggie. In the back of the

shop is a café serving hot and cold drinks (espresso, too), soup, sandwiches, and tasty baked goods.

Furniture

Benchmade Windsor chairs are the specialty at **M&E Gummel Chairworks** (600 Shore Rd., Castine, 207/326-8122, www.gummelchairworks.com). The father-and-son team utilizes 18th-century methods when handcrafting the chairs, Colonial dining tables, and bowls, one at a time in their 1895 barn workshop.

ACCOMMODATIONS

Inns

Castine is blessed with three fine traditional inns. This is not the place to come if you require in-room phones, air-conditioning, or fancy bathrooms. Rather, the pace is relaxed and the accommodations reflect the easy elegance of a bygone era.

The three-story Queen Anne–style **◖ Pentagöet Inn** (26 Main St., Castine, 207/326-8616 or 800/845-1701, www.pentagoet.com, May–late Oct., $115–245 in peak season) is the perfect Maine summer inn, right down to the perennial gardens, the lace curtains billowing in the breeze, the soft floral wallpapers, and the intriguing curiosities that accent, but don't clutter, the rooms. Congenial innkeepers Jack Burke, previously with the foreign service, and Julie Van de Graaf, a pastry chef, took over the century-old inn in 2000 and have given it new life, upgrading rooms and furnishing them with Victorian antiques, adding handsome gardens, and carving out a niche as a dining destination. Their enthusiasm for the area is contagious. The inn's 16 rooms are spread out between the main house (with Wi-Fi service) and the adjoining house. A hot buffet breakfast and afternoon refreshments are provided. Jack holds court in Passports Pub (chock-full of vintage photos and prints and exotic antiques) every afternoon, advising guests on activities and opportunities. A shopping nook in the dining room features unusual little gifts, many bird-related. Borrow one of the inn's bikes and explore around town or simply walk—the Main Street location is convenient to everything Castine offers. Better yet, just sit on the wraparound porch and take it all in.

The three-story **Castine Inn** (33 Main St., Castine, 207/326-4365, www.castineinn.com, May–late Oct., $105–300) earns a stellar rating for its stunning semiformal gardens and extremely helpful staff. The 16 rooms and three suites, updated from their 1890s origins, vary in style, from simple Maine to simple elegance (if you're looking for bathrooms with whirlpool tubs, this is the place). Lots of interesting artwork is everywhere and there's a very simpatico and unpretentious air. Rates include a continental breakfast; unfortunately the dining room no longer serves dinner except by special arrangement.

Once the summer "cottage" of Arthur Fuller, a South Boston Yacht Club commodore, **The Manor Inn** (76 Battle Ave., Castine, 207/326-4861 or 877/626-6746, www.manor-inn.com, $115–275) overlooks town and harbor from five mostly wooded acres elevated above Battle Avenue. Though the atmosphere is informal, there are lots of elegant architectural touches. Nancy Watson and Tom Ehrman took over in 1998, upgrading beds, linens, and furniture. They've expanded the dining room and continue to improve the inn each year. The 14 second- and third-floor rooms are an eclectic mix—some with canopied beds and fireplaces, all with private baths. A separate guest building has a TV and games as well as Nancy's yoga studio; guests are welcome to join her morning Iyengar classes (Mon., Wed., and Fri.; $12 drop-in fee). Wi-Fi is available. The trailhead for Witherle Woods is close by. The inn is often the site of weddings and receptions; ask before you book unless you don't mind being the odd man out. It's open mid-February to late December.

Rental Properties

Several Castine real estate agents have listings for summer cottage rentals; start with **Saltmeadow Properties** (7 Main St., Castine, 207/326-9116, www.saltmeadowproperties .com) or **Castine Realty** (5 Main St., Castine, 207/326-9392, www.castinerealty.com).

FOOD
Local Flavors

New owners in 2009 are breathing new life into **Castine Variety** (1 Main St., Castine, 207/326-8625, 7 A.M.–8 P.M. in summer, reduced hours in off season), a village institution since 1920. Go for the vintage feeling and the inexpensive breakfasts, lunches, and ice cream.

Another institution is **❰ The Breeze** (Town Dock, Castine, 207/326-9200, 11 A.M.–7 P.M. daily), a waterfront takeout stand with reliably good basics like burgers, fried clams, and ice cream. You can't beat the location or the view.

When everything else in town is closed, your best bet for late night eats is **The Reef** (8 Sea St., Castine, on the wharf, tucked underneath the bank facing the parking area and harbor, 207/326-4040, 11 A.M.–1 A.M.). Best bets are the hand-tossed gourmet pizzas, available in three sizes and 10 varieties, as well as a design-your-own choice. There are plenty of pub-style favorites, too. The atmosphere is more bar than restaurant, with a pool table in the back and a small stage area for live entertainment.

Casual Dining

Here's a doubleheader: **Bah's Bakehouse** (26 Water St., Castine, 207/326-9510, www .bahsworld.com, 7 A.M.–5 P.M. daily) and, sharing the same location, **Stella's Jazz Nocturnal** (207/326-9710, 5–11 P.M. Tues.–Sun., food service 5–9 P.M.). Upstairs is Bah's, a higgledy-piggledy eatery of three rooms and a deck at the end of an alleyway tucked between Main and Water Streets. Its slogan is "creative flour arrangements," and creative it is. Stop here for coffee, cold juices, pastries, interesting snacks and salads, homemade soups, wine or beer, good sandwiches, and, if you're lucky, fish cakes. Be forewarned: If it's crowded, go elsewhere—the kitchen is quickly overwhelmed and service can be slow to frustrating. Underneath the deck is Stella's, an intimate dining room and

© TOM NANGLE

Craving fried clams or a lobster roll? The Breeze is the place.

lounge where live jazz is performed Thursday through Sunday.

On a warm summer day, it's hard to find a better place to while away a few hours than **Dennett's Wharf** (15 Sea St., Castine, 207/326-9045, 11 A.M.–9 P.M. daily May–mid Oct.), next to the Town Dock. It's a colorful barn of a place with an outside deck and front-row windjammer-watching seats in summer. Service is leisurely; don't dine here if you're in a hurry. New owners in 2008 have rearranged the place a bit and gussied up the menu (and the prices; $9–40).

The Pine Cone Pub at The Manor Inn (76 Battle Ave., Castine, 207/326-4861) serves a light menu, with such choices as Caesar salad and fish-and-chips.

Fine Dining

Jazz music plays softly and dinner is by candlelight at the ◖ **Pentagöet** (26 Main St., Castine, 207/326-8616 or 800/845-1701, www.pentagoet.com, opens at 6 P.M. daily July and Aug., Mon.–Sat. May, June, Sept., and Oct.).

In fine weather, you can dine on the porch. Choices vary from roasted *loup de mer* to slow-cooked lamb shank, or simply make a meal of small plates, such as lamb lollipops and crab cakes and a salad. Don't miss the lobster bouillabaisse or the chocolate *budino*, a scrumptious warm Italian pudding that melts in your mouth (a must for chocoholics). Can't make up your mind? Order the Taste of the Pentagöet sampling platter ($45), with tasting portions of the most popular dishes. Most entrées are in the $18–29 range.

The bi-level dining room at **The Manor Inn** (76 Battle Ave., Castine, 207/326-4861, 6–8:30 P.M. Tues.–Sat. in summer, Thurs.–Sat. in the off season) overlooks the gardens and lawn. Dinner is served from an extensive menu accented with Asian tastes, Indian curries, and other world flavors, accompanied by home-baked breads, and always including vegetarian choices (most entrées $16–24). Reservations are essential on weekends and for the annual Fourth of July pig roast. It's open from Valentine's Day to late December.

© TOM NANGLE

Stop into Castine Variety for a quick bite to eat.

INFORMATION AND SERVICES

Castine has no local information office, but all businesses and lodgings in town have copies of the Castine Merchants Association's visitors brochure/map. For additional information, go to the **Castine Town Office** (Emerson Hall, 67 Court St., Castine, 207/326-4502, www.castine.me.us, 8 A.M.–3:30 P.M. Mon.–Fri.).

Libraries

Check out **Witherle Memorial Library** (41 School St., 207/326-4375, www.witherle.lib.me.us). Also accessible to the public is the Nutting Memorial Library, in Platz Hall on the Maine Maritime Academy campus.

Public Restrooms

Castine has public restrooms on the town dock, at the foot of Main Street.

BLUE HILL PENINSULA

DEER ISLE AND ISLE AU HAUT

After weaving your way down the Blue Hill Peninsula and crossing the soaring pray-as-you-go bridge to Little Deer Isle, you've entered the realm of island living. Sure, bridges and causeways connect the points, but the farther down you drive, the more removed from civilization you'll feel. The pace slows; the population dwindles. Fishing and lobstering are the mainstays, lobster boats rest near many homes, and trap fences edge properties.

Deer Isle is an artists' and artisans' colony, in equal parts due to the inspiring scenery and to the inspirational Haystack Mountain School of Crafts. Top-notch galleries and working studios are found throughout the island.

Deer Isle is also home to numerous small preserves, ideal for easy hiking and bird-watching, and its bevy of nearby islands beckon sea kayakers.

While dreamers and summer rusticators are plentiful, Stonington is first and foremost a working waterfront dominated by lobster and fishing boats and the remnants of once-active granite quarrying operations. It's also the jumping-off point for trips to Isle au Haut, an offshore gem that's gained fame thanks to author Linda Greenlaw.

The biggest attraction on Isle au Haut is a remote section of Acadia National Park that's raw and rugged, beautiful, even breathtaking in parts. It's not as dramatic as the Mount Desert Island section, but it seduces visitors with its simplicity, peacefulness, and lack of cars. On the trails that hug the granite shoreline and climb the forested hills, perhaps more

© TOM NANGLE

HIGHLIGHTS

◖ **Haystack Mountain School of Crafts:** Don't miss an opportunity to visit this internationally renowned craft school with an award-winning architectural design in a stunning setting (page 198).

◖ **Arts and Crafts Galleries:** Given Haystack's presence and the inspiring scenery, it's no surprise to find dozens of fabulously talented artisans on Deer Isle (page 200).

◖ **Edgar Tennis Preserve:** Serene views and pleasant places to picnic are reasons enough to hike the easy trails (page 203).

◖ **Barred Island Preserve:** Bring binoculars to sight nesting eagles on the island (page 204).

◖ **Sea Kayaking:** Paddle between the plentiful islands off Stonington and into hidden coves (page 205).

◖ **Guided Island Tours:** Captain Walter Reed knows these waters and is an expert on the flora and fauna (page 207).

◖ **Acadia National Park:** Isle au Haut's limited access makes this remote section of the park truly special. It's unlikely you'll have to share the trails – or the views – with more than a couple other souls (page 214).

LOOK FOR ◖ TO FIND RECOMMENDED SIGHTS, ACTIVITIES, DINING, AND LODGING.

than in any other section of the park, you can feel truly removed from civilization.

PLANNING YOUR TIME

If your ultimate destination is the section of Acadia National Park on Isle au Haut, the drive down Deer Isle serves to help disconnect you from the mainland. To reach the park's acreage on Isle au Haut, after wending your way through Little Deer Isle and Deer

Isle, you'll board the Isle au Haut ferryboat for the 45-minute trip down Merchant Row to the island. In summer, you can go directly to the park's Duck Harbor landing; other months, it's a hike through the woods.

Deer Isle and Isle au Haut are inexorably linked yet distinctly separate and very different. Both seduce visitors with their rugged independence and undeveloped landscapes. Deer Isle's main town of Stonington is a metropolis compared to Isle au Haut (about 1,200 souls versus fewer than 70). The sidewalks roll up relatively early in Stonington, but there's not much even in the way of pavement on Isle au Haut. Deer Isle has stepped tentatively into the 21st century; Isle au Haut remains pretty much in the 20th—and the early 20th at that. (Let it be said, though, that electricity came to Isle au Haut in 1970; telephone service soon followed—although cellular service is spotty at best.)

Deer Isle

"Deer Isle is like Avalon," wrote John Steinbeck in *Travels with Charley,* "it must disappear when you are not there." Deer Isle (the name of both the island and its midpoint town) has been romancing authors and artisans for decades, but it's unmistakably real to the quarrymen and fishermen who've been here for centuries. These long-timers are a sturdy lot, as even Steinbeck recognized: "I would hate to try to force them to do anything they didn't want to do."

Early-18th-century maps show no name for the island, but by the late 1800s, nearly 100 families lived here, supporting themselves first by farming, then by fishing. In 1789, when Deer Isle was incorporated, 80 local sailing vessels were scouring the Gulf of Maine in pursuit of mackerel and cod, and Deer Isle men were circling the globe as yachting skippers and merchant seamen. At the same time, in the once-quiet village of Green's Landing (now called Stonington), the shipbuilding and granite industries boomed, spurring development, prosperity, and the kinds of rough hijinks typical of commercial ports the world over.

Green's Landing became the "big city" for an international crowd of quarrymen carving out the terrain on Deer Isle and nearby Crotch Island, source of high-quality granite for Boston's Museum of Fine Arts, the Smithsonian Institution, a humongous fountain for John D. Rockefeller's New York estate, and less showy projects all along the eastern seaboard. The heyday is long past, but the industry did extend into the 20th century (including a contract for the pink granite at President John F. Kennedy's

Arlington National Cemetery gravesite). Today, Crotch Island is the site of Maine's only operating island granite quarry.

Measuring about nine miles from north to south (plus another three miles for Little Deer Isle), Deer Isle today has a handful of hamlets (including Sunshine, Sunset, Mountainville, and Oceanville) and two towns—Stonington and Deer Isle—with a population just under 3,000. Road access is via Route 15 on the Blue Hill Peninsula. A huge suspension bridge, built in 1939 over Eggemoggin Reach, links the Sargentville section of Sedgwick with Little Deer Isle; from there, a sinuous 0.4-mile causeway connects to the northern tip of Deer Isle.

Deer Isle is an artisans' enclave, anchored by the Haystack Mountain School of Crafts. Studios and galleries are plentiful, although many require noodling along back roads to find them. Stonington, a rough-and-tumble fishing port with an idyllic setting, is slowly being gentrified, as more and more galleries and upscale shops open for the summer each season. Long-empty downtown buildings have recently been purchased, and locals are holding their collective breath hoping that any improvements don't change the town too much (although most visitors could do without the car racing on Main Street at night). Already, real estate prices and accompanying taxes have escalated way past the point where many a local fisherman can hope to purchase, and in some cases maintain, a home.

SIGHTS

Sightseeing on Deer Isle means exploring back roads, browsing the galleries, walking the trails,

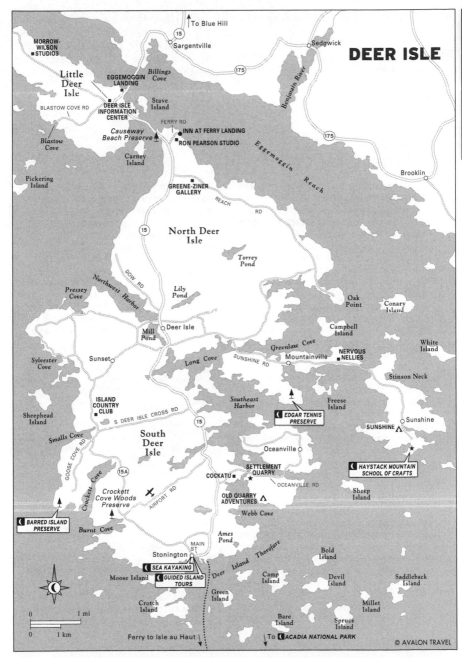

DEER ISLE

© AVALON TRAVEL

hanging out on the docks, and soaking in the ambience.

◖ Haystack Mountain School of Crafts

The renowned Haystack Mountain School of Crafts (Sunshine Rd., Deer Isle, 207/348-2306, www.haystack-mtn.org) in Sunshine (see the sidebar *Getting Crafty*) is open to the public on a limited basis, but if it fits in your schedule, go. Tours of the campus ($5) are given at 1 P.M. every Wednesday. These include a video, viewing works on display, and the opportunity to tour some studios. Free slide programs, lectures, demonstrations, and concerts, presented by faculty and visiting artists, start at 8 P.M.

GETTING CRAFTY

Internationally famed artisans – sculptors and papermakers, weavers and jewelers, potters and printmakers – become the faculty each summer for the unique **Haystack Mountain School of Crafts.** Founded in 1950 by Mary Beasom Bishop (1885–1972) and a group of talented Maine artisans as a studio research and study program, Haystack has grown into one of the top craft schools in the country.

Under the direction of beloved former director Francis Merritt, the school opened its first campus near Haystack Mountain, in Montville, Maine, in 1951. Ten years later, when the state unveiled plans to build a new highway (Route 3) that would bisect that campus, the school relocated to its present 40-acre oceanfront location at the end of the Sunshine Road in Deer Isle. Good move.

You would be hard-pressed to find a more artistically stimulating and architecturally stunning environment. Architect Edward Larrabee Barnes's award-winning campus perfectly complements its dramatic setting. The angular, cedar-shingled buildings are connected via walkways and teaching decks and a central staircase that cascades like a waterfall down the wooded hillside to the rocky coast below. The visual impression is one of spruce and ledge, glass and wood, islands and water.

One thing that makes Haystack work is its diverse student body. Students of all abilities, from beginners through advanced professionals, come from around the globe for the two- to three-week summer sessions, taking weekday classes and enjoying round-the-clock studio access to follow their creative muses. In a recent year, students ranged in age from 18 to 75, and represented professions from retired teacher to physicist. What brings them all here, says current director Stuart Kestenbaum, is the "direct making experience." That experience draws not only those who make but those who collect. For a collector of fine craft, he says, taking a class is a "great way to get insight into the making process; it gives a different relationship with the craft being collected." Each session also includes a range of craft. These may include blacksmithing, drawing, metals, wood, beads, clay, fiber/design, printmaking, glass, weaving, mixed media, paper, and baskets.

© TOM NANGLE

During a tour of the campus, you might see students at work.

on varying weeknights from early June to late August. Perhaps the best opportunities are the End-of-Session auctions, held on Thursday nights every two or three weeks, when you can tour the studios for free 4–6 P.M. and see the works the teachers and students have produced, then return for the auction preview at 7:30 P.M., followed by the auction at 8 P.M. It's a great opportunity to buy craftwork at often very reasonable prices.

Historic Houses and Museums

There's more to the 1830 **Salome Sellers House** (416 Sunset Rd./Rte. 15A, Sunset Village, 207/348-2897, 1–4 P.M. Wed. and Fri. July–mid-Sept., free but donations appreciated) than first meets the eye. A repository of local memorabilia, archives, and intriguing artifacts, it's also the headquarters of the **Deer Isle-Stonington Historical Society.** Sellers, matriarch of an island family, was a direct descendent of Mayflower settlers. She lived to be 108, a lifetime spanning from 1800 to 1908, earning the record for oldest recorded Maine resident. The house contains Sellers's furnishings, and in a small exhibit space in the rear is a fine exhibit of baskets made by Maine's Native American tribes. Behind the house are the archives, heritage gardens, and an exhibit hall filled with nautical artifacts. Bringing all this to life are enthusiastic volunteer guides, many of them island natives. They love to provide tidbits about various items; seafarers' logs and ship models are particularly intriguing, and don't miss the 1920's peapod, the original lobster boat on the island. The house is just north of the Island Country Club and across from Eaton's Plumbing.

Close to the Stonington waterfront, the **Deer Isle Granite Museum** (51 Main St., Stonington, 207/367-6331) was established to commemorate the centennial of the quarrying business hereabouts. The best feature of the small museum is a 15-foot-long working model of Crotch Island, center of the industry, as it appeared at the turn of the 20th century. Flatcars roll, boats glide, and derricks move—it all looks very real. The museum is open in July and August, but it's best to call for current days

and hours of operation. The recommended donation is $5 per family.

Another downtown Stonington attraction is a Lilliputian complex known as the **Miniature Village.** Some years ago, the late Everett Knowlton created a dozen and a half replicas of local buildings and displayed them on granite blocks in his yard. Since his death, they've been restored and put on display each summer in town—along with a donation box to support the upkeep. The village is set up on East Main Street (Route 15), below Hoy Gallery.

Pumpkin Island Lighthouse

A fine view of Pumpkin Island Light can be had from the cul-de-sac at the end of the Eggemoggin Road on Little Deer Isle. If heading south on Route 15, bear right at the information booth after crossing the bridge and continue to the end.

Penobscot East Resource Center

The purpose of the Penobscot East Resource Center, in Stonington (207/367-2708, www.penobscoteast.org), is "to energize and facilitate responsible community-based fishery management, collaborative marine science, and sustainable economic development to benefit the fishermen and the communities of Penobscot Bay and the Eastern Gulf of Maine." Bravo to that! It operates a **Lobster Hatchery** (Stonington Lobster Coop No. 1, 51 Indian Point Rd.), which was constructed by volunteers from the lobster industry in donated space with $25,000 raised locally and a matching grant. Lobster production began in 2006. Guided tours are offered ($10 adults, $5 children); call 207/367-2708 for the schedule.

The man behind both ventures is Ted Ames, who won a $500,000 MacArthur Fellowship "genius grant" in 2005 (see the sidebar *Ted Ames, Genius*).

Flightseeing

Get aloft to spy lighthouses, coves, and islands on a sightseeing tour with **Penobscot Island Air** (207/596-7500, www.penobscotislandair.net), with a base at the Stonington Airport.

TED AMES, GENIUS

That's what Ted Ames, the man behind the Penobscot East Resource Center and the Lobster Hatchery, in Stonington, is. In 2005, he was awarded a $500,000 MacArthur Fellowship. These prestigious "genius grants" are awarded to "talented individuals who have shown extraordinary originality and dedication in their creative pursuits and a marked capacity for self-direction." The foundation credited Ames with fusing "the roles of fisherman and applied scientist in response to increasing threats to the fishery ecosystem resulting from decades of over-harvesting." Criteria for selection are: exceptional creativity, promise for important future advances based on a track record of significant accomplishment, and potential for the fellowship to facilitate subsequent creative work. No question, they found the right guy in Ted Ames.

A humble, soft-spoken man with dogged determination, Ames found little time to bask in the limelight from the award. While he certainly appreciated the money and the attention paid to his causes, the numerous interviews with TV, radio, and newspaper reporters took up valuable time, time he would rather use researching fisheries, collecting data, and devising ways to develop community-based fisheries management.

Ames is a fascinating guy, a combination of fisherman, lobsterman, and research scientist with deep Maine roots. "My family were some of the original settlers of Vinalhaven," he says. His ancestors on his father's side arrived in 1757, on the island off Rockland in Maine's mid-coast. "My mother's side came from Mount Desert." They were the original settlers on Bartlett's Island. When King George told the family to leave, they refused and stayed put. Ames grew up in a fishing family on Vinalhaven and went on to earn a master's degree in biochemistry from the University of Maine. But fishing was in his blood, and he eventu-

◖ ARTS AND CRAFTS GALLERIES

Thanks to the presence and influence of Haystack Mountain School of Crafts, supertalented artists and artisans lurk in every corner of the island. Most galleries are tucked away on back roads, so watch for roadside signs. Many have studios open to the public where you can watch the artists at work. Here's just a sampling.

Little Deer Isle

On Little Deer Isle, don't miss **Morrow Wilson Studios** (455 Eggemoggin Rd., 207/348-6871, www.morrowwilsonstudios.com), Doug and Jennifer Morrow-Wilson's gallery. Doug has turned blacksmithing into an art form, while Jennifer makes paper by hand and uses it in three-dimensional collages that often include internal lighting. Their collaborations are especially nice. Both often open their studios to visitors.

North End of Deer Isle

Although **Ronald Hayes Pearson** has died, his innovative and beautiful jewelry lives on in his eponymous studio and gallery (29 Old Ferry Rd., 207/348-2535), where artisans continue to create his designs under the watchful eye of his wife. Do take time to visit the studio, and be sure to also visit the forge out back where Farrell Ruppert works.

The nearby **Greene-Ziner Gallery** (73 Reach Rd., 207/348-2601, www.melissagreene .com) is a double treat. Melissa Greene turns out incredible painted and incised pottery (she's represented in the Smithsonian's Renwick Gallery) and Eric Ziner works magic in metal sculpture and furnishings. Your budget may not allow for one of Melissa's pots (in the four-digit range), but I guarantee you'll covet them. The gallery also displays the work of several other local artists.

ally returned to the sea as a lobsterman and groundfisherman.

His years on the water gave him firsthand experience watching the changes in Maine's fisheries. He watched Maine's coastal economy change as fishing ports became more gentrified: Commercial piers gave way to oceanfront homes, and marine-related businesses gave way to fancy boutiques. His education combined with his experiences gave him tools and the insight needed to work toward developing new fisheries management practices and supporting fishing communities. He studied fishing patterns in the Gulf of Maine, noting spawning and habitat, and he complemented his research with listening to the stories and experiences of aging fishermen. By doing so, he was able to establish a fishing timeline beginning with historical patterns and following their evolution to current ones.

The Penobscot East Resource Center, which he founded with his wife, Robin, a former marine resources commissioner, and the Lobster Hatchery both are designed as research facilities as well as places for community members and others to learn more about fishing, meet commercial fishermen and women, and learn about their lifestyles in order to help support them and preserve the tradition and the economy. Ames, a master at gaining community support (due perhaps to his impeccable Maine credentials), managed to raise $25,000 from local fishing families, businesses, and individuals in an area not known for wealth.

Ames is using the unrestricted MacArthur Fellows Program money to continue his fisheries research and to develop ways for "community-based groundfishing management to make it sustainable, so coastal fishing communities can survive into the next century. That's a challenge, but we're in the midst of it." No better person to be on the forefront than Ted Ames.

Deer Isle Village Area

One of the island's premier galleries is Elena Kubler's **The Turtle Gallery** (61 N. Deer Isle Rd., Rte. 15, 207/348-9977, www.turtlegallery .com), in a handsome space formerly known as the Old Centennial House Barn (owned by the late Haystack director Francis Merritt) and the adjacent farmhouse. Group and solo shows of contemporary paintings, prints, and crafts are hung upstairs and down in the barn; works by gallery artists are in the farmhouse; and there's usually sculpture in the gardens both in front and in back. It's just north of Deer Isle Village—across from the Shakespeare School, oldest gallery on the island.

When founder Mary Nyburg died, the future of her famed **Blue Heron Gallery** (15 Main St., 207/348-6041, www.blueherondeerisle.com) was blowing in the wind. Supporters, Haystack alumni, and friends rose to the occasion, and now the gallery is secured in a fabulous new space, built on the foundation of what was once the town's hardware store. It remains a retail outlet for the work of the school's internationally renowned faculty—printmakers, blacksmiths, potters, weavers, papermakers, glassworkers, and more.

Just a bit south is **Dockside Quilt Gallery** (33 Church St., 207/348-2531, www.docksidequiltgallery.com), where Nancy Knowlton, her daughter Kelly Pratt, and daughter-in-law Rebekah Knowlton stitch heirloom-quality quilts. Also here are Re-Bears, one-of-a-kind teddy bears handcrafted from vintage furs and fabrics by ninth-generation islander Heather Cormier. Custom quilts and bears can be ordered.

The **Deer Isle Artists Association** (13 Dow Rd., 207/348-2330, www.deerisleartists .com) is headquartered less than a mile northwest of the village. The co-op gallery features two-week exhibits of paintings, prints, drawings, and photos by local pros. Horse fans won't want to miss Penelope Plumb's upstairs gallery, **Equine Art** (207/348-6892, www .penelopeplumb.com).

Just down the street, the **DOW Gallery** (19 Dow Rd., 207/348-6498, www.dowstudiodeerisle.com) shows pottery, metalwork, jewelry, prints, and drawings by Ellen Wieske, Carole Ann Fer, and Susan Webster.

New in 2008 was **RED DOT Gallery** (3 Main St., 207/348-2733, www.reddotgallery .net), showing the works of 10 artists creating in varied media.

Sunshine Road

Now for a bit of whimsy. From Route 15 in Deer Isle Village, take the Sunshine Road east 2.9 miles to **Peter Beerits Sculpture** (600 Sunshine Rd., 800/777-6845, www.nervousnellies.com). The meadows and woods surrounding the studio teem with whimsical wood and metal sculptures, including dragons, Huns on horseback, moose, and more (all for sale). The property is also home to Beerits's other enterprise, **Nervous Nellie's Jams and Jellies,** known for outstandingly creative

condiments; sampling encouraged. The best time to come is from May to early October, 9 A.M.–5 P.M., when the shop operates the ultracasual **Mountainville Café**, serving tea, coffee, and delicious scones—with, of course, Nervous Nellie's products. They're delicious—stock up, because they're sold in only a few shops.

Stonington

Cabinetmaker Geoffrey Warner features his work as well as that of other local woodworkers in rotating shows at **Geoffrey Warner Studio** (431 N. Main St., 207/367-6555, www.geoffreywarnerstudio.com). Warner mixes classic techniques with contemporary styles accented by Eastern, nature-based, and Arts and Crafts accents to create some unusual and rather striking pieces.

Bright and airy **Isalos Fine Art** (Main St., Stonington, 207/367-2700, www.isalosart .com) shows the work of local artists in rotating shows.

Debi Mortenson shows her paintings, photography, and sculptures at **D Mortenson**

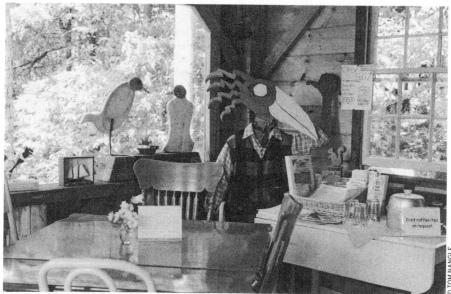

Nervous Nellie's tea room

Gallery (10 W. Main St., 207/367-5875, www
.debimortenson.com) year-round.

The **g.Watson Gallery** (68 Main St.,
207/367-2900) is a fine art gallery representing a number of top-notch artists working in
varied media.

More paintings, many in bold, bright colors, can be found at Jill Hoy's **Hoy Gallery** (E.
Main St., 207/367-2368, www.jillhoy.com).

A bit off the beaten path, but worth seeking
out is the **Siri Beckman Studio** (115 Airport
Rd., 207/367-5037, www.siribeckman.com),
Beckman's home studio-gallery featuring her
woodcuts, prints, and watercolors.

PARKS AND PRESERVES

Foresighted benefactors have managed to set
aside precious acreage for respectful public
use on Deer Isle. The Nature Conservancy
owns two properties, **Crockett Cove Woods
Preserve** and **Barred Island Preserve.** For
information, contact the Conservancy (14
Maine St., Fort Andross, Brunswick 04011,
207/729-5181). The conscientious steward of
other local properties is the **Island Heritage
Trust** (402 Sunset Rd., Sunset, 207/348-2455,
www.islandheritagetrust.org). At the office,
open daily in summer and 1–4 P.M. Wednesday
and Friday in winter, you can pick up notecards, photos, T-shirts, and helpful maps and
information on hiking trails and nature preserves. Proceeds benefit the IHT's efforts; donations are much appreciated.

Settlement Quarry

Here's one of the easiest, shortest walks in the
area, leading to an impressive vista. From the
parking lot on Oceanville Road (just under a
mile off Rte. 15), marked by a carved granite
sign, it's about five minutes to the top of the
old quarry, where the viewing platform (a.k.a.
the "throne room") takes in the panorama—all
the way to the Camden Hills on a good day.
In early August, wild raspberries are an additional enticement. Three short loop trails lead
into the surrounding woods from here. A map
is available in the trailhead box.

◀ Edgar Tennis Preserve

The 145-acre Tennis Preserve, off the Sunshine
Road, has very limited parking, so don't try to
squeeze in if there isn't room; schedule your
visit for another hour or day. But do go, and
bring at least a snack if not a full picnic to enjoy
on one of the convenient rocky outcroppings
(carry-in/carry-out, though). Allow at least
90 minutes to enjoy the walking trails, one of
which skirts Pickering Cove, providing sigh-
producing views. Another trail leads to an old
cemetery. Parts of the trails can be wet, so wear
appropriate footwear. And do bring binoculars
for bird-watching. The preserve is open from
sunrise to sunset. To find it, take the Sunshine
Road 2.5 miles to the Tennis Road, and follow
it to the preserve.

Shore Acres Preserve

This 38-acre preserve, a gift in 2000 from Judy
Hill to the Island Heritage Trust, comprises
old farmland, woodlands, clam flats, a salt
marsh, and granite shorefront. Three walking
trails connect in a 1.5-mile loop, with the Shore
Trail section edging Greenlaw Cove. As you
walk along the waterfront, look for the islands
of Mount Desert rising in the distance and
seals basking on offshore ledges. Do not walk
across the salt marsh, and try to avoid stepping on beach plants. To find the preserve, take
the Sunshine Road 1.2 miles, then bear left at
the fork onto the Greenlaw District Road. The
preserve's parking area is just shy of one mile
down the road. Park only in the parking area,
not on paved road.

Crockett Cove Woods Preserve

Donated to The Nature Conservancy by be-
nevolent, eco-conscious local artist Emily Muir,
98-acre Crockett Cove Woods Preserve is Deer
Isle's natural gem—a coastal fog forest laden
with lichens and mosses. Four interlinked walking trails cover the whole preserve, starting with
a short nature trail. Pick up the helpful map/
brochure at the registration box. Wear rubberized shoes or boots and respect adjacent private
property. The preserve is open from sunrise to

sunset daily all year. From Deer Isle Village, take Route 15A to Sunset Village. Go 2.5 miles to Whitman Road, then to Fire Lane 88. The local phone number is 207/367-2674.

◖ Barred Island Preserve

Owned by the Nature Conservancy but managed by the Island Heritage Trust, Barred Island Preserve was donated by Carolyn Olmsted, grandniece of noted landscape architect Frederick Law Olmsted, who summered nearby. A former owner of Goose Cove Lodge donated an additional 48 acres of maritime boreal fog forest. A single walking trail, one mile in length, leads from the parking lot to the point. At low tide, and when eagles aren't nesting, you can continue out to Barred Island. Another trail skirts the shoreline of Goose Cove, before retreating inland and rejoining with the main trail. From a high point on the main trail, you can see more than a dozen islands, many of which are protected from development, as well as Saddleback Ledge Light, 14 miles distant. To get to the preserve, follow Route 15A to Goose Cove Road, then continue to the parking area on the right. If it's full, return another day.

Holt Mill Pond Preserve

The Stonington Conservation Commission administers this town-owned preserve, where more than 47 bird species have been identified (bring binoculars). It comprises four habitats: upland spruce forest, lowland spruce/mixed forest, freshwater marsh, and saltwater marsh. A self-guided nature trail is accessed from the Airport Road (off Rte. 15 at the intersection with Lily's Café). Look for the nature trail sign just beyond the medical center. The detailed, trail brochure, available at the trailhead registration kiosk, is accented with drawings by noted artist Siri Beckman.

Ames Pond

Ames Pond is neither park nor preserve, but it might as well be. On a back road close to Stonington, it's a mandatory stop in July and August, when the pond wears a blanket of pink and white water lilies. From downtown Stonington, take Indian Point Road east, for just under a mile, to the pond. There's no official parking, so if you're shooting photos, pull off the road as far as possible, respecting private property.

Causeway Beach and Scott's Landing

If you're itching to dip your toes in the water, stop by Causeway Beach along the causeway linking Little Deer Isle to Deer Isle. It's popular for swimming and is also a significant habitat for birds and other wildlife. On the other side of Route 15 is Scott's Landing, with more than 20 acres of fields, trails, and shorefront.

Pine Hill

It's a very steep, rocky climb to the summit of Pine Hill, but for those up to the challenge, the reward is panoramic views of Deer Isle, Eggemoggin Reach, and beyond. Access to the base-area quarry and hill was provided in 2006, thanks to a donation of seven acres by Pat and Kurt Fairchild. To find it, follow Eggemoggin Road on Little Deer Isle 0.2 miles, turning left at the church on Blaistow Cove Road. The parking area is 0.2 miles farther, on the right.

Reach Beach

Yet another property owned by the Island Heritage Trust, the tidal Reach Beach is at Gray's Cove. Take Reach Road, off Route 15, and continue past the Greenlaw District Road. The road turns to dirt, and the beach is on your left.

RECREATION
Guided Walks

The Island Heritage Trust (402 Sunset Rd., Sunset, 207-348-2455, www.islandheritagetrust.org), along with the Stonington and Deer Isle Conservation Commissions, sponsors a Walks and Talks series. Guided walks cover topics such as "Birds and Bird Calls for Beginners," "The Geology of Deer Isle," and

THE MAINE ISLAND TRAIL

In the early 1980s, a "trail" of coastal Maine islands was only the germ of an idea. By the end of the millennium, the **Maine Island Trail Association (MITA)** counted some 4,000 members dedicated to conscientious (i.e., low- or no-impact) recreational use of about 150 public and private islands along 350 miles of Maine coastline between Kennebunkport and Machias.

More than a dozen of these islands (each year, new ones are added and others are subtracted) are in the Acadia region – between Isle au Haut and Schoodic Point. In fact, one of the best island clusters along the entire trail is in the waters off Stonington on Deer Isle.

Access to the trail is only by private boat, and the best choice is a sea kayak, to navigate shallow or rock-strewn coves. Sea kayak rentals are available in Bar Harbor, Southwest Harbor, Blue Hill, and Stonington, and several outfitters offer island tours. (See specific locations for details.) The best source of information is the Maine Association of Sea Kayaking Guides and Instructors (MASKGI), whose members agree to adhere to the Leave No Trace philosophy.

The trail's publicly owned islands – supervised by the state Bureau of Public Lands – are open to anyone; the private islands are restricted to MITA members, who pay $45 per individual or $65 per family per year for the privilege (and, it's important to add, the responsibility). With the fee comes the *Maine Island Trail Guidebook,* providing directions and information for each of the islands. With membership comes the expectation of care and concern. "Low impact" means different things to different people, so MITA experienced acute growing pains when enthusiasm began leading to "tent sprawl."

To cope with and reverse the overuse, MITA has created an "adopt-an-island" program, in which volunteers become stewards for specific islands and keep track of their use and condition. MITA members are urged to pick up trash, use tent platforms where they exist, and continue elsewhere if an island has reached its assigned capacity (stipulated on a shoreline sign and/or in the guidebook).

A superb complement to the *Maine Island Trail Guidebook* is a copy of *Hot Showers!* by Lee Bumsted, a former MITA staff member (see *Suggested Reading*). Recognizing the need for alternating island camping and warm beds (and hot showers), she has almost single-handedly alleviated island stress and strain. Some of the B&Bs and inns listed in her guide give discounts to MITA members.

Membership information is available from the **Maine Island Trail Association** (P.O. Box C, Rockland 04841, 207/596-6456, www.mita.org).

"Migrating Shorebird Walk." Call for information and reservations.

Biking

Unless you're an experienced cyclist, and even then, proceed with extreme caution. The main roads webbing Deer Isle are narrow and winding. That combined with the lack of shoulders and abundant blind corners can make it hazardous for bicycling. Side roads are a better choice, but even there, be proactive and ride single file, keeping far right. For bicycle rentals, see *Sporting Outfitters and Guided Trips.*

◖ Sea Kayaking

With lots of islets and protected coves, the waters around Deer Isle, especially off Stonington, are extremely popular for sea kayaking.

If you sign up with the **Maine Island Trail Association** (Box C, Rockland, www.mita.org, $45 per individual per year, $65 per family), you'll receive a handy manual that steers you to more than a dozen islands in the Deer Isle archipelago where you can camp, hike, and picnic—eco-sensitively, please. Boat traffic can be a bit heavy at the height of summer, so to best appreciate the tranquility of this area, try this in September, after the Labor Day

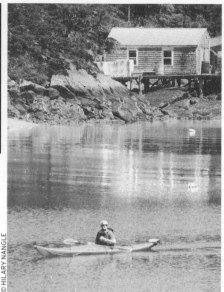

© HILARY NANGLE

Explore the islands around Deer Isle and Isle au Haut by sea kayak.

holiday. Nights can be cool, but days are likely to be brilliant. Do remember this is a working harbor.

The six-mile paddle from Stonington to Isle au Haut is best left to experienced paddlers, especially since fishing folks refer to kayakers as "speed bumps."

For equipment rentals or guided trips, see *Sporting Outfitters and Guided Trips.* Old Quarry Ocean Adventures is especially helpful and provides many services for kayakers.

Swimming

The island's only major freshwater swimming hole is the **Lily Pond,** northeast of Deer Isle Village. Just north of the Shakespeare School, turn in to the Deer Run Apartments complex. Park and take the path to the pond, which has a shallow area for small children.

Golf and Tennis

About two miles south of Deer Isle Village, watch for the large sign (on the left) for the **Island Country Club** (Rte. 15A, Sunset,

207/348-2379, early June–late Sept.), a nine-hole public course that's been here since 1928. Starting times are first-come, first-served, and greens fees are low; no credit cards are accepted.

Also at the club are three beautifully maintained tennis courts. Or just commandeer a rocking chair and watch the action from one of the porches. The club's cheeseburgers and salads are among the island's best bargain lunches.

Sporting Outfitters and Guided Trips

The biggest operation is **Old Quarry Ocean Adventures** (Stonington, 207/367-8977 or 877/479-8977, mobile 207/266-7778, www.oldquarry.com), with a broad range of outdoor adventure choices. Bill Baker's ever-expanding enterprise rents canoes, kayaks, sailboats, bikes, moorings, platform tent sites, and cabins. Bicycle rentals are $20 per day or $100 per week. Sea kayak rental rates are $57 per day for a single, $67 for a tandem. Half-day rates (based on a four-hour rental) are $42 and $52, respectively. Overnight 24-hour rental is available for a 10 percent surcharge. Weekly rentals are $300 single, $380 tandem. Canoes or rowboats are $42 per half day, $52 per full day, or $250 per week; sailboats are $80 or $100 per half day, $110 or $150 per full day. For all boat rentals, you must demonstrate competency in the vessel. They'll deliver and pick up anywhere on the island for a fee of $20.

All-day guided tours in single kayaks are $105; tandems are $175. Half-day tours are $55 and $110, respectively. Plenty of other options are available, including sunset tours, family trips, and gourmet picnic paddles.

Overnight kayaking camping trips on nearby islands are led by a Registered Maine Guide. Rates, including meals, begin at $285 per adult for one night; three-person minimum.

If you're bringing your own kayak, you can park your car ($7 per night up to two nights, $6 per night for three or more nights) and launch from here ($5 per boat for launching); they'll take your trash and any trash you find.

Old Quarry is off the Oceanville Road, less than a mile from Route 15, just before you reach the Settlement Quarry preserve. It's well signposted.

Next to the restaurant of the same name, and owned by the same family, is **Finest Kind** (Center District Crossroad, about halfway between Routes 15 and 15A, 207/348-7714). Bicycle rentals here are $15 per day or $75 per week. Kayak or canoe rentals are $35 per day for a single, $45 for a tandem, including paddles, lifejackets, spray skirts, delivery, and pickup.

EXCURSION BOATS
Isle au Haut Boat Company

If you're not up for self-propulsion, from mid-June through early September the *Miss Lizzie* or the *Mink* departs at 9 A.M. and 2 P.M. daily from the Isle au Haut Boat Company dock in Stonington for a narrated one-hour trip among the islands; on morning tours, the crew hauls a string of lobster traps. Cost is $18 adults, $8

kids under 12. Another option is to cruise over and back to Isle au Haut, without stepping foot off the boat, for half of the usual roundtrip fare ($34 adult, $17 child). Reservations are advisable, especially in July and August. Day parking is available at the pier for $4, or find a spot in town and save the surcharge. The *Miss Lizzie* and the *Mink* are owned by the Isle au Haut Boat Company (Seabreeze Ave., Stonington, 207/367-5193 or 207/367-6516, www.isleauhaut.com), the same company that operates the regular mailboat/passenger ferry service to offshore Isle au Haut.

◖ Guided Island Tours

Captain Walter Reed's Guided Island Tours (207/348-6789, www.guidedislandtours.com) aboard the *Gael* are custom-designed for a maximum of four passengers. Walt is a Registered Maine Guide and professional biologist who also is a steward for Mark Island Lighthouse and several uninhabited islands in the area. He provides in-depth perspective

© TOM NANGLE

One of the best ways to tour Deer Isle is by boat, perhaps aboard the Isle au Haut passenger ferry.

and the local scoop. The cost is $35 per person for the first hour plus $25 per person for each additional hour; kids under 12 are half price. Reservations required; box lunches are available for an additional fee.

Old Quarry Ocean Adventures

Yet another aspect of the Old Quarry Ocean Adventures (Stonington, 207/367-8977 or 877/479-8977, mobile 207/266-7778, www.oldquarry.com) empire are sightseeing tours on the *Nigh Duck*. The three-hour trips, one in the morning (9 A.M.–noon) and one in the afternoon (1–4 P.M.) are $40 for adults and $24 for children under 12. Both highlight the natural history of the area, as Captain Bill navigates the boat through the archipelago. Lobster traps are hauled on both trips (but not on Sunday); the morning trip visits Isle au Haut. The afternoon excursion features an island swimming break in a freshwater quarry. Also available is a 1.5-hour sunset cruise, departing half an hour before sunset, for $34 adults and $24 kids under 12. And if that's not enough, Old Quarry also offers puffin, lighthouse, whale-watching, and island cruises, with rates beginning at $55 per adult, $35 per kid. Of course, if none of this floats your boat, you can also arrange for a custom charter for $175 per hour.

Old Quarry also offers a number of special trips in conjunction with Island Heritage Trust. Most are noted on its website, but for reservations or more info, call 207/348-2455.

ENTERTAINMENT AND EVENTS

Stonington's National Historic Landmark, the 1912 **Opera House** (207/367-2788, www.operahousearts.org), is home to Opera House Arts, which hosts films, plays, lectures, concerts, family programs, and workshops year-round.

Mid-June, when lupine in various shades of pink and purple seem to be blooming everywhere, brings the **Lupine Festival** (207/348-2676 or 207/367-2420). The weekend festival includes art openings and shows, boat rides, a

Stonington's Opera House can be spotted from the harbor.

© HILARY NANGLE

private garden tour, and entertainment ranging from a contra dance to movies.

July through September is the season for **First Friday,** an open-house night held on the first Friday evening each month, with demonstrations, music, and refreshments, sponsored by the Stonington Galleries (www.stoningtongalleries.com).

Seamark Community Arts (207/348-2333, www.seamarkcommunityarts.com) hosts arts workshops for children and adults in areas such as book arts, nature crafts, pottery, drawing and painting, film and video, printmaking, basketry, textile arts, and more. The summer highlight is the themed annual auction; in 2008, local artists contributed their interpretations of that year's theme, "Gardens."

Mid-July brings the **Stonington Lobsterboat Races** (207/348-2804), very popular competitions held in the harbor, with lots of possible vantage points. Stonington is one of the major locales in the lobsterboat race circuit.

In early October is **Peninsula Potters Open Studios** (207/348-5681), during which more than two dozen potters welcome visitors.

Want to meet locals and learn more about the area? **Island Heritage Trust** sponsors a series of walks, talks, and tours from mid-June through mid-September. For information and reservations, call 207/348-2455.

SHOPPING

The greatest concentration of shops is in Stonington, where galleries, clothing boutiques, and eclectic shops line Main Street.

Food

In the May 2005 issue of the *Rosengarten Report,* Hickory-Smoked Salmon, Unsliced, by **Stonington Sea Products** (100 North Main St., Stonington, 207/367-2400 or 888/402-2729, www.stoningtonseafood.com), was named one of the "25 Best Products" the noted food critic has ever recommended, describing it in terms including "Wow!" and "Bravo!" See for yourself, or try any of the company's other smoked products. If you don't visit in person, shop online.

Antiques, Books, and Gifts

Two shops are in Deer Isle Village. **Old Fire House** (12 North Deer Isle Rd./Rte. 15, Deer Isle, 207/348-9978), just north of Main Street, is chock-full of old furniture and collectibles. Don't miss the downstairs. In "downtown" Deer Isle Village, you'll find **The Periwinkle** (8 Main St., Deer Isle, 207/348-2256), where Neva Beck carries a fine inventory of Maine books, as well as crafts, notecards, and gifts. Look for Neva's hand-braided rugs and chair pads and her baby quilts.

At the bottom of the island, **The Clown** (6 Thurlow's Hill Rd., Stonington, 207/367-6348) awaits. The imaginative owners came up with this combination of art, antiques, and...food and wine. Look, it works. Part of the key is the owners' farm in Tuscany, source of extra-virgin olive oil, wines, Deruta pottery, unusual furnishings, and other "necessities." Art openings are also wine-tastings—a fine idea.

The eclectic selection at **Bayside Antiques and Gifts** (131 Main St., Stonington, 207/367-8714) includes antiques, decorative accessories, and gifts, but the specialty is quality 18th- and 19th-century furniture and accessories from the Northeast.

Fine art and real antiques are featured at **Eagull Antiques** (Main St., Stonington, 207/367-5508, www.michaelconnorsantiques.com).

In downtown Stonington, below the Opera House, **Dockside Books & Gifts** (62 West Main St., Stonington, 207/367-2652) carries just what its name promises, with a specialty in marine and Maine books. The rustic two-room shop is open May to November. Don't miss the view from outside the shop.

In 2008, Janice Glenn moved her browsers' emporium, **Old Schoolhouse Antiques at Burnt Cove** (194 Burnt Cove Rd., Stonington, 207/367-2849), to Burnt Cove, across from the grocery store. It's a funky shop jam-packed with vintage clothing, kitchenware (organized by color), textiles, cookbooks, and other collectibles, with an especially nice collection of quilts, rugs, and samplers. No credit cards accepted.

Eclectic Shops

If you're looking for Maine pottery, weaving, metalwork, pewterware, imported tiles, or walking sticks, go directly to the **Harbor Farm Store** (Rte. 15, Little Deer Isle, 207/348-7755 or 800/342-8003, www.harborfarm.com). Based in a mid-19th-century schoolhouse a mile south of the Deer Isle suspension bridge, the shop carries thousands of very unusual, high-quality items, and it's all available by mail as well. The selection of tile from around the world draws buyers from well beyond Maine's borders.

Clothing

Women need to be cautious going into **The Dry Dock** (24 Main St., Stonington,

207/367-5528), where the merchandise instantly sells itself. Imported women's clothing from Nigerian, Tibetan, and Indian cottage industries; unique jewelry; and unusual notecards are just some of the options in one large room and a smaller back room.

ACCOMMODATIONS
Inns and Bed-and-Breakfasts

Pilgrim's Inn (20 Main St., Deer Isle, 207/348-6615, www.pilgrimsinn.com, $109–249) is a beautifully restored Colonial building and newer cottages overlooking the peaceful Mill Pond. The National Historic Register inn began life in 1793 as a boardinghouse named The Ark; be sure to check out the fascinating guestbook, with names dating back to 1901. A bit of a disconnect from the peacefulness is the recently added TV room (request a room far away from it, as the noise carries) and the downstairs tavern (formerly a fine-dining restaurant). It's open from early May to mid-October.

◖ The Inn on the Harbor (45 Main St., Stonington, 207/367-2420 or 800/942-2420, www.innontheharbor.com, $130–215 in peak season) is exactly as its name proclaims. Its expansive deck hangs right over the harbor. Although recently updated, the 1880s complex still has an air of unpretentiousness. Most of the 14 rooms and suites, each named after a windjammer, have fantastic harbor views and private or shared decks where you can keep an eye on lobster boats, small ferries, windjammers, and pleasure craft. (Binoculars are provided.) Rooms on the street can be noisy at night. Rates include a continental buffet breakfast. An espresso bar is open 11 A.M.–4:30 P.M. Nearby are antique, gift, and craft shops; guest moorings are available. The inn is open all year, but call ahead off-season, when rates are lower.

In downtown Stonington, just up the hill from the Inn on the Harbor and convenient for walking to everything (even a small sandy beach a mile away) is **Près du Port** (W. Main St. and Highland Ave., Stonington, 207/367-5007, www.presduport.com, $125–150), a bright B&B run by amiable innkeeper Charlotte Casgrain. After many summers at a Deer Isle French summer camp and a career as a Connecticut French teacher, she's settled here. Three rooms have detached baths, one has a private bath; there are vanity sinks in the rooms. Children are welcome, and there's even a toy cupboard to entertain them. Adults can relax in the water-view hot tub, or climb to Charlotte's Folly, a rooftop lookout, for the extensive views. No credit cards accepted. When Deer Isle beds are scarce at the height of summer, Charlotte is the best resource for dozens of last-minute overnight rooms in local homes. This location is ideal if you're en route to or returning from Isle au Haut.

Eggemoggin Reach is almost on the doorstep at **The Inn at Ferry Landing** (77 Old Ferry Rd., Deer Isle, 207/348-7760, www.ferrylanding.com, $120–175), overlooking the abandoned Sargentville–Deer Isle ferry wharf. The view is wide open from the inn's "great room," where guests gather to read, play games, talk, and watch passing windjammers. Professional musician Gerald Wheeler has installed two grand pianos in the room; it's a treat when he plays. His wife, Jean, is the hospitable innkeeper, managing three water-view guest rooms and a suite. A harpsichord and a great view are big pluses in the suite. The Mooring, an annex that sleeps five, is rented by the week ($1,500, without breakfast). The inn is open all year except Thanksgiving and Christmas; Wi-Fi is available throughout.

Motels

Right in downtown Stonington, just across the street from the harbor, is **Boyce's Motel** (44 Main St., Stonington, 207/367-2421 or 800/224-2421, www.boycesmotel.com, $60–130). Eleven units all have TV, phones, and refrigerators; some have kitchens and living rooms, and one has two bedrooms. Across the street, Boyce's has a private harborfront deck for its guests. Ask for rooms well back from Main Street to lessen the noise of locals cruising the street at night. It's open year-round.

Hostels

In 2009, the rustic-bordering-on-primitive **Deer Isle Hostel** (65 Tennis Rd., Deer Isle, 207/348-2308, www.deerislehostel.com), near the Tennis Preserve, opens. Owner Dennis Carter, a Surry, Maine, native and local stoneworker and carpenter, is modeling it on The Hostel in the Forest in Brunswick, Georgia. It's completely off the grid, with a pump in the kitchen for water and an outhouse. Carter expects guests to work in the extensive organic gardens, using produce for shared meals prepared on a wood stove, the sole source of heat. The three-story, timber-frame design is taken from a late-17th-century home in Massachusetts. Carter hand-cut the granite for the basement, and the timbers in the nail-free frame are hand-hewn from local blown-down spruce. Frills are limited to a sauna and a solar shower. The goal is sustainability, not profit, so rates are expected to be low.

Seasonal Rentals

For house and cottage rentals by the week, month, or season, contact **Sargent's Rentals** (207/367-5156, www.sargentsrentalsinc.com). Plan well ahead, as the best properties get snapped up as much as a year in advance.

Camping

Plan ahead if you want to camp at **Old Quarry Ocean Adventures Campground** (130 Settlement Rd., Stonington, 207/367-8977, www.oldquarry.com). It has both oceanfront and secluded sites for tents and just three RV sites. Each site has a 12-by-12-foot platform, a picnic table, deck chairs, and a fire grill. Tent sites are $34–50 for two, plus $17 for each additional person. An overflow site, without platform, table, or fire ring, is $24 per night for two. Kids younger than 5 are free; under 12 are $6. Leashed pets are permitted. Campground facilities include a swimming pond, hiking trails, laundry, a camp store (lobsters available), and a kayak launch. Parking is designed so that vehicles are kept away from most campsites, but you can use a garden cart to transport your equipment between your car and your site. The campground is adjacent to Settlement Quarry Park.

FOOD
Local Flavors

After browsing the shops, you just might need a double-dip cone from **Harbor Ice Cream,** across the street from The Periwinkle, in Deer Isle Village. Or a scoop of farm-made Smiling Hill Farm ice cream from **Island Cow Ice Cream,** on the main drag in Stonington.

Craving sweets? Head to **Susie Qu's Sweets and Curiosities** (40 School St., Stonington, 207/367-2415, 8 A.M.–3 P.M. Thurs.–Sun.). Susan Scott bakes a fine selection of cookies and pies, offers a limited selection of breakfast and lunch choices, and also carries antiques, books, quilts, toys, and other fun items. It's a Wi-Fi hotspot.

Best pizza on the island? Head for **Burnt Cove Market** (Rte. 15, Stonington, 207/367-2681, 6 A.M.–9 P.M., opens at 9 A.M. Sun.). Besides pizza, you can get fried chicken and sandwiches, plus beer and wine.

Creativity defines the menu at **Lily's Café and Wine Bar** (450 Airport Rd. at Rte. 15, Stonington, 207/367-5936, 7 A.M.–5 P.M. Mon.–Thurs., to 8 P.M. Fri.), mercifully expanded in 2008. It's all very casual; order at the counter and find a table either inside, on the upstairs deck, or outside in the garden. Or assemble a *haut gourmet* picnic: veggie and meat sandwiches, Mediterranean salads, cheeses, and homemade soups and breads. Upstairs is the Chef's Attic, with a smattering of antiques as well as works by local artists. Alas, it's closed on weekends. Beer and wine are served.

The Island Community Center (6 Memorial La., just off School St., Stonington) is the locale for the lively **Island Farmers Market** (10 A.M.–noon every Fri. May–Oct.), selling smoked and organic meats, fresh herbs and flowers, produce, gelato and yogurt, maple syrup, jams and jellies, fabulous breads and baked goods, ethnic foods, crafts, and so much more. Go early; it sells out quickly.

Family-Friendly Home Cooking

In July or August, don't show up at **Finest Kind Dining** (70 Center District Crossroad, Deer Isle, 207/348-7714, www.finestkindenterprises.com, 5–8:30 P.M. daily, May–Oct.) without a dinner reservation. This log-cabin family restaurant is no longer a secret. Expect home-style all-American food served conscientiously in a come-as-you-are setting. Pizza, pasta, prime rib, and seafood are all available, and there's a salad bar, too; most items are in the $8–20 range. And save room for dessert. Wheelchair access; liquor license. The restaurant, owned by the Perez family, is halfway between Route 15 and Sunset Road (Rte. 15A). The enterprising Perezes also own the adjacent **Round the Island Mini Golf** (same phone, open the same months) and rent canoes, kayaks, and bicycles.

Harbor Café (Main St., Stonington, 207/367-5099, 6 A.M.–8 P.M. Mon.–Thurs., to 9 P.M. Fri.–Sat., and to 2 P.M. Sun.) is *the* place to go for breakfast (you can eavesdrop on the local fisherfolk if you're early enough), but it's also reliable for lunch and dinner (especially on Friday nights for the seafood fry, with free seconds). Try to snag the front window table.

The views are top-notch from ◖ **Fisherman's Friend Restaurant** (5 Atlantic Ave., Stonington, 207/367-2442, 11 A.M.–9 P.M. Sun.–Thurs., to 10 P.M. Fri.–Sat.), which moved in 2005 from its longtime uptown digs to a harborfront location, complete with outdoor deck seating. The restaurant gets high marks for respectable food, generous portions, fresh seafood, outstanding desserts, and consistency, but it seems to have lost its soul in the move. Still, where else can you get lobster prepared 30 different ways? Prices are reasonable—the Friday night fish fry, with free seconds, is $7.99. It's open from early May to late October.

Casual Dining

Families are welcome at the **Whale's Rib Tavern** (20 Main St./Sunset Rd., Deer Isle Village, 207/348-5222, 5–8:30 P.M. daily, closed Tues. in May, Sept., and Oct.), a comfy white-tablecloth tavern in the lower-level of the

Pilgrim's Inn. Everyone can find something that appeals and is within budget on the menu, which varies from burgers to beef tenderloin, fish-and-chips to scampi.

You have a front seat—and a comfortable one at that—on all the harbor action at **Maritime Café** (27 Main St., Stonington, 207/367-2600, www.maritimecafe.com, 11:30 A.M.–3:30 P.M. and 5–8:30 P.M. daily). Big windows frame the harbor from the dining room, and there's also lunch seating on the harborside deck. The menu emphasizes seafood (no surprise), but there are other choices and always a vegetarian selection. Entrées run $18–28.

In 2007 **Cockatoo II Portuguese Restaurant** (Goose Cove Rd., Sunset, 207/348-2300, noon–9 P.M. daily) opened in the lovely Goose Cove Lodge. The views are the best on the island, and there is both indoor and outdoor seating and a full bar. Chef Suzen Carter prepares fresh, fresh, fresh seafood, most of it caught by her husband, Bradley, as well as chicken and meat. She was brought up in the Azores, so Portuguese-inspired preparations are the specialty, but you can get a classic Maine shore dinner here, too. Frankly, though, the Portuguese paella is the way to go. An order for two includes scallops, shrimp, mussels, and clams, most still in their shells, as well as a whole lobster, all served over Mozambique rice in a fabulous and slightly spicy sauce. Unless you're really big eaters, you'll likely have leftovers. Equally delicious is the Bacalhau ha Braz, shredded codfish with onions and crispy potatoes and peppers. Everything is cooked to order, and while, during its early operation, wait times were interminable, service and timing has improved. Still, go prepared for a leisurely meal. And with this location and these views, sit back and relax. Most choices are $18–38, although lunch rolls (fish, crabmeat, scallop) begin at $8.

INFORMATION AND SERVICES

The **Deer Isle-Stonington Chamber of Commerce** (P.O. Box 459, Stonington 04681,

207/348-6124, www.deerislemaine.com) has a summer information booth on a grassy triangle on Route 15 in Little Deer Isle, a quarter of a mile after crossing the bridge from Sargentville (Sedgwick).

Across from the Pilgrim's Inn is the **Chase Emerson Memorial Library** (Main St., Deer Isle Village, 207/348-2899). At the tip of the island is the **Stonington Public**

Library (Main St., Stonington, 207/367-5926).

Public Restrooms

Public restrooms are at the Atlantic Avenue Hardware pier and at the Stonington Town Hall, Main Street; at the Chase Emerson Library in Deer Isle Village; and behind the information booth on Little Deer Isle.

Isle au Haut

Eight miles off Stonington lies 4,700-acre Isle au Haut, roughly half of which belongs to Acadia National Park. Pronounced variously as "I'll-a-HO" or "I'LL-a-ho," the island has nearly 20 miles of hiking trails, excellent birding, and a tiny village.

About 60 souls call Isle au Haut home year-round, most of them eking out a living from

the sea. Each summer, the population temporarily swells with day-trippers, campers, and cottagers—then settles back in fall to the measured pace of life on an offshore island.

Samuel de Champlain, threading his way through this archipelago in 1605 and noting the island's prominent central ridge, came up with the name of Isle au Haut (High Island).

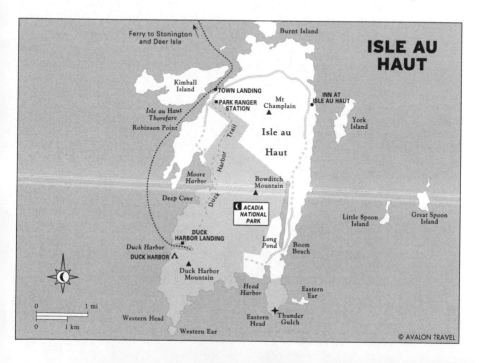

Appropriately, the tallest peak (543 feet) is now named Mount Champlain.

More recent fame has come to the island thanks to island-based author Linda Greenlaw, of *Perfect Storm* fame, who wrote *The Lobster Chronicles*. Although that book piqued interest in the island, Isle au Haut remains uncrowded and well off the beaten tourist track.

Most of the southern half of the six-mile-long island belongs to Acadia National Park, thanks to the wealthy summer visitors who began arriving in the 1880s. It was their heirs who, in the 1940s, donated valuable acreage to the federal government. Today, this offshore division of the national park has a well-managed 18-mile network of trails, a few lean-tos, several miles of unpaved road, and summertime passenger-ferry service to the park entrance.

In the island's northern half are the private residences of fishing families and summer folk, a minuscule village (including a market and post office), a five-mile stretch of paved road, and an inn. The only vehicles on the island are owned by residents.

If spending the night on Isle au Haut sounds appealing (it is), you'll need to plan well ahead; it's no place for spur-of-the-moment sleepovers. (Even spontaneous day trips aren't always possible.) The best part about staying overnight on Isle au Haut is that you'll have much more than seven hours to enjoy this idyllic island.

◖ ACADIA NATIONAL PARK

Mention Acadia National Park and most people think of Bar Harbor and Mount Desert Island, where more than three million visitors arrive each year. The Isle au Haut section of the park sees maybe 5,000 visitors a year—partly because only 48 people a day (not counting campers) are allowed to land here. The remoteness of the island and the scarcity of beds and campsites also contribute to the low count, leaving the trails and views for only a few hardy souls.

About a third of a mile from the town landing, where the year-round mailboat and another boat dock, is the **Park Ranger Station** (207/335-5551), where you can pick up trail maps and park information—and use the island's only public facilities. (Do yourself a

Isle au Haut Light

© HILARY NANGLE

favor, though: Plan ahead by downloading Isle au Haut maps and information from the Acadia National Park website, www.nps.gov/acad/.)

HIKING

Hiking on Acadia National Park trails is the major recreation on Isle au Haut, and even in the densest fog, you'll see valiant hikers going for it. A loop road circles the whole island; an unpaved section goes through the park, connecting with the mostly paved nonpark section. Walking on that is easy. Beyond the road, none of the park's 18 miles of trails could be labeled "easy"; the footing is rocky, rooty, and often squishy. But the park trails *are* well marked, and the views—of islets, distant hills, and ocean—make the effort worthwhile. Go prepared with proper footwear.

Duck Harbor Trail

- Distance: 4 miles one-way
- Duration: 2 hours
- Elevation gain: Minimal
- Effort: Moderate
- Trailhead: Park Ranger Station, north end of the island

The most-used park trail connects the town landing with Duck Harbor. (You can either use this trail or follow the island road—mostly unpaved in this stretch—to get to the campground when the summer ferry ends its Duck Harbor runs.)

Duck Harbor Mountain Trail

- Distance: 2.4 miles round-trip
- Duration: 3–4 hours
- Elevation gain: 300 feet
- Effort: Strenuous
- Trailhead: Western Head Road

Even though the summit is only 314 feet, this is the island's toughest trail. Still, it's worth the effort for the stunning, 360-degree views

from the summit. *Option:* Rather than return via the trail's steep, bouldery sections, cut off at the Goat Trail and return to the trailhead that way.

Western Head and Cliff Trails

- Distance: 2 miles one-way
- Duration: 2 hours
- Elevation gain: 150 feet
- Effort: Moderate
- Trailhead: Western Head Road

For terrific shoreline scenery, take these two trails at the island's southwestern corner that form a nice loop around Western Head. The route follows the coastline, ascending to ridges and cliffs and descending to rocky beaches, with some forested sections. *Option:* Close the loop by returning via the Western Head Road. If the tide is out (and *only* if it's out), you can walk across the tidal flats to the quaintly named Western Ear for views back toward the island. Western Ear is private, so don't linger. The Goat Trail adds another four miles (round-trip) of moderate coastline hiking east of the Cliff Trail; views are fabulous and birding is good, but if you're only here for a day, you'll need to decide whether there's time to catch the return boat. If you do have the time and the energy, you can connect from the Goat Trail to the Duck Harbor Mountain Trail.

Long Pond Trail

- Distance: 3 miles round-trip
- Duration: 2 hours
- Elevation gain: 150 feet
- Effort: Strenuous
- Trailhead: Main road, western side of the island

Big views are the rewards for this difficult loop hike that crosses from the west to the east side of the island and passes along a ridge paralleling Long Pond before climbing to the summit of Bowditch Mountain. *Option:* The trail intersects with the Median Ridge Trail (1.6 miles of moderate terrain to where it intersects with the main road) and the Bowditch Trail.

Bowditch Trail

- Distance: 4 miles round-trip

- Duration: 2 hours

- Elevation gain: 350 feet

- Effort: Moderate

- Trailhead: Off Duck Harbor Trail (1.5 miles from the ranger station)

The Bowditch Trail passes through bogs, forests, and wet ledges as it climbs to the mountain's 405-foot summit, where it connects to the Median Ridge Trail. Varied terrain and good views make the effort worthwhile.

Walks and Unmarked Hikes

Befriend a local and ask for directions to **Seal Trap,** an easy trail to a postcard harbor on the island's west side. The unmarked trail crosses private property, so do ask locally whether you can hike it, and practice good trail etiquette. Another unmarked trail that's worth discovering is **Mt. Champlain,** a moderate hike up to the 543-foot summit, which provides few views as it's heavily forested. Access is on the north end of the island.

When the water's rough, **Boom Beach,** on the island's east side, is the place to be. As crashing waves roll in over the round rocks, they rumble, hence the boom. The stormier it is, the wilder this spot becomes. It's an easy five-minute walk to the stone beach along a spruce-lined path edged with moss- and lichen-covered rocks. Bring a picnic, but don't even consider swimming here. Boom Beach is approximately one-quarter mile north of Long Pond beach; look for a grassy pullout, where there might be a few metal lobster traps. Ticks can be a problem here, so be wary.

If you're traveling counterclockwise around the island, just north of Head Harbor, take the first road on the right, when the road turns to

tar (you'll see a bright yellow house just down the road), and continue to a red and gray house, then look for a sign for **Thunder Gulch.** Follow the trail through the woods and down the middle of Eastern Head. Tension seems to build as you walk through the woods, then the trail emerges to open ocean views. Waves roll into a cleavage in the rock, before erupting in a tower of spray. One islander describes it as a Zen-like place "where all your questions will be answered."

BIKING

Pedaling is limited to the 12 or so miles of mostly unpaved, hilly roads, and while it is a way to get around, frankly, the terrain is neither exciting, fun, nor view-worthy. Mountain bikes are not allowed on the park's hiking trails, and rangers try to discourage park visitors from bringing them to the island. If you're staying at the Inn at Isle au Haut, you can borrow a bike, which is handy around the "village" and for going swimming in Long Pond. You can also rent a bike (about $22 per day) on the

A bicycle is one way to get around Isle au Haut.

island from the Isle au Haut Ferry Service or Old Quarry Ocean Adventures. It costs $18 round-trip to bring your own bike aboard the Isle au Haut Ferry. Both boats carry bikes *only* to the town landing, not to Duck Harbor.

SWIMMING

For freshwater swimming, head for Long Pond, a skinny, 1.5-mile-long swimming hole running north-south on the east side of the island, abutting national park land. You can bike over there, clockwise along the road, almost five miles, from the town landing. Or bum a ride from an island resident. There's a minuscule beach-like area on the southern end with a picnic table and a float. If you're here only for the day, though, there's not enough time to do this *and* get in a long hike. Opt for the hiking—or do a short hike and then go for a swim (the shallowest part is at the southern tip).

ACCOMMODATIONS AND FOOD

Options for food are extremely limited on Isle au Haut, so if you're coming for a day trip, bring sufficient food and water.

On the east side of the island is **The Inn at Isle au Haut** (Lighthouse Point, Isle au Haut, off-island 207/335-5141, www.innatisleauhaut.com, $275–350), a mansard-roofed waterfront Victorian home that Diana Santospago has turned into an inn. An accomplished cook, Diana whips up fabulous breakfasts, lunches, dinners for her guests; bring your own beer or wine. The downstairs room with private bath is most spacious. Three rather small rooms on the second floor share one bath; all but one have water views. Single-speed bikes are provided for guests, and it's an easy pedal to Long Pond for swimming or to connect with park trails. Special early- and late-summer packages at the inn include cruises, tours, and cooking classes with Linda Greenlaw. The inn is open from June 1 to September 30.

Camping

The only camping on Isle au Haut is in lean-tos at the Acadia National Park campground.

So you'll need to get your bid in early to reserve one of the five six-person lean-tos at **Duck Harbor Campground,** open May 15 to October 15. Before April 1, contact the park for a reservation request form (Acadia National Park, P.O. Box 177, Bar Harbor 04609, 207/288-3338, www.nps.gov/acad). From April 1 on *(not before, or the park people will send it back to you),* return the completed form, along with a check for $25, covering camping for up to six people for a maximum of five nights May 15–June 14, three nights June 15–September 15, and five nights again September 16–October 15. Mark the envelope "Attn: Isle au Haut Reservations." Competition is stiff in the height of summer, so list alternate dates. The park refunds the check if there's no space; otherwise, it's nonrefundable and you'll receive a "special-use permit" (*do not* forget to bring it along). There's no additional camping fee.

Unless you don't mind backpacking nearly five miles to reach the campground, try to plan your visit between mid-June and Labor Day, when the mail boat makes a stop in Duck Harbor. It's wise to call the Isle au Haut Company for the current ferry schedule before choosing dates for a lean-to reservation.

Trash policy is carry-in/carry-out, so pack a trash bag or two with your gear. Also bring a container for carting water from the campground pump, since it's 0.3 mile from the lean-tos. It's a longish walk to the general store for food—when you could be off hiking the island's trails—so bring enough to cover your stay.

The three-sided lean-tos are big enough (8-by-12-feet, 8 feet high) to hold a small (two-person) tent, so bring one along if you prefer being fully enclosed. A tarp will also do the trick. (Also bring mosquito repellent—some years, the critters show up here en masse.) No camping is permitted outside of the lean-tos, and nothing can be attached to trees.

Food

Isle au Haut is pretty much a BYO place—and for the most part, that means BYO food. Although the Inn at Isle au Haut is open to the public for dinner by reservation, you need to get there and back. Unless you're staying in a rental cottage with a car, there's no way to do so.

Thanks to the seasonal **Isle au Haut General Store** (207/335-5211, www.isleauhaut.net/islandstore.htm), less than a five-minute walk from the town landing, you won't starve. The inventory isn't extensive, but it can be intriguing, due to the store manager who travels worldwide and stocks the shop with her finds. On the other hand, food probably won't be your prime interest here—Isle au Haut is as good as it gets.

Even more intriguing is **Black Dinah Chocolatiers** (207/335-5010, www.blackdinahchocolatiers.com), just shy of a mile from the town landing. Steve and Kate Shaffer's little shop doubles as a café, serving pastries, organic coffees and teas, a few lunch-type offerings, and, of course, decadent handmade chocolates. It also has free Wi-Fi.

GETTING THERE

Until recently, unless you had your own vessel, the only access to Isle au Haut's town landing was the mail boat. That's still the only way to get there year-round, but two companies now offer transportation to and from the island. Use Isle au Haut Boat Company if your destination is the park, as it lands right at Duck Harbor twice daily during peak season. If money's no object, you can always arrange private charter.

Isle au Haut Boat Company

The Isle au Haut Boat Company (Seabreeze Ave., Stonington, 207/367-5193, www.isleauhaut.com) generally operates five daily trips Monday–Saturday, plus two on Sunday from mid-June to early September. Other months, there are 2–3 trips Monday–Saturday. The best advice is to request a copy of the current schedule, covering dates, variables, fares, and extras.

Round-trips from April to mid-October are $34 adults, $17 kids under 12 (two bags per adult, one bag per child). Round-trip surcharges include bikes ($18), kayaks/canoes ($36

minimum), and pets ($8). If you're considering bringing a bike, be sure to inquire about on-island bike rentals ($22 per day). Weather seldom affects the schedule, but be aware that ultraheavy seas could cancel a trip.

There is twice-daily ferry service, from mid-June to Labor Day, from Stonington to Duck Harbor, at the edge of Isle au Haut's Acadia National Park campground. For a day trip, the schedule allows you 6.5 hours on the island Monday–Saturday and 4.5 hours on Sunday. No boats or bikes are allowed on this route, and no dogs are allowed in the campground. A ranger boards the boat at the town landing and goes along to Duck Harbor to answer questions and distribute maps. Before mid-June and after Labor Day, you'll be off-loaded at the Isle au Haut town landing, about five miles from Duck Harbor. The six-mile passage from Stonington to the Isle au Haut town landing takes 45 minutes; the trip to Duck Harbor is 1.25 hours.

Ferries depart from the Isle au Haut Boat Company dock (Seabreeze Ave., off E. Main St. in downtown Stonington). Parking ($9 per day outside, $11 indoors) is available next to the ferry landing. Arrive at least an hour early to get all this settled so you don't miss the boat. Better yet, spend the night on Deer Isle before heading to Isle au Haut.

Old Quarry Ocean Adventures

The new kid on the block offering seasonal service to Isle au Haut, Old Quarry Ocean Adventures (Stonington, 207/367-8977 or 877/479-8977, mobile 207/266-7778, www.oldquarry.com) transports passengers on the recently renovated *Nigh Duck*. The boat usually leaves Old Quarry at 9 A.M. and arrives at the island's town landing one hour later. It departs from the same point at 5 P.M., arriving back at Old Quarry around 6 P.M. The fee is $35 round-trip for adults, $18 for children under 12. You can add an island bike rental for an additional $20 or a kayak for $10. Old Quarry also offers a taxi service to Isle au Haut for $140 per hour for up to six people.

ELLSWORTH AND TRENTON

The punch line to an old Maine joke is "Ya cahn't get they-ah from he-ah." Truth is, you can't get to Acadia without going through Ellsworth and Trenton. Indeed, when you're crawling along in bumper-to-bumper traffic, it might seem as if all roads lead to downtown Ellsworth. Truth is, many do.

While there are ways to skirt around a few of the worst bottlenecks, the region does have its calling cards. Ellsworth pluses are historical homes, a grand theater, a delightful bird sanctuary, an inviting downtown shopping area, and a few choice dining spots. Trenton, linked by a bridge to Mount Desert Island, is little more than a six- or seven-mile strip of restaurants, lodgings, shops, and activities.

One more plus for the area is the Bar Harbor Chamber of Commerce Information Center location on Route 3 in Trenton. If you're day-tripping to Mount Desert Island, you can leave your car here and hop aboard the free Island Explorer bus, eliminating driving and parking hassles.

PLANNING YOUR TIME

Route 1, the main thoroughfare along the coast, and Route 1A, which connects to Bangor, meet in downtown Ellsworth. Route 172 leads to the Blue Hill Peninsula and on to Deer Isle, Stonington, and the mailboat to Isle au Haut. Route 1 continues north, providing access to the Schoodic Peninsula and a remote section of the park. And the Bar Harbor Road (Route 3) is something of an Achilles heel—often a summertime bottleneck as it funnels all traffic to Mount Desert Island.

HIGHLIGHTS

◖ Woodlawn: This treasure-filled Georgian mansion has gardens, carriage houses, and walking trails (page 222).

◖ Birdsacre: Ornithologist Cordelia Stanwood's homestead is now a preserve, with a nature center, walking trails, and a bird reha-bilitation center (page 222).

◖ Kisma Preserve: Splurge on a behind-the-scenes tour of this preserve dedicated to conserving and protecting rescued and retired exotic animals (page 227).

◖ Aerial Touring: Get a proper introduc-tion to Mount Desert Island by gliding with the hawks or getting an eagle's-eye view from a small plane (page 228).

◖ The Great Maine Lumberjack Show: A must for kids, this show demonstrates all the old-time logging skills (page 229).

LOOK FOR ◖ TO FIND RECOMMENDED SIGHTS, ACTIVITIES, DINING, AND LODGING.

This became all too clear in June 2003, when a wealthy island summer resident had a mature apple tree moved from Ellsworth—via Trenton, of course—to his Northeast Harbor home. With no passing room to spare on the narrow two-lane roads, and the need to raise phone, cable, and electric wires along the entire route for the 20-foot-high tree, the traffic backed up halfway to Bangor—a costly 12-hour nightmare. Public works and local government officials learned a hard les-son, residents and commuters earned a public apology in the newspapers, and wags vowed to sneak in and sample those expensive ap-ples if and when the tree bears fruit in its new soil.

ELLSWORTH AND TRENTON

ELLSWORTH AND TRENTON

© AVALON TRAVEL

Ellsworth

Hancock County's shire town has mushroomed with the popularity of Acadia National Park, but you can still find handsome architectural remnants of the city's 19th-century lumbering heyday (which began shortly after its incorporation in 1800). Brigs, barks, and full-rigged ships—built in Ellsworth and captained by local fellows—loaded lumber here and carried it round the globe. Despite a ruinous 1855 fire that swept through downtown, the lumber trade thrived until late in the 19th century, along with factories and mills turning out shoes, bricks,

boxes, and butter. At local businesses, you can pick up a copy of *Historic Ellsworth: A Walking Tour and More* (www.downtownellsworth.com/Activities.htm), which details 17 downtown sites.

These days, Ellsworth is the region's shopping mecca. Antique shops and small stores line Main Street, which doubles as Route 1 in the downtown section; supermarkets, strip malls, and big-box stores line Routes 1 and 3 between Ellsworth and Trenton. Amidst all this roadside clutter, there are a few gems worth visiting.

SIGHTS
◖ Woodlawn

Very little has changed at the Woodlawn (Surry Rd./Rte. 172, Ellsworth, 207/667-8671, www .woodlawnmuseum.com, 10 A.M.–5 P.M. Tues.–Sat. and 1–4 P.M. Sun. June–Sept., 1–4 P.M. Tues.–Sun. May and Oct., $7.50 adults, $3 children 5–12, grounds are free) since George Nixon Black donated his home, also known as "the Black Mansion," to the town in 1928. Completed in 1828, the Georgian house is a marvel of preservation—one of Maine's best—filled with Black family antiques and artifacts. Enthusiastic docents lead hour-long tours, beginning on the hour, to point out the circular staircase, rare books and artifacts, canopied beds, a barrel organ, and lots more. Even kids appreciate all the unusual stuff. Afterward, plan to picnic on the manicured grounds, then explore two sleigh-filled barns, the Memorial Garden, and the two miles of mostly level trails in the woods up beyond the house. Restrooms are next to the parking area. On several Wednesday afternoons in July and August, there are elegant teas in the garden (or in the carriage house if it's raining). China, silver, linens, special-blend tea, sandwiches, pastries, and live music—all for $20 per person; reservations are required. The grounds are accessible all year. In winter, there's cross-country skiing on the trails. On Route 172, a quarter mile southwest of Route 1, watch for the small sign and turn into the winding uphill driveway.

◖ Birdsacre

En route to Bar Harbor, watch carefully on the right for the sign that marks Birdsacre (Rte. 3, Bar Harbor Rd., Ellsworth, 207/667-8460, www.birdsacre.com), a 200-acre urban sanctuary. Wander the trails in this peaceful preserve—spotting wildflowers, birds, and well-labeled shrubs and trees—and you'll have trouble believing you're surrounded by prime tourist territory. One trail, a boardwalk loop through woods behind the nature center, is wheelchair and stroller accessible. The

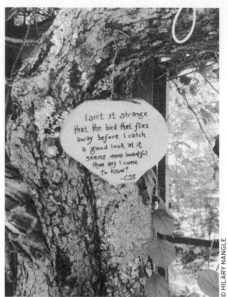

Markers accent the trails at Birdsacre, former home of ornithologist Cordelia Stanwood.

sanctuary is open all year, from sunrise to sunset. At the sanctuary entrance is the 1850 **Stanwood Homestead Museum,** with period furnishings and wildlife exhibits. Once owned by noted ornithologist Cordelia Stanwood, the volunteer-operated museum is open for tours by chance or appointment, from mid-May to mid-October. To be sure, call ahead for an appointment. Admission to the preserve and the homestead is free, but donations are needed and greatly appreciated. Birdsacre is also a wildlife rehabilitation center, so expect to see all kinds of winged creatures, especially hawks and owls, in various stages of rescue. Some will be returned to the wild, while others remain here for educational purposes. Stop by the Nature Center for even more exhibits.

The New England Museum of Telephony

What was life like before cell phones or touch-tone dialing? Find out at the New England Museum of Telephony (166 Winkumpaugh

Rd., Ellsworth, 207/667-9491, www.ells-worthme.org/ringring, 1–4 P.M. Thurs. and Sun. July.–Sept., $5 adult, $2.50 kids), a hands-on museum with the largest collection of old-fashioned switching systems in the East, including many from Maine. Place a call to see how these old systems work. To find the museum, head 10 miles north on Route 1A (toward Bangor), then go left on Winkumpaugh Road for one mile.

Ellsworth Historical Society
Kids love the **Old Hancock County Jail,** now home to the Ellsworth Historical Society Museum (State St., Ellsworth, 207/667-8943, 10 A.M.–3 P.M. Tues. and Thurs. July and Aug., free). Built in 1866, the building housed both the jail and the jailkeeper's residence, an interesting combo. Even more interesting is that each of the cells is named, a more contemporary twist, since these refer to local accommodations. The residence is filled with whatnot of Ellsworth's history, a hodgepodge of antiques and artifacts, with a decor reflecting the Victorian period.

RECREATION
Hiking
One of the newest efforts by the young Frenchman Bay Conservancy (207/422-2328, www.frenchmanbay.org) is the 13-acre **Indian Point Preserve.** The reward for following the footpath to the Union River shorefront is a lovely view of the city. Future plans call for a loop trail with wheelchair access. To find the preserve, drive south on Water Street, cross Card Brook, and, at the top of the next hill, look for Tinker Farm Way on your right. The road to the preserve's parking lot angles off to the right.

Nature trails lace **Birdsacre** (Rte. 3, Bar Harbor Rd., Ellsworth, 207/667-8460, www.birdsacre.com), a 200-acre urban sanctuary with three small ponds; one is wheelchair/stroller accessible. Two miles of mostly level trails can also be found behind the Black House at **Woodlawn** (Surry Rd./Rte. 172, Ellsworth, 207/667-8671, www.woodlawnmuseum.com).

Boat Launches
If you've brought your own boat, you can launch it into the Union River at the **Waterfront Park and Marina** (Water St.). To find it, head north on Route 1 and take a right at the first light in town. Another launch is on **Graham Lake,** just above the dam, on Route 180. To find it, take Route 1A north from downtown Ellsworth, then Routes 180/179 to the split, then Route 180. Look for the boat launch sign on your right, just after the dam.

Sports Facilities
Ellsworth has public basketball courts on Route 1A, heading north toward Bangor; a running track on Forest Avenue, off Route 1A; and tennis courts at Ellsworth High School, on Route 1A.

The **James Russell Wiggins Downeast Family YMCA** (238 State St., Ellsworth, 207/667-3086, www.defymca.org, 5:30 A.M.–9 P.M. Mon.–Fri., 8 A.M.–5 P.M. Sat. and Sun.) has a gym and indoor pool. A day pass is $8 per adult, $5 senior or college student, $3 youth, or $10 family. The Y is adjacent to the Skatepark and Ice Rink on Route 1A.

ENTERTAINMENT
The carefully restored art deco **Grand Auditorium** of Hancock County (100 Main St., Ellsworth, 207/667-9500, www.grandonline.org) is the year-round site of films, concerts, plays, and art exhibits.

A summer highlight is the **Ellsworth Concert Band** concert series, held Wednesday evenings in July and August in the plaza outside Ellsworth City Hall (an imposing building just north of Main Street). If it rains, it's held inside City Hall. Practice begins at 6:30 P.M.; concerts start at 8 P.M. The 50-member community band even welcomes visitors with talent and instruments. Just show up at practice time. The repertoire is mostly marches and show tunes; a prize goes to the person who correctly identifies a mystery tune.

SHOPPING
Antiques and Books

You're unlikely to meet a single soul who has left the **Big Chicken Barn Books and Antiques** (Rte. 1, 1768 Bucksport Rd., Ellsworth, 207/667-7308) without buying *something*. You'll find every kind of collectible on the vast first floor, courtesy of more than four dozen dealers. Climb the stairs for books, magazines, old music, and more. With 21,000 square feet, this place is addictive, offering free coffee, restrooms, and hassle-free browsing. The Big Chicken is 11 miles east of Bucksport, 8.5 miles west of Ellsworth.

A fine collection of antiquarian and used books fills the shelves of **Apple Tree Books** (71 Main St., Ellsworth, 207/667-7999).

The 40-plus-dealer **Old Creamery Antique Mall** (207/667-0522) fills two floors and 6,000 square feet, just of Main Street. It's a browsers emporium, with all manner of finds. It's fun to poke around.

Peruse a nice selection of used books in all genres at **The Book Shelf** (14 State St., Ellsworth, 207/667-1120).

Art and Artisans

Two shops specialize in handcrafted glasswork. At **Atlantic Art Glass** (25 Pine St., Ellsworth, 207/664-0222, www.atlanticartglass.com), Linda and Ken Perrin demonstrate glassblowing and sell their contemporary creations; they also offer workshops. **Seaglass Infusion** (56 Franklin St., Ellsworth, 207/667-0505, www.seaglassinfusion.com) is where Randy and Heather Ingraham craft jewelry and kaleidoscopes using sterling silver and glass that's been etched, frosted, and smoothed from decades of tumbling amidst the rocks at sea before washing ashore.

Inside the former Masonic Lodge that now houses Maine Grind is **SevenArts** (192 Main St., 207/667-1968, Ellsworth, www.sevenartsandcrafts.com), showing the works of seven local artisans working

Downtown Ellsworth's shops and restaurants invite lingering.

in varied media, along with selections from visiting artists.

Just south of downtown, in a National Historic Register property, the 1838 courthouse at the corner of Court Street and Route 1 is **Courthouse Gallery Fine Art** (6 Court St., Ellsworth, 207/667-6611, www.courthousegallery.com).

Eclectic Shops

Don't miss **Rooster Brother** (29 Main St., Rte. 1, Ellsworth, 207/667-8675 or 800/866-0054, www.roosterbrother.com), for gourmet cookware, cards, and books on the main floor; coffee, tea, candy, cheeses, a huge array of exotic condiments, fresh breads, and other gourmet items on the lower level; and discounted merchandise on the second floor, open seasonally. You can easily pick up all the fixings for a fancy picnic here. The shop is in a handsome old riverside building on busy Route 1. Access to the store's parking lot can be tricky at times because of traffic patterns, so be cautious and patient.

It's hard to categorize **J & B Atlantic Co.** (142 Main St., Rte. 1, Ellsworth, 207/667-2082). It takes up a good portion of the block, with room after room filled with furniture, home accessories, gifts, books, and antiques.

John Edwards Market (158 Main St., Ellsworth, 207/667-9377) is a two-fold find. Upstairs is a natural foods store. Downstairs is the Wine Cellar Gallery, a terrific space showcasing Maine artists throughout the year.

Sporting Goods and Toys

For an extensive sporting-gear inventory, plus advice on outdoors activities, stop in at **Cadillac Mountain Sports** (34 High St., Rte. 1, Ellsworth, 207/667-7819).

Safe toys for all ages can be found at **Four the Fun of It** (100 Main St., Rte. 1, Ellsworth, 207/667-2252, www.forfuntoys.com).

Discount Shopping

You can certainly find bargains at the **L.L.Bean Factory Store** (150 High St., Rte. 1, Ellsworth, 207/667-7753), but this is an outlet, so scrutinize the goods for flaws and blemishes before buying.

Across the road is **Reny's Department Store** (Ellsworth Shopping Center, 185 High St., Rte. 1, Ellsworth, 207/667-5166, www.renys.com), a Maine-based discount operation with a you-never-know-what-you'll-find philosophy. Trust me, you'll find something here.

In an adjacent shopping plaza is **Marden's** (225 High St./Rte. 1A, Ellsworth, 207/669-6036, www.mardenssurplus.com), another Maine bit-of-this, bit-of-that enterprise with the catchy slogan "I shoulda bought it, when I saw it." Good advice.

ACCOMMODATIONS
Motels

Lodging isn't Ellsworth's strong suit. National chains (Comfort Inn, Holiday Inn, Travelodge) and independent motels line High Street (Rtes. 1 and 3), a densely commercial stretch in Ellsworth, and continue southward through Trenton toward Mount Desert Island. (Bar Harbor is 20 miles from downtown Ellsworth.)

White Birches (20 Thorsen Rd., facing Rte. 1, Ellsworth, 207/667-3621 or 800/435-1287, www.whitebirchescountryclub.com) is a clean, generic, somewhat dated motel with 67 rooms ($70–105; kids 16 and younger free). It's popular with tour groups. The resort has a nine-hole par-three course ($20 per visit). Request a room overlooking the course. Rooms have phones and cable TV; some have air-conditioning. It's open all year.

Bed-and-Breakfasts

Simple accommodations are provided at **Mrs. Bancroft's Bed & Breakfast** (6 Wood St., Ellsworth, 207/667-4696, $65), a rambling 1876 home in a quiet, residential neighborhood within walking distance of downtown shops and restaurants. Each of two rooms has a private, but detached bath. A full vegetarian breakfast is served.

FOOD
Local Flavors

Order breakfast anytime at **The Riverside Café** (151 Main St., Ellsworth, 207/667-7220, 6 A.M.–2 P.M. Mon.–Thurs., to 8 P.M. Fri., 7 A.M.–8 P.M. Sat., 7 A.M.–2 P.M. Sun.). The fresh-squeezed juices are fabulous, the buckwheat pancakes are outstanding, and there's even a vegetarian menu with vegan choices. The lunch menu includes homemade soups, salads, sandwiches, grilled sandwiches, and high-cal desserts. Sunday brunches are legendary. Breakfast is served all day; lunch service begins at 11 A.M. And the cafe's name? It used to be down the street, overlooking the Union River.

Less creative but no less delicious are the home-style breakfasts at **Martha's Diner** (Reny's Plaza, 151 High St., Ellsworth, 207/664-2495, 6 A.M.–2 P.M. Mon.–Sat., 7 A.M.–1 P.M. Sun.), where lunch is also served weekdays 11 A.M.–2 P.M. Almost everything on the menu is less than $5, booths are red leatherette and Formica, and the waitresses likely will call you "doll."

Breakfast and deli sandwiches, salads and wraps, smoothies and sweets are all available at **The Maine Grind** (192 Main St., Ellsworth, 207/667-0011, www.mainegrind.com, 7:30 A.M.–5:30 P.M. Mon.–Sat., 8 A.M.–4 P.M. Sun.). There's free Wi-Fi service, too.

Although the emphasis is on vegan and vegetarian at **Frankie's Café** (225 High St., Ellsworth, 207/667-7701, www.frankiescafe .info, 8 A.M.–8 P.M. Mon.–Fri., to 6 P.M. Sat., 9 A.M.–4 P.M. Sun.), sharing space with Mr. Paperback in the Maine Coast Mall, other possibilities include roast beef, fresh roast turkey, and other not-so-green sandwiches.

Ice cream doesn't get much finer than that sold at **Morton's Ice Cream** (13 School St., Ellsworth, 207/667-1146), a tiny shop with a deservedly giant reputation for homemade Italian gelato, sorbet, and ice cream. It's well worth the slight detour.

The **Ellsworth Farmers Market** gets underway behind 245 East Main Street, in the parking lot of the Maine Community Foundation, from mid-June to late October, 2–5:30 P.M. Monday and Thursday and 9:30 A.M.–noon Saturday. It features fresh produce as well as jams, pickles, maple syrup, homemade breads, and homespun yarns.

Ethnic Fare

◖ **Cleonice Mediterranean Bistro** (112 Main St., Ellsworth, 207/664-7554, www .cleonice.com, 11:30 A.M.–9 P.M. daily in summer, but call ahead in the off-season) is named for chef-owner Richard Hanson's mother, Cleonice Renzetti. (It helps if you learn how to pronounce it: klee-oh-NEESE.) Gleaming woodwork and brass lighting fixtures combine for a golden glow in the long dining room, lined with wooden booths on one side, a 32-foot wooden bar, dating from 1938, on the other. The tapas and meze selection alone, served 2:30–5 P.M., is worth the trip—covering the Mediterranean circuit (spanakopita, hummus, manchego cheese with pear sauce, and even *brandade de morue*); most are around $5. Dinner entrée range is $12.50–30.

A refurbished 1932 Windsor dining car now serves as the bar area at **Calypso** (156 Main St./Rte. 1, Ellsworth, 207/667-6554, www.calypsodining.com, 11 A.M.–9 P.M. Mon.–Sat., 5–9 P.M. Sun.), where the eclectic menu varies from burgers and mac and cheese to duck breast and tenderloin ($10–30). Good service, good food, and live music on Saturday nights.

The area's best pizza is served at **Finelli Pizzeria** (12 Rte. 1, Ellsworth, 207/664-0230, 11 A.M.–8 P.M. Mon.–Thurs., to 9 P.M. Fri. and Sat.), where the pizza dough and focaccia bread are made fresh daily. The specialty is New York–style, thin-crust pizza, but other options include calzones, pastas, subs, and salads.

Ellsworth even has a popular Thai restaurant. **The Bangkok Restaurant** (321 High St., Rte. 3, Ellsworth, 207/667-1324, 11 A.M.–9 P.M. Mon.–Sat. and 4–9 P.M. Sun., all year) does a more-than-creditable job, and the always-popular pad Thai is a winner. Entrée range is $7–16.

Lobster

Of course you can get lobster. Brian and Jane Langley's **Union River Lobster Pot** (8 South St., Ellsworth, 207/667-5077, www.lobsterpot .com, 11:30 A.M.–9 P.M. mid-June–early Sept., then 5–9 P.M. through mid-Sept.) is tucked behind Rooster Brother, right on the banks of the Union River. Lobster's the main attraction, but the menu delivers everything from burgers, steaks, and ribs to sandwiches, chowder, and fried food. And remember to save room for the pie— especially the blueberry.

INFORMATION AND SERVICES

It can be hard to spot the **Ellsworth Area Chamber of Commerce** (163 High St., Ellsworth, 207/667-5584, www.ellsworth-chamber.org) amid the malls and fast-food places lining High Street (Route 1). Watch for a small gray building topped by an Information Center sign (on the right, close to the road, when heading toward Bar Harbor, just before Shaw's Plaza).

Libraries

Don't miss a chance to visit one of the state's loveliest libraries, the **Ellsworth Public Library** (46 State St., Ellsworth, 207/667-6363, www .ellsworth.lib.me.us). George Nixon Black, grandson of the builder of the Woodlawn Museum, donated the National Historic Register Federalist building to the city in 1897.

Public Restrooms

Public restrooms can be found in City Hall, downtown Ellsworth, open 24 hours a day, seven days a week; the library; the Chamber of Commerce; and the picnic area/boat launch on Water Street.

GETTING AROUND

If your destination is the Schoodic region, at the intersection of Route 1A and Main Street/ Route 1 in downtown Ellsworth, stay on Main Street and avoid the Route 1 strip. Main Street eventually will become the Washington Junction Road and will reconnect with Route 1 beyond the Route 3 split for Mount Desert Island and the worst congestion.

Trenton

Unless you're arriving by boat, you can't get to Mount Desert Island without first going through Trenton, straddling Route 3 from Ellsworth southward. Big-box stores, restaurants, motels, amusements, and gift shops line the congested six-mile strip, and some are worth at least a genuflection. If you're traveling with children, count on being begged to stop.

SIGHTS
◖ Kisma Preserve

I can't stress this enough: Kisma Preserve (446 Bar Harbor Rd., Rte. 3, Trenton, 207/667-3244, 9:30 A.M.–dusk daily, $12) is *not* a zoo; it's a nonprofit educational facility and everything revolves around preserving and

protecting the animals, most of which are either rescues or retirees. Rules are strictly enforced—no running, loud voices, or disruptive behavior is permitted. The only way to view the animals is on a guided tour. Guides educate visitors about the biology of the animals, how they came to be here, and whether they'll be returned to the wild. For serious animal lovers, the preserve offers behind-the-scenes tours and close-ups for fees beginning at $25 per person; there even are options for staying in the preserve overnight. It truly is a special place, with more than 100 exotic and not-so-exotic creatures—reindeer, bison, wolves, moose, big cats, and more. Donations are essential to Kisma's survival. Yes, it's pricey, but so too is feeding and caring for these animals.

ELLSWORTH AND TRENTON

© TOM NANGLE

Kisma Preserve is a sanctuary for retired or relocated exotic animals.

Aerial Touring

It's difficult to envision the Acadia National Park region without getting aloft. Two businesses provide a variety of ways to get an eagle's-eye view of the area—allowing you to see that although it takes miles of road to connect the various sections, they're all quite close on the water. Both are based on the Route 3 side of Hancock County/Bar Harbor Airport, just north of Mount Desert Island and 12 miles north of downtown Bar Harbor. Opt for a clear day, if possible.

Scenic Flights of Acadia (Bar Harbor Rd., Rte. 3, Trenton, 207/667-6527, www.maine-coastalflight.com) offers low-level flightseeing services in the Mount Desert Island region. Flights range 22–60 minutes and begin around $50 per person, with a two-passenger minimum.

Scenic Biplane and Glider Rides (968 Bar Harbor Rd./Rte. 3, Trenton, 207/667-7627, www.acadiaairtours.com) lets you soar in silence with daily glider flights. The one- or two-passenger gliders are towed to at least an altitude of 2,500 feet and then released. An FAA-certified pilot guides the glider. Rates begin at $199 for a 20-minute flight for two,

$149 for one. Or ride in a biplane: A 20-minute ride in an open-cockpit plane is $225 for two, $175 for one. All flights are subject to an airport fee.

RECREATION
Lamoine State Park

Lamoine State Park (23 State Park Rd., Rte. 184, Lamoine, 207/667-4778, $3 adults, $1 ages 5–11) features a pebble beach and a picnic area with a spectacular view, a children's play area, and campsites. If you've brought your own boat, the park also provides a boat ramp for launching. Careful, though, the currents are strong here. Though the 55-acre park isn't officially open in winter, it's popular for cross-country skiing and snowshoeing. This is strictly do-it-yourself fun, as there are no marked trails.

Golf

Try to keep your eye on the ball rather than the views at the challenging 18-hole **Bar Harbor Golf Course** (junction of Rtes. 3 and 204, Trenton, 207/667-7505, www.barharborgolf-course.com). Despite the name, it's not in the island community, nor even on the island.

ENTERTAINMENT
◖ The Great Maine Lumberjack Show

Ace lumberjack "Timber" Tina Scheer has been competing around the world since she was seven, and she shows her prowess at The Great Maine Lumberjack Show (Rte. 3, 207/667-0067, www.mainelumberjack.com, 7 P.M. daily mid-June–late Aug., $8.50 adult, $6.50 ages 4–11). During the 75-minute "Olympics of the Forest," you'll watch two teams compete in 14 events, including ax throwing, crosscut sawing, log rolling, speed climbing, and more. Some are open to participation. (Kids can learn log rolling by appointment.) Performances are held rain or shine. Seating is under a roof, but dress for the weather if it's inclement. The ticket office opens at 6 P.M.

SHOPPING

Adults can browse the books, antiques, and even wine selections housed in **Country Store Antiques** (410 Rte. 3/Bar Harbor Rd., Ellsworth, 207/667-5922), a huge red barn with 30 dealers selling a wide range of goods. While the parents shop, older kids can skedaddle over to **Dutch Treat Ice Cream** next door for homemade flavors.

Stock up on Maine-made jams, syrups, honeys, and other specialty foods at **Maine's Own Treats** (68 Rte. 3/Bar Harbor Rd., Trenton, 207/667-8888, www.mainesowntreats.com).

ACCOMMODATIONS

Most of the motels and cabin complexes along the Trenton stretch are small, family-owned operations—not fancy, but their rates are far lower than what you'd find on Mount Desert.

Family-owned, nicely landscaped, and meticulously maintained, the ◖ **Open Hearth Inn** (1147 Bar Harbor Rd., Rte. 3, Trenton, 207/667-2930 or 800/655-0234, www.openhearthinn.com, $70–130) is on the Island Explorer bus route, less than a quarter mile from the bridge connecting Trenton to Mount Desert, and within walking distance of four lobster restaurants. Choose an inn room with a three-course breakfast, or opt for a cottage or motel room (both with continental buffet breakfast) or apartment with kitchen. All have TV, fridge, air-conditioning, and Wi-Fi. Also on the premises is an enclosed family hot tub. The only drawback might be the traffic noise. Kids under 12 are free; two pet-friendly rooms are an additional $25. Free pickup at Bar Harbor Airport. It's open year-round.

Camping

Equally convenient (or not) to the Schoodic Region and Mount Desert Island is the 55-acre **Lamoine State Park** (23 State Park Rd., Rte. 184, Lamoine, 207/667-4778), which is just off the shortcut route from Mount Desert Island to Schoodic. Park facilities include a pebble beach and a picnic area with a spectacular view, a boat-launch ramp, and a children's play area. Day-use admission is $3 adults, $1 children 5–11. Camping (62 sites) is $25 per site per night for nonresidents ($15 for Maine residents), plus a $2-per-night fee for reservations. No hookups are available; two-night minimum stay, 14-night maximum. (Camping season is mid-May–mid-Sept. Reserve online at www.state.me.us/doc/parks/reservations using a credit card, or call 207/624-9950 or 800/332-1501 in Maine, weekdays.) Leashed pets are allowed, but not on the beach, and cleanup is required.

For RVers, the 200-site waterfront **Narrows Too Camping Resort** (1150 Bar Harbor Rd./Rte. 3, Trenton, 207/667-4300, www.barharborcampgrounds.com), a sibling of the Narrows campground on Mount Desert Island, has everything and then some. Peak rates for two adults and two children younger than 18 range from $49 for a site with water and electric to $99 for an oceanfront site with water, sewer, and electric. Also available are rental log cabins ($500 per week) and resort cottages ($1,500 per week). Facilities include a heated pool, grocery, laundry, video arcade, exercise room, canoe and kayak rentals, and even live entertainment. The site is on the Island Explorer shuttle bus route. It's open late May through mid-October.

FOOD

Route 3 (Bar Harbor Road) is lined with eateries, including several lobster pounds that deserve a stop. One of the best-known and longest-running (since 1956) is **Trenton Bridge Lobster Pound** (1237 Bar Harbor Rd., Trenton, 207/667-2977, www.trentonbridgelobster.com, 11 A.M.–7:30 P.M. Mon.–Sat. Memorial Day–Columbus Day), on the right next to the bridge leading to Mount Desert Island. Watch for the "smoke signals"—steam billowing from the huge vats; the lobster couldn't be much fresher.

In 2008, a branch of hugely popular (**Pectic Seafood** (367 Rte. 3, Bar Harbor Rd., Trenton, 207/667-7566, http://pecticseafood.com) opened, complete with indoor and outdoor seating and restrooms. The menu ranges from burgers and subs to fried seafood dinners and fresh lobster rolls at prices from $4–16. In addition, Pectic sells prepared heat-and-eat foods such as seafood Newberg, baked stuffed haddock, vegetable lasagna, and chicken soup, and it sells a wide array of fresh fish and specialty foods.

Edging the ocean at Mount Desert Narrows is the **Thompson Island Picnic Area** (Rte. 3, Thompson Island, Trenton). It has picnic tables, fire grills, a water fountain, and restrooms. At low tide, you might see locals raking the mud flats for clams.

INFORMATION AND SERVICES

The **Thompson Island Visitor Center** (Rte. 3, Thompson Island, Trenton, 207/288-3411) represents the Mount Desert Island Regional Chambers of Commerce, which includes the Trenton Chamber of Commerce. The center opens for the season in mid-May and is open 8 A.M.–6 P.M. daily until mid-October.

The **Ellsworth Area Chamber of Commerce** (163 High St., Ellsworth, 207/667-5584, www.ellsworthchamber.org) also covers Trenton.

Also, in Trenton, en route from Ellsworth on Route 3, and shortly before you reach Mount Desert, you'll see (on your right) the **Bar Harbor Chamber of Commerce** (Rte. 3, Trenton, 207/288-5103 or 888/540-9990, www.barharbormaine.com). You'll find all sorts of info about the island and other locations, as well as restrooms, phones, and a helpful staff.

GETTING AROUND

Route 1 of the **Island Explorer** (www.exploreacadia.com) bus system, which primarily serves Mount Desert Island with its fleet of propane-fueled, fare-free vehicles, connects the Hancock County/Bar Harbor Airport with downtown Bar Harbor between late June and mid-October.

If you're approaching from the south on Route 1, and your destination is Mount Desert Island, you can avoid downtown and the strip. When you cross the bridge in Ellsworth, turn right at the traffic light onto Route 230/Water Street, and follow it about 6.5 miles, turning left onto Goose Cove Road, which rejoins Route 230. (You can stay on Route 230; it's just longer as it loops around the point.) Bear left on Route 230, then right at the T intersection with Route 3. The causeway connecting to Mount Desert Island is less than a mile away.

Before or after visiting Mount Desert Island, if you're headed farther Down East—to Lamoine, the eastern side of Hancock County, and beyond—there's a good shortcut from Trenton. About five miles south of Ellsworth on Route 3, just north of the Kisma Preserve, turn east onto Route 204.

BACKGROUND

The Land

IN THE BEGINNING . . .

Maine is an outdoor classroom for Geology 101, a living lesson in what the glaciers did and how they did it. I tell anyone who will listen that I plan to be a geologist in my next life—and the best place for the first course is Acadia National Park.

Geologically, Maine is something of a youngster; the oldest rocks, found in the Chain of Ponds area in the western part of the state, are only 1.6 billion years old—more than 2 billion years younger than the world's oldest rocks.

But most significant is the great ice sheet that began to spread over Maine about 25,000 years ago, during the late Wisconsin Ice Age. As it moved southward from Canada, this continental glacier scraped, gouged, pulverized, and depressed the bedrock in its path. On it continued, charging up the north faces of mountains, clipping off their tops, and moving southward, leaving behind jagged cliffs on the mountains' southern faces and odd deposits of stone and clay. By about 21,000 years ago, glacial ice extended well over the Gulf of Maine, perhaps as far as the Georges Bank fishing grounds.

© HILARY NANGLE

But all that began to change with meltdown, beginning about 18,000 years ago. As the glacier melted and receded, ocean water moved in, covering much of the coastal plain and working its way inland up the rivers. By 11,000 years ago, glaciers had pulled back from all but a few minor corners at the top of Maine, revealing the south coast's beaches and the intriguing geologic traits—eskers and erratics, kettleholes and moraines, even a fjord—that make Mount Desert Island and the rest of the state such a fascinating natural laboratory.

Mount Desert's Somes Sound (named after pioneer settler Abraham Somes)—which may be (experts disagree) the only fjord on the eastern seaboard—is just one distinctive feature on an island loaded with geologic wonders. There are pocket beaches, pink granite ledges, sea caves, "pancake" rocks, wild headlands, volcanic "dikes," and a handful of pristine ponds and lakes. And once you've glimpsed the Bubbles—two curvaceous, oversized mounds on the edge of Jordan Pond—you'll know exactly how they earned their name.

CLIMATE

Acadia National Park fits into the National Weather Service's **coastal** category, a 20-mile-wide swath that stretches from Kittery on the New Hampshire border to Eastport on the Canadian border. In the park (and its surrounding communities), the proximity of the Gulf of Maine moderates the climate, making coastal winters generally warmer and summers usually cooler than elsewhere in the state.

Average June temperatures in **Bar Harbor,** adjoining the park, range 53–76°F; July and August temperatures range 60–82°F. By December, the average range is 20–32°F.

The Seasons

Maine has four distinct seasons: summer, fall, winter, and mud. Lovers of spring weather need to look elsewhere in March, the lowest month on the popularity scale, with its mud-caked

vehicles, soggy everything, irritable temperaments, tank-trap roads, and occasionally the worst snowstorm of the year.

Summer can be idyllic—with moderate temperatures, clear air, and wispy breezes—but it can also close in with fog, rain, and chills. Prevailing winds are from the southwest. Officially, summer runs from June 21 to September 23, but consider summer June, July, and August. The typical growing season is 148 days long.

A poll of Mainers might well show autumn as the favorite season—days are still warmish, nights are cool, winds are optimum for sailors, and the foliage is brilliant—particularly throughout Acadia. Fall colors usually reach their peak in the park in early October, about a week before Columbus Day. Early autumn, however, is also the height of hurricane season, the only potential flaw this time of year.

Winter, officially December 21 to March 20, means an unpredictable potpourri of weather along the park's coastline. But when the cold and snow hit this region, it's time for cross-country skiing, snowshoeing, and ice-skating. The park receives an average of 61 inches of snow over the season.

Spring, officially March 20 to June 21, is the frequent butt of jokes. It's an ill-defined season that arrives much too late and departs all too quickly. Spring planting can't occur until well into May; lilacs explode in late May and disappear by mid-June. And just when you finally can enjoy being outside, black flies stretch their wings and satisfy their hunger pangs. Along the shore, fortunately, steady breezes often keep the pesky creatures to a minimum.

Northeasters and Hurricanes

A northeaster is a counterclockwise-swirling storm that brings wild winds out of—you guessed it—the northeast. These storms can occur at any time of year, whenever the conditions brew them up. Depending on the season, the winds are accompanied by rain, sleet, snow, or all of them together.

ACADIA FACTS

Acadia National Park was established by Congress in 1929, after previous incarnations as Lafayette National Park (1919) and Sieur de Monts National Monument (1916).

- Acadia covers more than 47,000 mainland and island acres, including more than 11,000 acres protected by conservation easements. Its permanent boundaries were established by Congress in 1986.

- Acadia has 26 mountains ranging in height from 284 feet (Flying Mountain) to 1,530 feet (Cadillac). Cadillac is the highest point on the eastern seaboard of the United States.

- Nine "great ponds" (covering more than 10 acres) lie within the park boundaries. Five others abut parkland. The depths of these lakes and ponds range between 7 feet (Aunt Betty Pond) and 150 feet (Jordan Pond). Mount Desert Island's lakes and ponds have restrictions on swimming and personal and motorized watercraft.

- Acadia has about 130 miles of hiking trails. At the height (so to speak) of trail construction, in the early 20th century, there were some 230 miles. Some of the discontinued trails are being rehabilitated via the Acadia Trails Forever program, a joint project of the park and Friends of Acadia.

- Acadia has more than 2 million visitors each year, most in the months of July, August, and September, making it one of the most-visited national parks in the country.

- The "creature counts" in Acadia, on Mount Desert Island, and in the surrounding waters include 338 species of birds, more than 6,500 insect species and subspecies, at least 5 reptile species, 24 species of fish, at least 11 species of amphibians, and at least 40 mammal species.

- The Park Loop Road is 20 miles, with an additional 7 miles for a round-trip to the summit of Cadillac Mountain.

- The park has 45 miles of car-free, broken-stone carriage roads for walking, biking, and horseback riding, as well as cross-country skiing and snowshoeing in winter; 12 miles of privately owned carriage roads south of Jordan Pond are usable by walkers and horses but not bicycles.

- Acadia has three campgrounds – two on Mount Desert Island, one on Isle au Haut. Only one (Blackwoods) is open all year. Backcountry camping is not allowed in Acadia. (A dozen or so commercial campgrounds are located on Mount Desert Island beyond park boundaries.)

- The Schoodic Peninsula is the only park acreage that's on the mainland; all other park properties are on islands. A bridge connects Mount Desert Island to the mainland town of Trenton, but other parcels must be reached by boat.

Hurricane season officially runs from June through November, but hurricanes are most active in late August and September. Some years, Maine remains out of harm's way; other years, head-on hurricanes and even glancing blows have eroded beaches, flooded roads, splintered boats, downed trees, knocked out power, and inflicted major residential and commercial damage. Winds—the greatest culprit—average 74–90 mph. A hurricane watch is announced on radio and TV about 36 hours before the hurricane hits, followed by a hurricane warning that indicates that the storm is imminent. Find shelter away from plate-glass windows, and wait it out. If especially high winds are predicted, make every effort to secure yourself, your vehicle, and your possessions. Resist the urge to

© HILARY NANGLE

Fog adds a mystical quality to a boat-filled harbor.

head for the shore to watch the show; rogue waves combined with ultrahigh tides have been known to sweep away unwary onlookers. Schoodic Point, the mainland section of Acadia, is a particularly perilous location in such conditions.

Sea Smoke and Fog

Sea smoke and fog, two atmospheric phenomena resulting from opposing conditions, are only distantly related. But both can radically affect visibility and therefore be hazardous. In winter, when the ocean is at least 40°F warmer than the air, billowy sea smoke rises from the water, creating great photo ops for camera buffs but seriously dangerous conditions for mariners.

In any season, when the ocean (or lake or land) is colder than the air, fog sets in, creating nasty conditions for drivers, mariners, and pilots. Romantics, however, see it otherwise, reveling in the womblike ambience and the muffled moans of foghorns.

Storm Warnings

The National Weather Service's official daytime signal system for wind velocity consists of a series of flags representing specific wind speeds and sea conditions. Beachgoers and anyone planning to venture out in a kayak, canoe, sailboat, or powerboat should heed these signals. The signal flags are posted on all public beaches, and warnings are announced on TV and radio weather broadcasts, as well as on cable TV's Weather Channel and the NOAA broadcast network.

Flora and Fauna

In the course of a single day at Acadia National Park—where more than two dozen mountains meet the sea—the casual visitor can pass through a landscape that lends itself to a surprising diversity of animal and plant life. On one outing, you can explore the shoreline—barnacles encrust the rocks, and black crowberry, an arctic shrub that finds Maine's coastal climate agreeable, grows close to the ground alongside trails. On the same outing, you can wander beneath the boughs of the leafy hardwood forest that favors more southern climes, as well as the spruce-fir forest of the north. A little farther up the trail are subalpine plants more typically associated with mountain environments and neotropical songbirds providing background music.

Acadia's creatures and plants will endlessly intrigue any nature lover; the following are but a sampling of what you might encounter during a visit.

OFFSHORE

Acadia National Park is surrounded by the sea—from the rockbound Schoodic Peninsula jutting from the mainland Down East to the offshore island in Penobscot Bay that Samuel de Champlain named Isle au Haut. While the park's boundaries do not extend out to sea, the life that can be found there draws tourists and scientists alike.

The Maine coastline falls within the Gulf of Maine, a "sea within a sea" that extends from Nova Scotia to Cape Cod and out to the fishing grounds of Brown and Georges Banks. It is one of the most biologically rich environments in the world. Surface water, driven by currents off Nova Scotia, swirls in counterclockwise circles, delivering nutrients and food to the plants and animals that live there. Floating microplants, tiny shrimp-like creatures, and jellyfish benefit from those nutrients and once supported huge populations of groundfish, now depleted by overfishing.

These highly productive waters lure not only fishing vessels but also **sea mammals.** Whales may rarely swim into the inshore bays and inlets bounded by Acadia, but whale watch cruises based on Mount Desert Island ferry passengers miles offshore to the locales where whales gather. Whales fall into two groups: toothed and baleen. Toothed whales hunt individual prey, such as squid, fish, and the occasional seabird; they include porpoises and dolphins, killer whales, sperm whales, and pilot whales. Baleen whales have no teeth, so they must sift food through horny plates called baleen; they include finback whales, minke whales, humpback whales, and right whales. Any of these species may be observed in the Gulf of Maine.

Harbor porpoises, which grow to a length of six feet, can be spotted from a boat in the inshore waters around Mount Desert Island, traveling in pods as they hunt schools of herring and mackerel. The most you'll usually see of them are their gray backs and triangular dorsal fins as they perform their graceful ballet through the waves.

Of great delight to wildlife watchers is catching glimpses of **harbor seals.** While the shores of Mount Desert Island are too busy with human activity for seals to linger, they are usually spotted during nature cruises that head out to the well-known "seal ledges." Check the tide chart and book an excursion for low tide. Seals haul themselves out of the ocean at low tide to rest on the rocks and sunbathe. Naps are a necessity for harbor seals, which have less blubber and fur to insulate them from the frigid waters of the Gulf of Maine than other seal species. Hauling out preserves energy otherwise spent heating the body, and it replenishes their blood with oxygen.

At high tide, you might see individual "puppy dog" faces bobbing among the waves as the seals forage for food. Harbor seals, sometimes called "sea dogs," almost disappeared along the coast of Maine in the early 20th century. It was believed they competed with fishermen for the much-prized lobster and other valuable catches, and they were hunted nearly into oblivion. When it became obvious that the absence of seals did not improve fish stocks, the bounty placed on them was lifted. The Marine Mammal Protection Act of 1972 made it illegal to hunt or harm any marine mammal, except by permit—happily, populations of harbor seals now have rebounded all along the coast.

Every now and then, park rangers receive reports of "abandoned" seal pups along Acadia's shore. Usually it's not a stranded youngster, but rather a pup left to rest while its mother hunts for food. If you discover a seal pup on the shore, leave it undisturbed and report the sighting to rangers.

ALONG THE SHORE

Whether walking the shore or cruising on a boat, there is no symbol so closely associated with the coast as the ubiquitous **gull.** Several species of gulls frequent Acadia's skies, but none is more common than the herring gull. Easily dismissed as brassy sandwich thieves (which, of course, they are), herring gulls almost vanished in the 20th century as a result of hunting and egg collecting. Indeed, many seabird populations declined in the early 1900s due to the demand for feathers to adorn ladies' hats. Conservation measures have helped some of these bird species recover, including the large, gray-backed herring gull, an elegant flyer that often lobs sea urchins onto the rocky shore from aloft to crack them open for the morsels within.

Common **eider duck** females, a mottled brown, and the black-and-white males (nicknamed "floating skunks") congregate in large "rafts" on the icy ocean during the winter to mate. When spring arrives, males and females separate. While the males provide no help in raising the young, the females cooperate with one another, often gathering ducklings together to protect them from predators. Adult eiders may live and breed for 20 years or more, though the mortality rate is high among the

young. Present along Acadia's shore all year long, they feed on mussels, clams, and dog whelks, their powerful gizzards grinding down shells and all.

A smaller seabird regularly espied around Acadia is the **black guillemot,** also known as the "sea pigeon" and "underwater flyer" because it seems to fly through the water. Guillemots learn to swim before they learn to fly. Black-and-white with bright red feet, guillemots are cousins to puffins. They nest on rock ledges along the shore, laying pear-shaped eggs that won't roll over the edge and into the waves below.

Bald eagles and **ospreys** (also known as fish hawks) take advantage of the fishing available in Acadia's waters. Both of these majestic raptors suffered from the effects of the pesticide DDT, which washed down through waterways and into the ocean, becoming concentrated in the fish the raptors consumed. As a result, they laid thin-shelled eggs that broke easily, preventing the development of young. The banning of DDT in the United States has resulted in a strong comeback for both species and the removal of the bald eagle from the federal endangered species list. Along the coast of Maine, however, the bald eagle's return has been less triumphant than in other parts of the country. Biologists continue to seek explanations for the lag, and the bald eagle remains on state and federal lists as a threatened species.

Boat cruises (some with park rangers aboard) departing from several Mount Desert Island harbors offer good chances for sightings. They allow passengers to approach (but not too closely) nesting islands of eagles and ospreys. Both species create large nests of sticks, from which they can command a wide view of the surrounding area. Some osprey nests have been documented as being 100 years old, and researchers have found everything from fishing tackle to swim trunks entwined in the sticks of the nests.

Look also for eagles and ospreys flying above inland areas of the park. Ospreys hunt over freshwater ponds and lakes, hovering until a fish is sighted, then plummeting from the sky into the water to grab the prey. For aerodynamic reasons, they carry the fish headfirst.

Acadia visitors often ask rangers if there are sea otters in the park. After all, there is an Otter Creek, which flows into Otter Cove, which is bounded by Otter Cliffs. At one time, Gorham Mountain was known as Peak of Otter! With all these place names devoted to the otter, it would be logical to assume that Mount Desert Island teems with them. In fact, though, there are no sea otters along the entire eastern seaboard of the United States—perhaps the earliest European settlers mistook sea minks (now extinct) for sea otters. River otters do reside in the park, though they are reclusive and spend most of their time in freshwater environments. You might observe one during the winter frolicking on a frozen pond.

INTERTIDAL ZONE

Some of the most alien creatures on earth live where the ocean washes the rocky shoreline. The creatures of this intertidal zone are at once resilient and fragile, and always fascinating. Some of the creatures and plants live best in the upper reaches of the intertidal zone, which is doused only by the spray of waves and the occasional extra-high tide. Others, which would not survive the upper regions, thrive in the lower portions of the intertidal zone, which is almost always submerged. The rest live in rocky pockets of water in between, and all are influenced by the ebb and flow of the tide. Temperature, salinity, and the strength of crashing waves all determine where a creature will live in the intertidal zone.

As you approach the ocean's edge, the first creatures likely to come underfoot are **barnacles**—vast stretches of rock can be encrusted with them. Step gently, for walking on barnacles crushes them. Their tiny, white volcano-shaped shells remain closed when exposed to the air, but they open when submerged to feed. Water movement encourages them to sweep the water with feathery "legs" to feed on microscopic plankton.

Despite the tough armor with which barnacles cover themselves, they are preyed upon by **dog whelks** (snails), which drill through the barnacle shells with their tongues to feed on the creature within. A dog whelk can be distinguished from the common periwinkle by the elliptical opening of its shell. Periwinkles have teardrop-shaped openings.

Sea stars find blue mussels yummy. Blue mussels siphon plankton from the water and anchor themselves in place with byssal threads. Sea stars creep up on the mussels, wrap their legs around them, and pry open their shells just enough to insert their stomachs and consume the animal inside. Look for sea stars and mussels in the lower regions of tide pools.

Related to sea stars are **sea urchins**—spiky green balls most often seen as empty, spineless husks littered along the shoreline (they are frequently preyed upon by gulls). If you come upon a live sea urchin, handle it with care. While their spikes are not poisonous, they *are* sharp. Gently roll a sea urchin over to see its mouth and the five white teeth with which it gnaws on seaweed and animal remains. (While the green sea urchins found in Acadia do not possess poisonous spines, some of their counterparts in other regions do.)

Limpets, with cone-shaped shells, are snails that rely on seaweed for food. They suction themselves to rocks, which prevents them from drying up when exposed at low tide. Do not tear limpets from rocks—doing so hurts the animal.

Many intertidal creatures depend on seaweed for protection and food. **Rockweeds** drape over rocks, floating with the waves, their long fronds buoyed by distinctive air bladders. **Dulse** (edible for people) is common along the shore, as is Irish moss, used as a thickener in ice cream, paint, and other products.

Tide Pool Tips

The best way to learn about the fascinating world that exists between the tides is to look for creatures in their own habitats, with a good field guide as a reference.

- Go at low tide—there are two low tides daily, 12 hours apart.

- Tread carefully. Shoreline rocks are slippery.

- Do not remove creatures from their habitats; doing so could harm them.

- Be aware of the ocean at all times. Sudden waves can wash the shore and sweep you to your death.

- Join a ranger-guided shoreline walk to learn more about this unique environment. Check the *Beaver Log,* Acadia's official park newspaper, for the schedule and details.

FRESHWATER LAKES AND PONDS

Known best for its rocky shoreline and mountains, Acadia National Park cradles numerous glistening lakes and ponds in its glacially carved valleys. Several lakes serve as public water supplies for surrounding communities, and swimming is prohibited in most. Echo Lake and the north end of Long Pond are excellent designated swimming areas. Freshwater fishing requires a state license for adults. Please obey posted regulations.

TIDES

Nowhere is the adage "Time and tide wait for no man" more true than along the Maine coastline. The nation's most extreme tidal ranges occur in Maine, and they become even more dramatic as you head "Down East," toward the Canadian Maritime provinces. Every six hours or so, the tide begins either ebbing or flowing, so you'll have countless opportunities for observing tidal phenomena.

Tides govern coastal life, and everyone is a slave to the tide calendar or chart, which coastal-community newspapers diligently publish in every issue. Each issue of the official park visitor guide, the *Beaver Log,* also contains a tide chart (as well as times of sunrise and sunset). In tidal regions, boats tie up with extra-long lines, clammers and worm-diggers schedule their days by the tides, hikers have to plan ahead for shoreline exploring, and kayakers need to plan their routes to avoid getting stuck in the muck.

Average tidal ranges (between low tide and high tide) in the area around Acadia National Park are 10 or 11 feet, and extremes are 12 or 13 feet.

Tides, as we all learned in elementary school, are lunar phenomena, created by the gravitational pull of the moon; the tidal range depends on the lunar phase. Tides are most extreme at new and full moons – when the sun, moon, and earth are all aligned. These are **spring tides,** supposedly because the water springs upward (the term has nothing to do with the season). And tides are smallest during the moon's first and third quarters – when the sun, earth, and moon have a right-angle configuration. These are **neap tides** ("neap" comes from an Old English word meaning "scanty"). Other lunar/solar phenomena, such as the equinoxes and solstices, can also affect tidal ranges.

The best time for shoreline exploration is on a new-moon or full-moon day, when low tide exposes mussels, sea urchins, sea cucumbers, sea stars, periwinkles, hermit crabs, rockweed, and assorted nonbiodegradable trash. Rubber boots or waterproof treaded shoes are essential on the wet, slippery terrain.

Caution is also essential in tidal areas. Unless you've carefully plotted tide times and heights, don't park a car or bike or boat trailer on a beach; make sure your sea kayak is lashed securely to a tree or bollard; don't take a long nap on shoreline granite; and don't cross a low-tide land spit without an eye on your watch.

A perhaps apocryphal but almost believable story goes that one flatlander stormed up to a ranger at a Maine state park one bright summer morning and demanded indignantly to know why they had had the nerve to drain the water from her shorefront campsite during the night. When it comes to tides...you just have to go with the flow.

The voice of the northern wilderness belongs to the **common loon,** whose roots are so ancient it is the oldest bird species found in North America. During the summer months, loons are garbed in striking white-and-black plumage, which fades to gray during the winter when loons migrate to the ocean's open waters. Graceful swimmers, loons are clumsy on land. Their webbed feet are set to the rear of their bodies, making them front-heavy. Land travel is a struggle. Consequently, they nest very close to the water's edge, which makes them vulnerable to such manmade hazards as the wakes of motorized watercraft.

The loon's mysterious ululating call can be heard echoing across lakes on most any summer evening, an eerie sound not quickly forgotten.

Evening is actually an excellent time to observe wildlife. Creatures that seem shy and reclusive by day tend to be most active at dawn and dusk (crepuscular) or at night (nocturnal). Carriage roads along Eagle Lake, Bubble Pond, and Witch Hole Pond make nighttime walking easy. (Hint: Go at dusk so your eyes adjust with the darkening sky, and keep in mind that flashlight use abruptly ruins night vision.)

Frog choruses form the backdrop to the cries of loons. In Acadia, there are eight **frog and toad species,** which tend to be most vocal during the spring mating season. Close your eyes and listen to see if you can distinguish individual species, such as the "banjo-twanging" croak of the green frog and the "snore" of the leopard frog.

The onset of moonlight may reveal small winged creatures swooping, darting, and careening over lakes and ponds. Acadia is home to several species of **bats,** including the common little brown bat. Don't scream! Bats have no desire to get entangled in your hair. Their echolocation (radar) is so fine-tuned that it can detect a single strand of human hair. Bats are far more interested in the mosquitoes attracted to your body heat. True insect-munching machines, a single pinky-size little brown bat can eat hundreds, if not thousands, of insects in one evening.

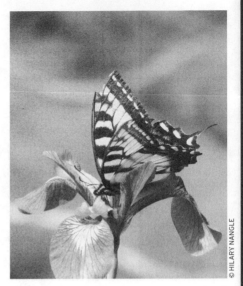

© HILARY NANGLE

Bandit-faced **raccoons** are also creatures of the night, and they sometimes can be found scampering alongside the shore. They are omnivorous, dining on anything from grubs, frogs, and small mammals to fish, berries, and garbage. Rabies is present in Maine, and raccoons are common carriers of the disease. Do not approach sick-acting animals (seeing them during the daytime may indicate illness), and report any strange behavior to a park ranger. When camping or picnicking, stow food items in your vehicle and dispose of scraps properly. Raccoons are opportunistic thieves that have been known to claw their way into tents to find food.

And where are the moose? The question is asked often at Acadia's visitors center, and wildlife watchers are disappointed to learn that moose, the largest member of the deer family, are rarely sighted in the park. Moose are more frequently observed in western and northern Maine, in the Moosehead Lake and Baxter State Park regions. However, individuals are spotted from time to time on Mount Desert Island, and there may even be a small family group residing on the west side. Moose like to dine on aquatic vegetation, such as the tubers of cattails and lily pads, and they frequent marshes and lakes to escape biting flies. Bass Harbor Marsh is inviting habitat for moose, but good luck spotting one.

A prehistoric-looking creature sometimes encountered on carriage roads near ponds is the **snapping turtle.** An average adult may weigh 30 pounds or more. Keep well clear of the snapper's powerful beak, which is lightning-quick when grabbing prey; it can do real damage, such as biting off fingers. Adult snappers have no predators (except people), and they will dine on other turtles, frogs, ducklings, wading birds, and beaver kits.

By midsummer, many of Acadia's ponds are beautifully adorned with yellow water lilies and white pond lilies. Lily pads are a favorite food of beavers. **Beavers** emerge from their lodges—large piles of sticks and mud—at dusk and dawn to feed and make necessary repairs to their dams. Beavers create their own habitat by transforming streams into ponds. They move awkwardly on land, so they adjust the water level close to their source of building materials and other favored foods: aspen and birch trees. Doing so limits their exposure to dry land and predators.

Beavers are large rodents that were trapped excessively for centuries for the fur trade. They have since made a strong comeback in Acadia—to the point that their ponds now threaten roads, trails, and other park structures. Resource managers try to keep ahead of the beavers by inserting "beaver foolers" (PVC pipes) through dams that block road culverts. This moderates pond levels and prevents damage to roads by allowing water to drain through the culvert. Sometimes the beavers, however, get ahead of the resource managers. They have been known to plug the beaver foolers with sticks and mud, or to chew through them with their strong teeth.

Amazingly adapted for life in the water, beavers are fascinating to watch. A very accessible location along the Park Loop Road, just past Bear Brook Picnic Area, is Beaver Dam Pond, featuring a few lodges, a dam, and an active beaver population. The best viewing times are dawn and dusk. In the fall the beavers are

busiest, preparing food stores for the winter to come. The park often presents a beaver-watch program at that time of year, which is a great way to learn more about the habits and adaptations of the beaver.

Beavers act as a catalyst for increasing natural diversity in an area. Their ponds attract ospreys, herons, and owls; salamanders, frogs, and turtles; insects and aquatic plants; foxes, deer, muskrats, and river otters. Their ponds help maintain the water table, enrich soils, and prevent flooding.

While beavers may bring diversity to a wetland, an invader has been endangering Acadia's ponds and lakes. **Purple loosestrife,** a showy stalked purple flower nonnative to North America, was introduced into gardens as an ornamental. Highly reproductive and adaptive and with no natural predators, purple loosestrife escaped the confines of gardens and has literally choked the life out of some wetlands by crowding out native plants on which many creatures depend and creating a monoculture. Few native species find purple loosestrife useful.

Purple loosestrife has been contained at Acadia, but it's an ongoing process. Uprooting it seems to encourage more to grow, and jostling stalks at certain times of the year disperses vast numbers of seeds, so resource managers have resorted to treating individual plants with an approved herbicide in a way that does not harm the surrounding environment.

WOODLANDS

A dark, statuesque **spruce-fir forest** dominates much of Acadia's woodlands and does well in the cooler, moist environs of Maine's coast. Red spruce trees are tall and polelike and often cohabit with fragrant balsam fir. The spruce grows needles only at the canopy, sparing little energy for growing needles where the sun cannot reach. Because the sun barely touches the forest floor, little undergrowth emerges from the bump and swale of acidic, rust-colored needles that carpet the ground, except for more tiny, shade-loving spruce, waiting for their chance to grow tall.

FALL FOLIAGE

The timing and quality of Maine's fall foliage owes much to the summer weather that precedes it, but the annual spectacle never disappoints. In early September, as deciduous trees ready themselves for winter, they stop producing chlorophyll, and the green begins to disappear from their leaves. Taking its place are the spectacular pigments – brilliant reds, yellows, oranges, and purples – that paint the leaves and warm the hearts of every "leaf-peeper," shopkeeper, innkeeper, and restaurateur.

The colorful display begins slowly, reaches a peak, then fades – starting in Maine's north in early to mid-September and working down to

Eagle Lake

the southwest corner by mid-October. **Peak foliage** in Acadia National Park typically occurs in early to mid-October, with the last bits of color hanging on almost until the end of the month.

The fall palette is stunning, especially in Acadia. The leaves of white ash turn purple; sumac and sugar and red maples turn scarlet; mountain ash, beech, basswood, and birch trees turn various shades of yellow.

Trees put on their most magnificent show after a summer of moderate heat and rainfall. A summer of excessive heat and scant rainfall means colors will be less brilliant and disappear more quickly. Throw a September or October northeaster or hurricane into the mix, and estimates are up for grabs.

So predictions are imprecise, and you'll need to allow some schedule flexibility to take advantage of optimum color. From early September to mid-October, check the foliage section on the state Department of Conservation's website (www.mainefoliage.com) for frequently updated maps, panoramic photographs, recommended driving tours, and weekly reports on the foliage status (this is gauged by the percentage of "leaf drop" in every region of the state). Between early September and early October, you can even sign up via the website for weekly email reports (Acadia straddles zones 1 and 2 in the report maps). The state's toll-free fall foliage hotline is 888/624-6345.

Fall foliage trips are extremely popular and have become more so in recent years, so lodging can be scarce. Plan ahead and make reservations; sleeping in your car can be mighty chilly at that time of year.

The spruce-fir forest can be uncannily quiet, especially in the middle of the day. The density of the woods and the springy, needle-laden floor seem to buffer noise from without. Listen closely, however, and you may hear the cackle of ravens, the squabble of a territorial red squirrel, or the rat-a-tat of a woodpecker.

Red squirrels are energetic denizens of

the spruce-fir forest, scolding innocent passersby or sitting on tree stumps scaling spruce cones and stuffing their cheeks full of seeds. Observant wildlife watchers will find their middens (heaps of cone scales) about the forest. Squirrels are especially industrious (even comical) in autumn as they frantically prepare for the winter by stocking up on food, tearing about from branch to branch with spruce cones poking out of their mouths like big cigars.

Woodpeckers favor dead, still-standing trees, shredding the bark to get at the insects infesting the trunk. The pileated woodpecker—a large black-and-white bird with a red cap—is relatively shy, so you are more likely to encounter evidence of its passage (rectangular and oval holes in trees) than the bird itself. Other common woodpeckers you might observe are the hairy and the downy.

The face of Acadia's woodlands changed dramatically in 1947. That fall, during a period of extremely dry conditions, a fire began west of the park's present-day visitors center in Hulls Cove. Feeding on tinder-dry woods and grasses, and whipped into an inferno by gale-force winds, the fire roared across the eastern half of Mount Desert Island, miraculously skirting downtown Bar Harbor but destroying numerous year-round and seasonal homes. In all, 17,000 acres burned (10,000 in the park).

Researchers have studied 6,000 years of the park's fire history by pulling core samples from ponds to analyze the layers of pollen and charcoal that have settled in their bottoms over time, the latter indicating periods of fire. The most significant layer of charcoal appeared in the period around 1947, indicating the intensity of the great fire.

The aftermath of the fire—the scorched mountainsides and skeletal, blackened remains of trees—must have been a devastating sight. Loggers salvaged usable timber and removed unsafe snags. Seed was ordered so replanting could begin in earnest. Soils needed to be stabilized and the landscape restored.

Then a curious thing happened the following spring: As the snow melted, green shoots began to poke up out of the soils among the sooty remains. "Pioneer plants," such as lowbush blueberry and Indian paintbrush, took over the job of stabilizing soils. By the time the ordered seeds arrived two years later (demand had been overwhelming, for much of Maine had burned in 1947), nature was already mending the landscape without human intervention.

What had been blackened showed promise and renewal in green growing things.

Over the decades since then, a mixed deciduous forest has grown up from the ashes of the fire, supplanting the dominance of the spruce-fir forest on Mount Desert Island's east side. **Birch, aspen, maple, oak,** and **beech** have embraced wide-open sunny places where shady spruce once thrived. The new growth not only added colorful splendor to the autumn landscape but also diversified the wildlife.

Populations of **white-tailed deer** benefited from all the new browse (and a lack of major predators), and by the 1960s, the island's deer herd had soared. Recent studies have shown the population to be healthy and stable—perhaps due to car-deer collisions and predation from the recently arrived eastern coyote.

Coyotes crossed the Trenton Bridge and wandered onto Mount Desert Island in the 1980s. They had been expanding their territory throughout the northeast, handily picking up the slack in the food chain caused when other large predators, such as the northern gray wolf and the lynx, were hunted and trapped out of the state. While coyote sightings do occur, you are more likely to be serenaded by yipping and howling in the night. Their vocalizations warn off other coyotes, or let them keep in touch with the members of their packs.

The **snowshoe hare,** or varying hare, is a main prey of the coyote. The large hind feet of these mammals allow them to stay aloft in the snow and speed away from predators. Camouflage also aids these fleet-footed hares—their fur turns white during the winter and brown during the summer, hence the name varying hare. Not all hares escape their predators. It is not uncommon to encounter coyote scat full of hare fur along a carriage road or trail.

Also along a carriage road or trail, you might encounter a **snake** sunning itself on a rock. Five species of snakes—including the garter snake, milk snake, and green snake—inhabit Acadia. None of these snakes are poisonous, but they will bite if provoked.

While autumn may cloak Acadia's mountainsides in bright beauty, spring and summer bring relief to Mainers weary of ice storms, shoveling, freezing temperatures, and short, dark days. Spring arrives with snowy clusters of star flowers along roadsides, and white mats of **bunchberry** flowers (dwarf members of the dogwood family) on the forest floor. Birdsong provides a musical backdrop. Twenty-one species of wood warblers migrate to Acadia from South America to nest—among them are the **American redstart, ovenbird, yellow warbler,** and **Blackburnian warbler.** At the visitors center, request a bird checklist, which names 273 species of birds that have been identified on Mount Desert Island and adjacent areas. Then join a ranger for an early morning bird walk. Check the *Beaver Log* for details.

The fire of 1947 may have transformed a portion of Acadia's woodlands, but change is always part of a natural system. While the broad-leafed trees that grew up in the wake of the fire continue to grow and shed leaves as the cycle of nature demands, young spruce trees poke up through duff and leaf litter, waiting in the shade for their chance to dominate the landscape once again.

MOUNTAINS

A hike up one of Acadia's granite-domed mountains will allow you to gaze down at the world with a new perspective. Left behind is the confining forest—the woods, in fact, seem to shrink as you climb. On the south-facing slopes of some mountains, you'll encounter squat and gnarled pitch pines. The fire of 1947 not only was beneficial to the growth of deciduous vegetation but it also aided in the regeneration of **pitch pines,** which rely on heat, such as that generated by an intense fire, to open their cones and disperse seeds.

Wreathing rocky outcrops and trailsides are such shrubs as **low-bush blueberry, sheep laurel (lambkill),** and **bayberry.** In the fall, their leaves turn blood-red. In the spring, **shadbush** softens granite mountainsides with white blossoms.

Green and gray lichens plaster exposed rocks in patterns like targets. Composed of algae and fungi, lichens were probably among the first organisms to grow in Acadia as the vast ice sheets retreated 20,000 to 10,000 years ago. Sensitive to air pollution and acid rain, lichens have become barometers of air quality all over the world.

On mountain summits, the trees are stunted. These are not necessarily young trees—some may be nearly 100 years old. The tough, cold, windy climate and exposed conditions of summits force plant life to adapt to survive. Growing close to the ground to avoid fierce winds is one way in which trees have adapted to life at the summit.

Other plants huddle in the shallow, gravelly soil behind solitary rocks, such as **three-toothed cinquefoil,** a member of the rose family that produces a tiny white flower in June and July, and **mountain sandwort,** which blooms in clusters from June through September.

While adapted to surviving the extreme conditions of mountain summits, plants can be irreparably damaged by feet trampling off-trail or by removal of rocks to add to cairns (trail markers) or stone "art." One has only to look at the summit area of Cadillac Mountain to see the damage wrought by millions of roving feet: the missing vegetation and the eroded soils. It may take 50 to 100 years for some plant life, if protected, to recover. Some endangered plant species that grow only at summits may have already disappeared from Cadillac due to trampling.

To protect mountain summits and to preserve the natural scene, follow Leave No Trace principles of staying on the trail and on durable surfaces, such as solid granite. Do not add to cairns or build rock art, a form of graffiti that not only damages plants and soils but also blemishes the scenery for other visitors.

Autumn provides a terrific opportunity to observe **raptors** of all kinds. In the fall, during their southward migration, raptors take advantage of northwest winds flowing over

Acadia's mountains. Eagles, red-tailed hawks, sharp-shinned hawks, goshawks, American kestrels, peregrine falcons, and others can be spotted. (The peregrine, a seasonal mountain dweller, has been reintroduced to Acadia after a long absence; see the sidebar *Peregrine Falcons* in the *Acadia on Mount Desert Island* chapter.) From late August to mid-October, join park staff for the annual Hawkwatch atop Cadillac Mountain (weather permitting) to view and identify raptors. Check the *Beaver Log* for details. In 2002, hawk watchers counted 1,659 raptors from 10 species (down a bit from the annual average of 2,500). The most prevalent species are American kestrels and sharp-shinned hawks.

WILDLIFE-WATCHING TIPS

- Seek out wildlife at dusk and dawn when it is more active. Bring binoculars and a field guide.

- Leave Rover at home—pets are intruders into the natural world, and they will scare off wildlife. If leaving your dog behind is not an option, remember that in the park, pets must be restrained on a leash no longer than six feet. This is for the safety of both the pet and wildlife, and it is courteous to other visitors.

- Never approach wildlife, which could become aggressive if sick or feeling threatened. Enjoy wildlife at a distance.

- Do not feed wildlife, not even gulls. Feeding turns wild animals into aggressive beggars that lose the ability to forage for themselves, and often ends in their demise.

- Join walks, talks, hikes, cruises, and evening programs presented by park rangers to learn more about your national park and its flora and fauna. Programs are listed in the *Beaver Log,* readily available at the Hulls Cove Visitor Center, the Sieur de Monts Nature Center, and park campgrounds, as well as online at www.nps.gov/acad/.

- Visit the Nature Center at Sieur de Monts Spring, where exhibits show the diversity of flora and fauna in the park and the challenges that resource managers face in protecting it.

(The Flora and Fauna *section of this chapter was written by Kristen Britain, former writer/editor for Acadia National Park.)*

Environmental Issues

You've already read about some of Acadia's major environmental issues, but still others exist. Tops among these are air pollution and overcrowding. Of utmost importance is the matter of "zero impact," addressed by the Leave No Trace philosophy actively practiced at Acadia.

AIR QUALITY

In 2002, a study by the private National Parks Conservation Association revealed that Acadia National Park had the fifth-worst air quality of all the national parks; Acadia allegedly has twice as much haze as the Grand Canyon.

Most scientists and environmentalists attribute the problem primarily to smoke and haze from power plants in the Midwest and South. New England is the end of the line, so to speak, for airborne pollutants, and it's estimated that 80 percent of Maine's pollution arrives from other regions. Maine has the highest asthma rate in the nation, rivers and lakes have high concentrations of mercury, and rainfall at Acadia is notably acidic. Maine's four legislators, and others in the region, have been especially active in their efforts to strengthen the Clean Air Act and improve conditions at Acadia and in the rest of New England.

LEAVE THE ROCKS FOR THE NEXT GLACIER

Acadia's relatively small size among national parks (compared to Yosemite, say, or Yellowstone) and high volume of visitors have necessitated a very active campaign to heighten sensitivity to the park's ecosystem. While you're in Acadia, do your part to "Keep Acadia Beautiful" by adhering to principles (guidelines, really) developed by the national Leave No Trace (LNT) organization, based in Boulder, Colorado (www.lnt.org):

- Plan ahead and prepare.

- Travel and camp on durable surfaces.

- Dispose of waste properly.

- Leave what you find.

- Minimize campfire impacts.

- Respect wildlife.

- Be considerate of other visitors.

While all seven of these are important, two are especially critical for Acadia:

- **Travel and camp on durable surfaces.** Since there is no backcountry camping in Acadia, and park rangers do their best to monitor the park's three "front-country" campgrounds (two on Mount Desert, one on Isle au Haut), the focus is on hiking – and use of the trails. Stay on existing trails – paying attention to signposts, blazes, and cairns – and don't be seduced by false trails where hikers have begun to stray. Walk single file down the center of a trail to avoid trampling the sensitive vegetation alongside; slow-growing lichens are particularly fragile. Remember, plants grow by the inch and die by the foot. Every footstep can make a difference. If you must step off the trail, step onto a durable surface. Acadia's most fragile sites are the summits and ridges. Especially vulnerable is the summit of Cadillac – it's a matter of sheer numbers. Yes,

walk the summit loop for its great views, but, above all, stick to the trail or at least step on solid rock.

- **Leave what you find.** That means *take NO souvenirs.* Save the wildflowers for the next visitors to enjoy, and leave the tide pool creatures where you find them. Above all, don't mess with cairns, the carefully constructed stone trail markers. Resist the urge to build or unbuild or rebuild cairns along the way – in some instances, removal or addition of a single stone can threaten a cairn's stability. It's a safety issue, too – a collapsed cairn becomes a missing link in the trail-marking system. Follow cairns, don't build them. As the slogan has it, "leave the rocks for the next glacier." Imagine if every one of the park's nearly three million visitors each year removed one cobble or rock. (Unfortunately, enough already have. Bar Harbor Airport screeners, under heightened security regulations, have been seeing visitors departing with beach rocks. But what to do with them? Who can say exactly where they came from? Please leave them where you found them.) If you're planning to camp at one of the park campgrounds, bring firewood – you'll see dozens of "Firewood for Sale" signs along the roads leading to the park. Stop and buy a bundle; it'll set you back a few dollars.

Also essential – anywhere, not just in Acadia – is the carry-in/carry-out message. If you're planning a picnic, enjoy it (on a durable surface – there's plenty of granite in Acadia), then remove all evidence of it. Carry trash bags and use them.

To keep wildlife wild, *do not feed* any of the park's wildlife – a problem of increasing concern at Acadia. Animals become dependent on humans and risk being hit by cars or otherwise meeting their end.

We all love the park, but we can't love it to death.

To heighten public awareness of pollution problems, a new government/private joint program has initiated **CAMNET,** an intriguing monitoring system that provides real-time pollution and visibility monitoring. Acadia is one of the nine New England sites with cameras updating images every 15 minutes. Log on to www.hazecam.net for data on current temperature and humidity, wind speed and direction, precipitation totals, visual range, and the air-pollution level (low, medium, or high). The site also includes a selection of photos showing the variations that have occurred in the past at Acadia. In the "clear day" photo, visibility was pegged at 199 miles! Ozone alerts (according to EPA standards) usually occur at Acadia a couple of times each summer. When they do, rangers put out signs to caution visitors—particularly hikers and bikers—to restrict strenuous activity.

While pollution is an Acadia issue—affecting the park, its vegetation and wildlife, and its visitors—the solution must be a national one. Stay tuned.

PARK CAPACITY

With more than two million visitors each year, Acadia and National Park Service officials are wrestling with a question: How many people are too many people? Other national parks have initiated visitor limitations, but Acadia has so far not done so. The time may come, however.

The establishment of the propane-powered Island Explorer bus service has greatly alleviated traffic (and thus also auto, SUV, and RV emissions) during the months it operates (late June to early October) and freed up space in Acadia's parking areas, but will it encourage more visitors?

Cruise-vessel visits in Bar Harbor have multiplied exponentially in recent years. Most passengers spend at least some time in the park, but it's minimal time—often just a carriage ride or a visit to Jordan Pond House or the Cadillac summit. (Bar Harbor merchants, of course, welcome the influx.)

The heaviest use of the park occurs in July and August, with marginally less use in September, yet there are still quiet corners of the park. It's a matter of finding them. The best advice, therefore, is to visit in "shoulder" periods—May and June, late September, or early October. You take your chances then with weather and temperature, but if you're flexible and adaptable, it could be the best vacation you've ever had.

History

NATIVE AMERICANS

As the great continental glacier receded northwestward out of Maine about 11,000 years ago, some prehistoric grapevine must have alerted small bands of hunter-gatherers—fur-clad Paleo-Indians—to the scrub sprouting in the tundra, burgeoning mammal populations, and the ocean's bountiful food supply. Because they came to the shore in droves—at first seasonally, then year-round. Anyone who thinks tourism is a recent phenomenon in this part of Maine need only explore the shoreline of Mount Desert Island, where cast-off oyster shells and clamshells document the migration of early Native Americans from woodlands to waterfront. "The shore" has been a summertime magnet for millennia.

Archaeological evidence from the Archaic period in Maine—roughly 8000–1000 B.C.—is fairly scant, but paleontologists have unearthed stone tools and weapons and small campsites attesting to a nomadic lifestyle supported by fishing and hunting (with fishing becoming more extensive as time went on). Toward the end of the tradition, during the late Archaic period, there emerged a rather anomalous Indian culture known officially as the Moorehead phase but informally called the Red Paint People; the name comes from their curious trait of using a distinctive red ocher (pulverized hematite) in burials. Dark red puddles and stone artifacts have led excavators to burial pits in Ellsworth and Hancock, close to Mount Desert Island. Just as mysteriously as they had arrived, the Red Paint People disappeared abruptly and inexplicably around 1800 B.C.

Following them almost immediately—and almost as suddenly—hunter-gatherers of the Susquehanna Tradition arrived from well to the south, moved across Maine's interior as far as the St. John River, and remained until about 1600 B.C., when they, too, enigmatically vanished. Excavations have turned up relatively sophisticated stone tools and evidence that they cremated their dead. It was nearly 1,000 years before a major new cultural phase appeared.

The next great leap forward was marked by the advent of pottery making, introduced about 700 B.C. The Ceramic period stretched to the 16th century, and cone-shaped pots (initially stamped, later incised with coiled-rope motifs) survived until the introduction of metals from Europe. During this time, at Pemetic (their name for Mount Desert Island) and on some of the offshore islands, Native American fishermen and their families built houses of sorts—seasonal, wigwam-style birch-bark dwellings—and spent the summers fishing, clamming, trapping, and making baskets and functional birch-bark objects.

ARRIVAL OF THE EUROPEANS

The identity of the first Europeans to set foot in Maine is a matter of debate. Historians dispute the romantically popular notion that Norse explorers checked out this part of the New World as early as A.D. 1000. Even an 11th-century Norse coin found in 1961 in Brooklin (near Blue Hill, the next peninsula west of Mount Desert) probably was carried there from farther northeast.

Not until the late 15th century, the onset of the great Age of Discovery, did credible reports of the New World (including what's now Maine) filter back to Europe's courts and universities. Thanks to innovations in naval architecture, shipbuilding, and navigation, astonishingly courageous fellows crossed the Atlantic in search of rumored treasure and new routes for reaching it.

John Cabot, sailing from England aboard the ship *Mathew,* may have been the first European to reach Maine, in 1498, but historians have never confirmed a landing site. There is no question, however, about the account of Giovanni da Verrazzano, a Florentine explorer commanding *La Dauphine* under the French flag, who reached the Maine coast in 1524. Encountering less-than-friendly Indians, Verrazzano did a minimum of business and sailed onward toward Nova Scotia. (Four years later, he died in the West Indies.) His brother's map of their landing site (probably on the Phippsburg Peninsula, near Bath) labels it "The Land of Bad People." Esteban Gomez, a Portuguese explorer sailing under the Spanish flag, followed in Verrazzano's wake in 1525, but the only outcome of his exploits was an uncounted number of captives whom he sold into slavery in Spain. A map created several years later from Gomez's descriptions seems to indicate he had at least glimpsed Mount Desert Island.

More than half a century passed before the Maine coast turned up again on European explorers' itineraries. This time, interest was fueled by reports of a Brigadoon-like area called Norumbega (or Oranbega, as one map had it), a myth that arose, gathered steam, and took on a life of its own in the decades following Verrazzano's voyage.

By the 17th century, when Europeans began arriving in more than twos and threes and getting serious about colonization, Native American agriculture was already underway, the cod fishery was thriving on offshore islands, Indians far to the north were hot to trade furs for European goodies, and the birch-bark canoe was the transport of choice when the Penobscots headed down Maine's rivers toward their summer sojourns on the coast.

MOUNT DESERT ISLAND "DISCOVERED"

In the early 17th century, English dominance of exploration west of the Penobscot River (roughly from present-day Bucksport down to the New Hampshire border and beyond) coincided roughly with increasing French activity east of the river—including Mount Desert Island and the nearby mainland.

In 1604, French nobleman Pierre du Gua, Sieur de Monts, bearing a vast land grant for *La Cadie* (or Acadia) from King Henry IV, set out with cartographer Samuel de Champlain to map the coastline. They first reached Nova Scotia's Bay of Fundy and then sailed up the St. Croix River. Mid-river, just west of present-day Calais, a crew planted gardens and erected buildings on today's St. Croix Island while de Monts and Champlain went off exploring. The two men and their crew sailed up the Penobscot River to present-day Bangor (searching fruitlessly for Norumbega) and next "discovered" the imposing island Champlain named *l'Isle des*

Monts Déserts, because of its treeless summits. Here they entered Frenchman Bay, landed at today's Otter Creek in early September, and explored inlets and bays in the vicinity before returning to St. Croix Island to face the elements with their ill-fated compatriots. Scurvy, lack of fuel and water, and a ferocious winter wiped out nearly half of the 79 men in the St. Croix settlement. In spring 1605, de Monts, Champlain, and other survivors headed southwest again, exploring the coastline all the way to Cape Cod before returning northeastward and settling permanently at Nova Scotia's Port Royal (now Annapolis Royal).

Eight years later, French Jesuit missionaries en route to the Kennebec River (or, as some allege, seeking Norumbega) ended up on Mount Desert Island. With a band of about three dozen French laymen, they set about establishing the St. Sauveur mission settlement at present-day Fernald Point. Despite the welcoming presence of amiable Indians (led by Asticou, an eminent Penobscot sagamore), leadership

---

PRONOUNCING MOUNT DESERT: THE "SAHARA SCHOOL" VS. THE "ICE CREAM AND CAKE SCHOOL"

Noted maritime author Admiral Samuel Eliot Morison, in *The Story of Mount Desert Island* (published by Little, Brown, 1960) devotes a long footnote to the controversy over the pronunciation of *Desert* in Mount Desert. Here's his wry take on it:

[Explorer Samuel de Champlain's] exact words are: "Le sommet de la plus part d'icelles est desgarny d'arbres parceque ce ne sont que roches. Je l'ay nommée l'Isle des Monts-déserts." Right here we may grapple with the problem [of] how to pronounce it in English – whether we should follow what many people call the "Sahara School" and accent the penult, pronouncing it "Mount DEZ-ert," or what opponents call the "Ice Cream and Cake School," pronouncing it "Mount Dez-ERT,"

with accent on the last syllable. I should say that the spelling "Mount Desart" on The Atlantic Neptune and other old maps indicates that, like "clerk," "sergeant," and other words containing "er," it was pronounced "ar," and that the accent was then on the last syllable. Charles Tracy recorded, in his journal of 1855, that the natives called it "Mount Desert."

Let's let the park service have the last word. "[Champlain] named it "Isles des Monts Desert," with the accent on the last syllable, as it would be in the French language. He wasn't implying that it was a desert. The phrase means "island of barren mountains." That's why it's pronounced both as it is spelled and as the French phrase would be pronounced (dessert).

squabbles led to building delays, and English marauder Samuel Argall—assigned to reclaim this territory for England—arrived in his warship *Treasurer* to find them easy prey. The colony was leveled, the settlers were set adrift in small boats, the priests were carted off to the Jamestown colony in Virginia, and Argall moved on to destroy Port Royal.

Even though England yearned to control the entire Maine coastline, her turf, realistically, remained south and west of the Penobscot River. During the 17th century, the French had expanded from their Canadian colony of Acadia. Unlike the absentee bosses who controlled the English territory, French merchants actually showed up, forming good relationships with the Indians and cornering the market in fishing, lumbering, and fur trading. And French Jesuit priests converted many a Native American to Catholicism. Intermittently, overlapping Anglo-French land claims sparked messy local conflicts.

In the mid–17th century, the strategic heart of French administration and activity in Maine was Fort Pentagoet, a sturdy stone outpost built in 1635 in what is now Castine (on the next peninsula west of Mount Desert). From Pentagoet, the French controlled coastal trade between the St. George River and Mount Desert Island and well up the Penobscot River. In 1654, England captured and occupied Pentagoet and much of French Acadia, but, thanks to the 1667 Treaty of Breda, title returned to the French in 1670, and Pentagoet briefly became Acadia's capital.

A short but nasty Dutch foray against Acadia in 1674 resulted in Pentagoet's destruction ("levell'd with ye ground," by one account) and the raising of yet a third national flag over Castine.

THE REVOLUTION AND STATEHOOD

From the late 17th to the late 18th century, half a dozen skirmishes along the coast—often sparked by conflicts in Europe—preoccupied the Wabanaki (Native American tribes), the French, and the English. In 1759, roughly

midway through the Seven Years' War, the British came out on top in Quebec, allowing Massachusetts Governor John Bernard to divvy up the acreage on Mount Desert Island. Two bravehearts—James Richardson and Abraham Somes—arrived with their families in 1760, and today's village of Somesville marks their settlement. Even as the American Revolution consumed the colonies, Mount Desert Island maintained a relatively low profile (politically speaking) into the early 19th century. A steady stream of homesteaders, drawn by the appeal of free land, sustained their families by fishing, farming, lumbering, and shipbuilding. On March 15, 1820, the District of Maine (which included Mount Desert) broke from Massachusetts to become the 23rd state in the Union, with its capital in Portland. (The capital moved to Augusta in 1832.)

ARRIVAL OF THE "RUSTICATORS"

Around the middle of the 18th century, explorers of a different sort arrived on Mount Desert Island. Seeking dramatic landscapes rather than fertile land, painters of the acclaimed Hudson River School found more than enough inspiration for their canvases. Thomas Cole (1801–48), founder of the group, visited Mount Desert only once, in 1844, but his one-time student Frederic Edwin Church (1826–1900) vacationed here in 1850 and became a summer resident two decades later. Once dubbed "the Michelangelo of landscape art," Church traveled widely in search of exotic settings for his grand landscapes. After his summers on Mount Desert, he spent his final days at Olana, a Persian-inspired mansion overlooking the Hudson.

It's no coincidence that artists formed a large part of the 19th-century vanguard here: The dramatic landscape, with both bare and wooded mountains descending to the sea, still inspires everyone who sees it. Those pioneering artists brilliantly portrayed this area, adding a few romantic touches to landscapes that really need no enhancement. Known collectively as "rusticators," the artists and their

FREDERIC EDWIN CHURCH: CONSUMMATE ROMANTIC

One of the best-known second-generation members of the Hudson River School – 19th-century painters of vast landscapes, river-scapes, and seascapes – was Frederic Edwin Church. Born in 1826 in Hartford, Connecticut, Church was a contemporary of Winslow Homer, Fitz Hugh Lane, and James McNeill Whistler. By the time he first visited Mount Desert Island in 1850, Church had already studied under Hudson River School founder Thomas Cole and had been admitted to the National Academy of Design in New York. Cole proudly claimed that his one and only protégé had "the finest eye for drawing in the world." Captivated by Mount Desert's bare summits, broad vistas, and rough shoreline, Church produced dramatic, atmospheric paintings of the area.

Among the best known of Church's Mount Desert paintings are *Otter Creek, Mount Desert* (about 1850), *Twilight in the Wilderness* (1860), and *Mount Newport on Mount Desert Island* (ca. 1851-53); the latter fetched $4.2 million at auction in May 2000. (Mount Newport, named for Christopher Newport, captain of the 1607 Jamestown Colony fleet, is now Mount Champlain.)

One reviewer used an apt musical metaphor to describe the range of Church's extraordinary work: "The painter best known nowadays for what might be termed visual symphonies or operas also regularly created concertos, hymns, and smaller works – the equivalents of sonatas, études, and Lieder."

In 1853, Church set out for South America, following the route of German naturalist Alexander von Humboldt through New Granada (now Colombia) and Ecuador, and creating sketches he used for later paintings of the Andean region. Subsequent journeys to South America, the Canadian Maritimes, Mexico, and the Caribbean, as well as extended explorations of Europe and the Middle East in 1867, served as inspirations for Church masterpieces of the Parthenon, Petra, Baalbek, and Jerusalem.

In 1860, Church married Isabel Carnes, with whom he had six children (two died of diphtheria in 1865). Isabel died in 1899.

Debilitated by rheumatism during the last 15 years of his life, Church retreated to Olana, his Persian-inspired mansion on the Hudson River, designed by Calvert Vaux (a colleague of noted architect Frederick Law Olmsted). Church died in New York in 1900. In 1966, Olana became a New York State Historic Site, open to the public.

The last major painting from Church's easel was not of Peru or Petra or the Hudson River, nor even of Cadillac Mountain. It was an 1895 portrait of Katahdin, in what is now Maine's Baxter State Park – *Mount Katahdin from Millinocket Camp,* the view from his beloved Camp Rhodora, on Millinocket Lake, which he purchased in 1878.

The best collection of Church paintings – indeed, the best collection of work by the members of the Hudson River School – is at the Wadsworth Atheneum in Hartford, Connecticut (www.wadsworthatheneum.org).

coterie seemed content to "live like the locals" and rented basic rooms from island fishermen and boatbuilders. But once the word got out and painterly images began confirming the reports, the surge of visitors began—particularly after the Civil War, which had so totally preoccupied the nation. Tourist boarding-houses appeared first, then sprawling hotels— by the late 1880s, there were nearly 40 hotels on the island, luring vacationers for summer-long stays.

At about the same time, the East Coast's corporate tycoons zeroed in on Mount Desert, arriving by luxurious steam yachts and building over-the-top grand estates (quaintly called "summer cottages") along the shore northward from Bar Harbor. (Before long, demand exceeded acreage, and mansions also began appearing in Northeast and Southwest Harbors.) Their seasonal social circuit was a catalogue of Rich and Famous Families—Rockefeller, Astor, Vanderbilt, Ford, Whitney, Schieffelin,

Morgan, Carnegie—just for a start. Also part of the elegant mix were noted academics, doctors, lawyers, and even international diplomats. The "Gay Nineties" earned their name on Mount Desert Island.

BIRTH OF A NATIONAL PARK

Fortunately for Mount Desert—and, let's face it, for all of us—many of the rusticators maintained a strong sense of *noblesse oblige,* engaging regularly in philanthropic activity. Notable among them was George Bucknam Dorr (1853–1944), who spent more than 40 years fighting to preserve land on Mount Desert Island and ultimately earned the title "Father of Acadia."

As Dorr related in his memoir (see *Suggested Reading*), the saga began with the establishment of the Hancock County Trustees of Public Reservations, a nonprofit corporation modeled on the Trustees of Public Reservations in Massachusetts and chartered in early 1903 "to acquire, by devise, gift or purchase, and to own, arrange, hold, maintain or improve for

Spring House, Sieur de Monts Spring

public use lands in Hancock County, Maine [encompassing Mount Desert Island as well as Schoodic Point], which by reason of scenic beauty, historical interest, sanitary advantage or other like reasons may become available for such purpose." President of the new corporation was Charles W. Eliot, president emeritus of Harvard. Dorr became the vice president and "executive officer" and dedicated the rest of his life to the cause.

Dorr wrote letters, cajoled, spoke at meetings, arrived on potential donors' doorsteps, and even resorted to polite ruses as he pursued his mission. He also delved into his own pockets to subsidize land purchases. Dorr was a fundraiser par excellence, a master of "networking" decades before the days of instant communications. Gradually he accumulated parcels—ponds, woodlands, summits, trails—and gradually his enthusiasm caught on. But easy it wasn't. He faced down longtime local residents, potential developers, and other challengers, and he politely but doggedly visited grand salons, corporate offices, and the halls of Congress in his quest.

In 1913, Bar Harbor taxpayers—irked by the increasing acreage being taken off the tax rolls—prevailed upon their state legislator to introduce a bill to annul the corporation's charter. Dorr's effective lobbying doomed the bill, but the corporation saw trouble ahead and devised a plan on a grander scale. Again thanks to Dorr's political and social connections and intense lobbying in Washington, President Woodrow Wilson on July 8, 1916, created the Sieur de Monts National Monument from 5,000 acres given to the government by the Hancock County Trustees of Public Reservations. Dorr acquired the new title of Custodian of the Monument.

After the establishment of the National Park Service in late August 1916, and after Sieur de Monts had received its first congressional appropriation ($10,000), Dorr forged ahead to try to convince the government to convert "his" national monument into a national park. "No" meant nothing to him.

Not only did he schmooze with congressmen, cabinet members, helpful secretaries, and even ex-President Theodore Roosevelt, he also provided the pen (filled with ink) and waited in the president's outer office to be sure Wilson signed the bill. On February 26, 1919, Lafayette National Park became the first national park east of the Mississippi River; George Bucknam Dorr became its first superintendent. (Ten years later, the name was changed to Acadia National Park.)

THE GREAT FIRE OF 1947

Wildfires are no surprise in Maine—where woodlands often stretch to the horizon—but 1947 was unique in the history of the state and of Acadia. A rainy spring led into a dry, hot summer with almost no precipitation… and then an autumn with still no rain. Wells went dry, vegetation drooped, and the inevitable occurred—a record-breaking inferno. Starting on October 17 as a small, smoldering fire at the northern end of the island, it galloped south and east, abetted by winds, and moved toward Bar Harbor and Frenchman Bay before coming under control on October 27. More than 17,000 acres burned (including more than 10,000 in Acadia National Park).

Sixty-seven magnificent "cottages" were incinerated on "Millionaires' Row," along the shore north of Bar Harbor, with property damage of more than $20 million. Some of the mansions, incredibly, escaped the flames, but most of the estates were never rebuilt. Miraculously, only one man succumbed to the fire. A few other deaths occurred from heart attacks and traffic accidents, as hundreds of residents scrambled frantically to escape the island. Even the fishermen of nearby Lamoine and Winter Harbor pitched in, staging their own mini-Dunkirk to evacuate more than 400 residents by boat.

THE PARK TODAY

If only George Dorr could see today's Acadia, covering more than 46,000 acres on Mount Desert Island, the Schoodic Peninsula mainland, and parts of Isle au Haut, Baker Island, and Little Cranberry Island. The fire changed Mount Desert's woodland profile—from the dark greens of spruce and fir to a mix of evergreen and deciduous trees, making the fall foliage even more dramatic than in Dorr's day. If ever proof were needed that one person (enlisting the help of many others) can indeed make a difference, Acadia National Park provides it.

People and Culture

Maine's population didn't top the one million mark until 1970. Thirty years later, according to the 2000 census, the state had 1,274,923 residents.

Despite the longstanding presence of several substantial ethnic groups, plus four Native American tribes (about 1 percent of the population), diversity is a relatively recent phenomenon in Maine, and the population is about 95 percent Caucasian. A steady influx of refugees, beginning after the Vietnam War, forced the state to address diversity issues, and it continues to do so today.

POPULATION GROUPS
Natives and "People from Away"

People who weren't born in Maine aren't natives. Even people who *were* may experience close scrutiny of their credentials. In Maine, there are natives and *natives*. Every day, the obituary pages describe Mainers who have barely left the houses in which they were born—even in which their grandparents were born. We're talking roots!

Along with this kind of heritage comes a whole vocabulary all its own—lingo distinctive to Maine or at least New England. (For help in translation, see the *Glossary*.)

Part of the "native" picture is the matter of "native" produce. Hand-lettered signs sprout everywhere during the summer advertising native corn, native peas, even—believe it or not—native ice. In Maine, homegrown is well grown.

"People from away," on the other hand, are those whose families haven't lived here year-round for a generation or more. But people from away (also called flatlanders) exist all over Maine, and they have come to stay, putting down roots of their own and altering the way the state is run, looks, and *will* look. Senators Snowe and Collins are natives, as is Governor Baldacci, but former Governor King came from away, as did most of his cabinet members. You'll find other flatlanders as teachers, corporate executives, artists, retirees, writers, town selectmen, and even lobstermen.

In the 19th century, arriving flatlanders were mostly "rusticators" or "summer complaints"—summer residents who lived well, often in enclaves, and never set foot in the state off-season. They did, however, pay property taxes, contribute to causes, and provide employment for local residents. Another 19th-century wave of people from away came from the bottom of the economic ladder: Irish escaping the potato famine and French Canadians fleeing poverty in Quebec. Both groups experienced subtle and overt anti-Catholicism but rather quickly assimilated into the mainstream, taking jobs in mills and factories and becoming staunch American patriots.

The late 1960s and early 1970s brought bunches of "back-to-the-landers," who scorned plumbing and electricity and adopted retro ways of life. Although a few pockets of diehards still exist, most have changed with the times and adopted contemporary mores (and conveniences).

Today, technocrats arrive from away with computers, faxes, cell phones, and other high-tech gear and "commute" via the Internet and modern electronics. Maine has played a national leadership role in telecommunications reform—thanks to the university system's early push for installation of state-of-the-art fiber optics, although getting a cell phone signal is still a challenge in parts of the Acadia region.

Native Americans

In Maine, the *real* natives are the Wabanaki (People of the Dawn)—the Micmac, Maliseet, Penobscot, and Passamaquoddy tribes of the eastern woodlands. Many live in or near three reservations, near the headquarters for their tribal governors. The Passamaquoddies are at Pleasant Point, in Perry, near Eastport, and at Indian Township, in Princeton, near Calais. The Penobscots are based on Indian Island, in Old Town, near Bangor. Other Native American population clusters—known as "off-reservation Indians"—are the Aroostook Band of Micmacs, based in Presque Isle, and the Houlton Band of Maliseets, in Littleton, near Houlton.

In 1965, Maine became the first state to establish a Department of Indian Affairs, but just five years later the Passamaquoddy and Penobscot tribes initiated a 10-year-long land-claims case involving 12.5 million Maine acres (about two-thirds of the state) weaseled from the Indians by Massachusetts in 1794. In late 1980, a landmark agreement, signed by President Jimmy Carter, awarded the tribes $80.6 million in reparations. Despite this, the tribes still struggle to provide jobs on the reservations and to increase their overall standard of living. A 2003 referendum to allow the tribes to build a casino was defeated. The latest attempt to increase jobs and money is a controversial plan to bring a liquified natural gas port to tribal lands in Perry.

One of the true success stories of the tribes is the revival of traditional arts as businesses. The Maine Indian Basketmakers Association has an active apprenticeship program, and two renowned basket makers—Mary Gabriel and Clara Keezer—have achieved National Heritage Fellowships. Several well-attended annual summer festivals—including one in Bar Harbor—highlight Indian traditions and heighten awareness of Native American culture. Basket making, canoe building, and traditional dancing are all parts of the scene. The splendid Abbe Museum in Bar Harbor features Indian artifacts, interactive displays, historic photographs, and special programs. Fine craft shops also sell Native American jewelry and baskets.

LOCAL CULTURE

Mainers are an independent lot, many exhibiting the classic Yankee characteristics of dry humor, thrift, and ingenuity. Those who can trace their roots back at least a generation or two in the state and have lived here through the duration can call themselves natives; everyone else, no matter how long they've lived here, is "from away."

Mainers react to outsiders depending upon how those outsiders treat them. Treat a Mainer with a condescending attitude, and you'll receive a cold shoulder at best. Treat a Mainer with respect, and you'll be welcome, perhaps even invited in to share a mug of coffee. Mainers are wary of outsiders and often with good reason. Many outsiders move to Maine because they fall in love with its independence and rural simplicity, and then they demand that the farmer stop spreading that stinky manure on his farmlands, or they insist that the town initiate garbage pickup, or they build a glass-and-timber McMansion in the midst of white clapboard historic homes.

In most of Maine, money doesn't impress folks. The truth is, that lobsterman in the old truck and the well-worn work clothes might be sitting on a small fortune. Or living on it. Perhaps nothing has caused more troubles between natives and newcomers than the rapidly increasing value of land and the taxes that go with that. For many visitors, Maine real estate is a bargain they can't resist.

If you want real insight into Maine character, listen to a CD or watch a video by one Maine master humorist, Tim Sample. As he often says, "Wait a minute; it'll sneak up on you."

THE ARTS
Fine Art

In 1850, in a watershed moment for Maine landscape painting, Hudson River School artist par excellence Frederic Edwin Church (1826–1900) vacationed on Mount Desert Island. Influenced by the luminist tradition of such contemporaries as Fitz Hugh Lane (1804–1865), who summered in nearby Castine, Church accurately but romantically depicted the dramatic tableaux of Maine's coast and woodlands that even today attract slews of admirers.

Another notable is John Marin (1870–1953), a cubist who painted Down East subjects, mostly around Deer Isle and Addison (Cape Split).

Fine art galleries are clustered in Blue Hill, Bar Harbor, and Northeast Harbor.

Crafts

Any survey of Maine art, however brief, must include the significant role of crafts in the state's artistic tradition. As with painters, sculptors, and writers, craftspeople have gravitated to Maine—most notably since the establishment in 1950 of the **Haystack Mountain School of Crafts.** Started in the Belfast area, the school put down roots on Deer Isle in 1960. Each summer, internationally famed artisans—sculptors, glassmakers, weavers, jewelers, potters, papermakers, and printmakers—become the faculty for the unique school, which has weekday classes and 24-hour studio access for adult students on its handsome 40-acre campus. Many Haystack students have chosen to settle in the region. Galleries and studios pepper the Blue Hill/Deer Isle Peninsula. Another craft enclave is in the Schoodic region.

Down East Literature

Maine's first big-name writer was probably the early-17th-century French explorer Samuel de Champlain (1570–1635), who scouted the Maine coast, established a colony in 1604 near present-day Calais, and lived to describe in detail his experiences.

Today, Maine's best-known author lives not on the coast but just inland in Bangor—Stephen King (b. 1947), wizard of the weird. Many of his dozens of horror novels and stories are set in Maine, and several have been filmed for the big screen here. King and his wife, Tabitha, also an author, are avid fans of both education and team sports and have generously distributed their largesse among schools and teams in their hometown as well as other parts of the state.

CLASSIC WRITINGS ON THE REGION

Louise Dickinson Rich (1903–1972) entertainingly described her coastal Corea experiences in *The Peninsula,* after first having chronicled her rugged wilderness existence in *We Took to the Woods.*

Ruth Moore (1903–1989), born on Gott's Island, near Acadia National Park, published her first book at the age of 40. Her tales, recently brought back into print, have earned her a whole new appreciative audience.

Mary Ellen Chase was a Maine native, born in Blue Hill in 1887. She became an English professor at Smith College in 1926 and wrote about 30 books, including some about the Bible as literature. She died in 1973.

Two books do a creditable job of excerpting literature from throughout Maine—something of a daunting task. The most comprehensive is *Maine Speaks: An Anthology of Maine Literature,* published in 1989 by the Maine Writers and Publishers Alliance. *The Quotable Moose: A Contemporary Maine Reader,* edited by Wesley McNair and published in 1994 by the University Press of New England, focuses on 20th-century authors.

A WORLD OF HER OWN

For Marguerite Yourcenar (1903–1987), Maine provided solitude and inspiration for subjects ranging far beyond the state's borders. Yourcenar was a longtime Northeast Harbor resident and the first woman elected to the prestigious Académie Française. Her house, now a shrine to her work, is open to the public by appointment in summer.

ESSAYISTS AND CRITICS, NATIVE AND TRANSPLANTED

Maine's best-known essayist is and was E. B. White (1899–1985), who bought a farm in tiny Brooklin in 1933 and continued writing for *The New Yorker. One Man's Meat,* published in 1944, is one of the best collections of his wry, perceptive writings. His legions of admirers also include two generations raised on his classic children's stories *Stuart Little, Charlotte's Web,* and *The Trumpet of the Swan.*

Writer and critic Doris Grumbach (b. 1918), who settled in Sargentville, not far from Brooklin, but far from her New York ties, wrote two particularly wise works from the perspective of a Maine transplant: *Fifty Days of Solitude* and *Coming into the End Zone.*

MAINE LIT FOR LITTLE ONES

Besides E. B. White's children's classics, *Stuart Little, Charlotte's Web,* and *The Trumpet of the Swan,* America's kids were also weaned on books written and illustrated by Maine island summer resident Robert McCloskey (b. 1914), notably *Time of Wonder, One Morning in Maine,* and *Blueberries for Sal.*

ESSENTIALS

Getting There

ORIENTATION

Acadia National Park lies about three-fifths of the way up the Maine coast. The primary section, on Mount Desert Island, is located about 46 miles south of Bangor and 160 miles northeast of Portland. Here is where you'll find the park's visitors center. Although it's an island, Mount Desert is connected to the mainland by bridges and causeways, so you can arrive by car or bus. Not so with Isle au Haut, the most remote section of the park. Isle au Haut is located off the tip of the Blue Hill/Deer Isle peninsula (southwest of Bangor) and can only be reached by boat. Access is limited, unless you have your own boat, and facilities are few. The Schoodic section of the park tips a mainland peninsula east of Bar Harbor and is easily reachable by car or via passenger ferry from Bar Harbor.

There are no direct commercial flights from overseas to any of Maine's airports. The closest international airport is Boston's Logan Airport (BOS). Bus service to Portland, Bangor, and in season, Bar Harbor, is available from Logan; train service is available from Boston's North Station terminal to Portland. Rental cars are available at Logan.

© HILARY NANGLE

DRIVING ROUTES

The major highway access to Maine from the south is **I-95,** which roughly parallels the coast until Bangor. Other busy access points are **Route 1,** also from New Hampshire; **Route 302,** from North Conway, New Hampshire, entering Maine at Fryeburg; **Route 2,** from Gorham, New Hampshire, to Bethel, and a couple of crossing points from New Brunswick into Washington County in northeastern Maine.

The maximum speed on I-95 and the Maine Turnpike is 65 mph, 55 mph on some stretches. In snow, sleet, or dense fog, the limit drops to 45 mph; only rarely does the highway close. On other highways, the speed limit is usually 55 mph in rural areas and posted in built-up areas. Published distances can be deceptive— while the Turnpike and the Interstate have 65 and 55 mph limits, you'll never average even 55 mph on the two-lane roads.

The Maine Department of Transportation (800/877-9171, www.state.me.us/mdot) has general road information on its website and also operates the Explore Maine site (www .exploremaine.org), which has information on all forms of transportation in Maine. For real-time information on road conditions, weather, construction, and major delays, dial 511 in Maine, 866/282-7578 from out of state, or visit www.511maine.gov. Information is available in both English and French.

If you're arriving by car, the Maine Tourism Association operates state visitor information centers in Calais, Fryeburg (May–October), Hampden, Houlton, Kittery, and Yarmouth. These are excellent places to visit to stock up on brochures, pick up a map, ask advice, and use restrooms.

The Interstate and the Maine Turnpike

The interstate can be a bit confusing to motorists; it's important to consult a map and pay close attention to the green directional signs to avoid heading off in the wrong direction. Between York and Augusta, I-95 is the same as the Maine Turnpike (a toll highway). I-295 splits from I-95 in Portland and heads up the coast to Brunswick, before veering inland and rejoining I-95 in Gardiner. Between Kittery and Portland, there's one service area with gas and fast food, and that's in Kennebunk. All exit numbers along I-95 reflect distance in miles from the border. Exits on I-295 reflect distance from where it splits from I-95, just south of Portland at Exit 44.

Two exits off I-95 provide access to the Acadia region: From Exit 113, in Augusta, take Route 3 east to Belfast, which joins Route 1 north to Ellsworth. From Bangor, take Exit 182A merging on to Route 395 east to Route 1A north, which joins Routes 1 and 3 in Ellsworth. Be sure to follow signs for Ellsworth and Bar Harbor; avoid Route 1A south to Hampden and Stockton Springs.

The Maine Turnpike becomes mega-congested on summer weekends, especially summer *holiday* weekends. More than 300,000 vehicles use the turnpike on Memorial Day, Fourth of July, and Labor Day weekends. The worst times on the turnpike are Friday 4 P.M.–8 P.M. (northbound), Saturday 11 A.M.–2 P.M. (southbound; most weekly cottage rentals run from Saturday noon to Saturday noon), and Sunday 3 P.M.–7 P.M. (southbound). On three-day holiday weekends, avoid heading southbound on Monday between 3 and 7 P.M.

Route 1

Two lanes wide from Kittery in the south to Fort Kent at the top, U.S. Route 1 is the state's most congested road, particularly in July and August. Mileage distances can be extremely deceptive, since it will take you much longer than anticipated to get from point A to point B. If you ask anyone about distances, chances are good that you'll receive an answer in hours rather than miles. Plan accordingly. If you're trying to make time, it's best to take I-95; if you want to see Maine, take Route 1 and lots of little offshoots.

From Boston

It would be interesting to know the statistics on how many people drive directly from Boston to Acadia National Park without stopping en route. I'd guess not many (perhaps mostly those who have summer homes on Mount Desert Island or nearby). The trip is 268 miles, and not all of that trek is on multilane highway. You can't count on averaging 60 mph, especially in midsummer, when you hit the two-lane roads. Even on the four- and six-lane I-95, traffic can choke up at tollbooths. Also, you'll need bathroom breaks, snack breaks, maybe a gas fill-up—and all of Maine south of Acadia has its own attractions to lure you into detours (L.L.Bean and the Freeport outlet shops are major magnets).

But if you're determined to drive through from Boston, the best route is I-95, through 18 miles of New Hampshire (the Hampton tollbooths often cause major backups), into Maine and directly toward Bangor (the Maine Turnpike and I-95 are the same road for some stretches). Take Exit 182A for Route 395 and watch for signs for Route 1A to Ellsworth and then Route 3 to Bar Harbor. (*Do not* take Route 1A to Hampden, or you'll end up on the wrong side of the Penobscot River.) For the Schoodic section of the park, when Routes 1 and 3 split in Ellsworth, take Route 1 north to Gouldsboro, then head south on Route 186. For the Blue Hill Peninsula, Deer Isle, and Isle au Haut, from Ellsworth take Route 1 south to Route 172, then in Blue Hill, Route 15 south to reach Stonington and the boat to Isle au Haut.

TRAVEL HUB: BANGOR
Airport

Bangor International Airport (BGR; 299 Godfrey Blvd., Bangor, 207/947-0384 or 866/359-2264, www.flybangor.com) is northern and eastern coastal Maine's hub for flights arriving from Boston and points beyond. Bangor is the closest large airport to Bar Harbor, Acadia National Park on Mount Desert Island, and the park's other outposts. About half a million passengers annually move through Bangor International, a user-friendly facility on the outskirts of the city. Although flights tend to be pricier to Bangor than to

Portland or especially Boston, there's a big convenience factor when flying in here.

Despite the "International" in the airport's name, passenger service from international destinations to Bangor tends to be limited to charter airlines, which sometimes arrive here to clear customs (and refuel) and then continue on to points south and west; military flights; and terror alerts, in which badly behaving passengers are removed from international flights here. More typically, international visitors arrive in Bangor via New York or Boston gateways. Bad weather in Portland or Boston also can create unexpected domestic and international arrivals at Bangor's less-foggy airfield.

The airport's lower level has an interactive information kiosk, where you can contact local hotels and motels for rooms and airport shuttle service.

Suggested Driving Routes

Bangor is slightly less than 50 miles from Bar Harbor, but you'll be traveling almost entirely on two-lane roads; in summer, figure on an hour at the very least. Drive Route 1A to Ellsworth and then Route 3 to Bar Harbor. (*Do not* take Route 1A to Hampden, or you'll end up on the wrong side of the Penobscot River.) For the Schoodic section of the park, when Routes 1 and 3 split in Ellsworth, take Route 1 north to Gouldsboro, then head south on Route 186. For the Blue Hill peninsula, Deer Isle, and Isle au Haut, from Ellsworth take Route 1 south to Route 172, then in Blue Hill, Route 15 south to reach Stonington and the boat to Isle au Haut.

Car Rentals

In July, August, and September, it's essential to reserve a car a week or two before your arrival. On-airport car rental companies are: Avis (207/947-8383 or 800/831-2847, www.avis .com), Budget (207/945-9429 or 800/527-0700, www.drivebudget.com), Hertz (207/942-5519 or 800/654-3131, www.hertz.com), and National and Alamo (207/947-0158 for both, 800/227-7368 for National, 800/462-5266 for Alamo, www.nationalcar.com or www.alamo.com).

Bus and Taxi Services

Concord Coach Lines (1039 Union St., Rte. 222, Bangor, 800/639-3317 or 945-4000, www.concordcoachlines.com) provides daily bus service year-round from Logan Airport in Boston to Bangor via Portland. No reservations are accepted, but you can purchase tickets online. The Concord Trailways station in Bangor is less than a mile from the airport, but plan to take a taxi for that short distance.

Vermont Transit (800/552-8737, www.greyhound.com), a division of Greyhound, operates a once-a-day seasonal bus service between Bangor (Bangor Bus Terminal, 158 Main St.) and downtown Bar Harbor. You can buy tickets online for Vermont Transit. The run coordinates with continuing service to/from Boston via Portland.

Convenient and reasonably priced transportation between Bangor and Bar Harbor is provided by **Bar Harbor-Bangor Shuttle** (207/479-5911, www.barharborshuttle.com).

Round-the-clock **taxi service** is provided by Airport/River City Taxi (207/947-8294 or 800/997-8294) and Town Taxi (207/945-5671 or 800/750-9935). There are many other companies listed on the airport's website.

Accommodations

Bangor International Airport is approximately 45 miles from Bar Harbor. Depending upon when your flight arrives, you may wish to spend the night here and begin your journey refreshed. Most of the mid-rate chains have properties here. Your choice of a hotel or motel near the Bangor Mall or the Bangor Airport may depend on your frequent-flyer memberships or where you get the best auto club deal. There are lots of options, and most offer free shuttle service to and from the airport.

Many properties book far in advance for the fourth weekend in August, when the American Folk Festival is in town and traffic can be a bear. Avoid it, unless you're planning on attending—not a bad idea, actually; it's a free and fabulous event.

For early morning flights, you can't beat the convenience of the **Four Points Sheraton Hotel** (308 Godfrey Blvd., Bangor, 207/947-6721 or 800/228-4609, www.bangorsheraton.com, $170–190), which is linked to the terminal by a skyway. Renovated for 2009, it has a restaurant, a fitness room, a games room, and free Internet access. Pets are permitted, but a one-time fee is charged.

Next to the Bangor Mall, with restaurants and a food court, is the 96-room **Country Inn at the Mall** (936 Stillwater Ave., Bangor, 207/941-0200 or 800/244-3961, www.countryinnatthemall.net, $100), which includes continental breakfast, free lodging for kids rooming with parents, free local calls, and free HBO.

Twelve miles southeast of Bangor (and about 40 miles northwest of Bar Harbor) is **The Lucerne Inn** (Bar Harbor Rd., Rte. 1A, Holden, 207/843-5123 or 800/325-5123, www.lucerneinn.com, $79–199), a retrofitted early 19th-century stagecoach hostelry on a 10-acre hilltop overlooking Phillips Lake and the hills beyond. The fall panorama is spectacular. Despite the highway out front, noise is no problem in the antiques-filled, rear-facing rooms, all with lake view, gas fireplace, and whirlpool tub. Outside there's a pool. The Sunday brunch buffet (9 A.M.–1 P.M.) in the inn's dining room (where moderately priced dinners are served 5–9 P.M. nightly) is a big draw, as is the adjacent golf course. Rates include a continental breakfast. One-night packages, including dinner, are a good idea, as you're in the middle of nowhere and not likely to head out again once you get here.

Camping

On Bangor's western perimeter are two clean, well-managed campgrounds convenient to I-95 and Bangor. The emphasis is on RVs, but tent sites are available. Closest to the city is the 52-site **Paul Bunyan Campground** (1862 Union St., Rte. 222, Bangor, 207/941-1177, www.paulbunyancampground.com, mid-Apr.–Oct.), about three miles northwest of I-95 on Route 222 west. Facilities at this attractive campground include a recreation hall and huge outdoor heated pool; activities are offered most weekends in midsummer. Leashed pets are welcome (cleanup is required) and noise rules are strictly enforced. Sites (for two adults and two children) are $20–35.

About two miles farther out on Route 222, **Pleasant Hill Campground** (Rte. 222, 45 Mansell Rd., Hermon, 207/848-5127, www.pleasanthillcampground.com), also a Good Sampark, has 105 sites on 60 acres. Facilities include mini-golf, laundry, play areas, a rec room, a heated pool, free showers, and a small store. Pets are welcome. Rates are $21–40, and the campground is open May–mid-October.

Food

You'll find lots of fast food and family-friendly chains between the airport and the mall. Just south on I-95 at Exit 180 is **Dysert's** (Coldbrook Rd., Hermon, 207/942-4878), a 24-hour trucker's destination resort with good grub. For a nicer meal in a wine-bistro atmosphere, head downtown to **Café Nouveau** (84 Hammond St., Bangor, 207/942-3336, 11 A.M.–3 P.M. and 5–9 P.M. Tues.–Sat.), serving imaginative dishes at reasonable prices. Bangor's best fine dining option is **New Moon Cafe** (47 Park St., Bangor, 207/990-2233, 5–9 P.M. daily); most entrées are in the $20s.

TRAVEL HUB: PORTLAND

For anyone planning to go *just* to Acadia National Park, the primary gateway typically is Bangor. But if you're visiting Acadia as part of a Maine vacation, you might well choose Portland—160–180 miles south of Bar Harbor, depending on your route—as a springboard for getting to Acadia. Another consideration: Because the airport's serviced by JetBlue, prices tend to be lower.

Airport

Although it keeps expanding, **Portland International Jetport** (PWM; 207/774-7301, www.portlandjetport.org) is a small, easily navigable airport, where all flights leave from and arrive at the same building. Don't be fooled by the "International" in the airport's name; you can't even get a direct flight to Canada from here. Note that, being on the coast, the Portland airport is more subject to fog shutdowns than Bangor.

Portland's amenities include a newsstand/gift shop, a coffee shop, a restaurant/lounge, restrooms, a large waiting area, and an ATM. There's a business center in the gate area with Internet access. Visitor information is dispensed from a desk (not always staffed, unfortunately) between the gates and the baggage-claim area. No need to rush out to grab your luggage, though—Portland has one of the slowest baggage-claim operations in the country. Plan to stop at the restrooms, browse through the gift shop, and pick up tourism information after you arrive—and even then you may still have to wait for your luggage. Complaints to management elicit the response that Portland is the terminus of many airline routes, and the airline companies (who provide the baggage handlers and unloading equipment) give low priority to locations that don't require fast turnaround. As a result, carry-on luggage is a plus here. Baggage-handling offices surround the luggage carousels. Airlines are responsible for luggage, so if you have a problem, contact a representative from your airline. If you have an emergency, contact the airport manager at 207/773-8462.

Note: If your return flight is from Portland, allow extra time to pass through security. Portland has only one terminal and one security checkpoint, and the line often wraps around the second floor. People who don't allow enough time do miss flights. Early morning is especially busy.

Train

Amtrak's Downeaster (800/872-7245, www.thedowneaster.com) makes five daily round-trip runs between Boston's North Station and Portland's Transportation Center, with stops in Wells, Saco, and (seasonally) Old Orchard Beach (May 1–Oct. 31). Call or check the website for discounted fares and special rates for children and seniors.

Amtrak trains from Washington via New York arrive in Boston at South Station (not North Station). Believe it or not, there's no direct link between the two. While you can connect via the T (Boston's subway), it's a real hassle with baggage. Instead, splurge on a taxi or take the bus north from South Station.

Train service terminates in Portland. There are no train connections to the Acadia region.

Suggested Driving Routes

There are several routes for driving from Portland to Mount Desert Island. Route A follows the four-lane interstate for most of the way, then finishes up on two-lane roads. Route B is fifty-fifty: half interstate, half two-lane roads. Route C is almost all on two-lane roads—it's also the most scenic and the slowest route. As with most other Maine auto explorations, it's particularly helpful to use the DeLorme *Maine Atlas and Gazetteer* ($19.95, www.delorme.com).

For **Route A,** depart Portland northward on I-295 and continue to just south of Augusta, where it merges with I-95. Continue on I-95 to Bangor, and take Exit 182A merging onto Route 395 east toward Holden and Ellsworth (and Acadia). At the end of 395, you're also at the end of four-lane highways. It's two lanes for the rest of the way. Continue on Route 1A to Ellsworth, then Route 3 through Trenton to Mount Desert Island.

For Blue Hill, Deer Isle, and Isle au Haut, from Ellsworth, head south on Route 1/Main Street, through town, then take Route 172 south to Blue Hill, then Route 15 south to reach Stonington and the boat to Isle au Haut.

For the Schoodic Peninsula, in Ellsworth, take Route 1 north to Gouldsboro, then take Route 186 south to the park.

For **Route B,** start out the same way from Portland, on I-295 to I-95, then just north of Augusta, take Exit 113 for Route 3 east. (You'll now be on two-lane roads for the rest of the way.) Route 1 doubles as Route 3 from Belfast to the southern end of Ellsworth.

For the Blue Hill Peninsula, Deer Isle, and Isle au Haut, take Route 15 south from Orland. If your destination is Castine, take Route 175 south from Bucksport.

For the Schoodic Peninsula, stay on Route 1 to Gouldsboro, then Route 186.

Route C is the coastal route, where you'll be winding through and skirting small communities the whole way. This route lends itself to (no, requires!) stops—for photos, for exploring, for shopping, for overnights. Stopping only for lunch and restrooms, you'll still need to allow five or six hours from Portland to Bar Harbor. And all bets are off on Friday afternoons in summer, when towns such as Wiscasset and Camden can be major bottlenecks. (They're lovely towns, though—definitely worth a stop.)

To take Route C from Portland, you can start right off on two-lane Route 1, or you can go north on I-295 and I-95 (four lanes) to Brunswick, then cut over when you see the Coastal Route 1 sign. Follow Route 1 the rest of the way—through Bath, Wiscasset, Newcastle, Waldoboro, Thomaston, Rockland, Rockport, Camden, Belfast, Searsport, Bucksport, Orland and the turn-offs for the Blue Hill Peninsula, and on to Ellsworth, where you'll split off onto Route 3 and head for Mount Desert Island or stay on Route 1 to Gouldsboro and the Schoodic Peninsula.

Between Brunswick and Rockland, down each of the "fingers" east of Route 1, are even more towns and villages—Harpswell, Phippsburg, Georgetown, Boothbay Harbor, Damariscotta, Friendship, and Cushing.

Which brings us to the bottom line: You could spend *weeks* visiting Portland and making your way from there to Acadia!

Car Rentals

Five major rental agencies are located at the airport complex (Alamo's office is at the edge, but connected via shuttle). If you're arriving by bus or train, either take the free Explorer bus to the airport or a taxi.

Your choices are Alamo (207/775-0855 or 800/462-5266, www.alamo.com), Avis (207/874-7500 or 800/230-4898, www.avis.com), Budget (207/772-6789 or 800/527-0700, www.drivebudget.com), Hertz (207/774-4544 or 800/654-3131, www.hertz.com), and

National (207/773-0036 or 800/227-7368, www.nationalcar.com).

Bus Services

Concord Coach Lines (800/639-3317, www.concordcoachlines.com) departs downtown Boston (South Station Transportation Center) and Logan Airport for the 100-mile trip to Portland about 14 times daily, making pickups at all Logan airline terminals (lower level). All buses stop at the Portland Transportation Center on Thompson Point Road, just west of I-295 (Exit 5 northbound, Exit 5A southbound; it's well signposted); four buses continue express to Bangor.

Vermont Transit Lines (950 Congress St., Portland, 207/772-6587 or 800/552-8737 or 800/451-3292, www.vermonttransit.com), a division of Greyhound Bus Lines, serves Maine, the rest of New England, and beyond, connecting with Greyhound routes. The schedule is slightly less convenient than that of Concord Coach Lines, but rates are slightly lower and you can buy tickets online.

You can connect to Bar Harbor via Vermont Transit. There's one four-hour trip a day in each direction between Portland and Bar Harbor via Bangor (departing Portland in early afternoon, departing Bar Harbor very early in the morning).

Local Transportation

Portland airport's small size and practically downtown location are big pluses for many travelers. It's simple to get on I-95 headed north if you're heading right out. If you're planning on spending the night, you can be in downtown Portland within 10 to 15 minutes via taxi.

Accommodations and Food

You'll find most of the major chain hotels in the Greater Portland area. Also here are some lovely B&Bs and excellent independent hotels and inns (see www.visitportland.com). Some offer an airport shuttle service. The accommodations below are all near either the airport or bus terminals. Fast food and family-friendly chains are clustered near the Maine Mall, which is just a mile or two from the airport. If you're willing to venture into downtown Portland, the choices are abundant, with most restaurants concentrated in the Old Port and Arts District sections of the city.

Railroad tycoon John Deering built **The Inn at St. John** (939 Congress St., Portland, 207/773-6481 or 800/636-9127, www.innatstjohn.com) in 1897. The clean, comfortable, moderately priced 37-room hostelry welcomes children and pets and even has bicycle storage. Cable TV, air-conditioning, free local calls, free parking, free airport pickup, and continental breakfast are provided. Rooms vary from singles with shared bath, beginning at around $70, to superior kings with jetted tubs, beginning around $150. It's across the street from the Vermont Transit bus terminal and a short taxi ride from Portland's Transportation Center.

Close to the Portland Transportation Center, where both Concord Trailways and Amtrak arrive, is the **Clarion Hotel** (1230 Congress St., Portland, 207/774-5611, $139–259), with an indoor pool, restaurant, lounge, and free Wi-Fi and airport shuttle; pets possible.

Right at the airport, with free shuttles, are **Embassy Suites Hotel** (1050 Westbrook St., Portland, 207/774-2200, $189–249), with an indoor heated pool, restaurant, free full breakfast, and coin laundry, and the **Hilton Garden Inn** (145 Jetport Blvd., Portland, 207/7828-1117, $149–219), with an indoor heated pool and coin laundry.

Near the Maine Mall and providing a free shuttle is the **Comfort Inn** (990 Maine Mall Rd., South Portland, 207/7775-0409, $139–199), with free continental breakfast.

Just a couple doors down from the Inn at St. John is tiny **Dogfish Cafe** (953 Congress St., 207/253-5400, 11:30 A.M.–10 P.M. Mon.–Sat.), which packs 'em in for salads and sandwiches and grilled 'goodies, with heartier dinner specials served Wednesday–Saturday evenings.

The most incredible fries come from **Duckfat** (43 Middle St., Portland, 207/774-8080, www.duckfat.com, 11 A.M.–8 P.M. Mon.–Thurs., to 9 P.M. Fri. and Sat., noon–6 P.M. Sun.), an ultracasual, order-at-the-counter joint owned by chef Rob Evans (whose Hugo's restaurant earns foodie raves and awards), so you know it's not only good, but it has that spark, too. Fries, fried in duck fat, of course, are served in a paper cone and accompanied by your choice of sauce from six options; the truffle ketchup is heavenly. Want to really harden those arteries? Order the *poutine,* Belgian fries topped with Maine cheese curd and homemade duck gravy. In addition, Duckfat serves paninis, soups, salads, and really good milk shakes; wine and beer are available, too.

Another foodie fave is **Five Fifty-Five** (555 Congress St., Portland, 207/761-0555, www .fivefifty-five.com, 5–10 P.M. Mon.–Thurs., to 10:30 P.M. Fri. and Sat., 10:30 A.M.–2:30 P.M. (brunch) and 5–9:30 P.M. Sun.). The bi-level dining area is bright and elegant. Fresh, local, and seasonal are blended in creative ways on the ever-changing menu, which is divided into small plates, green plates, savory plates, cheese plates, and sweet plates, with prices ranging about $8–30. A five-course tasting menu is available with 24-hour notice. If you can't afford to splurge in the main restaurant, chef Corry serves lighter fare in the lounge.

BAR HARBOR AIRPORT

The most convenient air access to Acadia is **Hancock County–Bar Harbor Airport** (BHB; 207/667-7329, www.bhbairport.com). It's located 12 miles from downtown Bar Harbor, but this isn't a big-jet airport—in case you're squeamish about small planes. (Despite its name, the airport is located in Trenton, just north of Mount Desert Island.) US Airways Express/Colgan Air (207/667-7171 or 800/428-4322, www.colganair.com or www .usairways.com) operates daily commuter-plane service from Boston to Bar Harbor Airport, sometimes with a stop in Owls Head, near Rockland (Knox County Municipal Airport). Flight time from Boston to Trenton is about 70 minutes direct. (Driving time from Boston to Trenton would be a minimum of six hours, usually longer.)

Suggested Driving Routes

Lucky you; this one's quick and easy. Take Route 3 west for Mount Desert Island and Bar Harbor (just take a left when exiting the airport). For the Schoodic section of the park, head east on Route 3 to the junction with Route 1 in Ellsworth, then north on Route 1 to Gouldsboro, then south on Route 186. For the Blue Hill Peninsula, Deer Isle, and Isle au Haut, take Route 3 east through Ellsworth to Route 172, then, in Blue Hill, Route 15 south to reach Stonington and the boat to Isle au Haut.

Car Rentals

Hertz (207/667-5017 or 800/654-3131, www .hertz.com) provides on-site rental cars year-round. Enterprise (207/664-2662 or 800/325-8007) operates seasonally. In summer, be sure to reserve a car well in advance.

Bus

The free **Island Explorer** (207/667-5796, www.exploreacadia.com) stops at the airport between late June and early October. Connections service most of Mount Desert Island, including Bar Harbor, Southwest Harbor, and Acadia National Park.

THE CAT FERRY

An oceangoing car-and-passenger ferry *The Cat* (877/359-3760, www.catferry .com) links Portland and Bar Harbor with Yarmouth, in western Nova Scotia, Canada, with up to two daily trips from one port or the other between early June and mid-October. When making plans, remember that Yarmouth is on Atlantic time—an hour later than Maine's Eastern time. Check for the current operating schedule and fees, but expect a 5.5-hour journey when departing from Portland, 3 hours from Bar Harbor. The ferry carries up to 900 passengers and 240 cars. Here's the hitch: Because of maritime law, the ferry can't operate between Portland and Bar Harbor without a stop in Canada.

Getting Around

How will you get around once you get here? Europeans are always shocked at Maine's minimal public transport. The few larger cities have bus systems, but there's almost nothing in small towns. The national Amtrak system enters Maine only at its southern tip. Fortunately, buses link the major urban centers, such as Portland and Bangor—with stops in small towns when they happen to be along the way.

Among less-populated areas, Mount Desert Island stands out, thanks to its fare-free, propane-fueled **Island Explorer** bus system, subsidized by your park fees, Friends of Acadia, L.L.Bean, and local businesses. It services most of the island, as well as Bar Harbor Airport in Trenton. The good news is that it's a very efficient network; the bad news is that it runs only between late June and mid-October. So try to come during the Explorer's season, when you can rubberneck all you want from the comfort of a bus seat. No missed turns, no near misses. Less pollution, less frazzle. If you've arrived by car, leave it at your lodging and hop on the bus.

The Island Explorer also circulates around the southern end of the Schoodic Peninsula, from Winter Harbor to Prospect Harbor, with a loop through the park. It meets the passenger ferry that connects Bar Harbor to Winter Harbor, so you can visit the Schoodic section of the park from Mount Desert Island without needing a car.

The outer islands are also accessible from Mount Desert Island, although there are no public transportation systems on any of these. Most can be explored on foot or bicycle (rentals are available in Bar Harbor and Southwest Harbor). Passenger ferries from Southwest Harbor and Northeast Harbor cruise to the Cranberry Isles. A state car ferry services Swans Island and Frenchboro. From Stonington, a passenger ferry connects Deer Isle to Isle au Haut.

Water taxis are another way to reach islands.

© HILARY NANGLE

You'll need a car to explore the other regions covered in this book: Blue Hill Peninsula, Deer Isle, the Schoodic region beyond the Island Explorer's reaches, and Ellsworth.

DRIVING

Almost all gas stations in Maine are self-serve (pumps are marked "Self"; at those marked "Full," you'll pay more to have an attendant pump the gas for you), and most now allow you to pay at the pump with a credit card. (Many also have ATMs, but you'll usually have to pay a bank surcharge.) Note that Irving stations have extremely clean restrooms and usually have a good selection of teas and coffees in addition to fast foods.

Important Driving Regulations

Seat belts are mandatory in Maine. You cannot be stopped for not wearing one, but if you're stopped for any other reason, you can be fined if you're not buckled in. Maine allows right turns at red lights, after you stop and check for oncoming traffic. In rare cases, you'll see a no turn on red sign—in which case, heed it. *Never* pass a stopped school bus in either direction. Wait until the bus's red lights have stopped flashing and all children are well off the road. Maine law also requires drivers to turn on their car's headlights any time the windshield wipers are operating. Keep right on multi-lane roads except to pass.

Roadside Assistance and Road Conditions

Since Maine is enslaved to the automobile, it's not a bad idea for vacationers to carry membership in AAA in case of breakdowns, flat tires, and other car crises. Contact your nearest AAA office or AAA Northern New England (425 Marginal Way, Portland, 207/780-6800 or 800/482-7497, www .aaanne.com). The emergency road service number is 800/222-4357.

For real-time information on road conditions, weather, construction, and major delays, dial 511 in Maine or 866/282-7578 from out of state, or visit www.511maine.gov. Information is available in both English and French.

BUS SERVICES

Hancock County, including the Blue Hill Peninsula and Deer Isle, Ellsworth and Trenton, Mount Desert Island, and east to Gouldsboro, is serviced by a patchwork of local transportation systems designed for commuters, seniors, and residents without access to a vehicle. Providing an umbrella for it all is Downeast Transportation (207/667-5796, www.downeasttrans.org), with maps and schedules online. You can piece the region together, but each acts independently. Check online for details, as drivers require exact change.

MAPS

Request a free state map through the Maine Office of Tourism (888/624-6345, www .visitmaine.com). Acadia National Park maps are available at the visitors centers. Most local chambers of commerce have free local maps.

Maine Atlas and Gazetteer

Peek in any Mainer's car, and you're likely to see a copy of *The Maine Atlas and Gazetteer,* published by DeLorme Mapping Company, in Yarmouth. Despite an oversize format inconvenient for hiking and kayaking, this 96-page paperbound book just about guarantees that you won't get lost (and if you're good at map reading, it can get you out of a lot of traffic jams). Scaled at one-half inch to the mile, it's meticulously compiled from aerial photographs, satellite images, U.S. Geological Survey maps, GPS readings, and timber-company maps, and it is revised annually. It details back roads and dirt roads and shows elevations, boat ramps, public lands, campgrounds and picnic areas, and trailheads. DeLorme products are available nationwide in book and map stores, but you can also order direct (800/452-5931, www .delorme.com). The atlas is $19.95 and shipping is $4 (Maine residents need to add 5 percent sales tax).

© HILARY NANGLE

Use the free Island Explorer bus to explore Acadia National Park.

Tips for Travelers

FOREIGN TRAVELERS
Entering the United States

Since 9/11, security has been excruciatingly tight for foreign visitors, with customs procedures in flux. For current rules, visit www .travel.state.gov/visa, www.usa.gov/visitors/ arriving.shtml, and www.dhs.gov/xtrvlsec. It's crucial to plan well ahead, pack diligently, and have all necessary paperwork. It's also wise to make two sets of copies of all paperwork, one to carry separately on your trip and another left with a trusted friend or relative at home.

Foreigners visiting Acadia National Park typically arrive in the United States via major ports of entry, such as Boston or New York, and then continue to Maine; a smaller number arrive in Maine by road via Canada (New Brunswick or Quebec) or in Bar Harbor via *The Cat,* a fast catamaran ferry from Yarmouth, Nova Scotia. (The only customs facilities on Mount Desert Island are at the Cat Ferry Terminal in Bar Harbor. See the sidebar *Getting Away to Nova Scotia* in this chapter.)

For information on what can be brought across the border, check the website of the Customs and Border Protection division of the Department of Homeland Security (www .cbp.gov).

Money and Currency Exchange

Since Maine's Down East (geographically, northeast) coast borders Canada, don't be surprised to see a few Canadian coins mixed in with American ones when you receive change from a purchase. In such cases, Canadian and U.S. quarters are equivalent, although the exchange rate may be different. Most services (including banks) will accept a handful of Canadian coins at par, but you'll occasionally spot "No Canadian Currency" signs.

Other foreign currencies are not easily convertible (without losing in the exchange) at the small local banks on Mount Desert Island. Acadia National Park has no ATMs within its boundaries, but there are ATMs in Bar Harbor and other communities on Mount Desert Island.

For the most current exchange rate info, visit www.xe.com.

TIME ZONE

Acadia National Park (as well as the rest of Maine) is in the Eastern time zone—the same as New York; Washington DC; Philadelphia, Pennsylvania; and Orlando, Florida. If your itinerary also includes the Canadian Maritimes, remember that the provinces of New Brunswick and Nova Scotia are on Atlantic time—one hour later than eastern. Surprising to many first-time visitors is how early the sun rises in the morning and how early it sets at night in midsummer.

TRAVELING BY RV

Bringing a recreational vehicle (RV) to Mount Desert Island and Acadia National Park creates something of a conundrum. No question, the vehicles are convenient for carting kids and gear, but they're a major source of traffic problems on the island, and especially within the park. All of the island's roads are two lanes, and even though the island offers more designated bike lanes than almost anywhere else in Maine, bikes and RVs often have to share the road. RV parking is very limited, and even banned in some locales (such as downtown Bar Harbor). Ideally, you should consider bringing an RV to Acadia only between late June and Columbus Day—when you can park the vehicle in one of the island's dozen commercial campgrounds and travel around the island via the Island Explorer shuttle service.

Incidentally, be aware that the maximum trailer (or RV) length in the national park's two campgrounds is 35 feet, maximum width is 12 feet, and only one vehicle is allowed per site. Neither park campground has water or electric hookups. (More details on the two campgrounds appear in the *Acadia on Mount Desert Island* chapter.)

Plans are in the works (but no date has been set) to provide parking facilities and a shuttle stop in Trenton, which promises to be a major plus for day-trippers with RVs. Until then, however, you can park on a space-available basis near the park's Hulls Cove Visitor Center and in a designated area on Lower Main Street (watch for signs) in Bar Harbor.

TRAVELING WITH CHILDREN

Acadia National Park isn't a turn-the-toddlers-loose kind of place (too many cliffs and other potential hazards), but for school-age youngsters and cooperative teenagers, it's a fabulous family vacation destination. The *Beaver Log* has pages devoted to family activities. There are family-oriented kayak tours, Park Ranger tours, whale-watching trips, hiking and biking trails, carriage rides, and boat excursions. There's saltwater (literally breathtaking for adults, but not for kids) swimming at Sand Beach and freshwater swimming at several lakes and ponds. Incredibly, McDonald's and Burger King haven't invaded Mount Desert Island (although Subway has), but Bar Harbor and other towns have plenty of pizza and lobster joints, as well as two cinemas (one year-round, one seasonal) and several museums for rainy days.

Be forewarned that in-line skates and skateboards are not allowed anywhere within the park. The island communities surrounding the park are all small and—especially at the height of summer—congested. In-line skates can come in handy, but use them sensibly; skateboards, on the other hand, are a major hazard in these villages. Bikes are *not* allowed on any of the park's hiking trails, but the car-free carriage trail network is ideal for biking.

How about doing a family volunteer stint? Consider spending a morning on a trail-maintenance crew (8:20 A.M.–12:30 P.M. Tues., Thurs., and Sat., June–Oct.). You'll help cut back vegetation along trails and carriage roads, rebuild walls or drainages, clean up, and participate in other such

GETTING AWAY TO NOVA SCOTIA

Bar Harbor is the starting point for the summertime car and passenger ferry to **Yarmouth, Nova Scotia,** which shaves more than 600 miles off the driving route. From mid-May to mid-October, the high-speed 900-passenger catamaran called *The Cat*, owned by Bay Ferries, zips to Yarmouth in three hours.

The Cat is fast: It's powered by four 9,500-horsepower marine diesel engines, making it capable of speeds up to 55 mph. If you take it, be sure to make a trip to the back deck and watch the four water jets – they could fill an Olympic swimming pool in 33 seconds. *The Cat* is also comfortable, with onboard food service, a small casino, a duty-free shop, and two TV/cinema lounges. A couple of caveats: First, the ferry doesn't have a full kitchen aboard, so the menu is somewhat limited. What's available is okay, but you might be happier bringing takeout aboard, especially if you're fussy or have any dietary restrictions. Second, the air-conditioning keeps the boat very cool (which helps prevent seasickness). Even in the midst of summer, it's wise to bring a fleece jacket and perhaps warm-up pants to slip on if you're cold.

In summer, you can even go to Yarmouth for the day, without a car, departing in the morning and returning on the late-afternoon ferry. It's a long day, but a short time in Nova Scotia. If you're taking the day cruise without your car, consider making arrangements in advance for a 2.5-hour tour of the Yarmouth area. The tours get you out and about to other sights, while throwing in a good dose of history and heritage to boot. You can make reservations for a tour when you book the ferry or take your chances and try to sign up on the spot with an operator that might have space available.

---

activities. Bring water, insect repellent, and a bag lunch for a post-work picnic—the camaraderie is contagious. It's advisable to dress in layers, and do wear sturdy shoes. The nonprofit Friends of Acadia organization chalks up more than 8,000 volunteer hours every year. Check the website before you come (www.friendsofacadia.org), or call 207/288-3934 when you get here for the recorded schedule of work projects. (Volunteer crews meet at Park Headquarters on Rte. 233, Eagle Lake Rd.)

Earn a BA in Family Fun

Every summer, College of the Atlantic opens its doors to families, offering five sessions of its **Family Nature Camp** (800/597-9500, www.coa.edu/summer). This hands-on, participatory, naturalist-led program provides plenty of fodder for those "What I Did on My Summer Vacation" essays. The week-long sessions are designed to cure nature-deficit disorder, and include activities such as whale-watching, tidal pool exploration, wildlife-viewing expeditions, and more. Minimum age is five; extended family is welcome. The fee is $900 for ages 16 and older, $450 for 15 and younger. Camp runs Sunday afternoon through Saturday morning and includes campus lodging (bring your own sheets and towels), meals, field trips, and three boat tours; optional kayak and bike trips are additional.

TRAVELING WITH PETS

If you're used to traveling with your cat or dog, you should be accustomed to playing by the rules. In Acadia National Park, dogs are allowed *only* on leashes, and they are banned from several park locations: Sand and Echo Lake Beaches, Duck Harbor Campground (on Isle au Haut), park buildings, and any of the "ladder" hiking trails, which have iron foot- and handholds. (When you see the ladder trails, you'll understand why pets are forbidden.) Don't take pets on the Park Ranger tours, and do *not* leave your dog unattended (especially in an RV at one of the campgrounds). Be considerate of your pet as well as of other

If you prefer to explore on your own, make your first stop the information center one block up the hill from the ferry. It's staffed with friendly, knowledgeable folks and is filled with brochures and pamphlets on the region, covering topics including a Yarmouth walking tour, regional driving tours, and Nova Scotia birding. Special packages are available if you want to stay longer and explore Nova Scotia, with or without your car.

If you do go, you'll need a passport. Pets may be brought into Canada as long as they have a valid rabies vaccination certificate. For a list of goods that cannot be brought into Canada, visit www.inspection.gc.ca. For other questions about Canadian customs, call 506/636-5064 from the U.S. or 800/461-9999 from Canada, or visit www.cbsa-asfc.gc.ca.

The ferry splits its runs between Portland and Yarmouth and Bar Harbor and Yarmouth (unfortunately, by law, it cannot provide that ideal connection between Portland and Bar Harbor, but you might be able to connect Portland to Yarmouth and then on to Bar Harbor, if you don't mind an overnight en route). For a current schedule and fare information, contact **Bay Ferries** (207/288-3395 or 888/249-7245, www.catferry.com).

You can get information and make reservations or pick up reserved tickets (saving time and waiting in line in the morning) at the Bar Harbor ferry terminal (121 Eden St., Rte. 3, Bar Harbor) or at the office in downtown Bar Harbor (65 Main St., corner of Cottage St.), known locally as Cat Corner. In summer, Nova Scotia's **Yarmouth County Tourism Association** (207/288-9432 or 902/742-5355) has staff at both locations to help you plan your trip.

---

visitors. Of course, guide dogs are exempted from all rules.

To make the best of a visit to Acadia—so you can hike and bike and kayak without worrying about your pet—you might want to reserve kennel space for part of your stay. Mount Desert Island has the **Acadia Woods Kennel** (Crooked Rd., Bar Harbor, 207/288-9766, variable rates); on the mainland in nearby Ellsworth is **Downeast Boarding Kennel** (275 High St., Rte. 3, Ellsworth, 207/667-3062, variable rates). In July and August, be sure to call well in advance for a reservation. If you'd prefer to have a dog-sitter come to your hotel or campground, contact Wendy Scott at **Bark Harbor, Inc.** (150 Main St., Bar Harbor, 207/288-0404, www.barkharbor.com). She'll recommend someone who can help. If at all possible, call before you arrive to make arrangements, and when you get here, visit the store—a Toys"R"Us for pet owners. Bark Harbor maintains a list of pet-friendly restaurants and accommodations. Another resource is *Downeast Dog News* (www.downeastdognews.com), a free monthly tabloid available at pet-friendly locations and also online. It has a calendar of events. Also available is *Dog Parks, Beaches & Trails of Maine* (order online, $4.95), a booklet listing dog-friendly parks, beaches, and trails throughout the state, as well as info on public transportation, emergency veterinary clinic numbers, and other useful tidbits.

SENIORS

Age does have its privileges. U.S. citizens and permanent residents age 62 or older can purchase a **Golden Age Passport,** valid for admission to more than 300 national parks (including Acadia), historic sites, and monuments for $10, a one-time fee. It also entitles you to half-price camping. Many lodgings and many attractions and sights offer discounts to seniors. It never hurts to ask. Age varies; some begin their discounts for those as young as 55 (egad!). In any case, you'll need proof of age, such as a driver's license or passport.

Age also often brings achy knees and hips or other such maladies. Many of the accommodations in this area are small inns and B&Bs. If you have mobility problems or difficulty carrying your luggage up a flight of stairs or two, you'll want to make sure that your lodging has either first-floor rooms or elevators.

ACCESSIBILITY

Acadia National Park has been conscientious about providing as much accessibility as possible to people with disabilities. For a start, the Hulls Cove Visitor Center (the park's spring, summer, and fall information center) has a special parking area for easy wheelchair access, bypassing the 52 steps from the main parking area. When you get into the center, request a **Golden Access Passport,** which provides free lifetime entry to any national park (and half-price camping at park sites) for any citizen or permanent resident who is permanently disabled. (If you've broken your leg or have another temporary disability, you're not eligible.) The passport is also available at the park's two campgrounds, at park headquarters, and at the Sand Beach and Bar Harbor Village Green ticket booths.

Also at the Hulls Cove Visitor Center, pick up a copy of the *Acadia National Park Access Guide,* which provides detailed accessibility information (including parking, entry, restrooms, pay phones, and water fountains) for the park's visitors centers, the two campgrounds, picnic areas, beaches, and gift shops, as well as carriage rides, some boat cruises, and nonpark museums on Mount Desert Island. A few of the Park Ranger programs are wheelchair-accessible, as are all of the evening programs at the park's two campgrounds. Access to the carriage road network depends on your ability (there are some steep grades); even the easiest trails may require some assistance. Each of the Island Explorer shuttle buses—operating between late June and Columbus Day—has room for at least one wheelchair.

Parking lots at some of the park's most popular locales (such as Thunder Hole, the Cadillac summit, and Jordan Pond House) have designated handicapped spaces.

Wheelchair rentals are handled by **West End Drug Co.** (105 Main St., Bar Harbor, 207/288-3318).

To plan your Acadia trip in advance, order a Golden Access Passport online, then download the accessibility information from the park's website (www.nps.gov/acad/accessibility.htm). If you're reserving a campsite at the Blackwoods Campground online (www.recreation.gov), you'll need the Golden Access Passport beforehand.

For additional accessibility information, call 207/288-3338 (voice) or 207/288-8800 (TTY). For emergencies in the park or elsewhere on Mount Desert Island, dial 911.

While newer properties must meet the strict standards of the Americans with Disabilities Act, older and historic lodgings and restaurants often don't have accessible rooms or facilities. It's wise to ask detailed questions pertaining to your needs before booking a room or making a restaurant reservation.

ACCOMMODATIONS

For all accommodations listings, rates are quoted for peak season, which is usually July and August but may extend through fall foliage season (mid-October). Rates drop, often dramatically, in the shoulder and off-season at accommodations that remain open. Especially during peak season, many accommodations require a two- or three-night minimum stay. Unless otherwise noted, accommodations have private baths.

A note about B&Bs: If you've never stayed in a B&B, begin by putting aside any ideas you may have about them. No two are alike, but all are built on the premise that your experiences will be richer if it's easy to meet other travelers. You will find few of the old-style homestay B&Bs—where a number of rooms share one bath as well as the owner's living quarters—in the region, with the notable exception of offshore islands. Almost all B&Bs have private baths for each room and special areas for guests to relax and dine; some have in-room fireplaces or fancy bathrooms with jetted tubs. Many also provide private

MAINE FOOD SPECIALTIES

Everyone knows Maine is *the* place for lobster, but there are quite a few other foods that you should sample before you leave.

For a few weeks in May, right around Mother's Day (the second Sunday in May), a wonderful delicacy starts sprouting along Maine woodland streams: **fiddleheads,** the still-furled tops of the ostrich fern *(Matteuccia struthiopteris)*. Tasting vaguely like asparagus, fiddleheads have been on May menus ever since Native Americans taught the colonists to forage for the tasty vegetable. Don't go fiddleheading unless you're with a pro, though; the lookalikes are best left to the woodland critters. If you find them on a restaurant menu, indulge.

As with fiddleheads, we owe thanks to Native Americans for introducing us to **maple syrup,** one of Maine's major agricultural exports. The syrup comes in four different colors/flavors (from light amber to extra dark amber), and inspectors strictly monitor syrup quality. The best syrup comes from the sugar or rock maple, *Acer saccharum*. On Maine Maple Sunday (usually the fourth Sunday in March), several dozen syrup producers open their rustic sugarhouses to the public for "sugaring-off" parties – to celebrate the sap harvest and share the final phase in the production process. Wood smoke billows from the sugarhouse chimney while everyone inside gathers around huge kettles used to boil down the watery sap. (A single gallon of syrup starts with 30-40 gallons of sap.) Finally, it's time to sample the syrup every which way – on pancakes and waffles, in tea, on ice cream, in puddings, in muffins, even just drizzled over snow. Most producers also have containers of syrup for sale. For a list of participating sugarhouses, contact the Maine Department of Agriculture (207/287-3491, www.getrealmaine.com).

The best place for Maine maple syrup is atop pancakes made with Maine **wild blueberries.** Packed with antioxidants and all kinds of good-for-you stuff, these flavorful berries are prized by bakers because they retain their form and flavor when cooked.

Much smaller than the cultivated versions, wild blueberries are raked, not picked. Although most of the Down East barren barons harvest their crops for the lucrative wholesale market, a few growers let you pick your own blueberries in mid-August. Contact the Wild Blueberry Commission (207/581-1475, http://wildblueberries.maine.edu) or the state Department of Agriculture (207/287-3491, www.getrealmaine.com) for locations, recipes, and other wild blueberry information, or log on to the website of the Wild Blueberry Association of North America, headquartered in Bar Harbor: www.wildblueberries.com.

The best place to simply *appreciate* blueberries is Machias (an easy day trip from most anywhere in the Acadia region), site of the renowned annual Wild Blueberry Festival, held the third weekend in August. While harvesting is under way in the surrounding fields, you can stuff your face with blueberry everything – muffins, jam, pancakes, ice cream, pies. Plus you can collect blueberry-logo napkins, T-shirts, fridge magnets, pottery, and jewelry.

Another don't-miss while in Maine is Maine-made **ice cream.** Skip the overpriced Ben & Jerry's outlets. Locally made ice cream is fresher and better, and often comes in an astounding range of flavors. The big name in the state is Gifford's, with regional companies being Shain's and Round Top. All beat the out-of-state competition by a long shot. Even better are some of the one-of-a-kind dairy bars and farm stands. Good bets are Morton's, in Ellsworth, and MDI Ice Cream and Ben & Bill's, in Bar Harbor.

Finally, whenever you get a chance, shop at a **farmers market.** Their biggest asset is serendipity – you never know what you'll find. Everything is locally grown and often organic. Herbs, unusual vegetables, seedlings, baked goods, meat, free-range chicken, goat cheese, herb vinegars, berries, exotic condiments, smoked salmon, maple syrup, honey, and jams are just a few of the possibilities. For a list of all the markets (including those in inland areas), visit www.getrealmaine.com.

tables for breakfast—ask before booking, if you're just not up to being sociable first thing in the morning. The shared breakfast table does provide an opportunity to trade experiences with other guests. Some also provide afternoon refreshments, another opportunity to chat. Many B&Bs are quite exquisite and decorated with antiques and fine art, which means they're often inappropriate for young children. Others are equipped with in-room TVs, CD players, VCRs or DVD players, air-conditioning, phones, and other modern conveniences. A number of Mount Desert Island B&Bs are in grand historic cottages that survived the fire, providing a taste of that lifestyle and a peek into those rambling homes. Most B&Bs are operated by folks who live here year-round (some for generations), so they are able to provide recommendations based on their in-depth knowledge. B&Bs, especially, reflect their owners, so expect any to be different than described if they have new owners.

FOOD

Days and hours of operation listed for places serving food are for peak season. These do change often, sometimes even within a season, and it's not uncommon for a restaurant to close early on a quiet night. To avoid disappointment, call before making a special trip.

Outside of Ellsworth, do not expect to see much in the way of fast food in this region. There just isn't the year-round population base to support it.

ALCOHOL

As in the rest of the country, Maine's minimum drinking age is 21 years—and bar owners, bartenders, and serving staff can be held legally accountable for serving underage imbibers. Owners and employees also may be held liable for accidents caused by *legal* drinkers. Stiff anti-drunk-driving efforts in Maine (including random roadblocks, license revocation or suspension, hefty fines, and jail terms) have reduced but by no means halted the fatalities. If your blood alcohol level is 0.08 percent or higher, you are legally considered to be operating under the influence.

SMOKING

Maine now has laws banning smoking in restaurants, bars, and lounges as well as enclosed areas of public places, such as shopping malls. Most accommodations either ban or limit smoking, and many have instituted high fines for anyone who smokes in a nonsmoking room.

What's a smoker to do? If you're unable to find a smoking room, your best bet is probably a motel that allows smoking on the premises, although not in the room. Most motels open directly to the outdoors, so all you'll have to do is step outside for a puff. Do ask, however, as some don't permit smoking where the smoke might enter another guest's room through an open window.

Health and Safety

There's too much to do and see in Acadia National Park to spend even a few hours laid low by illness or mishap. Be sensible—get enough sleep, wear sunscreen and appropriate clothing, know your limits and don't take foolhardy risks, heed weather and warning signs, carry water and snacks while hiking, don't overindulge in food or alcohol, always tell someone where you're going, and watch your step. If you're traveling with children, quadruple your caution.

Even though Maine's public transportation network is woefully inadequate, and the crime rate is one of the lowest in the nation, it's still risky to hitchhike or pick up hitchhikers.

MEDICAL CARE
In the event of any emergency, dial 911.

Blue Hill and Deer Isle
Head to **Blue Hill Memorial Hospital** (57 Water St., Blue Hill, 207/374-3400, emergency 207/374-2836, www.bhmh.org) for emergency care.

Acadia and Schoodic Regions
There are two hospitals in this area: **Maine Coast Memorial Hospital** (50 Union St., Ellsworth, 207/664-5311 or 888/645-8829, emergency 207/664-5340, www .mainehospital.org); **Mount Desert Island Hospital** (10 Wayman La., Bar Harbor, 207/288-5081, www.mdihospital.org).

Alternative Health Care
Nontraditional health-care options are available on Mount Desert Island as well as on the Blue Hill Peninsula and Deer Isle. After some overambitious hiking or biking expeditions, a massage might be in order. Holistic practitioners, as well as certified massage therapists and acupuncturists, are listed in the Yellow Pages of local phone books. Also check the bulletin boards and talk to the managers at the health-food stores in Bar Harbor, Ellsworth, and Blue Hill. They always know where to find homeopathic doctors.

Pharmacies
The major pharmacy chain in and near Acadia is **Rite Aid;** Hannaford supermarkets also have pharmacy departments; and some towns have an independent drug store. All carry prescription and over-the-counter medications. There are no round-the-clock pharmacies. Some independent pharmacists post emergency numbers on their doors and will go out of their way to help, but your best bet for a middle-of-the-night medication crisis is the hospital emergency room.

If you take regular medications, be sure to pack an adequate supply, as well as a new prescription in case you lose your medicine or unexpectedly need a refill.

Bug Dope
If you plan to spend any time outdoors in Maine between early May and late September, insect repellent is critical for keeping at bay the state's winged annoyances—especially black flies, mosquitoes, and midges. Ben's and Cutter's work well, and Avon Skin-So-Soft lotion has become an inadvertent favorite recently (supermarkets and convenience stores seldom carry Avon products, but all carry the clone Skintastic, produced by the manufacturer of Off!). A new product getting good results is Lewey's, an all-natural repellent concocted by Alison Lewey, a Passamaquoddy/Maliseet Indian. It's widely available in Maine. Home remedies (try at your own risk) include eating garlic, drinking alcohol, or rubbing cider vinegar, tansy leaves, or crushed lemon thyme on your skin.

Not much daunts the black flies of spring and early summer, but you can lower your appeal by not using perfume, aftershave lotion, or scented shampoo and by wearing light-colored clothing.

ALLERGIES

If your medical history includes extreme allergies to shellfish or bee sting, you know the risks of eating a lobster or wandering around a wildflower meadow. However, if you come from a landlocked area and are new to crustaceans, you might not be aware of the potential hazard. Statistics indicate that less than two percent of adults have a severe shellfish allergy, but for those victims, the reaction can set in quickly. Immediate treatment is needed to keep the airways open. If you have a history of severe allergic reactions to *anything,* be prepared when you come to the Maine coast dreaming of lobster feasts. Ask your doctor for a prescription for an EpiPen, a preloaded, single-use syringe containing 0.3 mg of epinephrine—enough to tide you over until you can get to a hospital.

AFFLICTIONS
Lyme Disease

A bacterial infection that causes severe arthritis-like symptoms, Lyme disease (named after the Connecticut town where it was first identified in 1975) has been documented in Maine since 1986. Health officials monitor the situation carefully and issue cautionary warnings during prime tick season—mid-May into August. Atlanta's Centers for Disease Control and Prevention (www.cdc.gov) has cited the wooded, marshy areas of Maine's southernmost counties, York and Cumberland, as the highest-risk areas. From there northward along the coast to Mount Desert Island, the risk is considered low to moderate.

Lyme disease is spread by bites from tiny deer ticks (not the larger dog ticks; they don't carry it), which feed on the blood of deer, mice, songbirds, and humans. Symptoms include joint pain, extreme fatigue, chills, a stiff neck, headache, and a distinctive ringlike rash. Except for the rash, which occurs in about 80 percent of victims, the symptoms mimic those of other ailments, such as the flu, so the disease is hard to diagnose. The rash, which expands gradually and usually is not painful, may appear from three days to a month after a bite. If left untreated, Lyme disease eventually can cause heart and neurological problems and debilitating arthritis. Preventive measures are essential. If you suspect you've been exposed, seek medical assistance.

The best advice is to take precautions: Wear a long-sleeved shirt and long pants, and tuck the pant legs into your socks. Light-colored clothing makes the ticks easier to spot. Buy tick repellent at a supermarket or convenience store and use it liberally on your legs. Spray it around your cuffs and beltline. While you're hiking, try to keep to the center of trails, away from long grasses. After any hike, check for ticks—especially behind the knees and in the armpits, navel, and groin. Monitor children carefully. If you find a tick and suspect you have been bitten, head for the nearest hospital emergency room. If you spot a tick on you (or anyone else), remove it with tweezers and save it for analysis. Not all deer ticks are infected.

Rabies

Incidents of rabies—a life-threatening, nerve-attacking disease for which there is no cure unless treated immediately—have increased dramatically in Maine since 1994. No human has ever survived a case of rabies, and the disease is horrible, so *do not* approach, or let any child approach, any of the animals known to transmit it: raccoons, skunks, squirrels, bats, and foxes. Domestic dogs are required to have biennial rabies inoculations, thus providing a front line of defense for humans. If you're bitten by any animal, especially one acting suspiciously, head for the nearest hospital emergency room. For statewide information about rabies, contact the Maine Disease Control Administration in Augusta (207/287-3591).

Seasickness

Samuel Butler, the 19th-century author of *Erewhon,* wrote, "How holy people look when they are sea-sick." And he wasn't kidding. Seasickness conjures visions of the pearly gates and an overwhelming urge for instant salvation. Fortunately, even though the ailment seems to last forever, it's only temporary—depending on where you are, what remedies you have, and how your system responds. If you're planning to do any boating in Maine—particularly sailing—you'll want to be prepared. (Being prepared in fact may keep you from succumbing, since fear of seasickness just about guarantees you'll get it.)

Seasickness allegedly stems from an inner-ear imbalance caused by boat motion, but researchers have had difficulty explaining why some people on a vessel become violently ill and others have no problem at all.

To prevent seasickness, try to stay in good shape. Get enough sleep and food, and keep your clothing warm and dry (not easy, of course, on a heeling sailboat). Some veteran sailors swear by salted crackers, sips of water, and bites of fresh ginger. If you start feeling queasy, keep your eyes on the horizon and stay as far away as possible from odors from the engine, the galley, the head, and other seasick passengers. If you become seasick, keep sipping water to prevent dehydration.

Dramamine, Marezine, and Bonine, taken several hours before a boat trip, have long been the preventives of choice. They do cause drowsiness, but anyone who's been seasick will tell you he'd rather be drowsy. Another popular preventive is the scopolamine patch (available by prescription under the trademark Transderm Scop; not advised for pregnant women, the elderly, or children), which gradually releases medication into the bloodstream for up to three days. Discuss the minor side effects with the physician who gives you the prescription, and read directions and cautions carefully before using.

And some people swear by the pressure bracelet, which operates somewhat on the principle of acupressure, telling your brain to ignore the fact that you're not on terra firma. Great success has been reported with these prophylactics in the last decade. Before embarking, especially if the weather is at all iffy, go ahead and put on a patch or a bracelet. Any such preventive measure also improves your mental attitude, relieving anxiety.

Sunstroke

Since Acadia National Park lies above the 44th parallel, sunstroke is not a major problem, but don't push your luck by spending an entire day frying on Sand Beach or the granite shoreline. Not only do you risk sunstroke and dehydration, but you're also asking for skin cancer down the road. Early in the season, slather yourself, and especially children, with plenty of PABA-free sunblock. (PABA can cause skin rashes and eruptions, even on people not abnormally sensitive.) Depending on your skin tone, use sun protection factor (SPF) 15 or higher. If you're in the water a long time, slather on some more. Start with 15 to 30 minutes of solar exposure and increase gradually each day. When you're hiking, carry water. If you don't get it right, watch for symptoms of sunstroke: fever, profuse sweating, headache, nausea or vomiting, extreme thirst, and sometimes hallucinations. To treat someone for sunstroke, find a breezy spot and place a cold, wet cloth on the victim's forehead. Change the cloth frequently so it stays cold. Offer lots of liquids—strong tea or coffee, fruit juice, water, or soft drinks (no alcohol).

Hypothermia and Frostbite

Wind and weather can shift dramatically in Maine, especially at higher elevations, creating prime conditions for contracting hypothermia and frostbite. At risk are hikers, swimmers, canoeists, kayakers, sailors, skiers, and even cyclists.

When body temperature plummets below the normal 97–98.6°F, hypothermia is likely to set in. Symptoms include disorientation, a flagging pulse rate, prolonged shivering, swelling of the face, and cool skin. Quick action is essential to prevent shock and keep body temperature from dropping into the 80s, where cardiac arrest can occur. Emergency treatment begins with removal of as much wet clothing as possible without causing further exposure. Wrap the victim in anything dry—blankets, a sleeping bag, clothing, towels, even large plastic trash bags—to keep body heat from escaping. Be sure the neck and head are covered.

Or practice the buddy system—climb into a sleeping bag with the victim and provide skin contact. Do not rub the skin, apply hot water, or elevate the legs. If the victim is conscious, offer high-sugar snacks and nonalcoholic hot drinks (but, again, no alcohol; it dilates blood vessels and disrupts the warming process). As quickly as possible, transport the victim to a hospital emergency room.

When extremities begin turning blue or gray, with red blotches, frostbite may be setting in. As with hypothermia, add warmth slowly but do not rub frostbitten skin. Offer snacks and warm, nonalcoholic liquids.

Even during the height of summer, be on the alert for mild hypothermia when children stay in the ocean too long. Bouncing in and out of the water, kids become preoccupied, refuse to admit they are cold, and fall prey to wind chill.

To prevent hypothermia and frostbite, dress in layers and remove or add them as needed. Wool, waterproof nylon (such as Gore-Tex), and synthetic fleece (such as Polartec) are the best fabrics for repelling dampness. Polyester fleece lining wicks excess moisture away from your body. If you plan to buy a down jacket, be sure it has a waterproof shell; down will just suck up the moisture from snow and rain. Especially in winter, always cover your head, since body heat escapes quickly through the head; a ski mask will protect ears and nose. Wear wool- or fleece-lined gloves and wool socks.

HUNTING SEASON

During Maine's fall hunting season (October–Thanksgiving weekend)—and especially during the November deer season—walk or hike only in wooded areas marked "No Hunting," "No Trespassing," or "Posted." And even if an area *is* closed to hunters, don't decide to explore the woods during deer or moose season without wearing a "hunter orange" (read: eye-popping fluorescent) jacket or vest. If you take your dog along, be sure it, too, wears an orange vest. Deer hunters are required to wear two items of orange clothing—a hat and usually a vest. Orange gear is available in sporting-goods stores, hardware stores, and some supermarkets and convenience stores. Hunting is illegal on Sundays.

During hunting season, moose and deer are on the move and made understandably skittish by the hunters invading their turf. Moose are primarily found inland, but deer are everywhere, and even the occasional moose strays into coastal Maine. At night, particularly in wooded areas, these huge creatures often end up alongside or in the roads, so ratchet up your defensive-driving skills. Reduce your normal speed, use high beams when there's no oncoming traffic, and remain extra-alert. In a moose-vs.-car encounter, no one wins, and human fatalities are common. An encounter between a deer and a car may be less dangerous to humans (although the deer usually dies), but some damage is inevitable.

Information and Services

MONEY
Credit Cards and Travelers Checks

Bank credit cards have become so preferred and so prevalent that it's nearly impossible to rent a car or check into a hotel without one (the alternative is payment in advance or a hefty cash deposit). MasterCard and Visa (or EuroCard) are most widely accepted in Maine, and Discover and American Express are the next most popular; Carte Blanche, Diners Club, and EnRoute (Canadian) lag far behind. Be aware, however, that small restaurants (including some lobster pounds), shops, and B&Bs off the beaten track might not accept credit cards or nonlocal personal checks; you may need to settle your account with cash or travelers checks (preferably $50 or under, for ease of cashing in Maine).

Taxes

Maine charges a 5 percent sales tax on items such as gifts, snacks, books, clothing, and video rentals, and a 7 percent tax on all bar, restaurant, and lodging bills. Bear in mind, especially when making reservations by phone, that restaurants and lodgings usually do *not* include the 7 percent tax when quoting their prices. A whopping 10 percent tax is added to car rental rates.

Tipping

The longtime restaurant tipping standard—15 percent of the total bill—still prevails in most of Maine in most restaurants, but a big-city 20 percent rate isn't unusual in the upscale restaurants. Of course, the restaurant tip always should depend on the quality of the service. If you've ever worked in a restaurant, you know how much tips are appreciated—but they need to be earned. Don't penalize a waitperson for the kitchen's mistakes or incompetence, but do reduce the tip if the service is sloppy. If for any reason you don't tip, do let a host or hostess know the reason, so you're not just considered chintzy.

Taxi drivers expect a 15 percent tip; airport porters expect at least $1 per bag, depending on the difficulty of the job. If a porter simply unloads a suitcase from a car, 50 cents is plenty; if he has to escort you to a ticket counter—and especially if he arranges for speedier service—a dollar per bag is appropriate.

The usual tip for housekeeping services in accommodations is $1–2 per person, per night, depending on the level of service. It's not necessary to tip at B&Bs if the owners do the housekeeping.

Some accommodations add a 10 to 15 percent service fee onto rates; you don't need to tip on top of this.

TOURISM INFO
Maine Office of Tourism

The Maine Office of Tourism has an excellent website: www.visitmaine.com. You'll find chamber of commerce addresses, articles, photos, information on lodgings, and access to a variety of Maine tourism businesses. You can use the website to request a free state map and a copy of *Maine Invites You,* which details sights throughout the state and provides listings of chambers of commerce and other info helpful for travelers. The state's toll-free information hotline is 888/MAINE-45 (888/624-6345).

Local Chambers of Commerce and Tourism Offices

Tourism is Maine's second-largest source of revenue, so almost every community of any size has some kind of information office. Information on these is listed in the destination chapters.

COMMUNICATIONS AND MEDIA
Postal and Shipping Services

Post offices in Maine cities and towns are open six days a week, Monday–Saturday, usually 8 A.M.–5 P.M., although Saturday service in small communities typically is 8 A.M.–noon.

Cities and large towns have strategically placed Express Mail, UPS (800/742-5877), and Federal Express (800/463-3339) boxes. Other national/international delivery services available in Maine are Airborne Express (800/247-2676) and DHL (800/225-5345). Ask locally about businesses that provide packing and shipping services.

If you expect to receive mail while visiting Maine, have your correspondents address it to you c/o General Delivery in the town or city where you expect to be and mark it "Hold for arrival on [your estimated arrival date]." Be sure to give them that post office's correct zip code (every post office has a national zip code directory; overseas residents can check with the nearest U.S. embassy or consulate or log on to www.usps.com).

Area Code

Maine still has only one telephone area code, 207. To call long distance in state and out of state, dial 1 plus the area code before the number. For directory assistance, dial 411.

Toll-Free Calling

Any number with an area code of 800, 888, 877, 866, 855, 844, 833, or 822 is toll free.

Cell Phones

When you're on vacation, a ringing telephone should be the absolute last thing you want to think about, but needs do arise. Although transmission towers are sprinkled throughout Maine, there are some locations, such as down the peninsulas so prevalent in the Acadia region, where it's difficult, if not impossible, to get a signal. Getting reception often requires asking locals for the best places to stand (perhaps out on a dock), then doing the dance—moving left, right, up, and down to find the strongest signal.

Internet Access

Internet access is widely available at libraries and coffeehouses. Most hotels and many inns and B&Bs also offer Internet access; many provide dataports or Wi-Fi.

Newspapers

The **Mount Desert Islander** (www.mountdesertislander.com) began publication in 2001 under the respected leadership of the former *Bar Harbor Times* editor. Four times each summer, the *Islander* also co-publishes (with the *Ellsworth American*) a very helpful tabloid-format supplement, **Out & About in Downeast Maine,** which goes well beyond fluffy travel info. You'll find history, trail advice, dining and lodging listings, event info, maps, ferry info, and more (the online version of *Out & About* is at www.acadiavisitor.com). **The Bar Harbor Times** (www.barharbortimes.com), founded in 1914, is published each Thursday, with extensive calendar listings. Also worth picking up are the *Acadia Weekly,* a round-up of activities, sights, events, and more published monthly in spring and fall and weekly in peak season, and the annual *Bar Harbor and Mount Desert Island Menu Guide.* Both are free and published by Acadia Publishing.

In Blue Hill, look for the *Weekly Packet;* in Castine it's the *Castine Patriot;* and on Deer Isle, pick up *Island Ad-Vantages.* All are published on Thursday by the same company and contain similar info.

The Bangor Daily News, published Monday through Saturday, is the largest paper in the region. On Sundays, you can pick up a copy of the state's largest paper, the *Maine Sunday Telegram.*

RESOURCES

Suggested Reading

CARRIAGE ROADS

Abrell, D. *A Pocket Guide to the Carriage Roads of Acadia National Park*. Camden, ME: Down East Books, 1985, 1995. A dozen excellent carriage road loops (ranging from 1.2 to 11.1 miles) for hiking, biking, or horseback riding—presented in a portable format.

Roberts, A. R. *Mr. Rockefeller's Roads*. Camden, ME: Down East Books, 1990. The fascinating story behind Acadia's scenic carriage roads, written by the granddaughter of John D. Rockefeller Jr. (who created them).

HISTORY

Brechlin, E. *Bygone Bar Harbor: A Postcard Tour of Mount Desert Island and Acadia National Park*. Camden, ME: Down East Books, 2002. A charming little book with reproductions of 100 historic postcards.

Collier, S. F. *Mount Desert Island and Acadia National Park: An Informal History*. Rev. ed. Camden, ME: Down East Books, 1978. An oft-cited source for island and park history.

Dorr, G. *The Story of Acadia National Park*. 3rd ed. Bar Harbor, ME: Acadia Publishing, 1997 (reprinted, combining 1942 and 1948 originals). How Acadia began—and the roller-coaster struggles involved—related by George Dorr, "the Father of Acadia."

Duncan, R. F., E. G. Barlow, K. Bray, and C. Hanks. *Coastal Maine: A Maritime History*. Woodstock, VT: Countrymen Press, 2002. Updated version of the classic work.

Helfrich, G. W., and G. O'Neil. *Lost Bar Harbor*. Camden, ME: Down East Books, 1982. Fascinating collection of historic photographs of classic, turn-of-the-century "cottages," most obliterated by Bar Harbor's Great Fire of 1947.

Isaacson, D., ed. *Maine: A Guide "Down East."* 2nd ed. Maine League of Historical Societies and Museums, 1970. Out of print. Revised version of the Depression-cra WPA guidebook. Still interesting for background reading.

Judd, R. W., E. A. Churchill, and J. W. Eastman, eds. *Maine: The Pine Tree State from Prehistory to the Present*. Orono: University of Maine Press, 1995. The best available Maine history, with excellent historical maps.

Morison, S. E. *The Story of Mount Desert Island*. Islandport Press, 2001 (reprint of 1960 book). A quirky, entertaining little history—from Native Americans to 20th-century Americans—by the late maritime historian, a longtime Mount Desert summer resident.

Paine, L. P. *Down East: A Maritime History of Maine*. Gardiner, ME: Tilbury House, 2000. A noted maritime historian provides an enlightening introduction to the state's seafaring tradition.

LOBSTERS AND LIGHTHOUSES

Caldwell, W. *Lighthouses of Maine*. Camden, ME: Down East Books, 2002 (reprint of 1986 book). A historical tour of Maine's lighthouses, with the emphasis on history, legends, and lore.

Corson, T. *The Secret Life of Lobsters*. New York, NY: HarperCollins, 2004. Everything you wanted—or perhaps didn't want—to know about lobster.

Hartnett, R., and P. D. Bachelder. *Maine Lighthouse Map & Guide*. Hartnett House Map Publishing, 2000. An illustrated map and guide providing directions on how to locate all Maine beacons as well as brief histories.

Rezendes, P. *The Lighthouse Companion for Maine*. Windsor, CT: Tide-Mark Press, 2005. An easy-to-use directory of Maine lighthouses, arranged in alphabetical order and accompanied by photos, directions by land and sea, and contact information for arranging tours.

Thompson, C. *Maine Lighthouses: A Pictorial Guide*. 3rd ed. Mount Desert, ME: CatNap Publications, 2001. What they look like and how to find them (sometimes only by boat), with some historical and contemporary background.

Woodward, C. *The Lobster Coast: Rebels, Rusticators, and the Struggle for a Forgotten Frontier*. New York, NY: Viking, 2004. A veteran journalist's take on the history of the Maine Coast.

NATURAL HISTORY AND NATURE GUIDES

Butcher, Russell D. *Field Guide to Acadia National Park, Maine*. Lanham, MD: Taylor Trade Publishing, 2005. A detailed, illustrated guide to Acadia's flora, fauna, and geology, including some trail descriptions with what to look for along the way.

Conkling, P. W. *Islands in Time: A Natural and Cultural History of the Islands of the Gulf of Maine*. 2nd ed. Camden, ME: Down East Books and Rockland, ME: Island Institute, 1999. A thoughtful overview by the president of Maine's Island Institute.

Grierson, R. G. *Acadia National Park: Wildlife Watcher's Guide*. Minocqua, WI: NorthWord Press, 1995. You're not likely to see any creature in the park that isn't mentioned in this handy guide.

Kavanaugh, J., and R. Leung. *Acadia National Park Wildlife: An introduction to familiar species of birds, mammals, reptiles, amphibians, fish and butterflies*. Waterford Press, 2008. An easy-to-carry laminated guide.

Kendall, D. L. *Glaciers & Granite: A Guide to Maine's Landscape and Geology*. Unity, ME: North Country Press, 1993. Explains knowledgeably why Maine looks the way it does.

Newlin, William V. P. *Lakes & Ponds of Mount Desert*. Camden, ME: Down East Books, 1989. Covers more than the title reveals—includes great picnicking, hiking, and biking advice, from a longtime summer resident. Out of print, but try used bookstores.

Perrin, S. *Acadia's Native Flowers, Fruits, and Wildlife*. Fort Washington, PA: Eastern National, 2001. This handy reference to the park's flora and fauna runs chronologically through three seasons (spring through fall). It's not a complete field guide, but rather a selective collection of photos in a portable square format.

Pierson, E. C., J. E. Pierson, and P. D. Vickery. *A Birder's Guide to Maine*. Camden, ME: Down East Books, 1996. An expanded version of *A Birder's Guide to the Coast of Maine*. A valuable resource for any ornithologist, novice or expert, for exploring Acadia (and the rest of Maine).

Scheid, M. *Discovering Acadia: A Guide for Young Naturalists*. Mount Desert, ME:

Acadia Publishing, 1990. A delightful book for children—as well as the adults who accompany them.

OFFSHORE ISLANDS
Cranberry Isles

Eliot, C. W. *John Gilley: One of the Forgotten Millions.* Bar Harbor, ME: Acadia Press, 1989 (reprint of 1904 book). Poignant story of 19th-century life in the Cranberries, as told by the Harvard president who was instrumental in the establishment of Acadia.

Frenchboro (Long Island)

Lunt, D. L. *Hauling by Hand: The Life and Times of a Maine Island.* Frenchboro, ME: Islandport Press, 1999. A sensitive history of Frenchboro (a.k.a. Long Island), eight miles offshore, written by an eighth-generation islander, now a journalist.

Isle au Haut

Greenlaw, L. *The Lobster Chronicles.* New York, NY: Hyperion, 2002. Essays on island life, warts and all, by the talented writer and lobsterwoman who first gained fame as a swordfishing skipper in *The Perfect Storm.*

Pratt, C. *Here on the Island.* New York, NY: Harper & Row, 1974. An appealing, realistic portrait of life on Isle au Haut several decades ago.

PICTORAL

Blagden, T., Jr., and C. R. Tyson Jr. *First Light: Acadia National Park and Maine's Mount Desert Island.* Englewood, CO: Westcliffe Publishers and Bar Harbor, ME: Friends of Acadia, 2003. A gorgeous, large-format book with spectacular photographs.

Wilmerding, J. *The Artist's Mount Desert: American Painters on the Maine Coast.* Princeton, NJ: Princeton University Press, 1995. A respected art historian's perspective on Mount

Desert's magnetic attraction to such American artists as Thomas Cole, Frederic Church, and Fitz Hugh Lane.

RECREATION GUIDES
General

Evans, Lisa Gollin. *An Outdoor Family Guide to Acadia National Park.* Seattle, WA: The Mountaineers, 1997. An excellent resource for hiking, biking, and paddling with kids in Acadia.

Monkman, J., and M. Monkman. *Discover Acadia National Park: A Guide to Hiking, Biking, and Paddling.* 2nd ed. Boston, MA: Appalachian Mountain Club Books, 2005. Well-planned and well-written guide, in the Appalachian Mountain Club tradition, including foldout AMC map.

Biking

Minutolo, A. *A Pocket Guide to Biking on Mount Desert Island.* Camden, ME: Down East Books, 1996. A third-generation islander's expert advice; this book covers the whole island, not just the park.

Stone, H. *25 Bicycle Tours in Maine: Coastal and Inland Rides from Kittery to Caribou.* 3rd ed. Woodstock, VT: Backcountry Publications, 1998. Includes half a dozen Acadia routes.

Cruising Guides

Bilder, J. *A Visual Cruising Guide to the Maine Coast.* Camden, ME: Ragged Mountain Press, 2006. A spiral-bound guide, with 180 aerial photos providing visual guidance.

Taft, H., J. Taft, and C. Rindlaub. *A Cruising Guide to the Maine Coast.* 5th ed. Peaks Island, ME: Diamond Pass Publishing, 2008. Don't even consider cruising the coast around Acadia without this thoroughly researched volume.

Hiking

Gillmore, R. *Great Walks of Acadia National Park & Mount Desert Island.* Rev. ed. Goffstown, NH: Great Walks, 2004. Two dozen trails in Acadia—some stretch the limits of their definition of "walks."

Kong, D., and D. Ring. *Hiking Acadia National Park.* Guilford, CT: Globe Pequot/Falcon Guide, 2001. Excellent hiking guide, with useful, accurate descriptions of 94 trails on Mount Desert Island, Isle au Haut, and the Schoodic Peninsula. The authors include a list of their 25 favorites and advocate the Leave No Trace philosophy.

St. Germain, T. A., Jr. *A Walk in the Park: Acadia's Hiking Guide.* 10th ed. Bar Harbor, ME: Parkman Publications, 2004. Arguably the best Acadia hiking guide, in a handy Michelin-style vertical format. Bar Harbor resident St. Germain hikes a thousand miles a year in Acadia, so he's the expert. The book includes plenty of historical tidbits about the trails, the park, and the island. Part of the proceeds go to the Acadia Trails Forever campaign to maintain and rehabilitate the park's trails. The book is updated regularly; ask for the most recent edition.

Seymour, T. *Hiking Maine.* 2nd ed. Guilford, CT: Globe Pequot Press, 2002. Covers the state, but has good detail on more than 20 hikes in the region spanning Bucksport to Milbridge.

Kayaking and Canoeing

Brechlin, E. D. *A Pocket Guide to Paddling the Waters of Mount Desert Island.* Camden, ME: Down East Books, 1996. Registered Maine Guide Brechlin recommends 17 places to paddle your kayak or canoe—in saltwater as well as freshwater ponds and lakes. This little handbook (64 pages) includes locations for parking and launching areas, as well as route maps.

Bumsted, L. *Hot Showers! Maine Coast Lodgings for Kayakers and Sailors.* 2nd ed. Brunswick, ME: Audenreed Press, 2000. Excellent, well-researched resource for anyone paddling or cruising the shoreline and yearning for alternatives to a sleeping bag.

The Maine Island Trail Guidebook. Rockland, ME: Maine Island Trail Association, updated annually. Available only with MITA membership (annual dues $45, www.mita. org), providing access to dozens of islands along the watery trail, including many in the Acadia region between Schoodic Point and Deer Isle.

Miller, D. S. *Kayaking the Maine Coast.* 2nd ed. Woodstock, VT: Countryman Press/ Backcountry Guides, 2006. Thoroughly researched guide by a veteran kayaker; good maps and particularly helpful information. With this book and a copy of *Hot Showers!* you're all set.

Wilson, A., and J. Hayes. *Quiet Water Canoe Guide, Maine: Best Paddling Lakes and Ponds for All Ages.* 2nd ed. Boston, MA: Appalachian Mountain Club Books, 2005. Comprehensive handbook, with helpful maps, for inland paddling.

Rock Climbing

Butterfield, J. *Acadia: A Climber's Guide.* The most up-to-date and thorough climbing guide for the park.

REFERENCE

The Maine Atlas and Gazetteer. Yarmouth, ME: DeLorme, updated annually. You'll be hard put to get lost on the roads in this region or anywhere else in Maine if you're carrying this essential volume; it contains 70 full-page (oversize format) topographical maps with GPS grids.

Internet Resources

ACADIA NATIONAL PARK INFORMATION

Acadia National Park
www.nps.gov/acad/

A comprehensive site with extensive, detailed information about Maine's only national park. Download natural and cultural history articles, accessibility charts, list of hiking trails, FAQ, maps of the park and its outlying sections (Isle au Haut and the Schoodic Peninsula), and the latest issues of the *Beaver Log,* the park's summer newspaper. Also included is a link for on-line reservations at Blackwoods Campground, as well as info for making Isle au Haut camping reservations.

Friends of Acadia
www.friendsofacadia.org

A very active nonprofit organization that acts as a financial safety net for the park and also organizes frequent volunteer work parties for various maintenance projects in the park. Its newsletters are posted on the website, as is information about where and when you can volunteer.

Island Explorer Bus System
www.exploreacadia.com

Everything you need to know about using the propane-fueled, fare-free Island Explorer buses (operating late June–early Oct. on Mount Desert, late June–Labor Day on the Schoodic Peninsula). Included are suggestions for getting to Mount Desert without a car, as well as for exploring the park with the bus.

ARTS AND ENTERTAINMENT

Maine Archives and Museums
www.mainemuseums.org

The Maine Arts and Heritage Tourism Partnership has produced this useful site (a printed guide is also available) with links to dozens of major and minor museums, archives, historical societies, and historic sites. Opening hours and admission fees are provided, although some fees listed are out of date.

Maine Maritime Heritage Trail
www.maritimemaine.org

Information about and links to maritime museums, boatbuilding schools, lighthouses, historic homes, fishing, naval history, forts, historic sites, and much more.

FOOD AND DRINK

Maine Department of Agriculture
www.getrealmaine.com

Information on all things agricultural, including fairs, farmers markets, farm vacations, places to buy Maine foods, berry- and apple-picking sites, and more.

Maine Lobster Promotion Council
www.mainelobsterpromo.com

All lobster, all the time, with links for ordering Maine lobster and organizing your own lobster bake, plus recipes for preparing lobster in more ways than you ever thought possible.

Wild Blueberry Association of North America
www.wildblueberries.com

Information on blueberries as well as numerous recipes.

GENERAL INFORMATION

Maine Emergency Management Association
www.maine.gov/mema/weather/weather.htm

Five-day weather forecasts broken down by 32 zones.

Maine Information
www.maine.info

A privately operated site with a mother lode of links handy for vacation planners.

Maine Office of Tourism
www.visitmaine.com

The state's official tourism site is the biggest and most useful and comprehensive of all Maine-related tourism sites, with sections for where to visit, where to stay, things to do, trip planning, packages, and search capabilities. Also has lodging specials and a comprehensive calendar of events. See links to the Downeast and Acadia Region.

Island Institute
www.islandinstitute.org

The institute serves as a clearinghouse/advocate for Maine's islands; the website provides links to the major year-round islands.

State of Maine
www.maine.gov

Everything you wanted to know about Maine and then some, with links to all government departments and Maine-related sites. Buy a fishing license online, reserve a campsite at Lamoine State Park (near Acadia), or check the fall foliage conditions via the site's LeafCam. (You can also access foliage info at www. mainefoliage.com, where you can sign up for weekly email foliage reports in September and early October.) Also listed is information on accessible arts and recreation.

PARKS AND RECREATION

Bicycle Coalition of Maine
www.bikemaine.org

Tons of information for bicyclists including routes, shops, events, organized rides, and much more.

Department of Conservation, Maine Bureau of Parks and Lands
www.maine.gov/doc/parks

Information on state parks, public reserved lands, and state historic sites; details on facilities such as campsites, picnic areas, and boat launches. Make state campground reservations online.

Golf Maine
www.golfme.com

Lists member courses, stay-and-play packages, and golf links statewide.

Healthy Maine Walks
www.healthymainewalks.com

Lists places for walking statewide.

Maine Association of Sea Kayaking Guides & Instructors
www.maineseakayakguides.com

Information and links to about two dozen members who meet state requirements to lead commercial trips.

Maine Audubon
www.maineaudubon.org

Information about Maine Audubon's environmental centers statewide. Activity and program schedules are included.

Maine Birding
www.mainebirding.net

A must-visit site for anyone interested in learning more about birding in Maine, includes news, checklists, events, forums, trips, and more.

Maine Island Trail Association
www.mita.org

The mission and activities of MITA, as well as information on becoming a member and receiving the annual guidebook to the island trail.

Maine Land Trust Network
www.mltn.org

Maine has dozens of land trusts statewide, managing lands that provide opportunities for hiking, walking, canoeing, kayaking, and other such activities.

Maine Professional Guides Association
www.maineguides.org

Find Registered Maine Guides for sporting adventures, including sea kayaking, hunting, fishing, and recreation (such as canoeing trips and wildlife safaris).

The Nature Conservancy
www.nature.org/wherewework/
northamerica/states/maine/
Information about Maine preserves, field trips, and events.

REGIONAL INFORMATION

Bar Harbor Chamber of Commerce
www.barharborinfo.com
Access to information about Mount Desert Island's major town. In addition to its helpful website, with lodging links, its annual visitor booklet is published earlier than most, allowing trip planning to begin in January.

Blue Hill Chamber of Commerce
www.bluehillpeninsula.org
Information about where to eat and sleep and what to do on the Blue Hill Peninsula.

Deer Isle-Stonington Chamber of Commerce
www.deerislemaine.com
Where to sleep and eat on Deer Isle, en route to Acadia National Park on Isle au Haut.

DownEast & Acadia Regional Tourism
www.downeastacadia.com
Information about the region from Bucksport through Calais.

Schoodic Peninsula Chamber of Commerce
www.acadia-schoodic.org
Where to sleep and eat in Eastern Hancock County, near Acadia National Park's Schoodic Peninsula section.

Southwest Harbor/Tremont Chamber of Commerce
www.acadiachamber.com
Visitor information (including accommodations, restaurants, activities, and shops) for the southwest corner of Mount Desert Island. The chamber's visitor booklet is especially informative, and the chamber has a free map of hiking trails on the west side of Mount Desert.

SHOPPING

Maine Antiquarian Booksellers Association
www.mainebooksellers.org
Lists independent shops that specialize in used, antiquarian, and rare books.

Maine Antiques Dealers Association
www.maineantiques.org
Lists member dealers statewide by location and specialty and provides information on upcoming antiques events.

TRANSPORTATION

Bay Ferries
www.catferry.com
Schedule and fare information for the passenger and car high-speed catamaran ferry operating mid-May to mid-October between Bar Harbor and Yarmouth, Nova Scotia, and Portland and Yarmouth, Nova Scotia.

Explore Maine
www.exploremaine.org
Explore Maine is an invaluable site for trip planning, with information on and links to airports, rail service, bus service, automobile travel, and ferries, as well as links to other key travel-planning sites.

Maine Department of Transportation
www.511maine.gov
Site provides real-time information about major delays, accidents, road construction, and weather conditions. You can get the same info and more by dialing 511 in-state.

Glossary

alewives herring

ayuh yes

barrens as in "blueberry barrens"; fields where wild blueberries grow

beamy wide (as in a boat or a person)

beans shorthand for the traditional Saturday-night meal, which always includes baked beans

blowdown a forest area leveled by wind

blowing a gale very windy

camp a vacation house (small or large), usually on freshwater and/or in the woods

chance serendipity or luck (as in "open by appointment or by chance")

chicken dressing chicken manure

chowder (pronounced "chowdah") soup made with lobster, clams, or fish, or a combination thereof; lobster version sometimes called "lobster stew"

chowderhead mischief- or troublemakers, usually interchangeable with "idiot"

coneheads tourists (because of their presumed penchant for ice cream)

cottage a vacation house (anything from a bungalow to a mansion), usually on saltwater

culch (also cultch) "stuff"; the contents of attics, basements, and some flea markets

cull a discount lobster, usually minus a claw

cunnin' cute (usually describing a baby or small child)

dinner (pronounced "dinnah") the noon meal

dinner pail lunchbox

dite a very small amount

dooryard the yard near a house's main entrance

downcellar in the basement

Down East with the prevailing wind; the old coastal sailing route from Boston to Nova Scotia

dry-ki driftwood, usually remnants from the logging industry

ell a residential structural section that links a house and a barn; formerly a popular location for the "summer kitchen," to spare the house from woodstove heat

exercised upset; angry

fiddleheads unopened ostrich fern fronds, a spring delicacy

finest kind top quality; good news; an expression of general approval; also, a term of appreciation

flatlander a person not from Maine, often but not exclusively someone from the Midwest

floatplane a small plane equipped with pontoons for landing on water; the same aircraft often becomes a skiplane in winter

flowage a water body created by damming, usually beaver handiwork (also called "beaver flowage")

frappe a thick drink containing milk, ice cream, and flavored syrup, as opposed to a milk shake, which does not include ice cream (but beware: a frappe offered in other parts of the United States is an ice-cream sundae topped with whipped cream!)

from away not native to Maine

galamander a wheeled contraption formerly used to transport quarry granite to building sites or to boats for onward shipment

gore a sliver of land left over from inaccurate boundary surveys. Maine has several gores; Hibberts Gore, for instance, has a population of one.

got done quit a job; was let go

harbormaster local official who monitors water traffic and assigns moorings; often a very political job

hardshell lobster that hasn't molted yet (more scarce, thus more pricey in summer)

hod wooden "basket" used for carrying clams

ice-out the departure of winter ice from ponds, lakes, rivers, and streams; many communities have ice-out contests, awarding prizes for guessing the exact time of ice-out, in April or May

Italian long soft bread roll sliced on top and

filled with peppers, onions, tomatoes, sliced meat, and black olives, and sprinkled with olive oil, salt, and pepper; veggie versions are available

jimmies chocolate sprinkles, like those on an ice cream cone

lobster car a large floating crate for storing lobsters

Maine Guide a member of the Maine Professional Guides Association, trained and tested for outdoor and survival skills; also called a Registered Maine Guide

market price restaurant menu term for "the going rate," usually referring to the price of lobster or clams

molt what a lobster does when it sheds its shell for a larger one; the act of molting is called "ecdysis" (as a stripper is an ecdysiast)

money tree a collection device for a monetary gift

mud season mid-March to mid-April, when back roads and unpaved driveways become virtual tank traps

nasty neat extremely meticulous

near stingy

notional stubborn, determined

off island the mainland, to an islander

place another word for a house (as in "Herb Pendleton's place")

pot trap, as in "lobster pot"

public landing see "town landing"

rake hand tool used for harvesting blueberries

rusticator a summer visitor, particularly in bygone days

scooch (or scootch) to squat; to move sideways

sea smoke heavy mist rising off the water when the air temperature suddenly becomes much colder than the ocean temperature

select a lobster with claws intact

selectmen the elected men and women who handle local affairs in small communities; the First Selectman chairs meetings. In some towns, "people from away" have proposed substituting a gender-neutral term, but in most cases the effort has failed.

shedder a lobster with a new (soft) shell; molting generally occurs in July and August (making shedders more common then, thus less expensive than hardshells)

shire town county seat

shore dinner the works: chowder, clams, lobster, and sometimes corn on the cob, too; usually the most expensive item on a menu

short a small, illegal-size lobster

slumgullion tasteless food; a mess

snapper an undersize, illegal lobster

soda cola, root beer, etc. (often referred to as "pop" in other parts of the country

softshell see "shedder"

some very (as in "some hot")

spleeny overly sensitive

steamers clams (before or after they are steamed)

sternman a lobsterman's helper (male or female)

summer complaint a tourist

supper (pronounced "suppah") evening meal, eaten by Mainers around 5 or 6 P.M. (as opposed to flatlanders and summer people, who eat dinner between 7 and 9 P.M.)

tad slightly; a little bit

thick-o'-fog zero-visibility fog

to home at home

tomalley a lobster's green insides; considered a delicacy by some

town landing shore access; often a park or a parking lot, next to a wharf or boat-launch ramp

upattic in the attic

Whoopie! Pie the trademarked name for a high-fat, calorie-laden, cakelike snack that only kids and dentists could love

wicked cold! frigid

wicked good! excellent

williwaws uncomfortable feeling

Index

Map Index

Acknowledgments

For Dad

The only way to compile all the tidbits of information required for a guidebook is to be everywhere at once, which is physically impossible. While I spent the better part of my spring, summer, and fall in the Acadia region researching every aspect of this book, it seemed no sooner did I leave the Blue Hill peninsula for Mount Desert Island, than something changed. Restaurants open and close. Outfitters change their offerings. B&Bs are sold. New trails are cut; old ones rerouted. Museums expand. Hotels renovate. And on it goes. Which all goes to say, I couldn't have done this without the help of many people who served as additional eyes and ears.

I'll start with Kathleen Brandes, who wrote the first edition of this book and whose friendship I valued and whose work and dedication I respected long before I began working on this edition. My appreciation for her extensive research, her ability to capture a place or a person with a quick turn of phrase, and her dead-on accuracy remains without bounds.

Big thank-yous, too, to those who sat down with me and shared local info, sheltered me along the way, fed me, helped with arrangements, verified information, called me with updates, or simply encouraged me as I've researched each edition: Wanda Moran, Bill Haefele, Fred Cook, Risteen Masters, Anne Beerits, Barbara Maurer, Jeff and Judi Burke, Bill Baker, Sally and Jim Littlefield, Dom and Joanne Parisi, Sharon Broom, Tom Minutolo, Michael Good, Jeff and Terri Anderholm, Megan Moshier, Ben and Sonja Walter-Sundaram, Roy Kasindorf and Helene Harton, Don Jalbert, Javier Mntesinos, Jack Burke, Julie Van de Graaf, Ben Walter, Sonja Sundararm, Darren Kelly, Sarah Pebworth, Charlene Williams, Rose Whitehorse, and the rest of the gang at Nancy Marshall Communications. I couldn't have done this without all of your help and support.

More thank-yous are due to the folks at Avalon Travel who shepherded me through the process: Bill Newlin, Kevin McLain, Jane Musser, Kevin Anglin, Nicole Schultz, Dylan Wooters, Jen Rios, Grace Fujimoto, and especially my editor, Naomi Adler Dancis. Also, thank you to the many other behind-the-scenes Avalon staffers who worked on this book, and more thanks to those who are promoting it, especially Jodee Krainik.

I save my biggest thanks for my husband, Tom, who drove me everywhere and didn't complain (too much) when I made him backtrack two or three times along the same stretch of road, while seeking an elusive address; who waited patiently while I visited practically every restaurant, inn, and B&B in the Acadia region; who let me order for him in restaurants; who tackled research projects; and who supported me in every way possible throughout the entire process—all while shooting photographs for the book. I couldn't have done it without him.

And to you, dear reader, thank you for using this book to plan your visit to Acadia National Park.

www.moon.com

DESTINATIONS | ACTIVITIES | BLOGS | MAPS | BOOKS

MOON.COM is all new, and ready to help plan your next trip! Filled with fresh trip ideas and strategies, author interviews, informative blogs, a detailed map library, and descriptions of all the Moon guidebooks, Moon.com is all you need to get out and explore the world—or even places in your own backyard. As always, when you travel with Moon, expect an experience that is uncommon and truly unique.

MAP SYMBOLS

≡≡≡	Expressway	◖	Highlight	✈	Airfield	⚲	Golf Course
—	Primary Road	○	City/Town	✈	Airport	Ⓟ	Parking Area
≡	Secondary Road	◉	State Capital	▲	Mountain	▲	Archaeological Site
▪▪▪	Unpaved Road	⊛	National Capital	✦	Unique Natural Feature	⛪	Church
----	Trail	★	Point of Interest			⛽	Gas Station
··········	Ferry	•	Accommodation	⌇	Waterfall	◌	Glacier
▬▬▬	Railroad	▼	Restaurant/Bar	⛊	Park		Mangrove
▬▬▬	Pedestrian Walkway	▪	Other Location	⊤	Trailhead		Reef
▥	Stairs	⋀	Campground	⛷	Skiing Area		Swamp

CONVERSION TABLES

°C = (°F - 32) / 1.8
°F = (°C x 1.8) + 32
1 inch = 2.54 centimeters (cm)
1 foot = 0.304 meters (m)
1 yard = 0.914 meters
1 mile = 1.6093 kilometers (km)
1 km = 0.6214 miles
1 fathom = 1.8288 m
1 chain = 20.1168 m
1 furlong = 201.168 m
1 acre = 0.4047 hectares
1 sq km = 100 hectares
1 sq mile = 2.59 square km
1 ounce = 28.35 grams
1 pound = 0.4536 kilograms
1 short ton = 0.90718 metric ton
1 short ton = 2,000 pounds
1 long ton = 1.016 metric tons
1 long ton = 2,240 pounds
1 metric ton = 1,000 kilograms
1 quart = 0.94635 liters
1 US gallon = 3.7854 liters
1 Imperial gallon = 4.5459 liters
1 nautical mile = 1.852 km

MOON ACADIA NATIONAL PARK
Avalon Travel
a member of the Perseus Books Group
1700 Fourth Street
Berkeley, CA 94710, USA
www.moon.com

Editor: Naomi Adler Dancis
Series Manager: Kathryn Ettinger
Copy Editor: Teresa Elsey
Graphics Coordinator: Lucie Ericksen
Production Coordinator: Lucie Ericksen
Cover Designer: Nicole Schultz
Director of Cartography: Mike Morgenfeld
Map Editor: Kevin Anglin
Cartographers: Chris Markiewicz, Kat Bennett
Indexer: Greg Jewett

ISBN-10: 1-56691-985-1
ISBN-13: 978-1-56691-985-2
ISSN: 1546-8062

Printing History
1st Edition – 2004
3rd Edition – April 2009

5 4 3 2 1

KEEPING CURRENT

If you have a favorite gem you'd like to see included in the next edition, or see anything that needs updating, clarification, or correction, please drop us a line. Send your comments via email to feedback@moon.com, or use the address above.